Trading Spaces

Trading Spaces

The Colonial Marketplace and the Foundations of American Capitalism

EMMA HART

The University of Chicago Press

CHICAGO AND LONDON

The University of Chicago Press, Chicago 60637
The University of Chicago Press, Ltd., London
© 2019 by The University of Chicago
Published 2019
Paperback edition 2024
Printed and bound by CPI Group (UK) Ltd, Croydon, CR0 4YY

33 32 31 30 29 28 27 26 25 24   1 2 3 4 5

ISBN-13: 978-0-226-65981-7 (cloth)
ISBN-13: 978-0-226-83327-9 (paper)
ISBN-13: 978-0-226-65995-4 (e-book)
DOI: https://doi.org/10.7208/chicago/9780226659954.001.0001

Library of Congress Cataloging-in-Publication Data

Names: Hart, Emma, 1972– author.
Title: Trading spaces : the colonial marketplace and the
foundations of American capitalism / Emma Hart.
Other titles: American beginnings, 1500–1900.
Description: Chicago ; London : The University of Chicago Press, 2019. |
Series: American beginnings, 1500–1900 |
Includes bibliographical references and index.
Identifiers: LCCN 2019017219 |
ISBN 9780226659817 (cloth : alk. paper) |
ISBN 9780226659954 (e-book)
Subjects: LCSH: United States—Commerce—History. | Markets—
United States—History. | Great Britain—Colonies—America—Economic
conditions. | United States—History—Colonial period, ca. 1600–1775.
Classification: LCC HF3025 .H35 2019 | DDC 381.0973—dc23
LC record available at https://lccn.loc.gov/2019017219

♾ This paper meets the requirements of ANSI/NISO Z39.48-1992
(Permanence of Paper).

Contents

INTRODUCTION

In 2014, inspired by campaigns highlighting the tax-dodging habits of large global corporations, Londoner Steve Pottinger decided to take direct action. He found out that his coffee shop of choice, British chain Caffé Nero, was not paying any corporation tax, so he returned his loyalty card with an explanatory letter, which he posted on Facebook. He pointed out that if he was going to be loyal to Caffé Nero, the owners needed to give back to the society where they traded. "Until such time as you start showing the same loyalty to the common good that you expect your customers to give to your business," Pottinger signed off, "I'll be buying my coffee elsewhere." The Facebook post soon garnered sustained attention, and Caffé Nero was forced to defend itself, excusing its actions on the grounds that it was not engaging in the notorious practice of transfer pricing that Starbucks and Amazon used to avoid tax.[1]

Pottinger's protest is, of course, part of a much larger movement that opposes globalized markets. Our era of "turbocapitalism," its participants argue, has sponsored the emergence of a global megarich elite who trade free from national regulatory regimes to maximize their wealth and impoverish ordinary workers. These protests, like Pottinger's words, reveal a central characteristic of markets past and present. When markets dramatically increase their reach, aspects of exchange begin to move beyond the horizon of individual consumers and their customary frame of reference. In doing so, they break through the parameters defined by government and society for their operation. As a consumer, Pottinger felt cheated by a company that had abandoned its national obligations. Caffé Nero was able to do this, he thought, because a borderless market had permitted complex company structures that made an international elite richer while depriving ordinary British coffee drinkers of basic rights such as properly funded health care. Pottinger had bought into the idea that, as markets become ever more transnational, they elude effective regulation and, if left unchecked, take on a rampant capitalist character.[2]

This book is about a similar step change in the scale of the market that occurred as the British colonized North America. Shining a light on the still murky process of colonial market making, I tell the story of an American market revolution that unfolded from the earliest moments of the continent's European contact. This revolution occurred in the everyday spaces frequented by ordinary trading Americans. Across the seventeenth and eighteenth centuries, Europeans tried, but failed, to recreate their familiar trading spaces and regulatory institutions. Their initial failure was grounded in the tricky proposition of building marketplaces on an extensive and distant continent. It was the scale of America that especially prompted colonists to create novel types of places, tailored to their desire to freely and easily exchange their abundant property. As customers, commodities, and market agents, Native Americans, Africans, and poor white colonists were very important to the emergence of new marketing practices. Together, colonial people created marketplaces that depended on the free trade of private property by individuals uninhibited by government regulation.

Over the eighteenth century, however, governing colonists' discomfort with the active role of Native American and African American people in the exchange of property prompted them to recreate European-style marketplaces that made orderly trade for the "public good" a priority. This quest took on a new urgency during the chaos and uncertainty of the Revolution. Once independence was won, the quest to regulate the market was swept up in white freeholders' desire to harness the powers of state government and build a virtuous republic of commercial citizens. By charting a revolutionary market crisis born of the nature of the colonial marketplace, this book reveals the centrality of the eighteenth century to longer histories of America's economic culture. It also invites us to rethink the beginnings of the United States' pioneering brand of capitalism by considering that its contemporary character may be rooted in dynamics that began to unfold not only during, but before, the birth of the nation.

The Steve Pottingers of eighteenth-century North America did not have loyalty cards for their lattes, but when they bought coffee they too became actors in a marketplace that had been profoundly changed by its creation during this first wave of globalization. When a Philadelphia consumer purchased coffee, the person who sold it had obtained it from a wholesaler, who had gotten it from a merchant, who had imported it from the Caribbean, where it had been grown by enslaved people themselves traded from Africa. Both the Philadelphia merchant and the Caribbean plantation owner likely were quite wealthy, partly because they had dodged many government regulations to gather as much profit as possible from their coffee. When the coffee arrived in Philadelphia the merchant landed it at a wharf that was owned and regulated not by the city authorities, but by the owner of the waterside lot, who ran it for his own profit. The wharfinger derived his wealth by charging merchants, ship owners, and tradespeople for the use of his property, often at rates unregulated by the government. British customs officials were a bothersome presence on these wharves, but not the professed masters of the waterfront that they were in London or Bristol. Since early American cities lacked guilds or a powerful corporation, the wholesaler and the retailer faced little regulation of their dealings. Consumers therefore found themselves in a freewheeling marketplace that operated according to principles quite unfamiliar to many early modern people. Not least, they might well have purchased their coffee at an auction, a novel method of retail almost unique in its colonial popularity. Expanding the scale of the marketplace had sponsored a move beyond the kind of regulated local markets that characterized much early modern commerce. As a result, property holders such as Philadelphia's wharfingers had become very rich while the Africans who grew the coffee suffered in extreme poverty.[3]

By reconstructing consumption networks like these, historians have shattered the remarkably enduring myth that early Americans were mostly self-sufficient Jeffersonian yeoman farmers. In reality, very few white and black American colonists, or Native Americans, operated completely outside the reach of the market economy, which was a driving force of Britain's American colonization project. From the early eighteenth century onward American men and women created an Atlantic market economy that consumed people as much as it consumed exotic new goods like coffee. This market was built on hemispheric commercial connections that would foreshadow the global economic systems so troubling to many people today.[4]

All-encompassing as this market expansion was, historians have looked at only a handful of its most striking aspects: the vast fortunes accumulated by the leading Atlantic merchants, the importance of credit to its operation, the ubiquity of new consumer goods, the gendered character of commerce, and the horrifying trade in human beings that lay at its foundations. These are important issues, but they overlook many of the nitty-gritty details of colonial America's commercial spaces and their political economy. Consequently we still know very little about the changes colonization wrought in everyday economic exchange.[5]

Yet just as the emergence of a global, internet-based, market has killed the high street while making our couches into stores, so the scale shifts involved in creating the colonial marketplace deeply affected the way people purchased their bread, butter, and indeed coffee in the early modern era. There remain numerous unanswered questions about these changes. Once they got to America and encountered Native Americans, Europeans and Africans traded in an extensive space that lacked anything they might recognize as a marketplace. What did the marketing spaces they then created look like? Where were they? What were the rules of exchange, and who made them? Europe's early modern markets were structured around particular expectations of location, appearance, and social hierarchy. How did colonists react when these assumptions were applied to an unfamiliar landscape?[6]

Lacking precise answers to these questions, colonial historians have cordoned themselves off from conversations about later American markets. To date, they have developed chronologies of market development that begin with debate about the nature of economic structures created at the Revolution. Aside from a few notable exceptions, this timeline has only become more entrenched since the domestic political economy emerged as a central theme of the recently revivified "history of American capitalism." This is a history that focuses on how a nascent banking industry, frontier boosterism, and the efflorescence of the American corporation formed the basis of a rich, and often deeply unstable, institutional scaffolding that encouraged the westward expansion of the market economy after 1776. On these grounds scholars have reached a consensus that the interplay of individual capitalists, the promise of the West, and the creation of a republican political economy formed the foundations of American capitalism.[7]

However, there is much less agreement about the forces underpinning the colonial and the Revolutionary economy. Historians of the early republic's market revolution have variously described its fundamentals as being loyal to "ancient English legal traditions," as already dominated by the capital accumulation of seaport merchants, or as both. Certainly we cannot yet call the prerevolutionary marketplace "American" in any meaningful way. While it did share a number of features across all the mainland territories—the presence of enslaved people, for example—it had not yet developed characteristics that made it anything other than colonial. The market's spaces were created by interactions between Europeans, Africans, and Native Americans that were colonial in character and were theoretically governed by British laws and institutions.[8]

Historians' uncertainty about the character of domestic marketplaces is equally connected to their recent outward-looking, Atlantic focus. After the end of long-running debates about farmers and capital, the merchant and the planter have, over the past twenty years, had attention lavished on them as the linchpins of an Atlantic economy of consumption and slavery. Certainly farmers have been acknowledged as the buyers of these goods, but we still know relatively little about how individuals—farmers, merchants, and others—related economically to places and governments. Trading as part of an Atlantic economy did not merely involve navigating the demands of British customs officials, their mercantilist policies, and an ocean infested with foreign pirates and privateers. Nor did it only comprise going to a store to barter goods that had arrived from Europe for things produced in America. Rather, it demanded that colonists exchange a wide variety of goods and property across the varied landscapes, rural and urban, in which they had planted themselves.[9]

What is more, these spaces of exchange, and the political and legal infrastructures created to regulate them, were the forerunners of those structures underpinning the nineteenth-century growth of an American capitalism. So we cannot understand the character of the latter without knowing what came before; not least because when we look carefully at the ground zero of European-patronized markets in the immediate pre- and postrevolutionary eras, they appear remarkably similar.[10]

Understanding the highly complex character of this colonial marketplace requires an approach that embeds it in its multiple scales. A scalar method demands that this investigation do two things. First, we must recreate a detailed sense of the everyday market transactions that constituted the economic ligaments connecting colonial Americans. We need to find out more about the character of these connections and, in turn, what that character reveals about colonial economic culture more broadly. The demands of this task led me to concentrate my analysis on two colonies: Pennsylvania and South Carolina. By getting down to ground level in the varied landscapes of these two places—urban and rural, east and west, land and water—I aim to provide a comprehensive picture of the spaces and practices of market exchange that evolved between 1660 and 1800. Europeans, African, and Native Americans each moved through many places over their trading lives, making a "joined up" approach essential to grasping both the mobile and the fixed elements of the colonial marketplace.[11]

What is more, only by uncovering the physical expressions of the market can we access the complex processes by which a native American landscape became a colonial space and also a commercial place frequented by Europeans, Africans, and Indians alike. People made certain spaces into market*places* by repeatedly using them for buying and selling. The rules of trade within these places emerged as much from the habitual procedures their users adopted as from the legal culture embraced by individuals and institutions seeking to govern them. In early America these processes of place making assumed outsize importance because they unfolded as part of colonization, which was itself a conscious effort to possess and shape invaded territory and its people. To grasp the nuts and bolts of how American marketplaces were made, it is therefore necessary to keep the discussion at ground level, in clearly defined spaces.[12]

Situating ourselves in Pennsylvania and South Carolina meets this need while providing diverse canvases on which to picture the evolving marketplace. What is more, the two colonial projects were set in motion within twenty years of each other after the restoration of the English monarchy in 1660. While their owners, William Penn and the Earl of Shaftesbury (with his fellow proprietors), had quite different ambitions, they were nevertheless working from assumptions shaped by their common background. Over their colonial eras, both places developed major cities, Philadelphia and Charleston, that acted as Atlantic hubs for largely agrarian economies. Colonists in both places engaged extensively in trade with Native Americans who, until the 1760s at the very earliest, were powerful enough to define the western limits of each colony. Consequently Pennsylvania and South Carolina shared chronologies of imagining, making, and ordering commercial space.[13]

Yet it is clear to even the most casual observer that these two colonial projects also had very divergent histories. South Carolina flourished because of its foundational commitment to a system of enslaved African labor, while Pennsylvanians relied more heavily on indentured servants to work the land. For over a century the slave society mainly produced one crop, rice. The mid-Atlantic's natural resources lent themselves to a more multifaceted economy that exported wheat but also produced iron, linen, and glass. Although the Pennsylvania landscape was rural by modern standards, it was dotted with a handful of small towns like Lancaster. South Carolina, on the other hand, had a few small villages, such as Camden, beyond Charleston but no significant inland towns. These contrasts, along with different climates, peoples, and natural geographies, informed the making of markets in these locations. However, some of the ingredients for colonization were the same, as people, institutions, and landscapes combined to create a market. It is possible to tell a broader story of economic development constituting a shared process of market making, albeit with sometimes contrasting points of emphasis.[14]

To underline these common strands of space and practice in the marketplace, I discuss examples from across the colonies and from other British regions. Yet I do not claim that all marketplaces were the same; generations of historians on both sides of the Atlantic have worked to prove the importance of regional difference to these processes and practices. Nevertheless, it is equally critical to recognize that there were also moments of shared experience. Indeed, colonial commonalities are often thrown into bold relief when placed alongside British practice. It is hard to uncover what was colonial about the marketplace without situating it among the other marketing cultures that influenced it and functioned alongside it.[15]

In Britain, I concentrate on trading people and places situated in the northeast of England and the southwest of Scotland, locations that had a similarly distant relationship with the very particular developments affecting the nature of commercial exchange in London and the southeast of England. Like Pennsylvania and South Carolina, northern British markets were undergoing commercialization, but not with same intensity as London's. Glasgow and Newcastle both grew steadily across the seventeenth and eighteenth centuries. Their rural hinterlands were also enmeshed in national processes such as industrialization and land enclosure that changed some elements of the British economy. Nevertheless, looking carefully into the spaces and institutions of provincial commerce demonstrates fundamental ways that new trading patterns emerged in dialogue with long-held customary practices. Plotting the creation of colonial marketplaces along a British axis of time and space thus centers our attention on the short European history of places that lacked centuries of custom and tradition.[16]

As all this talk of space and place suggests, this book is more a history of economic life, its character, and its values than a purely economic history. While I have deployed some statistics in my analysis, I have not discussed matters of growth or wealth, nor have I sought to quantify the extent of the domestic marketplace or the total value of the deals within it. This approach has partly been informed by the evidence available. Although customs records permit quite reliable estimates of the value of colonial overseas trade, and tax lists or probate records afford glimpses of wealth distribution, calculating the value of domestic commerce is not easy. It might be possible to use merchant and farmer account books to analyze where and how imported goods were sold. Yet the exchange of American crops for British imports, or even the free labor market, made up only a fragment of the dealing that took place in colonial trading spaces. What is more, account books rarely reveal much about the logistics and spaces of trade; they tell us little of where the goods were sold and what type of institutional structures were relevant to the deals.

Consequently, I rely instead on a very wide selection of qualitative sources—diaries, letters, court testimony, statutes, newspapers, maps, corporation and guild records—to uncover the most frequent spaces and mechanisms of buying and selling. In these sources people discussed the places they most often visited in their daily commercial circuits. English court testimonies, for example, yield numerous mentions of visits to fairs and to town marketplaces, whereas their colonial counterparts seldom, if ever, recorded such locations. Rather, colonists regularly noted trips to auctions and stores. Such contrasts are just as critical to our understanding of the early American economy as are the distinctive features of the labor market or the importance of cash crops.

Qualitative accounts of trade also afford an assessment of the relation between practice and ideology in an American setting, where rhetoric about private interest and the public good in economic life would eventually become integral to national identity. Right from the beginning of England's colonial project, the practices and spaces of marketing frequently failed to match up with the ideologies and ambitions harbored by colonists. As in Britain itself, the clashes that unfolded when commercial practice met ideological aspiration were expressed in the language of a "private interest" that undermined the "common good" or "public good." These were slippery terms whose definition depended on who was using them; much ink is still spilled today in trying to work out where private interest ends in the marketplace and the public good begins.

Yet the importance of such ideas to early modern people meant that they remained determined to identify where that line fell. Their devotion to demarcating the limits of the public good in the marketplace was not motivated solely by ideology, however; trading in the name of the public good sanctioned economic power. Thus the concept's malleability was also a tool for the many groups jostling to legitimize their economic interest at a time of imperial opportunity. Even after they had declared independence from Britain, colonists remained committed to the values and the utility of the public good in the marketplace. Since it was a flexible concept, they could reinterpret it to suit their purposes. Consequently, an early modern idea of the "public good" was entangled with the experience of American colonization,

eventually becoming redefined to suit the demands of the republican project. Placing the more qualitative features of the colonial marketplace front
and center thus allows continuities to emerge between eras that have customarily been considered discrete phases of the nation's development.

Given these continuities, I start the story of the colonial American marketplace in the commercial spaces its participants were most familiar with,
namely the markets of Britain, West Africa, and early contact North America.
People's experience in these locations determined how colonizers thought
local exchange would (and should) work. The colonial situation, however,
was not conducive to the quick and easy re-creation of the ideal European
marketplace. Populated by Indians, Europeans, and Africans roaming over
a vast landscape and characterized by a superabundance of private property
in the form of people, land, and consumer goods, Britain's American colonies gave rise to new places of market exchange, new ideas about how they
should be ordered, and new sources of conflict within them.

By the middle of the eighteenth century, local market exchange in America already looked quite different from its European counterpart. New modes
of buying and selling and novel spaces of trade created a much more contested role for Europe's customary places and institutions. Well before Adam
Smith had proposed a "free" market from the comfort of his Kirkcaldy study,
Americans had created one in the toil of making new marketplaces. Critical to the "bottom-up" nature of this market evolution, moreover, was the
involvement of Indians, Africans, women, and men. The markets' character,
and their centrality to local trade, relied on the support of all of these traders, who ensured their success by using them for everyday needs.

However, as colonial governments became more powerful across the
middle of the eighteenth century, they started trying to resurrect the spaces
and tools of market order still popular in Europe. The support of white governing men for such regulation was especially strong when it provided a
means of ordering people they deemed unruly: Indians, Africans, and poorer
whites. These efforts were not uniformly successful, but while peace reigned
the novelties and instabilities of these distinctive colonial marketplaces were
incidental to their success. With the onset of imperial crisis following the
Treaty of Paris and British officials' renewed determination to order their
American colonies, the functionality of these marketplaces collapsed. Many
people suffered as a result, but those white property-owning men who had
benefited most from the system felt the pinch in their pockets for the first
time. This galvanized them into more concerted action, setting in motion a
sustained effort to reorder markets for a "public good." Bringing uniformity

to America's marketplaces no longer involved reintroducing early modern ideas about them, however. When colonial experiences, diverse populations, and propertied white men combined in a new republic, the result was a new sense of the "public good" as it should operate in the marketplace.

Both this public good and the other ideological forces it encountered were grounded in a particular character formed throughout the colonial era. Because this was a republic, it was essential for ruling men to argue for a marketplace that met the "good of the whole" by ensuring a regular trade performed by a virtuous citizenry. Widely advertised in print and practice, professing adherence to such an ideal became an important part of being a good republican. Yet its application was uneven at best. In short, the concept was fundamental to the way whites governed blacks, women, and poor whites in the marketplace, but it remained contested among propertied whites themselves. By the 1790s, therefore, the American public good had become something very different from the common good that had shaped the British marketplace. Much less embedded in a set of values that centered on a godly commonwealth in which reciprocity and duty governed the way an entire society related to one another in the economy, the American public good was an ideology to be trumpeted loudly and applied selectively. Traders who were most likely to be the subject of its selective application were those who had been highly visible in creating the free-trading marketplace of the colonial era: Africans, Indians, and women.

The republic's rulers had therefore created an economy that purported to meet the "good of the whole" but in reality operated mostly for the benefit of the white male freeholders who governed it. This creation was solely the product neither of colonization nor of the Revolution. Instead, it was sparked by the friction between these two critical eras. Whereas the colonial decades had witnessed the emergence of a hybrid marketplace melding novel and customary places and practices, the Revolutionary era had threatened that culture. Recognizing their precarious supremacy, propertied rulers were motivated by the chaos to recommit to the idea of trading spaces regulated to function for the public good. Crucially, this was a new definition of an old concept, designed especially to work for a multiethnic society emerging from its status as a colonial outpost of the British Empire. However novel, though, it still faced a struggle with those property owners who strongly adhered to the ideal that they should have the liberty to trade as they pleased, unmolested by any government. Since this was a right embedded in the very trading spaces of America, they were not about to give it up easily.

PART I

The Early Modern Marketplace and Its Colonial Encounter

CHAPTER ONE

A Journey through Early Modern Trading Spaces

According to neoclassical economics, markets share a set of rules regulating their operation irrespective of any particular historical or spatial attributes. The market is imagined to be an autonomous system and an omnipresent organizational principle, structuring our social and economic relationships in an efficient and beneficial manner. The proponents of this point of view draw support from Adam Smith, who explained that traders were "led by an invisible hand" to increase their own wealth and that of their nation. Following this famous characterization of the market, Smith explained how "by pursuing his own interest" man "frequently promotes that of the society more effectually than when he really intends to promote it." Smith was suspicious of traders who said they gave priority to the common good and claimed he had "never known much good done by those who affected to trade" in its name.[1]

During this era of rapid economic change, the market was certainly becoming less a place and more a set of rules. Among the merchants and manufacturers Smith considered in *The Wealth of Nations*, the market was often a concept spanning the global trading networks discussed in their correspondence. When they asked about "the state of the market" or requested "the market price," these entrepreneurs were not inquiring after the conditions in a particular place. They might link descriptions to a port city—the "Liverpool market" or the "New York market," for example—but such comments referred not to a fixed location but rather to a system constituted by demand and supply. In its most tangible form, this market was a list of "prices current" in local newspapers, merchant guides, or a fellow trader's letter. This idea of the market is very easy for us to grasp in the twenty-first century, where the market is on the internet, in the stock exchange, and in the algorithms dreamed up by hedge-fund managers to increase their profits and those of their wealthy clientele. The market is most definitely not on the high street, which is constantly in decline.[2]

However, looking at the early modern market in its proper context rather than on the terms refracted through a present-day lens, such interpretations are lacking in two ways. First, Adam Smith did not deploy the phrase "invisible hand" in the way it has been understood by his neoliberal interpreters. Using the term only three times, Smith did not advocate an omnipresent, self-regulating market primarily to promote efficiency; he was offering his ideas as an alternative to the power relationships permeating the markets he observed. To loosen the grip of vested interests, Smith favored a system in which individuals made their own economic choices free from the oppressive hand of regulation. *The Wealth of Nations* promoted a laissez-faire market as the solution to a problem of self-interested intervention by corrupt governing elites. The market should be free, thought Smith, because that was the only way to stamp out interest groups that so often masqueraded as the "public good." Free markets were the solution to a political issue rather than to a solely economic problem of "optimal allocation." Smith instead offered a vision for an improved market rooted in Britain's emerging commercial scene. He centered this vision on industrialization and the imperial economy, dreaming of the further advantages they could offer if only the shackles of custom, interest, and misconceived support of the "common good" might be thrown off.[3]

Yet, as Smith was only too aware, this was a manifesto for "the market," not an outline of the actual frameworks structuring everyday buying and selling. Ideological agendas aside, therefore, his outlook is helpful precisely because of its focus on the British economy's "problems," namely institutions and their interests. Smith's aspirations nudge us toward a better understanding of the early modern market's particularities. As Keith Wrightson has explained, while this economy "bore the face of a commercial civilisation, it remained still a mixture of forms, structurally, geographically, culturally and in its congeries of social identities, shot through with ambiguities and inconsistencies." All at once people's economic lives embraced new structures and practices while still proceeding within familiar places, hierarchies, and cherished traditions. To explain more fully how this dynamic influenced marketing, we must cast our eye over the changing array of places where Britons went to trade goods. A *tableau vivant* of the physical spaces where people traded with each other, this outline appraisal of day-to-day marketing will be critical when we shift our attention to America.[4]

The stage for activity was the places hosting early modern commercial exchange. These spaces were critical because fixing commerce in a physical location was one of the primary ways institutions in England and Scotland sought to maintain their "interest" in it. Fairs, provisions markets, and shops were familiar commercial spaces where traders converged and associated social, economic, and political hierarchies were rehearsed. Institutions such as guilds, city corporations, manors, and national governments historically preferred that commerce take place in these locations because it eased the collection of tolls, the enforcement of quality control and price regulations, and the exclusion of people not trading in the interest of such groups. Bound up in these laws and protocols were social and political hierarchies. City corporations, for example, were composed of a town's wealthiest citizens, who expected deference to their authority from the urban population because they regulated marketing for the common good. Individuals who attempted to trade away from these structures, and who seemed to reject the public interest and the hierarchies and institutions embedded within it, still faced censure even in the last quarter of the eighteenth century.

Since physical, regulated market spaces remained important, a central strand in the story of eighteenth-century commercialization is the increasing distances and volume of trade that dislodged marketing from them. Given the intimate relationship between the political economy of marketing and its settings, this process was neither straightforward nor undisputed. In addition to challenging the authority of those interests used to overseeing trade, it tested the hierarchies ensconced within them. Thus the second portion of this chapter outlines the new marketing spaces and practices that emerged over the eighteenth century, explaining how they departed from this economy of geographically embedded interests, though they often developed in reference to it.

Existing simultaneously within single marketing spaces, therefore, were new marketing habits, existing spaces put to novel purposes, and also novel habits absorbed into traditional patterns of commerce. To obtain an idea of what "the market" meant to ordinary Britons—and what sense of the thing they took with them to Britain's American colonies—our picture must incorporate this complex interplay between the new and the old. We should acknowledge the multiple ways they were layered together, existing in dialogue with one another. These interlocking layers were indeed very complex; framing them as tradition versus novelty, or as a market economy versus a moral economy, drastically oversimplifies the situation. These dynamics were entangled with the local landscape in a process where setting, people, and institutions constantly interacted.

With an understanding of this dynamic in provincial Britain comes a better appreciation of how North American colonization disrupted it. Once in America, colonists encountered a vast landmass devoid of what they defined as marketplaces. Initially they were without the institutions that overlaid those marketplaces, managing interests in the name of the common good. Thus settlers were equally detached from the hierarchies rooted within these structures. Ultimately, the complexity of the British marketplace made remapping it onto a colonial landscape a tricky business.

At the same time, the nature of the colonizing enterprise presented Europeans with unprecedented trading opportunities in Native Americans. Carolinians also had numerous Africans in their midst from the very start of their project. So, while we acknowledge the importance of European market cultures, it is equally necessary to decipher the character of trading places and practices frequented by the people of color so critical to them. As many historians now recognize, in the chaos of early colonial society, Europeans were heavily dependent on the knowledge and labor of Indians and Africans. For a substantial number of decades, therefore, these people's habits and spaces of local market exchange were very influential. Even at the dawn of the eighteenth century, they would continue to hold substantial power over Europeans' ability to profit from market exchange in their colonies. Thus we must be aware of the values driving Indians and Africans as they also sought to sustain themselves in an American landscape that was a New World for all.

THE SPACES OF EARLY MODERN BRITISH TRADE

At the heart of English and Scottish marketing were three fixed commercial locations that had endured for centuries: the fair, the urban marketplace, and the shop. These spaces endured partly because they responded to change. As James Davis has explained in his history of the English marketplace before 1500, it was "an intense and complex arena of cultural negotiation between a variety of forces—ideology, laws, economics, vested interests and social needs." This dynamic endured well into the eighteenth century, and although the field of negotiation shifted with the emergence of new markets, the types of interests involved and the dynamic between them remained familiar. Exploring these interests at work in fairs, in urban marketplaces, and in shops allows us to see how the market, like so many other aspects of early modern society and culture, was still profoundly local. All three of these commercial spaces were embedded in local political economies and institutions and as such were places for rehearsing local power struggles as well as for conducting trade. So it is also essential to grasp the larger political and social environment in which these struggles occurred.[5]

Our tour starts in the marketplace most unfamiliar to the twenty-first-century reader—the fair. In Britain, fairs now conjure up images of gaudy rides, giant plush toys, and cotton candy. In America the state fair also includes craft displays, deep-fried butter, and funnel cakes. All such enticements remained peripheral to the early modern fair, which was a wholesale and retail trading opportunity customarily occurring two times a year on the same piece of ground. Fairs came in many shapes and sizes and also welcomed agricultural laborers looking for an annual contract. Most renowned were the very large events at which international merchants gathered to buy and sell goods wholesale. Such fairs took place all over Europe and in its New World territories too. At Cartagena and Portobello, Spanish creole merchants traded their precious metals for European commodities, with the timing of the event decided by the seasonal visits of the flota, which took colonial treasures safely back to Spain. In the German lands, merchants gathered in Leipzig and Frankfurt. In England, Stourbridge was among the most renowned fairs, Daniel Defoe noting in 1724 that "scarce any trades are omitted—goldsmiths, toyshops, braziers, turners, milliners, haberdashers, hatters, mercers, drapers, pewterers, china-warehouses, and in a word all trades that can be named in London; with coffee-houses, taverns, brandy-shops, and eating houses, . . . all in tents, and booths." Defoe's description particularly notes that fairs were not always just wholesale events but also sold retail to visitors from the surrounding areas.[6]

As revealed in *Owen's Book of Fairs*, first published in 1756, Stourbridge was the zenith of a rich provincial British fair culture. Throughout the country, fairs were a major location of trade for all sorts of livestock, foods, labor, and manufactures. They took place at times of the year dictated by customary calendars of church holy days and local cultural activities. *Owen's* guide, first published to clarify the confusion over dates after the shift to the Gregorian calendar in 1752, was an exhaustive list of county fairs in England and Wales, the 152 printed pages a testimony to the sheer number of such events. The entry for one county—Northumberland—reveals the fairs' common qualities. Twenty fair locations are listed, and since many fairs took place twice a year, this included thirty-five separate events. Because fairs were linked to the high points of the church year or the agricultural year, many were noted as being not on a particular date, but on "Whit-Tuesday," "Whitsun Eve," "Old Michaelmas," or "Palm Sunday Eve." Each fair specialized in a different array of goods, partly dependent on the season. At Allentown buyers would find "horned cattle, horses, linen cloth, green and dry hides"; at Harbottle "great quantities of linen and woolen, and scotch cloth"; at Morpeth "Wed. for horned cattle, Thurs. for sheep, Frid. For horses, &c"; and at Newcastle's nine-day fair livestock for the first three days, then "cloth, woollens, and various other goods to the end."[7]

Mentioned frequently in accounts of trade and of daily life, fairs were embedded in the commercial culture of the nation until the early nineteenth century. Newspapers carried regular reports of fair trade, both locally and farther afield, to give readers a barometer of economic health. Farmers kept timetables of local fairs at hand to know when they might sell their produce or buy additional livestock. Giving accounts of themselves in court, witnesses and the accused used fairs to contextualize their actions, provide a sense of time, or offer a reason for their movements. John Ladler, a Northumberland yeoman, caught his neighbors in the act of slaughtering a stolen sheep because he had come by their house early in the morning on his way to Hexham fair. John Robertson, a Newcastle laborer, found himself the victim of theft on the city's quayside when the perpetrators correctly guessed he had cash on him since he had "been at some Fair or Hopping" selling nuts and gingerbread. In a 1778 accusation of defamation the Wooler fair, scheduled to take place about the time of the incident, was a recurring theme in the testimony of those involved. Two deponents heard about the "ill words" spoken on their way back from the fair, and a third heard while she was selling eggs to a neighbor "one day in the week before Wooller fair."[8]

These testimonies reveal that the fair, as an event and as a marketplace, was part of local economy and society. Often such customs spilled over into popular political culture. In Northumberland, trading cattle at fairs was entangled with the region's border status and with a frontier of English identity in a Britain relatively recently formed. At Newcastle's 1768 Lammas fair, when many of the 10,000 cattle offered for sale were brought south by Scottish drovers, the politics of the day got dragged into the haggling. As the *Newcastle Courant* reported, "Some English and Scotch Drovers went into a Tent to drink a Glass over a Bargain, when the former calling for a Toast, the latter gave Lord Bute, and went round: After which one of the English Drovers gave Mr Wilkes, but the Scotchman refusing, saying 'Troth he was noa gude Man,' and persisting in it, the Toaster of Mr Wilkes put his Finger in his Mouth, and gave the Scotchman his Wine and his Toast back again on his Breast, which occasioned some confusion among them, but at last they parted good Friends." Drinking, toasting, and bargaining, eventually opposing political views clashed to sully the atmosphere in the fair tent—but at least a cordial deal was achieved in the end.[9]

However, fairs had not emerged as trading places just because people happened to find them useful or especially liked them. Fairs ensured that commerce took place for the benefit of various interest groups in local society looking to take a cut of the proceeds of trade while also expressing their power to govern it. Although anyone was free to come and trade, their dealings were subject to surveillance by these groups, who had created the fair precisely to concentrate deals in a single easily observable place. Watching traders were local elites and corporate bodies aiming to order dealing according to the idea of the common good. Fairs were often held at the behest of a local aristocrat who had been granted a royal charter bestowing the privilege to hold the event on his estate. Groups of local worthies also gathered to run a fair in their joint names. In the Scottish highlands "the principal gentlemen, drovers, and other dealers" of Doun in Perthshire assembled for this purpose. The palatinate of Durham's fair was a privilege granted to the bishop but then conferred by him on the freemen of Durham. The right to run a fair was thus viewed as a valuable privilege to be enjoyed among provincial gentry and better sorts, as individuals and also as a group assembled in a body corporate.[10]

The enduring value of this privilege motivated the conflicts that arose over whose right it was to enjoy them. At a Herefordshire fair, the local lord attempted to use the event to unify local society, entertaining first "the Gentlemen and Ladies" and then "the Freeholders" in several large tents. However, the neighborly peace was broken when a nearby landowner "threatened to pull down the Booths, saying, they were on his ground." Likewise, a group of Argyllshire justices of the peace intervened when some rival gentlemen farmers advertised a competing fair scheduled at the same time as their established event. The justices opined that they could only imagine their competitors were acting in this way "to promot[e] their own private interest." The new fair had none of the facilities needed to accommodate cattle at the fairground or to guarantee owners a good price for their stock. As an incentive, the justices in charge of the long-standing event promised sellers that unsold beasts "would be purchased upon the risque of the shire."[11]

These aristocrats and gentlemen fought to control fairs because the events enhanced both the power and the wealth of local elites. Fairs were ruled

FIGURE 1.1 Broadside announcing the Cornhill Fair, Newcastle, 1714. Courtesy of the Haggerston Family and Northumberland Archives.

by intricate charters distributing benefits and authority among recipients, who were usually society's "better sorts." A broadside announcing the fair at Cornhill in Northumberland thus explained "by order of the Honorable Sir Carnaby Haggerston, Baronet" that attendees must not "break his Majesty's Peace" on pain of a forty-shilling fine. Anyone who drew blood in a fight either at the fair or on the way to it would have to pay a hefty one hundred shillings to be "Levy'd of the Goods of the offenders." With George I's crest heading up the broadside, there could be little doubt concerning the ultimate authority overseeing this fair, which was susceptible to the unrest that dogged this border region in an era of Jacobitism.[12]

Fairs were further regulated by thirteen clauses in various acts of Parliament, accumulated over centuries. These statutes asserted the right of the charter holder to run the fair on a specific piece of ground, determine the tolls charged sellers at the fair, recruit toll collectors, and decide what fee these "farmers" would enjoy. Each fair was supposed to keep a record of all goods sold—especially livestock—with special clauses instructing the clerk of the fair what to do if stolen animals were brought for sale. Officials were also charged with enforcing standard measures for any goods sold by weight or quantity and with limiting the size of traders' tents, which could be raised only within a stipulated time before the fair. With these regulations in place, the fair officials might be sure they would benefit financially from the event, but also that trade would fulfill the principles of "the common good"—that bargains would be honest, prices fair, deals observed, and stolen goods prevented from entering the marketplace. It was benefits like these—tangible to so many elements in local commercial society—that meant new fairs were still founded over the course of the eighteenth century.[13]

As I have noted, the prince bishop and the palatinate of Durham granted a fair charter to the city's freemen. The "gift" also bestowed on the citizens the privilege of running the town's marketplace. This bundling of authority over the two markets illustrates the way that, throughout Britain, they formed the twin pillars of the customary marketplace. Together these commercial locations provided fixed and observable sites for trade, convenient to buyers and sellers of all sorts of commodities, at all times of year, in both city and country. Much that was characteristic of the fair's spaces, its culture, and its political economy also applied to the year-round town marketplace. Perhaps even more than the fair, this was a space where commerce and the competing interests of the local political economy came together to conduct trade according to the common good. As an important location of everyday commerce, the marketplace also figured largely in popular economic culture.

The urban marketplace remained a central space where wholesale and retail food transactions took place throughout the eighteenth century. In Glasgow the city's provisions markets expanded and shifted to keep pace with population growth. Following a 1636 charter from Charles I, Glasgow "magistrates and council as representing the community of the city" had been "vested with full power of holding and excrasing weekly markets three days every week vizt Monday Wednesday and Friday . . . with all the tolls customs rights privileges and immunities." These powers they duly exercised, undertaking a constant program of "improvement" over the eighteenth century. In 1701 they built a fish market "at the West syde of the Candlerig," and by 1755 the city's markets consisted of an "Old Beef Market to be rebuilt for a Green Market . . . Markets in Kings Street vizt a Large Beef Market, a Large Mullon Market, Market for Country Butchers, a Fish Market on Clyde Side vizt a Slaughter House, a market for Live Cattle." In total, these markets were estimated to bring thousands of pounds a year into the city coffers. They remained bustling and well patronized right to the end of the eighteenth century, the Incorporation of Gardeners' records showing that the "green market" opened in 1758 with sixty-five stalls remained fully occupied into the nineteenth century.[14]

Like the fairs, such marketplaces occupied a central place in everyday commercial life and culture. Manuals advising housewives on issues of household "oeconomy" interpreted marketing as going to the central marketplace to buy beef, brawn, butter, and eggs. Court testimonies betrayed how closely the act of buying and selling was still associated with trade in the town marketplace. Identifying himself to the magistrates, one Jonathan Staines of Pickering in Yorkshire explained that "he is a dyer & keeps Kirby Markett." Mary Chapman, a joiner's wife, opportunistically stole a tankard when she went "to seek a man to carry her marketings home." Servant Sarah Marshall was sent by her master to Sheffield "to make some Markett, and to buy some necesaries for the family." These uses of the word, unfamiliar to us today, were well understood among ordinary people going about their daily commercial lives. "Market" was a verb and "marketings" was a noun, with both terms owing their meaning to their close connection with the physical space visited to transact trade.[15]

As at fairs, such transactions were overseen by local interest groups who saw it as their responsibility to ensure they were executed, so they claimed, for the "common good." Sellers should charge a fair price, goods should not be sold before they reached the publicly owned piece of ground that was the market, trade should begin and end at an appointed time, the market infrastructure should be orderly and kept in good condition, and goods offered for sale should be of a decent quality. Usually the statutes governing urban marketplaces concentrated on the duties of the clerk of the market, the maintenance of standard weights and measures, and the three related offenses of forestalling, engrossing, and regrating. (Forestallers bought up provisions before they reached the marketplace; engrossers held on to supplies of essential food and fuel to drive up the price; and regraters bought in the marketplace then sold to householders at a higher price.) Breaking any of the regulations, or simply trading lawfully in the marketplace, usually involved paying a toll or a fine. As Glasgow's city accounts demonstrate, such charges, along with stall rentals, produced a steady income for the authorities.[16]

With both year-round profits and the fundamental "order" of trade at stake, it is no wonder that those in charge of the marketplace were at least as keen to maintain their power as those who had jurisdiction over the fair. The wide variety of institutions claiming a stake in the marketplace made this a tricky proposition, however. The space might be under the jurisdiction of a local aristocrat, the manor, the town corporation, or the bishop. No matter what entities were granted ultimate authority, they frequently suffered challenges from other interest groups, making the market's management as much a political task as an economic one. In both Hexham and Durham, long-running conflicts between freemen and ruling elites influenced the ordering of this central commercial space. With the manor still a powerful authority in eighteenth-century Hexham, its lord, Sir Walter Blackett (a divisive figure at the best of times), had to tread carefully with the town's freemen. Following a 1755 move to enclose four thousand acres of common land surrounding the town, a riot broke out in the marketplace in which fifty-one people died. In an effort to restore cordial relations in 1766, Blackett funded the construction of a new shambles out of his own pocket.[17]

Discord was not so easily smoothed over in the Durham marketplace, however, where a dispute over a grain toll called scavage lay unresolved for over a hundred years. First coming before the Chancery Court in the seventeenth century, the disagreement centered on freemen's claims that they were exempt from this toll, some of whose proceeds were due to the bishop of Durham. This, claimed the freeman, was a privilege bestowed on them after the early seventeenth-century charter increasing the city corporation's power. As a protest against the corporation's continued subservience to the bishop, freemen repeatedly refused to collect the toll, allowing the toll-free marketing of grain in the marketplace. Grain marketing in Durham thus became a pawn in an ancient dispute between the palatinate's secular and religious authorities.[18]

Shops, the final location on our itinerary, were equally enmeshed in local political economy. Certainly they were the sites of an emergent consumer economy, but they were also customary spaces regulated by guilds and corporations. Hence they remained among the local, fixed marketing locations frequented by buyers and sellers. In provincial cities like Glasgow and Newcastle, both guilds and corporations still claimed authority over shops in the eighteenth century. The city government owned commercial properties, which it rented out to tradesmen, often dictating the terms of use. Newcastle's corporation was particularly interventionist in this respect, ordering tradesmen to desist from trading, banning "foreigners" from using shop stalls in the main streets, allowing shopkeepers to give up their leases only with the Common Council's permission, chasing unincorporated wig makers out of their shops, forbidding tobacconists to sell tobacco outside their fixed shops, and dictating whether residential properties might be turned over to retail.[19]

Consequently, all three of the most popular sites of day-to-day retail were governed by the hierarchies and duties embodied in the idea of a market that functioned for the common good. Many of the economic interactions that took place within the fair, the market, and the shop involved exchange between individuals and authorities who occupied different places in a social hierarchy: the prince bishop and the freeman, the tobacco seller and the corporation were not equals. Yet under the auspices of a trade that functioned for a common good, their inequality did not necessarily mean the rich could act as they pleased in the marketplace while the poor had no choice but to obey the laws laid down by their betters. Rather, each had their duties and their roles. In a contemporary ballad, a West Country plowman told the "fine folk" of the city how "For all your Rich Jewels you starving may dye, / If we do not bring in a daily supply." Such reciprocity was also embedded within the process of petitioning, used by so many poor Britons to make requests to their betters; petitioners stressed their diligence as humble people while reminding wealthy magistrates and lords of their duties to assist them by ensuring that the local economy was fair for all participants. The early modern market was thus embedded in the local landscape, at the center of economic, social, and political life. Trading in these spaces was part of a familiar "way of doing," and across all social classes buying and selling were interwoven with the values and places that structured local communities.[20]

With the fair, the market, and the shop nested so tightly within the web of local social and economic relations, it comes as no surprise that men and women who attempted to trade away from these spaces, or who were not well known to a community, suffered extreme hostility. Even though the Atlantic world had dramatically increased mobility among some sectors of society, peripatetic traders—whose "market" was abstract and not closely tied to an identifiable physical space in which acknowledged authorities and power structures operated—provoked strong reactions.[21]

For many people, the peddler and the hawker most embodied the dangers inherent in straying from physical market spaces. Reaction to such traders throws further light on the enduring importance for early modern Britons of "locating" trade in a particular space. It is especially in the long-running campaign by shopkeepers to completely remove peddlers and hawkers from the retail scene that the importance of fixed market spaces emerges. Complaints against these itinerants appeared in print throughout the eighteenth century, but they reached fever pitch in the 1770s and were quelled only in the 1780s when Pitt's government raised the cost of peddling licenses to a prohibitive level. Local authorities proclaimed shrilly on the necessity of protecting "the resident trade . . . from the depredations of itinerants" who came to town before a fair and sold goods at local inns. Newspaper editors looked forward to banning peddlers, who were so "injurious to the settled fair trader." Allowing full expression to his dislike of these traders, the editor of the *Newcastle Courant* asked his readers to consider "what sort of people these hawkers are," arguing that a moment's contemplation would surely reveal them to be "a body of strolling, idle people, composed of all nations and countries, wandering about from town to town, vending deceitful wares, under colour of a licence." With this invective the editor takes us to the very heart of the reasons the market as an abstraction, instead of a fixed place, remained a dangerous anomaly for so many; it undermined the industrious local community who traded quality wares at fair prices and always looked out for the "common good" over private interest. Peddlers dislodged the market, and in doing so they threatened to undermine the very fabric of society. Conversely, the "fair trader" was an individual who respected the privileges and hierarchies of the marketplace and who thus represented the forces of social and economic order.[22]

THE BRITISH MARKETPLACE, EMPIRE, AND COMMERCIALIZATION

Our modern perceptions of the market may get in the way of understanding its early modern incarnation, but they can also help us see that these late eighteenth-century invectives against peddlers came at a moment when this social group was far from alone in challenging the customary spaces of commerce. Indeed, any rise in the number of such traders was surely linked with the industrial and consumer revolutions and the expansion of Britain's empire. Quite possibly the anxieties that arose as a result of this economic change sustained opposition to peddlers and hawkers, who may have seemed part of a larger assault on the familiar spaces and habits of trade and on the normative social relationships they embodied.[23]

Historians, who like to document change, have usually focused on the novelties of British retail in the eighteenth century. We are alert to the new methods of marketing that emerged in this era but are less familiar with the endurance of longer-standing ones. In this emerging consumer society, scholars have identified an array of innovations shaping British retail before the "invention" of the department store in the second quarter of the nineteenth century. Shops sold more specialized goods than ever before. Shop interiors acquired an air of sophistication, catering to the emerging preoccupation with shopping as a leisure activity. In an effort to gentrify the urban environment, messy and noisy provisions markets were sometimes relocated away from the center of towns. Inns and taverns became retail spaces, hosting traveling salesmen who brought goods from London to the provinces. Shops proliferated in rural Britain too, and soon even large villages accommodated a number of fixed outlets offering much more than a butcher, a baker, and a candlestick maker. Many of these new shopkeepers were grocers, who supplied local communities with tea, sugar, coffee, chocolate, and tobacco—the exotic offerings of empire. Increasing numbers of auctions, a form of retail that also took place away from the controlled, corporate space of the market, fair, or shop, offered consumers across the country the opportunity to buy novel goods secondhand, even permitting middling sorts to get their hands on the cast-off possessions of the aristocracy. Such changes in the spaces and practices of commerce touched many localities in eighteenth-century Britain, but inevitably their impact was greater in some parts of the nation than in others.[24]

Only recently, however, have historians turned their attention back to the market's enduring qualities. This shift in focus has forced recognition of the important national economic discussions, such as debates about the wool trade, unfolding around traditional assumptions rooted in a balance of economic interests. Similar motivations underpinned the local marketplace. In Scotland, burgh (town) institutions continued to play a much greater role in organizing urban trade than did their counterparts in southern English towns. Likewise, guilds remained more influential in Newcastle than in Birmingham, where manufacturing expanded and organized without regard for the privileges still claimed by freemen elsewhere. Other cities where the industrial economy had taken hold, such as Sheffield, London, and Manchester, also grew without close corporate surveillance.[25]

Consequently some buyers and sellers visited fairs or marketplaces less frequently than their compatriots elsewhere in the country. City merchants were the group most likely to conduct their commercial business in an abstract "market." So, while our court witnesses used terms related to markets and marketing in ways that are strange to us in the twenty-first century, we encounter more familiar usages of the word in the letterbooks of these traders. For the British overseas merchant, it was the size of the market that made it an abstraction; the Caribbean sugar plantation, the Chesapeake wharf, or the backcountry store was unimaginable to many such men, who shipped goods to the port city's wholesalers, the dealers responsible for breaking bulk to move them through local retail channels.[26]

However, as national markets emerged for certain agricultural products, "the market" ceased to be an actual place among some inland merchants too. Markets became even more abstracted as places when these merchants were joined from the early eighteenth century by factors, who acted as brokers and transporters in the cheese, cattle, and grain trades. These middlemen not only made the route from producer to consumer more complex, they also played a role in setting prices and shifting commercial activity to new "private" sites away from the gaze of local officials. Rather than being fixed upon in the marketplace under the watchful eye of the clerk, the moment of transaction might now happen in the miller's house or the local inn, not at the public wharf or dedicated market house. The Kentish grain trade, customarily anchored at London's Bear Quay market, was bypassed as dealers agreed on a price before shipping. Hoyman-factors or merchant millers struck deals with farmers in Kent, the grain arriving in London with the price already decided. Dealing in a provision in demand across Britain and America, Cheshire cheese factors similarly moved trade from a single, fixed place so that by the 1760s the grocery's price was under the control of a clutch of London agents.[27]

The emergence of new marketing places and practices certainly diverted trade from both the spaces and the political economies of longer-standing locations of commerce. Nevertheless, there were many ways such innovations existed in dialogue with more familiar locations. Although E. P. Thompson, and the many early American historians who followed in his footsteps, emphasized two-way conflict between the traditional "moral economy" and the novelties of a market-driven model, on the ground contrasts were often far from stark. Local courts saw an increase in interpersonal credit litigation, but magistrates also still heard many cases where the common good was the driving principle. Scotland's burgh courts, and its court of sessions, regularly adjudicated disputes concerning the rights and privileges of guilds and corporations and the use of common lands for private profit. Inhabiting this entangled landscape of old and new commercial practice, Adam Smith observed that traders who sought to operate away from this entrenched network of corporate interests faced an uphill struggle. Smith's intense dislike of the system of apprenticeship stemmed from his belief that these institutions stifled trade with their closed shops as well as their determination to exclude individuals who would not conform to their rules.[28]

But one man's opprobrium could not end a centuries-old institution. In an economic culture valuing tradition, even traders involved in newer marketplaces still retained habits and links to existing institutions and practices. Customary values influenced popular perceptions and critiques of marketing, and the persistence of the early modern marketplace in its historic form meant that all novelties would exist, in some way, in reference to established habits. Rather than being a clear-cut battle between patricians and plebeians or between a free market and a moral economy, the conflicts of this era thus represented moments of complex negotiation between new and old. As they contested the disputed terrain of "provisions politics," farmers, consumers, merchants, and magistrates took apart the "building blocks of which marketing and trade were made . . . and when the crisis was over they were rarely reassembled in precisely the same way." While the new ways of dealing among grain merchants and middlemen were changing the way they traded, all such change took place amid the existing customary reference points of the marketplace.[29]

This dynamic characterized disputes unfolding beyond the explosive conflicts involving the grain supply. When Glasgow's "warehouse keepers" and property owners in the genteel Saint Andrew's Square complained that a newly relocated butter, egg, and fowl market was devaluing their properties and kicking up dust that ruined their stock, the city's magistrates refused to make any concessions to the rights of these traders, dealing as they were in nonessential goods from their private properties. The magistrates sniffily suggested that "in this wet climate . . . it is but seldome that dust can be any annoyance to the neighbouring warehouses" while underlining their right and duty as the city's rulers of "regulating the public markets . . . in such a manner as appeared to them to suit best the public convenience which is the primary and fundamental object of such an establishment." In short, the customary marketplace trumped the entrepreneur selling exotic imports in his warehouse, the authorities requiring that the two cordially deal side by side.[30]

Thus, even the shop selling novel imports existed with reference to the older marketplace and its egg sellers. This relationship between novel and customary marketplaces took many forms. As Jon Stobart has argued, early modern grocery retailers conducted their sale of exotic goods on customary foundations. While grocers slowly expanded in number and their stock increased in variety as consumables poured in from across the British colonies, the supply networks linking wholesale to retail did not change dramatically from the sixteenth century to the late eighteenth.[31]

Although they favored older distribution networks, grocers did sometimes advertise in newly founded provincial newspapers. Often, however, they avoided them for fear they might attract undesirable customers. More broadly, the increase in newspaper advertising is a window onto the ways customary market spaces, relationships, and institutions continued to insinuate themselves even into the most novel innovations of eighteenth-century British marketing. The newspaper was exactly the kind of "abstract," virtual marketplace that lies at the heart of our contemporary perceptions of trade. Yet there were multiple ways beyond the wariness of grocers that traders, rather than embracing the new, looked to merge novelty with older modes of marketing or, indeed draw it into historical economic debates hinging on marketplace relations.[32]

Even that most traditional of marketplaces, the fair, became entangled with the novelties of print. As I have already suggested, one indicator of the fair's continued importance during the eighteenth century was the multiple reports of such events appearing in newspapers. The reports almost always included an assessment of trade at the fair, summarizing, for example, how "at Worcester Fair on Thursday Se'nnight, there were about 2500 Pockets of Hops, 2099 of which were sold; the prices from about 41 4s to 61 per Hundred—The Cheese Fair was uncommonly large; some prime Old Sold from 34s to 35s per Hundred; One meal from 26s to 28s and two meal from 24s to 28s."[33]

With these reports, the "actual" market became part of a bundle of abstract market information, often including the prices of essential commodities in various locations around the country. One notice even demonstrated that the fair had been drawn into the transatlantic market: at Stokesley in 1776, just as the Declaration of Independence was being read, "black cattle went off slowly: cows and calves sold well; raw linen web very high, on the demand for America." We can see how traders who read this information and treated it as an abstract "state of the market" report were still connected to customary spaces, which continued to be relevant long into the eighteenth century.[34]

While editors merged the abstract and the actual marketplace in their quest to make themselves a useful information source for readers, some subscribers recognized the newspaper as a useful tool for bringing long-running economic arguments to the attention of a wider public. As a political mouthpiece, the newspaper provided a novel outlet for ancient local economic grievances. Here we can return to the perennial dispute over grain tolls in the Durham marketplace. Although the conflict that sprang up in the 1750s was a repeat performance of a clash between the Durham bishop and the freemen before the Chancery Court in the 1620s, there was one major difference: the eighteenth-century episode included a separate case brought by the bishop's lawyer against one of the most vocal freemen, William Appleby. The suit objected to Appleby's placing newspaper advertisements in the *Newcastle Journal* and the *Courant*. These notices defended the freemen's conduct and accused the bishop's men of fraudulently adjusting the relevant charters. In particular, the bishop's lawyer indicted Appleby for "continually writing Advertisements to inflame the Minds of the People against the relators and their cause and indeed they had very bad effects. The chancellor on many occasions took notice of the impropriety of their behaviour and always recommended it to him to be quiet, but his good advice had little effect." Appleby's determination to bring up this deep-seated disagreement over the political economy of the Durham marketplace—a dispute that was embedded in local corporate power structures and inequalities—provoked horror among his elite opponents, who regarded the newspaper as wholly unsuitable because it drew on a much broader definition of the "public" than they were comfortable with.[35]

As a small town on England's east coast, Durham was not at the forefront of the nation's emerging commercial economy. Rather, Atlantic-facing cities on the west coast were at the cutting edge of these changes, and it is therefore the economic lives of their resident merchants that best embody this interplay between new and old marketing practices. As we have seen, these merchants faced outward toward oceans and empires. Historians have duly focused on their entanglement in commercial networks structured by expertise, commercial "intelligence," and trust. Such qualities, along with new financial instruments and the growth of marine insurance, created novel institutions that greased the wheels of overseas trade and overcame the limitations of the face-to-face economy. It was in letters among themselves, discussing the conditions of this international trade, that merchants most often referred to "the market" in the abstract.[36]

Such letters, however, relate to only one aspect of their economic dealings. Elsewhere we can find surprising ways that Britain's merchants remained deeply entangled in the local marketplace, its economic culture, and its political economy. Among the principal channels for this involvement were the merchant guilds and city corporations many traders belonged to.

These institutions were deeply invested in sustaining the regulated market-ing practices, guided by interests and hierarchies, that Adam Smith had so strongly objected to. First of all, they strove to protect the trading interests of their particular towns against potential British competitors. In the sev-enteenth century, Newcastle's merchants frequently mounted objections to competitors' from London, and even from nearby York, trading in the north-east. Well into the eighteenth century, Glasgow's corporation viewed itself as competing with nearby burghs for the profits of the Atlantic trade, a situa-tion reflected in its efforts to improve Port Glasgow in the face of Greenock's expansion as a more convenient harbor for ships bound for America and the Caribbean. Bristol's Society of Merchant Venturers and its city corporation attempted to maintain the city's premier position in trade by sinking public money into improving its quays and dredging the river Avon, which was in real danger of silting up and ending the port's preeminence altogether.[37]

There were many more mundane ways merchants' deep roots in the ur-ban corporate environment drew them into the politics of the local market-place, often in support of its customary practices. Merchant elites tackled food shortages by establishing funds and clubs to buy provisions and sell them to the poor at an agreed "fair" price. Hence the merchant as freeman reasserted his role as an elite patron to the urban poor, who were expected to return the favor with grateful deference and obedience to their masters. Such dynamics were rehearsed in multiple urban marketplaces, including Bristol, where in February and March 1772 "several gentlemen" formed a committee for provisions and "entered into a subscription to raise a fund to purchase meat, in order to reduce the present most exorbitant price of that article, and finally to check the infamous practice of forestalling; which has been the principal means of raising both bread and meat in this city, to the great distress of the inhabitants." Similar schemes were contrived during grain shortages, when local committees purchased wheat to sell to the poor at "fair" prices. In Glasgow, 1772 was also a bad year for the local economy. The city's worthies responded with a scheme "for the relief of Indigent People Especially of People out of Employ especially tradesmen" whereby traders placed money in a box lodged in "Arthur Robeson's shop," the final total to be distributed to those most in need. Responsibility for the poor state of the Bristol and Glasgow economies may have lain with the vicissitudes of the transatlantic "market," but the solutions merchants sought were grounded in the customary political economy of the urban marketplace.[38]

One man directly involved in the Glasgow scheme was John Brown, a linen manufacturer, merchant, and gentleman farmer whose working life had started in the city at the height of its Atlantic-fueled growth in 1754. Brown had connections to the Bogle family, who had agents in the Chesapeake. His own entanglement in the Atlantic economy came through his export of Scottish linen to South Carolina, Pennsylvania, and Virginia. In 1770 he also got into shipping insurance, the same year that he was "taken into the Merchants house and made a Member of the Dean of G[u]ild Court," thus becoming a member of the city corporation. Brown's "recollections," kept sporadically from 1754 to 1777, are a remarkable testament to the persistence of customary perceptions of the marketplace alongside the more abstract notions characterizing the transatlantic trade. As part of his recollections, Brown offered an annual assessment of the state of the economy, such as the following in December 1757:

> Provisions this year extremely dear oatmeal at 10 per Peck and all other grain & Provisions in proportions. Many a day not a grain of meal in Glasgow Market, it was so scarce or kept for even a great Price on the Parliament Seting down an act Passd prohibiting the Exportation of all kinds of grains which had a very good effect on the Market, and Brought down grain ⅓ in a very short time. All kinds of Coulourd Work this year has been very Cheap, Best ¾ handks at 5/... North Country yarns out of a shop at 22 ½ & 23 ... Lawn Borded hanks and thred gazes has sold pritty weal this Season and a Considable quantity of them Exported to the West India Islands.[39]

Brown thus interpreted "the market" both as the physical space in Glasgow where prices were set by corporate authority and as a more abstract entity spanning the British imperial world, where supply and demand determined the cost of things. Such competing definitions and spaces appeared elsewhere in his economic habits and thoughts: Brown supported protectionist measures and bounties to encourage domestic trade, and he frequently used fairs and marketplaces to transact business. Yet he also traded away from them, establishing personal connections with weavers and middlemen throughout the Scottish lowlands as he traveled around the country buying up linen to finish in his own bleach fields in the Glasgow hinterland for export across the Atlantic.[40]

The complex connections between novelty and custom in local markets were forged equally by men and women dealers. Married or single, urban or rural, British women had long been visible and important presences in marketplaces, fairs, and shops. Commercialization merely drew them into the market more frequently as it offered new avenues for economic activity. Women continued to market agricultural produce, to brew and sell beer, and to spin or sew. However, some wives, spinsters, and widows now diversified to take advantage of emerging financial instruments and retail opportunities created by the expanding imperial economy. Middling families in particular discovered that they could achieve success, or at least security, by developing a "family strategy" that pooled resources to expand business into new areas opening up in the economy. In Glasgow, women shopkeepers made their way by selling exotic groceries, while a number of widows, spying the increased demand for credit among Atlantic traders, took to lending money at interest. Since neither activity was regulated by the urban authorities, male-created corporate barriers had little impact. The city's women maintained their role in customary household marketing while incorporating Atlantic opportunities into their dealings.[41]

Whether traders were women or men, their routine market entanglements underline the complex interactions between old and new in the local economy. The two forces were sometimes antagonistic, with those who favored new ways of doing things coming into direct conflict with existing corporate interests, patterns of behavior, and customary beliefs and with the spaces that were the physical manifestation of these values in the local landscape. Yet conflict was not always part of the equation. The traditional marketplace and its political economy quietly insinuated itself into trading lives and cultures, even among those individuals and areas of commerce most deeply associated with industrial revolution, a consumer society, and the capitalization of the British economy.

Therefore, if we identify the eighteenth century as a moment when the customary marketplace "lost" the fight against the free market, the corporate economy died, or the gradual separation of household and market took hold, we end up with an oversimplified image of the British marketplace. Rather, we must view long-standing market spaces and political economies as the principal reference points in practices and discourses of commerce. Even as new patterns of trading and new ways of conceptualizing the market were emerging, the ongoing influence of institutions that had endured in some form since the medieval era ensured their continued importance. When people continued to trade in these spaces, they endorsed their value, as they did when they deployed discourses long established by their political economies.

TRADING SOCIETIES BEYOND EUROPE

Commercialization rattled the dominance of customary marketing places and practices in Britain. It forced those who wanted to trade in new ways to reckon with the old and to justify their practices to others who supported the status quo. However, such genteel elisions of old and new were a luxury not afforded to the peoples that England's Atlantic commercial exploits brought them into contact with. Rather, by the time England's colonizing projects in Pennsylvania and Carolina were under way in the late seventeenth century, West Africans and Native Americans had had to reckon for at least a century with new forces challenging their habitual economic relations. This challenge came with the arrival, often in waves, of Europeans intent on exploiting their potential as trading partners, as commodities, and as residents of continents identified as offering great commercial promise.

Two vital features of West African and Native American local economies are critical to this age of North American market making. First we must understand them as commercial societies. When Europeans traded with the Siin or Dahomey polities in the Senegambia region of West Africa, or with Creeks or Cherokees in the American Southeast, they were not imposing market relations on primitive, subsistence societies: they were engaging in commerce with people who knew a market when they saw one and even shared some marketing habits with their European contemporaries. Equally important to note, however, is the character of trade in these societies, which had implications when Englishmen came to America en masse in the late seventeenth century. Indians and Africans were part of trading societies founded on fluid and varied market models, well suited to the expansive landscapes they inhabited. The intensification of interaction with Europeans during the 1600s and 1700s merely increased the mobility of their marketplaces.

It is comparatively difficult to outline precisely the phases of market development after 1500 in both West Africa and the native societies of the American Southeast and Mid-Atlantic. The principally archaeological basis of the evidence, and scholars' approach to it until very recently, means we often know the spatial characteristics of the local economy only generally. Since these societies were themselves highly variegated, it is hard even to pinpoint a single model of the marketplace.[42]

Among those West African societies enmeshed in the slave trade, marketplaces adopted many forms. It is clear that Africans patronized local markets; the archaeology and history of settlement patterns has found significant contrasts in the expression of commercial places at ground level. Along the Falemme River in Senegambia, early eighteenth-century settlements were often temporary and military in character; the reaction of the Siin people on the Senegambian coast to regional conflict caused by the slave trade was to move inland and stay mobile. In contrast, the Aro, residents of the Bight of Biafra, at Bonny and northward, created nimble marketing networks reconfigured in response to an increasing demand for slaves over the middle of the eighteenth century. Any trade in this region would thus have contrasted with the experience of the Segou, whose society produced very durable mercantile cities that nevertheless were separated from more transitory state-centered settlements.[43]

This variety demonstrates that we must dispense with any notion that during the sixteenth and seventeenth centuries these people inhabited purely subsistence societies. West Africans were commercial people who shared some marketing practices and spaces with Europeans. Archaeologists have identified mercantile hubs well beyond the coastal forts of Europeans. Ede-Ile, in the expanding Oyo empire, and the place variously known as Savi, Hueda, and then Ouidah after its conquest by the Dahomey in 1727, were both hubs in regional market systems, distributing a wide range of commodities. Excavations at Ede-Ile have uncovered large quantities of cowrie shells, the currency of the region, as well as evidence of a regional trade in earthenware and metalware. From Savi comes proof of a frequent market in which local traders, among them many women, sold foods, cloth, and household goods. Rulers exacted tolls on subjects engaged in such trade, which they had to pay before offering goods for sale.[44]

After 1750, a number of West African towns had market economies similar to their counterparts around the Atlantic world. Women's central role in urban marketing was particularly notable. At Saint-Louis and Gorée in Senegambia, the *signores* were the mistresses of households that thrived on their pivotal place in the local exchange of agricultural staples and consumer goods. In Angola's capital, Luanda, women were among the principal traders in manioc flour, supplying the staple product to African and European consumers alike. Agents of local trade came in many guises, and the canoemen of the Lagos lagoon and Ouidah, who were the sinews of exchange in these watery landscapes, represented just one adaptation to the demands of local geography.[45]

Equally important is the varied and agile character of West Africa's markets, which stretched across the extensive landscape in the precolonial Atlantic era. British marketing institutions relied on a collection of fixed spaces, regulated by numerous overlapping institutions that sought to enforce their interest by making traders conduct commerce within them. West African trade, in contrast, leaned more heavily on the articulation of kinship, cultural, or political networks that could reach over long distances to bring commodities downriver (or overland) to coastal settlements. The success of the Aro's networks relied on the rotation of fair locations and the mobility of brokers between Old Calabar and Bonny. A network of family clans in the polity then used their influence in villages to move people toward the coast—and European slave ships.[46]

The Africans who were in Carolina from the beginning of its Atlantic era therefore not only were a trading people, but were used to achieving their commercial goals by forming fluid networks, stretching across large distances, to move goods to a central coastal place. At the same time, they had little investment in English ideas of a fixed marketplace. In short, they were more familiar with articulating markets in landscapes very similar to those where they found themselves on arriving in Carolina.[47]

Shifting our gaze to this North American landscape, we find Native Americans restructuring their market systems to accommodate the Europeans who had been in their midst from the 1500s onward. In the Southeast, a trade in slaves and guns animated the towns and the paths joining them across the region. Visited first by Spanish adventurer Hernando de Soto, then by his successor Juan Pardo on a mission to settle Florida, and finally by Virginian Englishmen trekking southward, the polities of natives who lived in what would become the western reaches of Virginia, the Carolinas, and Georgia were fully enmeshed in this trade when Carolina projectors arrived in the late 1600s. It was a commerce that relied on, and promoted, mobility between agents who crisscrossed a landscape punctuated by Indian towns joined by well-used paths. While chiefdoms such as Cofitacheque (at present-day Camden, South Carolina) had enjoyed superior power in the sixteenth century, access to trade shifted hierarchies and even incited some groups, such as the Guatari, to move their towns closer to the main paths. By the turn of the seventeenth century, the Southeast's people were participants in regional markets powerful enough to reconfigure both native landscapes and natives' political economy, redirecting them toward increased access to trade goods.[48]

Native groups positioned in the middle of the eastern seaboard, such as the Lenapes and the Susquehannocks, had a similar experience. Finnish-Swedish settlers, then Dutch and English, arrived in this region between present-day Maryland and New Jersey at the beginning of the seventeenth century. Native Americans in the vicinity quickly sought trading relations with Europeans. The attraction of trading with William Claibourne, an English planter who had set up a trading post on Kent Island, prompted the Susquehannocks to battle their rivals for access to the goods he offered, for which they exchanged skins. Victorious in this dispute, the Susquehannocks proved awesome customers for Claibourne, who was already well out of his comfort zone having to deal from "a small shallop" staffed by a handful of Europeans. As the Indians rummaged through the wares on offer, the dealer complained that "it is not convenient or possible to keep an account in that trade for every axe knife or string of beads or for every yard of cloth, especially because the Indians trade not by any certain measure or by our English weights and measures." Willing to enter into violent competition to sell beaver skins, the Susquehannocks then forced their trading partners into a mode of marketing that was unfamiliar to Europeans, contravened their customary expectations, and felt more than a little threatening. In the process, Indians also changed their own ideas of commercial exchange.[49]

Anthropologist Robbie Ethridge has used the idea of a "shatter zone" to evoke the fluid landscapes that emerged when European commercial colonizers mingled with the region's Native Americans. The phrase is apt not only because it captures how contact could affect native societies, but also for its facility in communicating the shock waves of intensified commerce reverberating through the structures of Indian life, rearranging them and aggressively pushing some to breaking point. After two hundred years of living in the shatter zone, the Southeast's Indians were repeatedly caught up in violent conflicts such as the Tuscarora and Yamasee Wars. The slave trade was a violent experience for Africans too, and historians have often focused on the increase in warfare that came with it.[50]

This violence was an important part of the asymmetric relationships that eventually evolved when European commercial colonizing ventures used Indians and Africans as profitable commodities. However, a long era of adaptation also had advantages for people of color. They had something that we have seen the British did not possess, even though they too were part of a commercializing society: the experience of newly articulating markets across expansive landscapes. While British marketing remained rooted in customary landscapes, governed by powerful institutions and their accompanying ideologies, Indians and Africans operated in commercial systems already proven to be capable of responding to new economic topographies.

In Britain, new goods and novel marketplaces became so entangled with a familiar landscape of commerce that in everyday economic life it remained almost impossible to pull apart the new and the old. When in 1776 James Bailey, a sometime resident of Carlisle in Westmoreland, North West England, came before the assizes charged with stealing "a box which contained a set of silver shoe buckles gold wire earrings and other goods wares and merchandize," this intertwined quality emerges from the testimonies of the witnesses.

Four years before, Bailey had stolen these toys, metalware, and trinkets—the stuff of Britain's new consumer economy. Made in Birmingham, London, and Sheffield, the buckles and jewelry were manufactured by industries that excelled in turning out ranges of goods affordable to consumers of all backgrounds. Such items were small, light, and easily transported. Across the years that it took for Bailey's crime to come to light, items from the stolen box changed hands at locations around the North West from Whitehaven to Cockermouth to Westlinton-in-Cumberland.

As they circulated among owners, bargains struck along the way reveal both new consumer opportunity and new marketing places. After stealing the jewelry, Bailey pawned some of it to yeoman Richard Brown, probably at the White Swan inn run at Westlinton by Brown's wife, Sarah. It is hard to imagine that Bailey would have been able to get cash for goods at an inn so easily a century earlier, when desirable, movable, affordable wares were a rarity. But more customary markets also had their role. The crime was detected when Carlisle-based licensed peddler Hugh Adamson stopped in at the White Swan, opened his pack for Brown, and exchanged some silver spoons for the pawned goods, which Bailey had never redeemed. Adamson knew the victim of the original theft, a fellow Carlisle jeweler named John Robson, and at once recognized the gem-encrusted shoe buckles that Robson had talked about losing a few years earlier. Robson's goods had been stolen at Cockermouth fair, which he customarily attended to sell his wares. Adamson himself was at the inn as part of his familiar trek to Dumfries fair.

So, although both men dealt in consumer goods, they were part of resident community of jewelry sellers and makers in Carlisle who maintained an intimate knowledge of each other's movements and dealings. When they sold goods outside the town they followed familiar itineraries that included an annual round of fairs, which had taken place at the same times and in the same locations for centuries. In the end it was the opportunities and knowledge produced by these networks of "settled" traders that brought Bailey, a "sometime" resident, to court. The availability of consumer goods had allowed Bailey to elude these networks of community surveillance and profit from his opportunistic theft, but even four years after the act, their enduring effectiveness led to his capture.[51]

When European immigrants came to North America, this was the market environment they were familiar with, right up until 1776, the year James Bailey found himself at the Northern Assizes charged with stealing a set of silver shoe buckles. The early modern canvas on which European Americans sought to redraw their marketing places was both tangible and enduring. However, there are three central features of early modernity in the marketplace that bear particular emphasis. First, we must foreground the importance of space to the eighteenth-century market. As we have seen, European economic ideals remained closely tied to a particular place, and removing trade from that space frequently caused anxiety. On arrival in their New World, the British came face-to-face with landscapes devoid of such places, as well as with distances between marketing spaces greater than anything they knew in the Old World. Second, Old World marketing spaces were layered with overlapping institutions competing for authority in the marketplace. As Adam Smith appreciated, the laissez-faire market was a radical proposition only in the context of an existing economy where the possibility of being a "free agent"—someone who had private property and could manipulate it freely in a market space—was minimal. Yet given that they viewed both Native Americans and Africans not as a "restriction" on their trade, but as an opportunity to enlarge it, this was exactly the situation confronting Europeans in America.

Finally, we must grasp how social hierarchies continued to govern economic interactions. Market dealings of all sorts in Britain and Europe were structured by traditional ideas about how participants should relate to each other: the freemen who should show deference and gratitude to the bishop of Durham; the aristocrat who was granted the "privilege" of the fair and market by the king and who then collected tolls from the local people when they came to buy and sell in that space; the lord of the manor who created a court in which local traders could air their grievances about the order of the marketplace; and the trade guilds and urban corporations that determined who could trade where, and how they could trade. These complex relationships were structured by social difference and deference to long-standing hierarchy. None of this is to say that the spaces, institutions, and relationships of the marketplace in Britain were insulated from change in the eighteenth century. All of these entities experienced, responded to, and influenced change as the islands underwent more intensive imperial expansion and industrial revolution.

The Native Americans and West Africans who were fundamental to this expansion, however, experienced economic change from a different perspective. Many were familiar with market exchange and with the commercial ambitions of Europeans. Indeed, it was these ambitions that had drawn them into more intensive trading relationships from the sixteenth century onward. As they responded to commercial opportunity in an expansive landscape, Africans and Indians demonstrated the agility and flexibility of their trading networks. At the same time, unlike their European counter-parts, these peoples did not have a unified market vision embedded in gen-erations of experience, custom, and relative stability.

While some historians have claimed that Americans were particularly drawn to Adam Smith's ideas because they could use him as a guide "in a newly formed country that could design its politico-economic institutions and policies free of the weight of old ideals and popular superstitions," in re-ality nothing could have been further from the truth.[52] By the Revolutionary era, colonial Americans had a long history of market experience behind them; they had to trade if they were to make a living, to eat, and ultimately to survive. Into these marketplaces, Europeans had brought their own ideas and their commitment to a regulated marketplace set up to answer the com-mon good. Yet it was in these very spaces that colonists would encounter Native American and African actors. With their own sets of expectations and their own experience of economic change, such people were not about to conform to European customs, especially ones that made so little sense in the expansive continent they all now inhabited.

CHAPTER TWO

The Market Turned Upside Down

We start with trees. The dense and limitless forests were often what made arrival on North America's shores so astounding, and foreboding, to Europeans. Such abundant woodland produced awe and wonder among early colonists, who marveled at how a vast wooded landscape hugged equally grand rivers. Woods were places that Indians knew but Europeans got lost in, both sacred spaces and places that induced fear. They were a source of wood for fuel and housing but a hindrance to European agricultural practices. Those who could gaze on the forest at leisure endorsed William Penn's rustic celebration of the woods as a sylvan paradise "adorned with lovely Flowers." Those who had fought their way through the seemingly endless American forests were less positive, complaining that they were "dark and thick," impeding ignorant European travelers.[1]

Whether colonists found the woods fascinating or foreboding, there was one thing about the abundance of trees that all could agree on: the landscape bore none of the spaces and places familiar to them in their daily economic lives. There were no towns with market squares, and there was no room for a quay, since the trees often crept right down the riverbanks to the water's edge. Clearings in which one might hold a fair were also hard for disoriented Europeans to find as they blundered around, blind to ways Native Americans managed the woods to their advantage.

But discomfort with America's woods did not preclude an appreciation of their commercial potential. Fear was not enough to prevent colonists from looking at a forest and wondering how much money they might make by chopping down the trees. For these early modern people, however, the question of who should profit from such acts was far from straightforward. Deciding who should "own" trees, who could sell them, where they could be sold, whom they might be sold to, and what price should be put on them was not an easy task. In an early modern marketplace structured by interests and privileges, government officials assumed that the sale of trees, even those found in places of uncertain ownership, should not take place just anywhere, anytime, at any price, by anyone.[2]

It was certainly not acceptable for individual colonists to cut down trees and sell them on the spot. In Britain itself, the "forest law" of the medieval period had lapsed by the later seventeenth century despite Charles I's best efforts to revive royal control over woodlands in the years leading up to his deposition in 1642. Nevertheless, an assumed scarcity of timber in a wooden world prompted a pan-European intensification of forest management, ostensibly for the common good. Government, aristocratic, and corporate interests sought to prevent the poor from freely obtaining, using, or selling wood. Their interventionist attitude was motivated by a fear that woods might be decimated. No doubt it was equally prompted by the suspicion that the "wrong" interest would benefit if they themselves gained nothing from this decimation.[3]

With these ideals of forest management in mind, leading colonists moved quickly to secure North American wood for the "right" customers. John Stewart, a resident of the Scottish settlement of Stewart Town, Carolina, in the 1690s, urged the colony's proprietors to create laws that would prevent the "stealing of cedar or cutting it off other men's land." William Penn, attempting to manage his colony from England, wrote letters to Pennsylvania's governors asserting his privilege over the woods. Why, asked Penn, had colonists ignored the woodsman he had appointed to cut timber and sell it at a fixed price? Why were people cutting down and carrying away timber as and when they wanted, when it was Penn's colony, Penn's wood, and therefore his right to benefit from the sale of this commodity? William Blathwayt, colonial undersecretary, was urged by one of his American officials to direct colonists to use the woods to produce potash for British industry rather than spending their time growing crops such as wheat that were "not of . . . use to their Mother Country."[4]

Indeed, there was a widespread idea that the woods should be used in the service of England, and more specifically the "public interest" of the monarch and his navy. Edward Randolph, a notorious colonial agent roving the colonies in the late seventeenth century, was an ardent proponent of this point of view. Randolph's first government assignment in Britain was formative, as he had traveled to Scotland to parlay a timber supply for the commissioners of the navy. The negotiations proved lengthy and complicated, and Randolph had to overcome the objections of a number of Scottish interests who sought to prevent the sale of this valuable commodity to their southerly neighbor. Once in Britain's North American colonies, Randolph again familiarized himself with the task of asserting the king's interest in valuable timber supplies. By 1685 he had procured the commission as "Surveyor of all the Woods and Timber growing upon any of the Main Lands or Islands within ten or twelve Miles of any Navigable River, Creek or Harbour, within the Province of Maine in New England," a post he hoped to pursue in "service" to the Crown rather than "at any private advantage."[5]

Like many of the other one-man crusades Randolph engaged in as the self-appointed embodiment of English royal authority, the job proved much harder than he first assumed. Colonists showed remarkably little regard for the king's right to the trees in their midst. Rather than thinking of the monarch's naval requirements, they persisted in chopping down the largest trees and selling them where and when they wanted, or they simply took them without payment to build and heat homes or to build their own ships. In a 1700 petition to William III, Samuel Allen, a proprietor of New Hampshire, expressed dismay with his fellow settlers on this account. Having "come to his Province with his whole family to settle," Allen discovered that "the inhabitants are a considerable trading people wholly governed by their own private interest." In particular, his compatriots had "lately made a contract with the Portuguese for sending timber for building great ships and are still felling the best masts in the Province, which is the best for your Majesty's service. Unless a speedy stop be put to these proceedings, the woods will in a little time be destroyed to the prejudice of England and your Navy." Settlers had still not reformed in 1721 when Martin Bladen reported to the Board of Trade that failure to enforce the king's privilege in America threatened "the preservation of the woods." Settlers' unrestricted felling of the trees was, stated Bladen, "of very great consequence to your Majesty's service." For decades settlers had been felling trees and selling them in the name of no one but themselves.[6]

However hard English officials in America tried, the sheer number of trees, the huge territory over which they were distributed, and settlers' ability to roam these ancient woodlands, stymied the king's men as they sought to enforce "legitimate" interests. The process of commodifying America's trees, so numerous and so scattered, reveals what happened when European expectations of how markets should function met conditions on the ground in England's colonies. When the invaders tried to apply their models of market management to the unfamiliar territory and its people, their efforts frequently foundered on the rocky shores or languished in the wooded glades of this expansive and unknowable landscape. Our story of the fate of the early modern market in America must therefore begin with a thorough exploration of the encounter between existing economic assumptions and the realities of colonization. Before we can inquire into the creation of European-style marketplaces in America, we need to find out what happened when colonists arrived to discover nothing that looked to them like a marketplace and few people who shared their vision.

COLONIZATION AND THE ECONOMY
OF INTERESTS

Edward Randolph's efforts to harvest America's forests for the king's profit was part of a late seventeenth-century drive by the Crown and its officials to bring its North American possessions under better surveillance. How this might be achieved depended on the position one took in the fast-moving debates that characterized English government in the choppy waters of Restoration politics. Some of Charles II's closest supporters sought an overhaul of colonial constitutions to align government with the royal interest while also promoting monopolies such as the Royal African Company and granting the monarch all customs income in perpetuity. William's cronies preferred to promote their commercial interest through the power of Parliament, a strategy they successfully pursued with royal support after they had installed the stadtholder on the English throne and got him to sign up to the Bill of Rights.[7]

Yet no matter one's stance on the relationship between monarch and Parliament, all were ultimately arguing for what they viewed as a balance of economic interests judiciously united to answer England's common good. As Perry Gauci has noted, economic policy-making in England at the local, national, and international levels was driven by this desire to achieve "an alignment of interests." Certainly competing factions passed power back and forth, constantly contesting the definition of a legitimate interest. Yet only a very few individuals dared to suggest abandoning the influence of interest groups over the national, local, or imperial economy. Colonial policy was therefore formulated on the assumption that it must steer American economic pursuits to answer England's common good. To meet this goal, the economy of interests in which all worked in harmony to meet this good must be remade in the colonies.[8]

The new Navigation Act of 1696 was the Whigs' way of applying their interpretation of this economy of interests to the colonies. The act contained no new laws but reinforced existing ones by introducing colonial vice admiralty courts, enforcing oaths and bonds of loyalty for English officials, and extending the Act of Frauds to give customs officers stronger search powers. Armed with more authority, the officers were better equipped to strong-arm settlers into paying their duties and trading only to England in English ships with mainly English crews. The new act was also a clear expression of the "economy of interests." The king and his agents believed the economic interest of the monarch had been left unregarded when officials failed to collect duties or to direct trade through official ports. Colonists had not met their obligation to trade for the common good. With a Whig government behind this move, the interests needing greater attention were those of London's rent-seeking commercial elite and their ally the king, which together constituted the public good.[9]

Because the economy of interests operated at all levels of English society, imperial initiatives were ideologically aligned with their authors' actions in their everyday economic lives. As landed gentlemen, both William Penn and the Earl of Shaftesbury had a stake in perpetuating local economies of interest. With estates in southern Ireland and the Kentish Weald, Penn had multiple tenants who paid him a total of two thousand pounds a year to farm his land. After he purchased his estate at Warminghurst in 1676 he took up residence in its grand house, employing numerous servants and offering lavish hospitality to his gentry neighbors, who filled the offices of local government. Although Penn's Quakerism prevented him from holding one of these offices himself, this would not have been enough to remove him from the political economic mentalities they represented; simply by being an estate owner with tenants, Penn became enmeshed in an economic relationship predicated on the idea that it should operate for the common good of all involved.[10]

At the same time the Earl of Shaftesbury, in writings about his Carolina project, clearly explained the need to recreate an economy of interests across the Atlantic. He hoped that, under his *Fundamental Constitutions*, Carolina would be a place where "every one in his place will but contribute his Part to the Promotion of the Common Good of the Plantation." By ensuring that all interests in the colony were balanced, Shaftesbury predicted that there would be a "quiet equall and lasting Government wherein every mans Right Property and Welfare may be soe fenc'd in and secured that the preservation of the Government may be every ones Interest." Both men were fully immersed in the institutions and mechanisms of the local economy that regulated fairs and markets, meted out commercial justice, and generally ensured that the interests of rich and poor were marshaled to meet the common good.[11]

The ideals expressed by Crown agents such as Edward Randolph and Martin Bladen and by proprietors such as William Penn and Lord Ashley all reflected a universal set of principles they hoped ordinary people would trade by in daily life. Their ideas resonated with those of their New England predecessors, who had also urged traders to deal for the "public spirit." Religious, political, and chronological differences aside, all shared basic assumptions about how markets should work. Once their colonizing enterprises got under way, all proceeded to apply them to their New World settings. From Massachusetts to Carolina, ideals of the early modern marketplace structuring local trade in the Old World—a fixed space in which commerce was governed by interests for a common good—were an integral component of these Atlantic designs.[12]

Given this mutual ideological commitment, it makes sense that schemes to order trade in the colonies relied on replicating the spaces and commercial practices foundational to England's economy of interests. Leading colonists looked to make a marketplace that, as far as possible, was situated in a fixed and observable location convenient for governing trade for the right interests. One way to achieve this goal was to locate the marketplace in a town, close to the eyes of the relevant officials. In a landscape devoid of towns, however, colonizers needed to create not only the marketplace but also the urban environment where it was to be situated. Penn's Frame of Government thus commanded that "the Governor and provincial Council shall, at all times, settle and order the situation of all cities, ports, and market towns in every county, modeling therein all public buildings, streets, and market places." Subsequently, in 1683 Penn pointed out that the "good beginning" of his colony was manifested by a "fair we have had, & weekly Marketts, to wch the ancient lowly Inhabitants come to sell their Produce to their Profit & our accommodation." The burgeoning trade with Native Americans also quickly came to Penn's attention, leading the proprietor to rule that all deals with Indians should "be performed in Publick Markett when such places shall be sett apart, or erected, where they shall pass the publick Stamp or Marke." In addition, any furs sold in the marketplace should "suffer the test whether good or bad" so that the "natives may not be abused nor provoked.[13]

Carolina's lords proprietor held similar ambitions for their marketplaces. Statutes in the *Fundamental Constitutions* deployed a range of measures to root domestic trade in an urban setting. The colony's high steward's court was responsible for establishing towns with fairs and markets. Since such places were all to be incorporated, they would have an additional authority overseeing their development; the mayor, aldermen, and common council were charged with ensuring that all items of trade would be loaded or unloaded in towns. No commerce should take place anywhere other than port towns, which would be situated on every major waterway. The lords proprietor exhorted colonists to establish manors in which "every week one market and two fairs every year" would take place, allowing "a court of pypowder in every fair, and with all liberties, tolls, customs, fines, & c. belonging to any market, fair, or court of pypowder in England." Both Penn and the Carolina proprietors were therefore in agreement that creating fairs and markets, situating them in towns, and installing a set of officials to oversee their proper function would guarantee the evolution of marketing according to acknowledged principles, replicating practices and settings familiar to Europeans in the Old World.[14]

Colonial officials, for their part, were suspicious of proprietary power but sought the creation of remarkably similar marketplaces. Hence the king's men held to the same reasoning when they promoted towns. Since colonists in Virginia all lived rurally, Henry Hartwell, author of a lengthy 1697 report to the Board of Trade on the state of the colony, concluded that "the causes of . . . misery are chiefly to be found in the first wrong measures of not seating the people in towns, and in the narrow selfish ends of most of them." Thus Hartwell and his fellow authors of this ten-point analysis of Virginia's shortcomings explicitly linked the poor state of the economy to the failure to fix marketplaces in an urban setting with the proper interests overseeing their operation. With no town marketplaces that tradesmen and farmers could resort to, labor was dear and there was no incentive for farmers to produce a surplus. "The matter would perhaps be more quickly and effectually settled," argued the authors, "if measures were taken to grant privileges to the ports and to discourage country-stores."[15]

Ardently committed to a marketplace centering trade in well-governed locations, young colonial authorities hoped for an easy recreation of their Old World commercial privileges of power and income. Prominent colonists implemented ongoing measures to support a trade that met the public good and the rights of those "fair traders" who held it foremost in their minds. Of course, these were flexible concepts, and one man's fair trader could easily be another's illegal interloper. Yet however the terms were defined, they nevertheless adhered to the principle that the "private interest"—that of individual colonists nakedly trading according to their own wishes—must not reign supreme.

Hoping that private interest would not win the day in his colony, Penn granted a charter to the Free Society of Traders, a group of Quaker merchants gathered as a joint stock company "calculated both to promote the publique good, and to Encourage the private." The charter of the Free Society may have claimed it was operating for the "publique good," but like many such claims it masked the reality of a body designed to give a group of wealthy and influential Quakers a generous stake in the nascent Pennsylvania domestic economy. By bestowing on his commercial Friends the privilege of overseeing trade in the Delaware Valley, Penn hoped to make his colony successful economically as well as a religiously and to reap the benefits accordingly. The society's articles sought to preserve profits from domestic trade in the hands of the subscribers by fixing commerce in the landscape. The organization was to have two "general factories" (trading posts) along the Delaware and the Chesapeake "for the more speedy conveyance of goods." Merchandise would be collected at these locations for resale. What is more, the society would "be Assisting to the Indians in their settling in Towns and other places, both by Advice and Artificers." Thus the society not only would contribute to the growth of Pennsylvania's trade but might also ensure that commerce proceeded in an orderly manner, guaranteeing the transfer of an early modern economy of interests on the ground in the New World.[16]

In Carolina, early colonists had similar plans. The colony's Assembly demonstrated a strong desire to build an economy of interests in the Lowcountry, albeit emphasizing different interests than those formerly promoted by Shaftesbury. The assemblymen contemplated "an act to punish forestallers and ingrossers and to ascertaine Weights and measures and a market place in Charles Towne." They pressed to outlaw trade between servants and enslaved Africans and Indians, to regulate the trade in beef and pork, thus "avoyding deceipts," and to appoint a clerk of the market. Seven years into their tenure, and in response to exhortations from the proprietors, the Assembly resolved that "ye Indjan Trade be Regulated." A committee of members then concluded that it should be managed "by a publick Stock for the use of ye publick" and should take place primarily on the plantations of Carolinians. In the Scottish frontier settlement of Port Royal, colonist John Stewart replicated this approach in his 1690 proposals for "Laws in number 5 or 600 for present conveniency," including many that applied to the domestic economy. Stewart also advocated for "inland Townes And frequent Villages ... which will prove the seeds of Towns and Cityes in tyme, lawfull obedience to Magistracy Indoctrinat vice and Laziness discouraged."[17]

These ideas were all familiar to imperial officials who, whether Whig or Tory, strove to create a more robust imperial regime grounded in a local economy operating for the "public good." On a journey through Pennsylvania, Maryland governor Francis Nicholson carefully observed the commercial habits of the colonists he encountered. What he saw did not please him, for he came across any number of locations "fit to manage illegal trade at, and the people generally inclined to make use of them whenever they can." As a result, Nicholson lamented how "prejudicial it is to the revenue and to the interest of all fair traders"—in other words, those who had the common good foremost in their minds. Robert Quary praised Nicholson himself as a man who had not "omitted any oppertunity of encouraging ye honest and fair Trade." Meanwhile, the Earl of Bellomont argued against making Perth Amboy a free port, since "the people will always prefer private gain to the general good of the English nation." As they voiced their frustration with colonists who refused to carry on a fair trade under the observation of His Majesty's customs officials, these men revealed that they shared a set of economic values with proprietors and governors even as they disagreed with the exact balance of power between king, colony, and individual. William Penn and the Board of Trade warred over the influence of their separate interests when the Quaker proprietor appeared in London in 1701 to defend his enterprise. Nevertheless, all were fully invested in an economy of interests, "balanced" only when the "right" amounts of hierarchy and reciprocity were achieved to meet the common good. When it came to creating and regulating markets, therefore, the competing factions of England's colonizing project had very little to disagree about aside from whose interest should prevail.[18]

FOUNDERING AMBITIONS

The men involved in England's colonial project spilled so much ink over regulating markets precisely because the task proved so difficult. It was not just the king's men who were frustrated, however: the ambitions of proprietors and their governing allies to order trade also suffered repeated blows. In the 1640s, New England's leaders had gradually abandoned their strictest efforts to regulate prices when the legislation proved ineffectual. In South Carolina and Pennsylvania, however, colonists' utter refusal to conform to any official commercial vision became apparent almost immediately after settlement. Resistance grew steadily into the early eighteenth century. Ordinary settlers were unenthusiastic about the spaces and regulations that proprietors had designed for trade. Local governing authorities proved slow and chaotic in their efforts to put their superiors' ambitions into action. Under these conditions, both the marketplace and its associated economy of interests quickly foundered. While the ambitions and reassurances of Penn and his Carolina counterparts might suggest the early flourishing of marketplaces and fairs in both Philadelphia and Charles Towne, the reality was somewhat different.[19]

Ten years after Penn's claim that the market in his chief town was functioning smoothly, the preoccupations of the Provincial Council reveal a different story. With no clerk in place to oversee Philadelphia's marketplace until 1693, colonists were butchering animals in town anytime they wished and selling them there every day of the week, regardless of official market days. Meanwhile inhabitants from the surrounding countryside sold their grain elsewhere because the roads were so poor they could not reach Philadelphia. When a clerk was finally appointed by the council in late 1693, he remained in the post only a few months, until accusations of corruption led to his dismissal in early 1694. The issue of recruiting a new clerk did not arise again in the council until 1699, when it emerged that bakers were selling light loaves, in complete contravention of prices set by the bread assize.[20]

Like their Pennsylvania counterparts, the Carolina assemblymen appeared happy to ignore the proper regulation of Charles Towne's marketplace, despite an initial burst of enthusiasm shortly after their 1691 inception. Fifteen years later, Governor Nathaniel Johnson, a former member of Parliament for Newcastle-upon-Tyne who certainly knew a well-regulated market when he saw one, pointed out to the colonial Assembly "the unreasonable huckstering and fforestalling this Town, to that End that you would think of having a Markett and regulation of Weights ffor it is a Crying Sin to See what light bread is Imposed upon those that necessitated to by it nay even when Corne is Cheap." Johnson's consternation extended to the poor quality of meat available to townspeople, even though "horses are become plentifull" and there were "Oxen fitt ffor the Plow." Used to an economy of interests that relied on official weights and measures, the integrity of the bread assize, and a corporate body checking the quality and price of meat sold by freeman butchers, Johnson was shocked to the core by the state of trade in the colony's chief town.[21]

As his complaints suggest, the growth of colonial towns had produced few citizens who diligently frequented the marketplace and respected the economic principles it embodied. The increasing commerce between Europeans and Native Americans failed to have a more salutary effect. Everywhere, colonists and Indians traded enthusiastically with one another, but nowhere did they do so in the locations proprietors had set aside for them. Nor did they seem to hold the common good in much regard. Penn's highly pro-scriptive instructions that the trade should take place in Philadelphia's mar-ketplace, and that it should on no account involve the sale of rum to Indians, were widely ignored. Settlers ended up before the court or the council for surreptitiously trading rum, often from their own houses. Bucks County res-ident Jacob Hall was found guilty of the crime in 1685 when a neighbor "saw an Indian carry away 3 bottles of rum wch contained 1 pt out of the said . . . Halls House." Hall was in good company, as residents of Chester County were also observed selling alcohol to Native Americans. And this was not a habit that died out. Twenty years later the provincial council received a messenger from the chief of the Conestogoe Indians informing them that "ye great Quantities of Rum, continually brought to their Town, insomuch that they are ruined by it, having nothing left but have laid out all, even their Cloaths for Rum, & may now when threatened with war, be surprised by their Enemies when besides themselves with drink, & so utterly be de-stroyed." As these complaints reveal, colonists neither adhered to regula-tions concerning what they could sell to Indians nor took notice of laws designed to control where they could trade with Native people. It was such disobedience that quickly undermined the success of the Free Society of Traders, whose members were already complaining in 1685 that the "genne-rall good of the whole" was rarely privileged by colonists "before their owne privat interest." The society's carefully planned trading warehouses had no chance of success when colonists found it preferable to sell rum to Indians in their houses and in the countryside, far from official attempts to prevent them.[22]

Early on in Pennsylvania, the trade in rum presented one threat to the official vision of a well-governed relationship between Europeans and In-dians, but a second threat came in the form of enslaved Indians imported from Carolina, some of whom provoked "umbrage for suspicion and dissat-isfaction." The arrival of these enslaved people was, of course, a result of the total refusal of Carolina's colonists to successfully regulate their trade with Indians, let alone obey any laws directing it for the public good. From London, the proprietors instructed settlers "to regulate all disputes in or about Trade or Comerce between Christians & Indians" and to adhere to metropolitan instructions. In 1683 the colony's proprietors had already noted that "wee are very Jealouse yt ye Private gaines yt some make by buying Slaves of ye Indians" and were of the opinion that "they ought to bee transported yr the publick safety or benefitt." As I have noted, some Carolinian settlers proposed that the Indian trade should be brought into the public realm through the establishment of a joint stock company. Nevertheless, it would be another twenty-four years before the Assembly passed an act requiring Indian traders to have a license and to stop trading people. While the Indian trade and its regulation arose numerous times as a matter of discussion for the Carolina representatives, that many of their fortunes rested on it prevented them from passing legislation. Eventually this failure would cost them dear when the deadly Yamasee War broke out in 1715, ending the extremes of the exploitative commerce by those merchants who had put their private profit above all else.[23]

Since colonists were so reluctant to conform to the principles and places of the early modern marketplace endorsed by their own leaders, who often lived among them, it follows that the Navigation Acts were also widely ignored. Underresourced and confronting an unfamiliar and expansive landscape, officials struggled to pin down not only "pirates" but the many landlubber colonists whose desire to heed the king's interest seemed limited. Robert Quary and Edward Randolph, two of the era's most active English agents, were frequently outraged at settlers' failure to pay due homage to the economy of interests. In a report that directly prompted the passing of the 1696 Navigation Act, Randolph described to his London masters how "Scotchmen coming by way of Berwick or Whitehaven to the plantations . . . land with a considerable quantity of goods, which they dispose of in a peddling manner by running small boats from creek to creek." By labeling traders as Scottish peddlers, Randolph immediately conjured up an image of colonists as a mobile, suspicious people whose commercial activity sought to undermine the common good and cheat the king's interest. From Pennsylvania, Quary likewise complained in 1699 of colonists who took seized cargo from the king's store and hawked "their prohibited goods publicly in boats from one place to another for a market." With these actions, settlers contravened the principle that marketing should occur in a fixed place and overrode the monarch's right to organize trade for his interest.[24]

Such complaints did not abate with the turn of the century, when a new batch of officials continued sending reports of colonists who assiduously avoided dealing in the places they were meant to trade. William Popple noted in 1702 that "sloops are purposely imployed to go out of the Capes and take on board goods brought by other vessells from Curacao, which they land at Philadelphia or elsewhere, and then the vessells that brought them come up to Philadelphia in ballast, as if they had brought nothing." The

Curaçao trade was equally alluring and elusive in Carolina, where reports noted how the absence of any customs officers in Port Royal had made the harbor a hot spot for the illegal landing of French imports, mahogany, and brandy. Since he was only an island in an ocean of interlopers, customs officer Richard Wigg was still struggling to stanch the flow of these goods in 1714. Thus when Board of Trade official Martin Bladen penned his comprehensive report on the state of the colonies in 1721 he argued that "daily experience shews that illegal trade is not to be prevented in a Proprietory Government." Reading through this catalog of complaints from governing colonists of all allegiances suggests that Bladen's assessment of the situation was close to the truth. Consistently presented with a vision of commerce reliant on central marketing places ordered by a select group of governing interests, many Europeans displayed a distinct lack of enthusiasm. Instead of colonists' embracing the opportunity to reestablish familiar hierarchies and spaces of trade, officials documented their retreat into remote coves, woods, and indeed their own homes to conduct bargains that snubbed the so-called public good while advancing only their private fortunes.[25]

MAKING COLONIAL MARKETS

While trying and, it seems, failing to get colonists to trade according to the economy of interests, English authorities remained committed to ensuring the policy's effectiveness at home. The late seventeenth century witnessed the launch of initiatives to protect the interests of English cattle farmers by blocking the import of Irish beef and butter. Local economies of interest were embellished with new fair and market charters, and government vigorously supported those who claimed their privileges in the marketplace had been undercut by "private interest." As the consternation voiced by colonial officials suggests, although widely held economic beliefs were tested by smugglers and middlemen in the metropole, few flouted the rules quite so openly as colonists dared to.[26]

Why was this so? In answering this question, we can identify what was different about the circumstances of colonial marketing while also delving further into the forces that produced this difference. There were two sides to the story. First, the lack of entrenched institutions in the colonies made enforcing an intricate economy of interests almost impossible. Compared with the situation in England, the paucity of regulations in early Pennsylvania and Carolina reveal a government ill-equipped to begin the herculean task of managing trade. Second, when these weak institutions were placed in an expansive landscape with a diverse population, their effectiveness was further diluted. In short, it made little sense to people to trade in towns under the watchful eyes of the authorities, and there was almost no way to prevent them from conducting commerce in the unobserved creeks and forests that constituted almost the entire colonial environment.

Colonial authorities lacked many of the tools essential to enforcing authority in European marketplaces. If only "they had towns, markets and money," argued Hartwell, "many inconveniences . . . might be avoided." Yet young governments not only missed these instruments of market control but confronted a society with poor communication networks and only a handful of functioning law courts. Even worse, novice governments were remarkably adept at undermining what little authority they did have. In both Pennsylvania and Carolina, factional conflict enabled piracy. While one government faction tolerated pirates and privateers and welcomed the boost their cash brought to the local market, the other worked to undermine them. Robert Quary observed just this situation in 1702 in Carolina, where the government "turned out Mr Trott, who had given security to the Commissioners of the Customs, and had their Commission to be Naval Officer at that Port, and have put in a man who hath spent all his time in carrying on illegal trade, in which he is still concerned. However," concluded Quary, "he is fit for their purpose."[27]

This factionalism also fostered a haphazard approach to creating legal regimes and spaces that might organize day-to-day trade. Over the decades before 1710, lawmakers' efforts to regulate the local economy were scant as factions blocked or reversed campaigns for legislation. At most, Pennsylvanians enacted twenty laws managing local trade, while their Carolina counterparts pushed through only sixteen. Mainly concerned with ensuring the quality of export goods and blocking the sale of alcohol to Indians, Pennsylvanians finally got a bread assize on the books in 1700, while Carolinians did not regulate bakers at all in this period. Overall, Pennsylvanians were more diligent legislators, but their achievements amounted to no more than an act "to prevent fraud and regulate abuses" and an effort to introduce standard weights and measures. The first courts established by Europeans were charged with enforcing these laws, but records suggest their effectiveness was limited. Sessions often had to be canceled because either the jury or the plaintiffs had not shown up, and Crown officers strongly doubted their ability to offer justice.[28]

Local governments that were understaffed and plagued by conflict found it both impossible and undesirable to construct complex institutional regimes

FIGURE 2.1 Pint measure, Glasgow, 1707. Courtesy of Glasgow Museums Collection.

of the sort that had evolved over centuries in England and Scotland. In the Restoration town, corporations, courts, and guilds all kept a close eye on market spaces and the commercial conduct of those within (and outside) them. At its late seventeenth-century sessions, Glasgow's burgh court cited unfreemen for packing goods on the town's Broomielaw wharf, and shoemakers in the neighboring jurisdiction of the Gorbals were accused of undercutting their Glasgow brethren by illegally coming to the city, measuring feet, and selling customers shoes at their houses rather than in the correct marketplace. Contemporaries in the Berwick-upon-Tweed corporation ordered "that noe burgesses shall buy any loading of timber at Holy Island or any other Creeks here adjacent and they shall give in their reasons ... why such a wholesome order shall not be continued for the towns good." In Newcastle, meanwhile, the corporation appealed to "Custome used since out of Mind" to prevent tobacconists from setting up tables and stands in the streets of the town to sell their wares. Traders in these towns thus not only were expected to abide by the essential regulations governing the size of loaves, weights and measures, the operation of the marketplace, and the privileges of guilds, but were also subjected to ongoing efforts to confine their commerce to spaces of the town that the authorities deemed proper. Laws were accompanied by an abundant material culture of market regulation. Weights and measures carried not only the crest of the town, but also that of the monarch. For Glasgow traders, 1707's Act of Union brought with it a daily reminder of their new status as Britons when their grain was measured out in the marketplace in a pewter vessel embossed with Queen Anne's coat of arms alongside the insignia of their city.[29]

Even beyond Britain's towns, the hand of multiple overlapping authorities loomed large in the marketplace. While corporations and guilds were sparse in rural areas, numerous other bodies stepped in to claim oversight of ordinary people's marketing. Courts were among the most important of these institutions. Their business not only was composed of the debt litigation, violent crimes, thefts, and policing of morality that has principally caught the attention of historians, but also involved enforcing order and the common good in the marketplace. The Northumberland quarter sessions certainly dealt with shop robberies, rapes, and brawls over ownership of church pews, but they also heard cases of innkeepers who cheated customers, high grain prices, illegal tailor shops, the sale of undrinkable ale, unlicensed butchers, forestalling the market, and drapers who misrepresented the source of their cloth. Hexhamshire's manor authority included a host of officials whose duty was to oversee marketing and prosecute those who broke the numerous regulations. The "scalerakers" appointed by the manor to supervise the Hexham marketplace not only had to assist the market keepers but were charged with keeping the space clean, well paved, and fenced off, collecting a grain toll for every sack brought to market, and ringing the bell to signal the start of trading. Other local officers received payment in a hay toll, which the authorities also had to collect.[30]

The comparative lack of institutional intervention in colonial commercial spaces at this time is striking. Neither Pennsylvania's Provincial Council, Carolina's Commons House of Assembly, nor their embryonic legal systems made it their business to meddle in settlers' mundane economic activities. The authorities played little part in promoting the development of regulated market spaces or in directing traders toward creating an economy that functioned for the common good. Instead, intermittent efforts by the courts to enforce early statutes forbidding trade with servants and slaves and the sale of alcohol to Indians, as well as the Navigation Acts, reveal a commercial culture rooted in spaces that settlers and Native Americans found most convenient to their individual needs. Ineffectual governments received little assistance from the courts. Lacking either the will or the legal framework to prosecute contraventions of the common good, they adjudicated the individual suits brought by creditors and nothing more.[31]

It is in these suits, therefore, that we glimpse a colonial market culture mostly formed around private bargains agreed to by individuals on their own property without the intervention of any corporate interest. In a sparsely peopled landscape, such modes of trade suited colonists, who saw little point in making the arduous journey to a central marketplace where there was no guarantee of buyers or sellers. Often the location of a deal was remote enough to allow easy exchange of stolen goods or nefarious commercial practices. Surveying the trading habits of early colonists firmly conveys the sense of a mobile marketplace that was convenient for dispersed settlers but risky for traders who did not keep their wits about them.

Early on, the marketplace had become anywhere colonists decided to trade their property. When Charles Thomas sold William Fforst a side of leather, the bargain was struck at the door of the buyer's mill. When Thomas Wither purchased a calf from Samuel Boyes, Boyes delivered the calf to the buyer in a canoe after the deal had been agreed on. Henry Pullin, a resident of Pennsylvania's Lower Counties, appealed to the court in 1685 because "he bought two coats of Mary Southin, A runaway woman," then had to watch his garments sold at auction after they were identified as stolen property. Others suffered inflated prices charged by sellers able to set their own terms of exchange. Writing from Goose Creek, seventeen miles north of Charles Towne, Anglican minister Francis Le Jau noted that since his family were not planting they relied on shopkeepers for provisions. However, since these shopkeepers had "contrived to make certain Tickets pass for current Coyn we are come by degrees to See nothing else current which considering how they sell all things reduce our Sallaries." Plantation owner and Indian trader John Wright and his wife Eleana turned their plantation into a tavern—without a license, of course—in which they gathered "Sufficient Quantityes of Wines and other Liquors not only for their own use but alsoe to Supply their Neighbours who frequently Set . . . for that purpose." When she was widowed, Eleana moved to Charles Towne, where she went into partnership in a shop with Francis LeBrasseur.[32]

In these seventeenth-century colonial markets, women like Wright enjoyed an unprecedented freedom to trade when, what, and where they pleased. Wives, widows, and spinsters from New England to Carolina were deeply enmeshed in local trading economies, which were foundational to market exchange. Women's widespread centrality to such business was greater there than in the heavily institutionalized trading environments of contemporary England; Wright could cross from rural to urban retailing at will without any corporate authority restricting what she could sell. Colonial men, with better access to property and credit, enjoyed still greater opportunity. Carolina merchants benefited from a market that rewarded those who could use their skill and credit in face-to-face bargaining to create market networks extending hundreds of miles across town and countryside. Benjamin Godin and his partners were based in Charles Towne, but they did not settle there to take advantage of any corporate privileges. Rather, their location put them at the pivot point of transatlantic and inland person-to-person credit networks and gave them access to the region's few courts. This allowed them to become the creditors of those traders who went west to deal with Indians and also permitted them to effectively call in those traders' debts when they failed to pay up. Men like Godin were just the type of merchants who had undermined the Society of Free Traders in Pennsylvania.[33]

Dealing anyplace that suited their efforts to make a profit, trading colonists fanned out across an expansive landscape. Commerce in such places could be risky for Europeans, but it represented the best option for people who lived far apart and were unhindered by government. However, these diffuse patterns of dealing were only partly due to Europeans' choices. As Godin's success suggests, the potential of the trade with, and in, Native Americans was critical to the emergence of these sprawling and mobile trading arrangements. Indeed, the importance of Indians and Africans to the marketplace—as agents and as commodities—played a large part in fashioning a commerce poorly aligned with European spatial expectations.

As we have seen, non-Europeans were most familiar with fluid trading networks that effectively bridged expansive landscapes. The situation in early Carolina and Pennsylvania gave them no reason to change these commercial habits. In the late seventeenth century Indians and colonists made a mobile marketplace that unfolded variously in their homes, their towns, and the places in between. In Pennsylvania's Lower Counties, the habit of selling to Indians from homes, creeks, and other convenient places was established by Swedish and Dutch settlers and continued by the English. Then, as Europeans became numerous and ventured farther west, the spaces of the Indian trade became yet more diverse and remote from colonial-created locations. Many deals were struck "at any Indian Town or other place in ye woods." Indians explained that traders were also intercepting men as they returned from hunting to sell them rum for skins before they reached their towns. Carolina officials regularly complained of traders who arrived in Creek and Cherokee towns, immediately bought slaves, then disappeared into the vast landscape before the deal could be questioned. Some traders such as John Seabrooke, who built a house between Charles Towne and the Savannah River, created commercial locations on the journey from coast to interior where they could "putt and secure" some of their goods. Early Carolina chronicler John Lawson noted that such places were "common in these parts, and especially where there is Indian towns, and Plantations near at hand."[34]

Native Americans sometimes objected to these huts, viewing them as a ploy by Europeans to root themselves farther west. When trader John Hans attempted to set up a dwelling among the Conestogoe, Shawanois, and Ganawense Indians in 1706, their chiefs reported to the Pennsylvania authorities that he was "building a Log house for Trade amongst them, which made us uneasie." As objectionable to Indians as Hans's log house was, it was equally offensive to Europeans. To conduct a lucrative trade with Indians, colonists had had to abandon almost completely their ideas of what a marketplace was and how it should function. At the very least they had accepted stores at, or in, Indian towns, operating according to Indian government, and in stark contrast to European towns and their regulatory regimes. If Indians decided they preferred dealing in the woods rather than at a fixed store, Europeans had to accept this choice if they were to obtain the skins and slaves that sustained many colonists, especially in South Carolina.[35]

As the weaker power on the continent, Europeans were rarely in a position to dictate where trade should take place, nor could they establish permanent marketing places without the assent of their Native customers. Even though the Yamasee War weakened the Native presence in the southeastern parts of Carolina, the new 1718 resolutions of the Commission for Indian Affairs continued to reject European market conventions and cater to the remaining "settlement" Indians in the region. The statute did not insist that Native traders come to Charles Towne; rather, it nominated nine men as agents who would supply Indians "at their respective plantations," located rurally at Wando, Ashley Ferry, Edisto, and New London. The trade with Indians had now permanently shifted perceptions of what constituted a legitimate marketplace, moving it well away from the coastal towns promoted by the proprietors of both Pennsylvania and Carolina.[36]

What is more, the Carolina government's unwillingness to put enough money into the project of public regulation provided the opportunity for Indians to step in and exercise even greater agency. Unable to afford pack-horses, the authorities moved "to employ Indians as Burtheners to fetch Goods and Carrie Skins." The Catawbas recruited for the job chose to distribute goods among their own townspeople at prices they determined, returning eastward with small numbers of skins only when it suited them. Carolinian efforts to set the terms of commerce were then further hampered by the arrival of Virginia traders selling goods at lower prices than those set by the Assembly. Since the Virginians brought goods to the Indian towns on horses, taking skins in exchange on the spot, a Carolina plan to create a fort and trading post at the Congarees foundered. Indians preferred Virginians because they let them inspect goods properly. The Carolina traders attacked them when they sought to enter a storehouse to get a proper look at what was on offer. At Chouee, Chote, Quanissee, and Tunissee, Catawbas demonstrated their displeasure with Carolina traders by breaking into stores and taking goods they wanted.[37]

Insisting that dealing take place in their towns, on their terms, Catawbas, Cherokees, and Creeks all used the advantage of distance from weak Carolina authorities to control the spaces and customs of marketing. The marketplaces hosting trade therefore possessed few of the physical or legal qualities the English authorities sought. In this respect the emerging geography of Indian-European commerce in these southeast contact zones shared much with those under construction elsewhere on the continent. To the north, Indians remained in control of Virginia's paths, even though in 1686 Europeans claimed ownership of them in the wake of Bacon's Rebellion. To the northwest, the French were beginning to establish Detroit as a hub for the fur trade in the Ohio River Valley. Although the colonists hoped to make their new fort into a commercial city in the European manner, the decisions of indigenous people, mostly women, determined an alternative role. Establishing "entrepôt trading villages" such as Miamitown and Sandusky on the Wabash, indigenous women transported the peltry from Detroit, locating face-to-face dealing in spaces they had created.[38]

Returning to Carolina, we find trading places made yet more unfamiliar to Europeans by African trading networks, which unfolded across their claimed territories. By 1686 the Carolina Assembly had already passed an act to prevent trade with slaves and servants because they had seen so many "indeirect bargaines between freemen, servants and slaves, amongst themselves, whereby some evilly disposed have adventured privately to embezzle, wast and sell divers of their master's goods." Laying aside for the moment the contradictions inherent in this attempt to regulate black traders by whites who saw little need to create rules to govern commerce among themselves, this statute evinces the critical role Africans played in decentering early Carolina's trade. At the same time, it underscores colonists' annoyance at how far blacks, as they freely traded their owners' property, had failed to pay due respect to the privileges of the white "elite."[39]

Striking these "indeirect bargaines," enslaved people became the linchpins of on-the-hoof deals sustaining travelers and residents alike. African cattle herders, roaming across vast distances as they gathered cows from open-grazing lands and moved them to market, would have had numerous opportunities to trade with passing Lowcountry inhabitants. African boatmen also facilitated the Lowcountry's "floating market" as skilled navigators of inland waterways and as dealers at plantations, ferries, and on boats. Men like Charles, who had spent five days paddling his master's canoe up and down the Ashley River when he was stopped and sent to the Charles Towne workhouse, made the most of their skills, fashioning themselves into the lines connecting the dots of a scattered market. Others emulated Charles, sometimes even with their owners' assent. Charles Towne residents Sarah Sommerville and Elizabeth Miles owned both enslaved people and watercraft, whom they likely deployed on the waterways to trade for their profit.[40]

As the constant objections of white authorities acknowledged, however, Africans used these opportunities to deal on their own account. Laws permitting whites to seize "all Boats and Canoes belonging to any Slaves," and requests to put a stop to enslaved Charlestonians "going in Boats and Canoes up the Country trading with Negroes in a clandestine Manner" could have little effect when the government lacked the means to effectively enforce such edicts. By the early eighteenth century, travelers knew they could rely on meeting an African who would appear at a landing, riverbank, or ferry offering food and supplies. As he journeyed through the creeks winding between the sea and the mainland, John Lawson noted that one among his party, possibly an African or a Native American, "purchas'd some small Quantity of Tobacco and Rice" from an African who had been left in charge of a plantation near Bull's Island.[41]

With fewer African inhabitants in Pennsylvania as well as fewer waterways, it is not clear whether enslaved Africans enabled Pennsylvania's early marketing in quite the same way. Yet it is evident that the expansive landscape also allowed servants and slaves to roam far and wide, buying and selling as they went. Joseph Trivithan, a resident of Bucks County, purchased "1 cloth Coate 1 p plush breeches 1 womans cloak" from a "negro woman" for the use of his neighbor's wife after she had fallen in the river. Here too, laboring people supplied the needs of colonists as they traversed the countryside; that they were evading masters and mistresses was no matter to customers looking to buy goods or provisions in a landscape devoid of shops and markets.[42]

While colonial authorities struggled with few committed officials in an extensive and unfamiliar landscape, colonists and Native Americans set about making their homes, waterways, and ferry landings into trading spaces. As he carried off the goods of fellow traders killed when Creeks attacked the Cherokee town of Nogutchee, rogue Indian trader John Sharp boasted that "no Laws they make in Carolina can hurt him for what he does here." Sharp was not an outlier but was representative of how day-to-day trading habits had developed across the first decades of colonization. Such a scattered pattern of unregulated commercial exchange bore little resemblance to the focused market spaces usually frequented by Europeans, but this was unimportant to the Africans and Indians central as actors and as commodities in these early networks. Indeed, it was the skills and demands of these Americans that contributed largely to the lack of enthusiasm for towns, customs officials, and marketplaces. Although Europeans were not in the habit of letting Africans and Indians dictate the direction of their colonizing enterprise, in the embryonic stages of the project, when making a deal was critical for survival, this is exactly what happened.[43]

The early era of English colonization in North America spanned two or three lifetimes—ample opportunity to forget customary habits of trade. This process of forgetting had begun in New England, where, during 1641's depression, John Winthrop had observed "a very sad thing" about the character of commerce: "how little of a public spirit appeared in the country, but of self-love too much." Soon after the establishment of Carolina some fifty years later, colonists saw a similar process at work. Almost on his deathbed, minister Francis Le Jau confessed he had "thought all the great noise they had made in Print at home was grounded upon true Zeal for the glory of God and the public chiefly spiritual good of this Province; but I assure you it is far from it, revenge, self-interest, engrossing of trade, places of any profit and things of that nature are the Mobile that gives a turn ... of our Affairs."[44]

Le Jau had the misfortune to find himself in one of the more chaotic regions of English America, but his contemporaries in the Middle Colonies came to similar conclusions. Penn answered accusations that he harbored smugglers by explaining that the geography of the New World, and the fluidity of young societies, meant that customs officials would always be easily corrupted and Customs Houses easily avoided. After a frustrating tenure as governor of New York, the Earl of Bellomont concluded that America simply was "naturally cut out . . . for unlawful trade." Having surveyed all the colonies in preparation for his lengthy report to the Board of Trade in 1721, Martin Bladen characterized the Massachusetts Assembly as "generally filled with people of small fortunes and mean capacities, who are easily led into any measures that seem to enlarge their liberties and privileges, however detrimental ever the same may be to Great Britain or your Majesty's Royal Prerogative." All therefore agreed that colonial circumstances made any efforts to get settlers to put aside their "private interests" and trade for the good of the British nation (or at least the greater good) were an uphill struggle.[45]

Others expressed much more than dismay. They feared that greed and private interest had irreversibly corrupted colonists. Not only were settlers trading openly in their private interest, their decades-long experience of commerce outside the norms of the customary marketplace meant they had altogether forgotten what the "public good" was. Writing from Annapolis, Governor Francis Nicholson observed that "people begin to pretend custom and to claim that it is common law, which, if it be not timely prevented, may be prejudicial to the King's interest. For if they be allowed the benefit of their old customs, it will be vain for me to prosecute illegal traders . . . or to endeavour to model the country either in church or state." In response to William Penn's defense of his colony at the Board of Trade, Robert Quary gloomily "considered the difficulty that must attend it from a people that had so long practiced illegal trade and found the sweet of it." Since Bostonians, lobbying against the centralization of marketing in their town, argued that hawking groceries was the "ancient custom" while a marketplace was an unwelcome imposition, these commentators may have had a point. Even in Puritan New England, settlers had cast aside centuries of good English tradition, deaf to the exhortations of those only too aware of the disaster that would befall a society trading outside the constraints of well-established custom and the common law.[46]

The alternative marketplaces made by Europeans, Africans, and Indians together featured dramatic changes in the spatial qualities of marketing. A statement offered to Indian trading partners by the Pennsylvania Assembly in 1715 suggests that spatial novelties prompted new thinking about how trade should work. In a statement, Governor Charles Gookin sought to explain to his native counterparts why the price of deer skins had dropped and they were now receiving only a meager income from them. "The governor is sorry" the council wrote,

> he Can't give ym. a more intire satisfaction in it, & remove every hardship they lie under; But that all trade is uncertain, Our own wheat *ye* last year yielded twice the price it does this; All our Goods yt they buy are brought from England, whither we also send theirs; That sometimes a habit that is in fashion one year is laid aside the next, and accordingly the skins they are made of will be of a higher or lower value. It is the same with all our other merchandize as with those that they buy, their own security & safety will be to trade with the honestest men, and those of the best Reputation, and prefer those who will give the most, that this is our Rule in all our business, and they must do the same.[47]

How should Indians seek to get a fair deal? Well, there were limits because no one—not the guild, not the corporation, the king's officers, the clerk of the market, or even the commissioner for Indian affairs could fix a price on something. The price of goods was taken care of by the market—not the market that was visible in the town square and was under the control of a municipally appointed clerk, but "the market" as an abstraction. Institutions were not responsible for ensuring that merchants traded fairly. Getting a fair deal was the duty of the buyer, who must capably assess the reputations of individual traders.

This assessment of trade's machinations sounds perfectly logical to us as inhabitants of an advanced capitalist society. Yet, in the context of early modern economic practice and thought, such reasoning flew in the face of the majority view. The governor's opinion came only one year after the publication of Bernard Mandeville's controversial *Fable of the Bees*, whose suggestion that individual consumers should buy as many luxuries as they wished because it would advance the wealth of the nation had prompted widespread condemnation. Others who had proffered similar arguments in favor of "free trade," such as London building entrepreneur Nicholas Barbon, were likewise regarded with great suspicion. It is highly likely that Gookin's view of the situation was strongly shaped by his experience of the marketplace as it had developed in early Pennsylvania, a space both physically and ideologically outside European economic norms.[48]

Such novelties caused great anxiety among leading colonists, who believed strongly in European rules of exchange. Very early on in the colonial project, Americans' market culture was changed for the worse by the geographical and institutional setting of settlement. Colonists traded for their private interest on their private property, often concealed from the view of governing institutions attempting to regulate commerce for the common good. Native Americans and Africans were only too willing to encourage such trading habits. Not only did they see little reason to abide by unfamiliar rules set by a group of people who had little chance of enforcing them, this was a mode of trade long proved to suit the expansive landscapes that characterized North America. According to some, the common good was no longer valued at all in marketplaces. The consequences of this amnesia were enormous.

PART 2

Remaking the Marketplace

CHAPTER THREE

Making a Colonial Marketplace

The early modern miller was essential to making wheat into bread, the staff of life. Because of his importance, greedy millers were stock characters familiar to many Europeans. Happy to pursue their own gain at the expense of the hungry community, these reviled figures hoarded grain and earmarked it for export while local people went hungry. Christian, principled millers, on the other hand, refrained from running their mills for their own profit, placing first the poor's need for affordable daily bread. So when grain shortages combined with commercialization at various points over the seventeenth century, invective against "bad" millers who worked their mills for their private interest reached fever pitch. By the eighteenth century, the conflict between the common good and the "private interest" of millers was a main topic of economic debate. Millers regularly faced calls for heavier policing of their trading and complaints that they despised laboring people.

During an acute failure of the grain supply in 1758, many British newspapers printed letters and comments on the situation. The year's first edition of the *Manchester Mercury* opened with a heated discussion about ending the shortage. Some writers favored greater government regulation, pointing at millers "who do most notoriously infest our Markets; and by their Eagerness to purchase, do certainly raise the Price, particularly of wheat." Mills could not be markets, and their owners must not be commercial men. When millers overstepped that principle to insert themselves into the marketplace as middlemen, entrepreneurs, merchants, or dealers, they were quickly condemned for contravening the common good.[1]

Meanwhile, in the embrace of colonial America's fertile soils and abundant land, eighteenth-century Pennsylvanians were busily building mills that thrived on their role as epicenters of the market. By 1767 the colony was home to 950 mills, many of them gristmills established to make a profit. Processing grain was just one element in a portfolio of market functions folded into the mill complex. The mill at Pottstown, the settlement founded by John Potts to the northwest of Philadelphia, was one such place. In addition to Potts's gristmill and his impressive estate, Pottsgrove Manor, the roughly nine-hundred-acre tract incorporated four iron forges, a smith's shop, and a company store selling provisions, alcohol, and dry goods to local people in exchange for labor, produce, and cash. In 1761 the success of his enterprise prompted Potts to announce that to promote "trade and commerce" he was "resolved to erect a town on the said tract" by dividing his land into lots and renting them for "Four Spanish Milled Dollars a year."[2]

As early colonists and imperial authorities had feared when they wrestled with the freewheeling commercial habits of traders, Potts's personal economic ambitions as a landowner, forge owner, and miller had come to master the market in his eponymous Pottstown. Without the interference of regulation by government or other collective economic interests, Potts became one of many Pennsylvania landowners to establish commerce in places that suited their own business needs. Innumerable mills like his enterprise emerged as marketing hubs reliant entirely on the entrepreneurial endeavors of individual landowners seeking their fortunes. Indeed, mills were so important to marketing networks that road petitions frequently argued for a new thoroughfare on the grounds that colonists required access to "mill and market." The symbiosis of these two locations, though highly questionable for Europeans, caused Americans no worry at all. Indeed, not a single complaint about the behavior of these millers is to be found before the Revolutionary era; instead, their entrepreneurial zeal is celebrated in the language of newspaper advertisements boasting of mills' "fine situation" and their suitability for "carrying on merchant and country business."[3]

What is more, mills were among many novel, privately owned marketing spaces scattered across the American landscape during the first half of the eighteenth century. They belonged to an ensemble of permanent and temporary locations emerging to serve trading people—Europeans, Indians, and Africans alike. Investigating the character and situation of these spaces, as well as the texture of commercial interactions taking place within them, uncovers a distinctive market culture under construction from the early eighteenth century to the 1760s. The importance of these distinctive spaces lay not only in their novelty, but also in the new dynamics governing the trade within them. Soon novel dynamics became colonial custom. According to these new customs, power in the marketplace sprang almost entirely from the ownership and use of private property. As a result, whereas commerce in Europe's marketplaces was also structured by complex webs of obligation and corporate interest, these novel American spaces were formed entirely according to the needs of those individuals who could most easily acquire and trade property.

A MARKET IN MOTION

Even though commercialization shifted some trade away from the market-place in Europe, traders continued to concentrate buying and selling in fixed spaces and familiar settings. Auctions became an acknowledged method of selling goods in Britain, and mobile middlemen inserted themselves into the grain trade. Yet the mobility of these traders remained shackled to long-established inns and taverns where they met for bidding and haggling. If commerce moved out of the marketplace, it nevertheless stayed in the town, which was still a corporate environment. Dealers continued to be uncomfortable with bargains struck completely outside familiar spaces and hierarchies. The nation's burgeoning provincial newspaper press, for example, seemed a little too novel for many traders. With large amounts of paid copy produced by quack doctors and patent medicine salesmen, the marketplace of print could ruin a reputation as easily as it could make it. Josiah Wedgwood was hesitant about placing newspaper advertisements in the 1760s; he viewed them as too brazen a form of publicity to attract the exclusive clientele he sought for his ceramics. Although Malachy Postlethwayt had conceded in 1757 that "advertising in the papers, at present times . . . seems to be esteemed," he felt the need to note that it had been considered "mean and disgraceful . . . a few years since." Well into the 1700s, English traders were sure to hold their noses and make suitable excuses before purchasing column space in their local newspapers. It was not until the 1750s that tradesmen began to embrace advertising columns more widely as a means of reaching out to customers.[4]

In a marketplace that still set so much store by bricks and mortar, easily surveyed by the community, individuals who dealt through novel channels frequently came under suspicion. Neighbors and local officers of the law or excise, who could quite easily be the same, were quick to conflate mobile traders with criminal activity. Eager buyers sneaked to a neighbor's house in the dark to purchase duty-free wine, while networks of brandy smugglers saw to it that the liquor was "run in order to carry it into ye country to sell." Strangers offered stolen bay mares for sale "in the publick streets" of cities rather than at the local fair or market, and householders became suspicious when they opened their front door to find their neighbors offering holland fabric for sale, anxious lest they had "not come honestly by it." Eli Longbothom purchased a stolen cow at 6:30 in the morning from a man he had never seen before and "paid . . . in the High Road without going to any house." When buying and selling took place in the middle of nowhere there was a strong chance that the goods were not the rightful property of the seller.[5]

Americans were less suspicious of transient commercial spaces. When they embraced the private bargain as a core method of buying and selling they demonstrated a widespread acceptance of marketplaces that were often not places at all. These virtual marketplaces assumed different forms in the colonial landscape, in the mechanisms of trade, and in the world of print. It is important to document and emphasize the centrality of the on the hoof, face-to-face dealing in America that, while it may appear to be a normative way of trading, was actually a novelty within an early modern marketplace customarily organized around communal marketing places set up to answer the common good.[6]

In the colonies, buying at roadside inns, in the street, or at a neighbor's house *could* be a sign that the goods were stolen. More often than not, however, this was not so. So much was bought and sold in locations that did not permanently exist as marketplaces that their unstable designation as trading spaces went unchallenged. When John Cornell appeared before the magistrates in Lancaster, Pennsylvania, he was not on trial for selling a horse from his house. Instead, the crime lay with Michael Mayer, who stole the horse after asking to saddle it and take it for a test ride. Likewise, Sarah McMaghan appeared in court because the men who entered her house under the pretext of buying some wheat she had gleaned had beaten and robbed her. That she was selling wheat from her house in the first place was unremarkable. Livestock dealer Jacob Hiltzheimer struck many a deal for horses and cows in the sellers' fields or at their houses. On the road to Pittsburgh, Indian trader James Kenny frequently purchased supplies from houses on the route and from people he encountered on his way, buying candles and beer from "Troters wife," bread from "Slater's wife," and sugar from "Crissops." Especially in sparsely populated areas, homes, fields, and river landings all temporarily became legitimate marketplaces as colonists struck bargains while traversing the extensive landscape.[7]

This style of dealing persisted from its seventeenth-century origins partly because it suited Europeans, but also because it remained grounded in well-established networks of local trade involving Native Americans and Africans. As they crossed on ferries, arrived at landings or wharves, and shuttled between plantations, men such as Abraham, a boatman owned by Carolina rice planter Henry Laurens, exchanged provisions with whites and blacks alike. Traveling "both by land and water" and offering groceries for hogs, fowl, rice, and corn, these African peddlers marketed to other slaves on plantations but also sold to anyone who would buy along the river. Their mobility caused Laurens to have a troubled relationship with his boatmen; they were essential to his market but could not be stopped from creating their own markets as they plied the Lowcountry's waterways.[8]

It is almost impossible to calculate the extent of Africans' marketing, or even to clarify its exact role in local commerce, but incidental accounts provide a glimpse of its extensive character. Charles Cattell's enslaved Africans, unaccompanied by whites, crossed at Mary Sureau's ferry on the Ashley River over one hundred times from 1752 to 1755. Is it really possible that not a single one of these people, making their way on long journeys from plantations to ferries and towns, took the opportunity to deal in some small goods along the way? Some certainly had the knowledge to do so. Although not named in the records, it is highly likely that one of these people was Sam, a "waiting man" who was "well known" in the area and later worked as a porter in Charleston for Richard Park-Stobo, who bought him at Cattell's estate auction in 1758. When Sam ran away from Stobo in 1760, his new owner speculated that he might frequent the Ashley River, which he no doubt knew well from his journeys up and down it, plying the waterways and trading as he went. Such opportunities presented themselves not just for Sam, but for many other Africans roving the Lowcountry without their masters. In 1777, Africans made approximately 650 solo journeys across the Cooper River at Strawberry Ferry. On foot or on wagons, chaises, or horses, these "boys" and "negroes," or occasionally "wenches" and "girls," shepherded cattle and sheep across the river, carried advertisements to Charleston, or simply undertook unspecified trips back and forth. Quite often their journey spanned two days. Sometimes only a one-way trip was recorded by the ferry keeper. On these hundreds of lengthy unsupervised excursions, enslaved people almost certainly traded both with each other and with willing white customers, who were similarly wandering the watery Lowcountry landscape. Since this environment still lacked abundant villages or stores, we can be sure the convenience of buying from these traders far outweighed concerns about the legality of the deal.[9]

While Africans crisscrossed the Carolina Lowcountry, putting a market in motion as they went, Native Americans likewise interacted with European traders farther west. Across large distances, commercial connections forged in the seventeenth century intensified. Native American dealers continually asked European authorities to stop unscrupulous traders from selling them rum and cheating them on the price and quantity of goods. Nevertheless, this did not mean Indians wished to fix trade in European-style spaces. Instead, as historians of the Indian trade in both Carolina and Pennsylvania have explained, a network in which paths and towns were equally important, and equally suitable as trading spaces, continued to host exchange. These spaces operated according to particular rules, culture, and etiquette, which traveling traders failed to acquaint themselves with at their peril. Indeed, to successfully negotiate paths as trading spaces, one had to master the dangers, distances, and horse management skills essential to moving along them, skills unnecessary in European marketplaces.[10]

Such paths—through woods, along rivers, over mountains, and across valleys—hosted many a deal before the Seven Years' War once again brought uncertainty to the region. Moravian traveler Bishop Cammerhoff observed in detail the network of paths these traders traversed along the Susquehanna River. Noting that "the country was populous with Indians," he estimated that "a trader with a train of twenty or thirty pack-horses, could in a very short time dispose of his wares." Another witness to the commerce remarked that Pennsylvania's traders went "where they might best dispose of their goods," becoming "numerous and scattered" across the landscape and running "up and down from one Indian town to another."[11]

In South Carolina and Georgia wandering Virginia traders continued to form a good proportion of the itinerant peddlers heading southward to trade with Cherokees and Creeks. They quickly found Indians who were willing to deal with them. South Carolina agent Ludovic Grant observed how trader Paris "had come from Stecoe on Tewtewah River and passing my House went to Docharty's where he bought two Cows and Calves. The Day after took his Journey for Great Terequa which he was to pass in his Way to Toquo where he resided with a remarkable Indian and a Warriour of Tannassee who had some Days before come over the Hills to Docharty's in order to pay a Debt he owed him." Carolina traders also conducted deals when and where they could. In a 1755 overview of the state of the trade, Grant explained to the governor that Europeans and Indians had traded "raw Skins in the Woods." The following year, the governor heard about "one Williams" who "went into the Woods, at or near a Place called the Honey Mountain, and there . . . traded with the Creeks and Cerickees a Quantity of Goods in their Hunting Ground for raw Skinns." These "Indian peddlers" knew they could find Indians ready to sell to them and eager to buy. Fortunately there were plenty of eastern merchants only too happy to supply them with goods on credit in exchange for skins.[12]

As the importance of these roving traders suggests, Penn's edict that Indians should always come to the Philadelphia marketplace to trade was never obeyed. Indian men and women did trade in the city when they came to town on diplomatic matters, but from the late 1750s onward most of the peltry for sale in the capital could be found under the Philadelphia Court House in Market Street, where the government had ordered it be sold by auction. Among other things, bidders could acquire deer, beaver, fox, raccoon, and otter furs at these sales, which took place almost monthly. However, auctions of "Indian goods" constituted only a fraction of all the sales held in colonial Pennsylvania, as this exchange mechanism emerged to become one of the chief enablers of the "mobile" marketplace in the colonies. By the 1760s hundreds of sales took place every year, making the vendue, as colonists called it, a core retail space. Their astonishing success was grounded in the seemingly endless supply of private property available for sale in the colonies. The vendue's popularity was then given a further boost by the adoption of 1732's Debtors Act, embraced everywhere except Virginia, which enabled land seized for debt to be sold at auction.[13]

All sorts of colonists attended vendues, for a multitude of reasons. Europeans and Africans bought and were sold. Elites purchased land or second-hand luxury goods. Poorer colonists frequented them to pick up cut-price groceries, shop-damaged imports, and books. Many purchased household or personal necessities, but small-time dealers also went to sales in search of stock for their shops. Although officially appointed city vendue masters were always men, free white women also constituted a large proportion of the attendees. Since women often acted as estate executors, they could be both sellers and buyers, organizing the vendue while also repurchasing items that went under the hammer to pay off their deceased husbands' debts. Auctions were an important price-setting mechanism in the colonial marketplace, and women's centrality to them reflected their major role in the development of such novel marketing methods.[14]

Because they were so popular, colonists frequently discussed their attendance at vendue sales. Animal trader Jacob Hiltzheimer noted visits by both him and his wife, where they perused and purchased livestock and household goods. Philadelphia and Charleston's merchants repeatedly explained to their correspondents that they turned to the vendue when they could not sell imported wares that were "stuck on hand." Philadelphia merchant

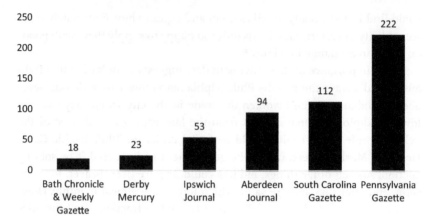

FIGURE 3.1 Number of auctions advertised in a selection of 1763 British and American newspapers. From Emma Hart, "A British Atlantic World of Advertising? Colonial American For Sale Notices in Comparative Context," in "Before Madison Avenue: Newspaper Advertising in Early America," special issue, *American Periodicals* 24 (Fall 2014): 110-27.

Benjamin Fuller was one of the quickest to recognize the vendue's commercial potential. After disposing of his own stock of "refuse goods" under the hammer, the merchant then imported wares specifically for sale at his "vendue house in the upper part of second street." The venture, Fuller proclaimed, soon "succeeded to my utmost wishes," enabling him "to support my family genteely." The draw of the auction even forced rural South Carolina minister Archibald Simpson to move the day of his 1761 New Year's sermon forward, since because of "a large publick vendue in the parish I would not get the people so generaly to attend."[15]

As Simpson's comment suggests, auctions were also a major conduit of rural commerce. While they sometimes were held in designated "vendue houses" or at city taverns similar to British venues, Americans favored auctions because they could take place anywhere. In both Pennsylvania and South Carolina, 40 percent of advertisements noting a sale location announced it would occur "on the spot," "on the premises," or "at the plantation of the deceased." In other words, the property under the hammer was itself the marketplace, but only until conveyed into the new ownership of the highest bidder. At that point the asset was stripped of movable goods—consumer durables and enslaved or indentured people—and once again returned to its function as an agricultural homestead. A 282-acre farm two and half miles from Christiana Bridge in Pennsylvania's Lower Counties temporarily became a marketplace when it was put up for auction in 1753. The only buildings there were "a good dwelling house and store house," where the bidding might well have taken place. Simultaneously, South Carolinians were gathering in a field, or at a house, on the colony's Wadmelaw Island, where they were bidding on "four valuable plantation slaves," livestock, provisions, and plantation tools. In both cases, once the purchased property was dispersed, the site resumed its bucolic character.[16]

Colonists favored auctions such as this Wadmelaw Island sale not only because they had so much property to dispose of, but also because that property often comprised people. It is of course immensely difficult for us to consider the "problem" of how to sell people, but this was precisely the issue faced by Carolinians, and also by some Pennsylvanians, for whom moving sentient beings across an expansive landscape to a central marketplace could be logistically challenging without the large-scale slave-trading networks of the antebellum era. Vendues represented the solution to this problem, and by embracing them colonists transformed multiple points in the South Carolina landscape—and to a lesser extent its Pennsylvania counterpart—into slave and servant marts. In all, advertised Carolina auctions from 1732 to 1765 listed for sale at least 17,464 individuals. People were on offer at 40 percent of vendues in the colony. While some of these "parcels" of people were offered by merchant importers selling cargoes directly from Africa, the vast majority were small groups of Africans sold from an existing workforce. By the early 1760s roughly five such auctions were advertised in the Lowcountry every month, of which fewer than a third took place in Charleston.[17]

In Pennsylvania, where owning people was not so widespread, only about one in ten vendues included people for sale. Nevertheless, with face-to-face negotiation a principal way of acquiring laborers, either for the period of an indenture or for a lifetime of slavery, the sale of people still underpinned the fluid nature of commercial space. Jacob Hiltzheimer bought two servants in the course of three years, one of whom he purchased at the wharf, directly from on board a recently arrived ship. Hiltzheimer then acquired a second laborer from future Philadelphia mayor and eminent Quaker Samuel Shoemaker, negotiating at Shoemaker's home. Cape May farmer Aaron Leaming bought people in a similar manner. On the last day of May 1761, Leaming "set out from home to go to Philada to buy a negro or two." The farmer did not

TABLE 3.1. Frequency of common commercial advertising phrases in provincial British Atlantic newspapers, 1764 and 1768

Phrase	Pennsylvania Gazette		South Carolina Gazette		Newcastle Courant		Caledonian Mercury		Ipswich Journal	
	1764	1768	1764	1768	1764	1768	1764	1768	1764	1768
To be sold	788	552	680	1992	57	55	153	158	55	52
Tea	112	85	192	176	47	46	44	80	33	54
Roup, auction, or vendue	259	157	154	404	26	28	156	163	53	51
Just imported	144	76	362	818	1	0	10	2	0	0
To be sold, just imported, and slave	3	7	52	131	0	0	0	0	0	0

Source: Emma Hart, "A British Atlantic World of Advertising? Colonial American For Sale Notices in Comparative Context," in "Before Madison Avenue: Newspaper Advertising in Early America," special issue, *American Periodicals* 24 (Fall 2014): 110–27.

visit public markets or auctions but instead "went over to Mr Dav Coopers where Willing & Morris has some negroes." Comparing the heights and ages of Troy, Sambo, and Lichfield, three Africans lodged there, with the heights of his own children, whom he had carefully measured before he left home, Leaming settled on Troy, purchased for £40. Before finishing his business, Leaming "paid the money to their store keepers and took a bill of sale."[18]

How did Aaron Leaming know that Willing and Morris had enslaved people for sale at Daniel Cooper's Jersey ferry store? We cannot be sure, but there is a strong chance the Cape May farmer had learned it from a May 7 advertisement in the *Pennsylvania Gazette*, which had announced "just imported from Barbados . . . a negroe man, and two new negroe boys, who are to be sold by Willing, Morris and Company." If he did enter the market through the newspaper's advertising section, Leaming would have been just one of many colonists who happily conducted trade this way, making the newspaper a third and final pillar of the portable colonial marketplace. Advertisements offering goods and services for sale were far more numerous in colonial newspapers than in their metropolitan counterparts. Both the *Pennsylvania Gazette* and the *South Carolina Gazette* were composed half of "news" and half of advertising copy. The *South Carolina Gazette* also periodically issued special supplements of additional advertisements. At the apogee of the colonial era, Franklin's newspaper contained over five hundred, and sometimes as many as seven hundred "for sale" notices a year. Peter Timothy's Carolina newspaper carried a similar number of notices, with 1768 a bumper year of almost two thousand. Including wares listed as being "just imported" or offered for vendue brings the number of announcements to more than three thousand.[19]

Directly comparing the advertising copy of American newspapers with that of their British contemporaries plainly reveals the greater commercialization of colonial print. Leading British provincial newspapers, such as the *Newcastle Courant* and the *Caledonian Mercury*, carried at most one-fifth the "for sale" notices of their American equivalents. They incorporated almost no notices placed by merchants announcing goods "just imported." Americans' peculiar reliance on the newspaper as an instrument of commerce suggests that the colonial setting had dislodged the market from fixed locations. Newspapers were foundational to the elaboration of a marketplace characterized by person-to-person deals driven primarily by individuals' trading needs rather than the corporate aspirations of commercial spaces governed by the common good.[20]

The advertising columns of early America's newspapers had become an instrument for free, white, literate people to trade property, a major reason for their popularity. Newspapers existed in a symbiotic relationship with both auctions and private bargains, making them possible in an extensive colonial landscape lacking spaces that Europeans customarily designated as markets. Closely examining a singular example illustrates how auction advertisements bridged the distances separating colonists:

> To be Sold at Vendue on Tuesday the 25th of April next, a Plantation, scituate upon round O *Savannah*, containing 584 acres of choice planting Land[,] Barn and some other convenient Buildings upon the same, the Plantation is well fenc'd in, and every Thing in good Order for planting the ensuing Crop. Any Person inclinable to purchase, may treat with Messrs *Yeomans* and *Escott* in *Charlestown*, Mr. *James Ferguson* at *Pon Pon*, or *Robert Wright* at *Dorchester*. [*South Carolina Gazette*, April 6, 1738.]

Announcing the vendue of a piece of land forty-two miles from Charleston at the Round "O," the Carolina advertisement alerted readers to the availability of a tract situated in what was regarded at the time as the backcountry. To overcome this remoteness, the seller lodged information at key points in the Lowcountry for buyers to consult; both Pon Pon and

Dorchester had become centers of commercial activity by this time, and Charleston, of course, was the region's capital. Using the newspaper, the seller not only was able to notify buyers of the sale but could also circulate advance information about the land on offer and the terms of purchase.[21]

However, vendue notices were far from the only type of commercial copy. As innumerable historians have noted, newspaper advertisements also drove early America's burgeoning consumer economy. When merchants and shopkeepers used print to virtually open the doors of their emporiums of imported necessities and luxuries to customers, they helped to create an entirely new market space. William Sitgreaves was one of countless merchants enticing newspaper readers into his "New Shop" with a carefully placed advertisement. His store at the corner of Philadelphia's Water and Arch Streets offered, among other things, "just imported Striped and flowered lustrings, crimson, blue and green damasks, sattins, black paduasoy, mantuas, blue, red, green, changeable and black taffeties, peelings, striped, cloth colour and black ell wd. persians, half yd. do. Figured modes, new fashioned check, Prussian cloaks, cardinals, poloners, with hats, newest fashioned sattin hats and bonnets."[22]

Although such exhaustive lists of fabrics, teas, ceramics, ribbons, and toys might look to the modern eye like a typical British Atlantic "inventory of consumer desire," their candid appeal to individual buyers was perhaps even more novel than the goods offered for sale. Colonial traders' heavy use of such advertisements suggests that they worked; and they worked because the American marketplace was, in large measure, a space structured by trade between individuals, free of embedded hierarchies and institutions. Unlike their European counterparts, colonial newspaper readers saw nothing suspicious about buying virtually, particularly when they could rely on networks of friends, servants, and family to verify the quality of the product. Advertisements could be used to alert men and women—fathers and mothers, uncles and aunts, nephews and nieces—to the availability of a product, which could then be procured either by shopping in person, sending enslaved or servant proxies to shop, or commissioning a relative in another city to visit the shop. To successfully attract buyers' attention, dealers like Sitgreaves had to reach colonists far beyond Philadelphia who nevertheless looked to the city for goods.[23]

If anything, transient spaces became more important to trading colonists over the course of the eighteenth century. Combining the communication potential of the newspaper with the large quantities of private property available for sale, former Europeans created a marketplace that was both nowhere and everywhere at the same time. The necessity of trading with Indians far from coastal regions enhanced these qualities, as did the creation of slave societies in which Africans were both roving market agents and commodities. By abandoning the requirement that a marketplace should be a distinct physical space permanently marking the landscape, colonists not only solved the problem of bridging the vast distances of the North American continent, they also created new and innovative ways of buying and selling. These innovations set them apart from their European counterparts, who still struggled with the ephemeral and impersonal marketplaces sponsored by commercialization.

MARKETS IN MOTION AND MARKETING HUBS

The impact of this portable marketplace on the geography and the character of American commerce was dramatic. Indeed, the novelty of American marketplaces was so striking that we can see it in the maps produced by the inhabitants of these colonial regions. In an Enlightenment quest to know and possess their surroundings, both Americans and Britons embraced the

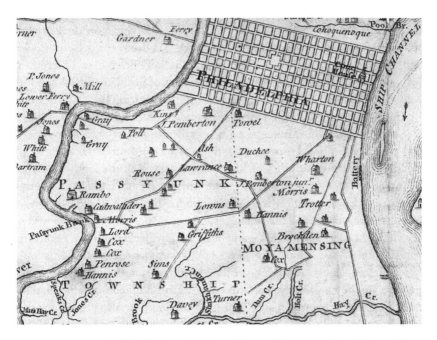

FIGURE 3.2 *Map of Philadelphia and the Parts Adjacent,* Nicholas Scull and George Heap, Philadelphia, 1753. Library of Congress, Geography and Map Division.

FIGURE 3.3 Charleston, Dorchester, and Jacksonboro–Pon Pon, from *A Map of the Province of South Carolina etc.*, James Cook, London, 1773. Library of Congress, Geography and Map Division.

newest surveying techniques to produce highly detailed representations of the landscape—the most "accurate" possible. Pennsylvanians, Carolinians, and North East Englanders all entered into the mapmaking endeavor with enthusiasm. From 1752 to 1770, elites in the three polities sponsored expensive surveys. The depictions that the surveyors—Scull and Heap, James Cook, and Andrew Armstrong—made laid bare numerous prominent differences between American and British elite visualizations of the landscape. When the colonial maps are laid beside their British counterparts, the strikingly distinctive footprint of the North American marketplace quickly comes into view.[24]

Let us consider these maps as a guide to the geography of local commercial practice. Andrew Armstrong's 1769 map of Northumberland (fig. 3.4) clearly marked the authority of his elite subscribers in the landscape. The country seats of the great and the good, which were the basis of their economic power, are carefully denoted by miniature houses. Nevertheless, these houses do not dominate the mapped landscape. Indeed, they are between the villages and towns that also populated the terrain, even in this relatively rural region of North East England. Each of these nuclear settlements harbored shared economic spaces, yet they were far from the only communal markers on the map. Armstrong was equally careful to label common lands, including Wooler Common and Corbridge Common. He also pinpointed the region's mills and its most important fairs; Stagshawbank, "where one of the greatest Fairs in England are held for Live Cattle" and Whitsun Bank, with "a fair held annually here." In producing the most detailed and "accurate" depiction possible of Northumberland, Armstrong had pleased his wealthy patrons, but he had also revealed the enduring presence of the commons in the local economy.[25]

The maps produced by Heap, Scull, and Cook of Pennsylvania and South Carolina are comparable in quality to their British counterparts. Nevertheless, they reveal the startling lack of common commercial space in these American colonies. Beyond the main cities, individual landowners dominated the landscape. Quite simply, in eastern Pennsylvania and Carolina common economic space appears to have largely disappeared from the map. The maps provide a bird's-eye view of colonial economic space without community, not surprising given the amount of trade conducted in temporary or "imagined" marketplaces such as the auction and the newspaper.

However, these maps do share some important commercial locations. Mills, agricultural estates, and urban waterfronts appear in all of them, as, of course, do towns and cities. Since these trading spaces were positioned at the leading edge of the Atlantic trading economy, we need to explore very carefully how trade was conducted within them. However, closely comparing their configuration, ownership, and institutional regimes only reinforces the particularities of the colonial setting. In Britain, a variety of institutional interests continued to guide the conduct of trade in all three locations. In

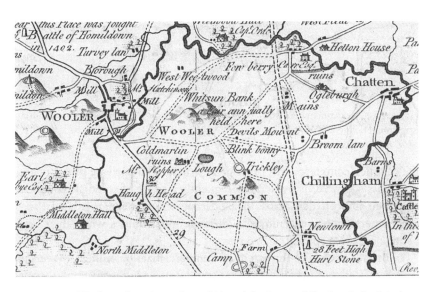

FIGURE 3.4 Wooler and environs, from *A Map of the County of Northumberland*, Andrew Armstrong, London, 1769.

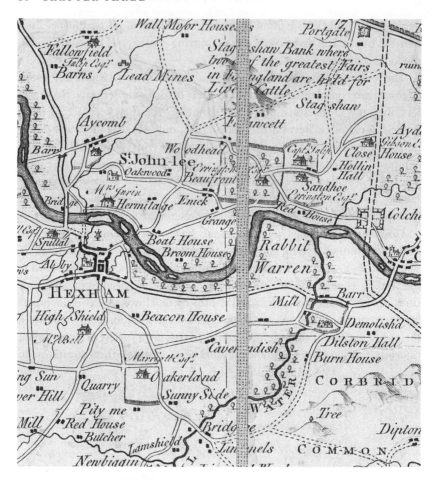

FIGURE 3.5 Hexham and environs, from *A Map of the County of Northumberland,* Andrew
Armstrong, London, 1769.

the colonies, commerce was principally structured by private property and
the rights accorded its owner. Consequently a range of colonists could exploit their ability to deal across the landscape without being regulated. Property owners, moreover, enjoyed additional opportunities when their land
became a trading space.

In Britain, no matter the extent of commercialization, millers, owners of
landed estates, and urban merchants could not evade the customary economy of interests. At every turn it intruded to structure their trading and
to shape the spaces where they operated. Millers, especially rural ones, did

become entangled in supply chains constituted through private bargaining, but many mills still functioned as part of a corporate economy. Glasgow's inventory of its assets and income in 1755 included at least four mills for grinding city residents' grain and malt. These water mills were let on three-year leases to individual townspeople, who competed for the privilege at auction. It was well into the eighteenth century before the monopoly of these corporate mills met with a challenge from millers building their own steam mills outside the city limits, undermining the privilege of town millers extant "since time immemorial."[26]

When English industrial entrepreneurs attempted to set up stores on their estates to supply their employees with groceries, consumables, and raw materials, the government stepped in. From the sixteenth century onward, authorities remained sympathetic to the appeals of cloth workers, nail-makers, and coal miners whose employers paid them in provisions or gave them less work if they refused to buy at company stores stocking only low-quality goods at inflated prices. Laborers objected to these practices on the grounds that masters were ensnaring them in an economic relationship for their private gain while failing to assume the patriarchal duties inherent in the common good. In the late seventeenth and eighteenth centuries Parliament introduced a number of bills designed to outlaw this "truck system," prompted by the belief that, while landed and industrial estates were not sites of economic equality, they nevertheless should operate according to long-standing expectations of the poor's right to "subsistence, custom, family, and community."[27]

Because they were almost exclusively in cities, Britain's wharves were among the commercial spaces subject to almost constant intervention by corporate forces. Local government owned and invested in wharves, so they expected to organize and regulate the commerce that took place on them. The bustling wharves of Newcastle and Glasgow were closely monitored to ensure that they remained a location for unloading and loading but not for buying and selling. In 1771 Newcastle's Common Council complained that "divers Persons do still continue the illegal and prejudicial Practice of Setting up Shambles and exposing Beef to sale thereon at the Keyside in this town, notwithstanding several of them have been indicted and convicted of, and fined for the same: It is ordered that the aforesaid Practice be wholly discontinued." In 1778, when Newcastle timber merchants started storing timber on the wharf, "divers persons" complained to the council that they were "making the quay a repository for private purposes instead of a public landing wharf." The council agreed with the petitioners, applying a strict limit to the length of time cargoes could be left at the quay. Even Glasgow's Broomielaw, which saw very little long-distance traffic, was governed by a shoremaster from the late 1780s onward. This individual, appointed by the city council and paid a regular salary, was charged with assigning berths to arriving ships, overseeing their loading and unloading, making sure cargoes lay on the wharf for no more than twenty-four hours, and keeping the wharf clean.[28]

In a multitude of ways corporate authorities, acting in the name of the public or common good, sought to direct trade in these British spaces. In the American iteration of these commercial settings, however, property owners were masters of their own domains, their trading pursuits untrammeled by the interference of communal or corporate interests. As we have seen, John Potts enjoyed the right to establish mills, ironworks, and company stores at Pottstown without the intervention of collective interests seeking to regulate his processing wheat or paying workers in provisions. The vast majority of Pennsylvania's farmers enjoyed a similar relationship with the market. Whereas four-fifths of British farmers rented their farms, by the Revolution no more than a quarter of white colonists were tenants. These owner-occupiers were free to trade as they wished, with little meaningful intervention by manors or estate managers. Indeed, mill owners even enjoyed the support of the government, which happily assented to the steady flow of millers' road petitions requesting better connections to customers and markets.[29]

The emergence of the colonial farm as a market space reached its apogee on southern and Caribbean plantations. As James Cook's map shows (fig. 3.3), more than even its Pennsylvania counterpart, the Carolina landscape was defined by the personal commercial empires of the region's planters. From their plantations, wealthy elites like Ralph Izard and Richard Drayton—whose names are clearly marked on the map—coordinated the movement of goods from plantation to ferry to rural store, or to town, and back again. Planter Richard Hutson negotiated by letter, no doubt carried by an enslaved African. In writing, the planter acknowledged the receipt of a cow and a calf from Charleston butcher Daniel Stroble and notified Mr. Davis that he was "in great want of a boat, I am willing to give you 180 pounds for her. . . . If you are willing to take that . . . I will send to Beaufort for her immediately." What Hutson meant, of course, was that he would send an enslaved boatman to collect the watercraft. As proxies who did the hard work of connecting white elites to the market, Africans were vital in sustaining a commerce where planters and their families rarely had to visit a common market space for either necessities or luxuries. Instead, they ran markets from their plantations. Many white planters, including Henry Laurens, purchased corn, honey, eggs, and poultry from the enslaved people on their properties in a trade that reinforced the plantation's status as a marketplace in which the land, the laborers, and all the movable goods operated as the owner pleased.[30]

Much less well understood than the plantation's emergence as a marketplace is the role of private property in shaping urban commerce. Property owners became particularly influential at the water's edge. Britain's city wharves were exclusively public landing facilities, but colonial wharves quickly became intensive sites of individual entrepreneurship. A few did operate under the aegis of the city authorities. However, as the finely executed plan of the waterfront and its immediate environs shown in figure 3.6 demonstrates, Charleston's eighteenth-century wharves were overwhelmingly in the hands of individual wharfingers who, to maximize their incomes, crammed as much commercial activity as possible onto them. Shops, stores, and workshops housed factors, auctioneers, tradespeople, and storekeepers. Wharfingers set their own rates for storing goods and mooring vessels. Many Charleston wharves had their own scale houses, making the wharfinger responsible for measuring and weighing all incoming and outgoing cargoes from his wharf, using his own set of weights and measures.[31]

In Charleston, and in Philadelphia, wharves thus became a prime location for buying and selling. Advertising in the *South Carolina Gazette*, one wharf owner notified the public that they would know fish was available when there was "a WHITE-FLAG hoisted at the upper-end of Capt. *Roper's* wharf, near the *Curtain-Line*." Even after the construction of the town's fish market in 1770, its wharves continued to be central places of trade as boats came ashore bringing livestock, wood, and corn. Their arrival at the wharves nearest the market, according to one commentator, often saw such commodities sold off to individual buyers before they reached the shambles. Another witness noted that when a boat arrived in town "with corn, hogs, sheep, calves or other provisions, for the *Charles-town* market, there are people who watch the wharves before day, to engross the whole. . . . This sort of fraud, is practiced both by white and black people." Once again, Africans were the sinews of this marketplace, helping the wharf to grow as a trading space rather than just a corporate-controlled landing.[32]

Africans were not so visible on Philadelphia's wharves, but the waterfront was as heavily commercialized as its Charleston counterpart. Among the commodities often sold there was wood harvested from the surrounding

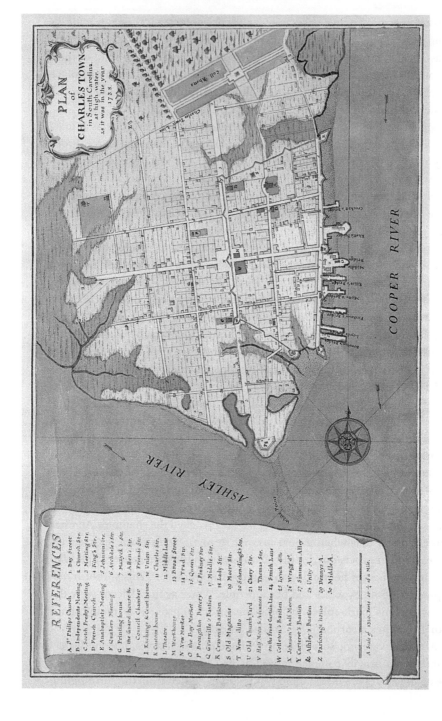

FIGURE 3.6 Hand-colored map of Charleston in 1738 with detail of its principal wharves, n.d. Courtesy of the Library Company of Philadelphia.

countryside. Cape May farmer Aaron Leaming marketed his red cedar posts by first gathering them into bundles on the beach near his home, then loading these bundles onto a boat for Philadelphia. On arrival, the posts were unloaded at "Anthony Wilkinson's wharf," where buyers came to purchase them. Perhaps Leaming was following the example of fellow sellers who sold wood at the Northern Liberties wharves just outside the city limits—in short measures, much to the ire of the officers of the nearby Callowhill market.[33]

When it came to the urban wharf, looks could be deceptive, since colonial wharves seemed to be common spaces functioning much like their European counterparts. Such an assumption was particularly easy to make about New York's wharves, which lacked the piers constructed by the entrepreneurial merchants who had taken responsibility for developing most of the waterfront in Boston, Philadelphia, Newport, and Charleston. However, moving from the birds'-eye view provided by regional maps to ground level brings an alternative perspective. In almost every colonial city the eighteenth-century wharf was a majority privately owned space in which entrepreneurs concentrated economic activity for their individual profit. Even in New York, where the Dutch-founded government had originally owned the shoreline, the process of privatizing and pier building was under way by the 1760s. Bernard Ratzer's 1767 map of the city depicted Beckman's Slip and Cruger's Wharf (among others) as East River landmarks, the personal empires of these trading men gradually conquering the waterfront as the corporation sold off lots to sponsor their improvement.[34]

This model of privatization was rolled out across the American countryside. Dotting the landscape were places that looked like communities but lacked any communal spaces. In these locations, such as Bacon's Bridge and Jacksonboro in South Carolina, or Pennypack Creek in Pennsylvania, auctions, inns, and stores clustered to create commercial hubs. Such spaces did not resemble Europeans' idea of a fixed marketplace, however, because they were a collection of privately owned commercial enterprises and therefore had no public marketplace. Rather, they were like rural wharves—privately owned and privately run.[35]

Situated roughly ten miles northeast of Philadelphia, Pennypack Creek and neighboring Busseltown was one such space. By the 1740s one mill was located there, and with a capacious tidal creek running through the tract, more followed by the 1750s. The potential of the location was realized by the early 1760s, when the creek had become home to at least two gristmills with adjoining cooper's shops, a bolting mill, and a fulling mill. By 1767 resident Elizabeth Thomas was selling cloth near the creek, and a number of vendue sales were held in the White Horse Tavern and at the mills themselves, which often changed ownership through this market mechanism. With stables and stone outhouses now adjoining the mills and plantations of Pennypack, a 1769 advertiser thought the location could safely be described as "in a good neighbourhood, and part of the country for business." Together these merchant mills, taverns, and homes represented a marketplace, being spaces where economic exchange was concentrated. They also nurtured settlers who embraced this innovative commercial setup; one of the first settlers of Pennypack was Quaker Thomas Livezey, who owned a farm and a quarter share of a mill at his death in 1759. Once he had reached adulthood Livezey's son, Thomas Jr., relocated to Roxbury, where he purchased land and established a similar mill settlement in his new township residence.[36]

South Carolina's rural parts incorporated many similar spaces. Jacksonboro-Pon Pon evolved into one such focal point. After the Yamasee War, Pon Pon developed into an Indian and English settlement where Native and European people forged alliances through trade and marriage. Starting in the late 1740s the place was increasingly known by its English name Jacksonboro' (later Jacksonboro). During the Revolutionary War a passing British army colonel described it as a "village containing about sixty houses" with "some large store houses for rice" connected "by water to Charleston market . . . well situated for trade." The town was laid out in lots by John Jackson in the early eighteenth century, but his planning did not encompass a market square. Instead, its commercial qualities sprang from the efforts of individual colonists who spied a convenient riverside location and the adjacent Parker's Ferry. By the 1740s Jacksonboro was home to an inn with a billiards table and probably more than one store. Both of these locations hosted auctions, which also took place in the village streets. Over the middle of the eighteenth century almost eighty auctions were held there. While transferring thousands of acres of land, these sales also included 716 enslaved people listed as individuals, in addition to unnumbered people mentioned only as part of a "parcel."[37]

As Jacksonboro continued to flourish, it became an attractive destination for traders seeking commercial opportunity beyond Charleston. In the 1750s shopkeeper Moses Pimento had opened a dry goods store in the capital, making forays into the countryside as a middleman in the indigo and livestock trade. However, Pimento had a hard time selling these commodities at a profit, and by the early 1760s he had relocated to Jacksonboro-Pon Pon, where he ran a store. Supplied by Charleston merchants Woodrop and Cathcart, the store was profitable enough for Pimento to make regular cash remittances of up to £150 to his city creditors. Pimento's death in 1765 prompted his wife Leah, who like many women had been appointed the estate's executor, to organize a vendue of his remaining stock. Lured to the event by printed broadsides and newspaper advertisements, the attendees were encouraged to bid generously with a ready supply of beer, punch, and meat over the "three days the sale lasted." It appears that the store then passed into the custody of Pimento's coreligionist Mordecai Myers.[38]

Such trading places also flourished because Native American and African American traders frequented them. The success of Camden, South Carolina, was partly due to its proximity to Catawba towns. Besides marketing goods imported from Britain and alcohol brewed in his recently constructed brewhouse, Camden's founder Joseph Kershaw likely sold River Burnished ware made by Catawba potters in the nearby Waxhaws district. In some ways early Camden was reminiscent of Shamokin, a settlement at the forks of the Susquehanna in the western reaches of the territory claimed by Pennsylvania. Until its destruction during the Seven Years' War, Shamokin was a collection of Native people and some Europeans who used it as a trading hub for European and Indian products.[39]

Places such as Pennypack and Jacksonboro–Pon Pon were not the only clusters of marketing activity emerging as colonists established businesses on creeks and rivers and at ferries. In South Carolina, Willtown, Bacon's Bridge, Ashley Ferry, Monck's Ferry, and Stono Landing grew to fulfill marketing needs. Pennsylvanians also founded multiple settlements around forges and mills—Elizabeth Furnace, Hopewell Furnace, Tulpehocken Forge, the mill complexes of the Brandywine Valley, and Manheim glassworks and forge, for example. Anchoring a distinctively colonial commercial landscape, these market spaces had flourished not because a government legislated them into existence. As they grew, they were subject to remarkably few corporate controls. If public marketplaces were eventually laid out, they often seemed an afterthought. Rather, such settlements functioned according to the ambitions of the men who owned the enterprises constituting them; men who hoped that the "fine situation for trade" would bring them and their families financial security.[40]

POWER AND AUTHORITY IN THE COLONIAL MARKETPLACE

William Streper lived on Wissahickon Creek, not far from Thomas Livezey Jr., northwest of Philadelphia and close to Germantown. Moses Pimento started out as a shopkeeper and factor in Charleston but struck out for Jacksonboro to run a dry goods store. The Pennsylvania German and the South Carolina Jew appear to have had very little in common.

Divided by religion and distance, the two colonists were nevertheless united by the unpleasant experience of facing public assaults on their character as creditable men of trade and property. In 1767, in a letter to the *Pennsylvania Gazette*, Streper fended off his neighbors' claims that he had blackened the name of one Nathaniel Shepherd. Streper had accused Shepherd of ruining a plot of land Streper had recently purchased by flooding it with a new mill dam. Shepherd had wanted the land himself, but failing to secure a deal he had decided that building the dam and ruining the plot was his best route to satisfaction. Both the original sale to Streper and the signing of the documents permitting Shepherd to construct the offending dam had taken place in private spaces with few or no witnesses present. As a result, the identity of the malicious party was unclear. Moses Pimento found himself similarly compromised when he went into the country and purchased a quantity of indigo from James McGirth at his plantation in Craven County. Possibly new to the business, Pimento was "intirely ignorant of the quality and goodness of indigo" but nevertheless believed the "assurances he had" from the seller that it was of high quality. Unfortunately McGirth was lying, and Pimento found himself the owner of unsalable indigo. Fortunately a witness had been present in McGirth's house at the time of sale, and Pimento won compensation in civil court on the grounds that the planter had intentionally deceived him.[41]

The predicaments of Streper and Pimento illustrate perfectly the perils of trading in obscure spaces free from the oversight—and the protection—of any corporate body. The two men were completely reliant on the word of friends and acquaintances, with whom they had to cultivate a reputation as honest individuals if they were to call on them for support when a deal went awry. Such conflicts tested their ability to successfully enter the marketplace. But as free, white, property-owning men, Streper and Pimento were not entirely vulnerable, since they could, and did, appeal to the law. Whereas early colonists like minister Francis Le Jau suffered at the hands of unscrupulous dealers because there were almost no functioning legal institutions, by the 1720s the creation of local criminal and civil courts provided recourse for those who had been cheated or slandered by another trader.[42]

It makes sense that Streper and Pimento turned to those courts to solve their marketplace disputes. The law took on an ever greater importance across the Atlantic world as credit increasingly greased the wheels of ex-

change. In America the growing legal power of Europeans was dangerous
to Indians and Africans; the law was as likely to be used by whites to divest
enslaved boatmen of their trade goods as to protect Pimento against the
losses he endured from McGirth's efforts to cheat him.[43]

Particular to the colonial marketing spaces we have visited here, moreover, was the singular importance of property and credit to economic power.
In Europe's long-established marketing spaces, credit undoubtedly played a
greater role in dictating market relations than it had done before the eighteenth century. Nevertheless, because of the persistent dialogue between
established institutions and novel practices in Europe's marketplaces, an
individual trader's credit was as yet just one component in a larger web of
values influencing economic relations. But with no corporate bodies claiming to work for the common good in the colonial marketplace, individuals' credit *overwhelmingly* determined their capacity to function effectively
within it. Economic power in the colonial marketplace was directly related
to ownership of property and the ability to manage (or defend) it successfully. Such a reliance on credibility was an advantage not only for European
men, but also for European women, many of whom were well apprised of
emerging financial instruments, the importance of good credit, and the legal
procedures for recovering bad debts.[44]

In early America's criminal and civil courts, credit's power in the marketplace was inscribed into the case papers scrutinized by judge and jury.
As colonial governor Thomas Pownall astutely observed in 1764, since the
common law was grounded in precedent, the experience of colonization
was bound to change it. A process would unfold, he wrote, in which "the
common law of these countries must, in its natural course, become different,
and sometimes even contrary [to], or at least incompatible with the common
law of England." This was certainly the case in Pennsylvania. On the face of
it, the colony's quarter sessions seemed to operate like their British cousins.
In both provincial Britain and Pennsylvania, sessions opened with the jury
surveying the state of the local infrastructure, issuing orders for bridge re-
pair, and reading petitions for new roads. Judges and juries then turned to
a depressingly familiar litany of poverty, misery, and violence. The destitute
poor, drunken fighters, pregnant unmarried women, petty thieves, and ne-
glectful masters and servants all appeared before a court of local worthies
charged with punishing them according to a familiar definition of criminal
behavior. At colonial quarter sessions, however, juries did not hear of crimes
against the common good in the marketplace. So when their British counterparts were still preoccupied in the 1700s with cases where the accused

had contravened or challenged the legal and institutional infrastructure of the marketplace, juries in Pennsylvania and Carolina almost never heard such complaints.[45]

The differing regulatory regimes of the British and American marketplaces thus are clearest at the crossroads of trade and the local court. English quarter sessions often preoccupied themselves with regulating the local market. In Northumberland, the cost of a bushel of wheat, rye, barley, oats, beans, pease, and bigg (a locally grown four-rowed barley) were set at the sessions at least until the middle of the eighteenth century. Not uncommon were disputes where traders had ignored the rights of corporate interests in the marketplace or had assaulted officers charged with upholding them. Brandy smugglers, those who had either insulted or assaulted customs and excise men, guild members who had charged excessive tolls to nonfreemen, butchers who had dressed rotten meat to make it look fresh, tallow chandlers who sold tallow from rotten sheep, rogues and cheats at fairs "throwing dice for gingerbread" who took profits away from honest biscuit sellers, and women who set out to forestall and engross the Newcastle market all had to answer to the charges of grand juries. Since most local disputes never made it as far as the quarter sessions, justices of the peace heard yet more cases in which cheating, commercial deception, or unfair dealing was the main accusation. Edmund Tew, a Durham justice of the peace from 1750 to 1776, dealt repeatedly with pawnbrokers who had detained goods unreasonably, bakers who had tried to cheat the bread assize, criminal peddlers, and those who stood accused of buying smuggled brandy and gin from their neighbors or of selling it to them.[46]

Pennsylvania juries, on the other hand, entertained barely any complaints concerning the economic common good. Traders neither enjoyed nor sought legal protection on this score. Instead, they entered into bargains at their own risk, relying on the word of friends or family—if any were present to vouch for them—when the deal went wrong. Lancaster County established its quarter sessions in 1742. Although the court was soon hearing multiple accusations of theft, assault, and fornication, there were no prosecutions for misselling, substandard goods, forestalling, engrossing, or assaulting duty collectors. Local magistrates had made no effort to dictate where commercial exchange should take place, on what terms, or what protections buyers and sellers were due regarding price and quality. Chester County's well-established quarter sessions operated on a similar remit, as did Philadelphia County's courts. Even the Philadelphia mayor's court maintained a similar caseload, with only a handful of prerevolutionary prosecutions for regrating in the city's marketplaces appearing before the justices in the 1760s. Instead, colonial criminal and civil courts proved most useful for people who had been swindled, had had property stolen, or were unpaid by a chronic debtor. In such cases there was plenty of support for individuals who enjoyed the right of trading their own private property to recover it, both at quarter sessions and in common pleas courts.[47]

Since the law provided an avenue of redress in the marketplace only when a complaint was grounded in property ownership, those who had the most property and the clearest right to recover it, or the capacity to defend their reputation as honest traders in that marketplace, enjoyed the most power. South Carolina's equity court, and a group of local supporters, proved to be the savior of William Logan, a factor and storekeeper who, like Pimento, started out in Charleston and then relocated to a rural store. Logan's problems began when his former master, merchant Thomas Stone, held a grudge against his erstwhile apprentice. Initially Logan enjoyed the advantages the unfettered marketplace bestowed on white men who were able to buy and sell freely. After the conclusion of Logan's apprenticeship in 1746, his master returned to London to work in the Carolina trade, leaving Logan to set himself up in Charleston. After working for two years as a clerk, Logan went into partnership with Lionel Chalmers, "a man of considerable fortune and credit." Thomas Stone agreed to become their London factor, supplying them with SC£5,500 worth of goods.

The partnership soon got into trouble when Stone wrote to Logan demanding he pay him back for the goods within six months rather than the nine that was "the Custom at that time among other Factors in England dealing to Carolina." On hearing this news Chalmers, on his attorney's advice, withdrew from the partnership. However, Logan still had options open to him as a free white man of property. With the financial and personal support of Richard Baker, an eminent planter and his father-in-law, Logan decided to "settle a store" at Bacon's Bridge on the Ashley River. Purchasing a lot with a store already on it, Logan soon had a "repository of goods, wares, and merchandize" whose popularity gave him "great encouragement."[48]

The ease with which Logan could obtain credit and property was central to his ability to salvage his situation. He could quickly take advantage of the growing commercial hubs springing up beyond Charleston. Bacon's Bridge, like Jacksonboro–Pon Pon and Ashley Ferry, was emerging by the late 1740s as a marketing place where a number of commercial outlets conveniently clustered. Merchants Smith and Scott maintained a store there, where they sold "parcels" of Africans and received deer skins from traders "at the

Charles-Town market price." There were frequent vendue sales, drawing in bidders who might also then purchase from Logan's store, in which he was careful to keep an up-to-date "assortment" of wares.[49]

Unfortunately, in 1752, just two years after he had set up the enterprise, the contents of Logan's store themselves fell under the hammer. Having returned to South Carolina, Stone was pursuing his grudge against his former apprentice with renewed vigor, this time putting Logan's stock-in-trade up for sale without his permission. Logan's efforts to recover his livelihood by purchasing a plantation were also scuppered by Stone, who, with the word of the provost marshal, once again offered Logan's property at vendue on the grounds that he was still indebted to him. When Logan inherited a portion of his father-in-law's estate, Stone swooped a third time. On this occasion, however, Logan had gathered a band of supporters who could testify to his honesty and credibility. These men helped him take his case to the chancery court, where Stone was ordered to pay SC£1,000 compensation. Operating as an individual trader in the Carolina marketplace, Logan found himself vulnerable to attacks on his credit from Stone. Nevertheless, as a free white man, the opportunities afforded by the easy purchase of property, and the possibility of defending his status as a creditable property owner, eventually saved Logan from destitution.[50]

A legal system fashioned to protect private property in the marketplace, but not corporate privilege, also benefited single white women traders. If they were widowed or could acquire feme sole status, such women could enjoy significant economic power. Mary Sureau, the proprietor of Ashley Ferry, was one such individual. Sureau's husband, Francis, originally ran the ferry and its adjoining inn, first advertising its services in the *South Carolina Gazette* in 1738. However, Francis died soon afterward, and Mary ran the show for at least fifteen years, until her own demise in 1755. As we have seen, at her death planter Charles Cattell owed her over SC£250 for ferrying horses, people, and carriages across the river, for stabling horses, and for innumerable drinks, dinners, and breakfasts. Sureau oversaw a number of vendues at the ferry, including that of Mrs. Mary Seabrook in 1753, when buyers snapped up practical items such as hoes and axes as well as luxury mahogany tables and silverware. Six enslaved people—women, men, and children—were the most expensive lots, however. Sureau also retailed food from her inn, and other debtors owed her for processed meats, butter, and calf skins. At her death she possessed an "old small canoe" at Dorchester that, perhaps piloted by an enslaved African boatman, plied the Ashley River. Her inventory also noted 173 outstanding debts, while Sureau owed money to Indian trader Patrick Brown. From her riverside location, Mary Sureau thus coordinated a one-woman marketplace through which flowed provisions, people, land, consumer durables, food, and drink.[51]

Urban women, if they could accumulate sufficient property through marriage or inheritance, could also thrive. With courts uninterested in the idea of towns as corporate spaces of male economic privilege, white woman who inherited enslaved people with skills, stock-in-trade, or property from spouses, parents, or siblings could trade without legal restriction. Charleston butcher Margaret Oliver was one such woman. Her husband Peter was already working in the city in 1735 and had declared bankruptcy in 1744. Sometime afterward he died, evidently having recovered his finances sufficiently for his wife Margaret to continue the business. Working until her own death in 1765, she obtained an enslaved male butcher and two enslaved women. The family business endured as Margaret's daughter Margaret, with brother James, continued it, "much obliged to their late mother's friends and good customers." The Olivers joined the numerous women in urban retail who succeeded in planting themselves at the heart of the city market. This was not a position that women in all English-speaking towns could expect to achieve. In cities like Newcastle and Glasgow, the corporate power of guilds and city councils often excluded female butchers from buying, slaughtering, and selling livestock unless they happened to be married to a butcher.[52]

A legal regime protecting the rights of property holders in the marketplace, but not concerned with the commons, created losers as well as winners. English cloth workers and nail-makers could draw on antitruck legislation when middlemen forced them to purchase overpriced necessities at a company store. Manorial authorities bestowed power over the local economy on the lord of the manor, but poor tenants successfully drew on their historic right to petition through the manor courts well into the nineteenth century. But, as Franklin's *Poor Richard* noted, in a marketplace governed purely by the individual creditor, that person "has authority, at his Pleasure, to deprive you of your Liberty, by *confining you in Goal* FOR LIFE, or to SELL YOU *for a* SERVANT if you should not be able to pay him!" Franklin's warning not only pointed up the primacy of credit, it also illustrated the helplessness of the propertyless—of married women, servants, and the enslaved—in a marketplace that was predicated on property ownership. Such individuals might find themselves in a far more precarious position than even the English Wiltshire clothier who had been forced to buy overpriced provisions at his employer's store, but whose complaints were heard on the grounds that such practices betrayed the principles of the common good.[53]

Through no fault of her own, this was exactly the precarious situation endured by Violet, an enslaved Carolinian. Violet knew well her status in the colonial marketplace, because she had been sold by vendue three times over. As a girl she lived on the plantation of William Perriman at Edisto Bluff. When Perriman died in 1746 Violet was sold to Jeremiah Knott, an Indian trader turned planter, along with one other (unnamed) woman and child, a bed, some iron pots, and thirteen head of cattle. The sale meant she had to move almost fifty miles upcountry to Knott's Cypress plantation in Dorchester. Just under eleven years later, Knott died too, and Violet once again faced the auction block. Retired factor and storekeeper William Logan became her new master when he purchased her along with Boston, another of Knott's enslaved people. It is not clear whether they were a couple, but together Violet and Boston traipsed another fifty miles eastward to the Cooper River, where Logan had established himself on a small plantation "with a few slaves for the support of his family." While no record of the vendue exists, we do know that Stone's suit forced Logan to sell his slaves—presumably including Violet—just two years after he had bought them in 1759. Violet's experience as a commodity in the marketplace shaped the course of her life. As a legal nonperson in a place where the law of the market recognized only legal persons and their property, there was almost nothing she could do about it.[54]

As Violet's experiences suggest, the lure of a profit in the marketplace easily trumped the emergent doctrine of planter-slave paternalism. Such talk was no more than a flimsy veneer of respectability in an economy that thoroughly commoditized her. In America, market transactions between individuals of unequal status had become completely disconnected from the reciprocal rights and duties still influencing (though not equalizing) similar economic relationships in Europe. The effects of this process were also apparent in the Indian trade. Since Europeans did not consistently consider Indians to be persons before their law and, in addition, often supposed them to be inferior, "honest" traders were a minority in the swarm of dealers who felt little compulsion to apply the principles of "fair trade" to commerce. When they took Indians as slaves or made up their own pricing schedules, traders must have known that since Native people were unlikely to appear in court as witnesses against them, they could do as they pleased, free from any larger community retribution that might ruin their future prospects. That courts were rarely established in the places where such dealing took place was merely an additional boon to the Indian trader. To "get the same Trade" as other tribes, argued the Cherokees, the Creeks must badger whites, because "you need never expect it by Fairness." By the Seven Years' War, Indians were fully aware that whites would not go out of their way to treat them well in such circumstances, even though the worst excesses of mass enslavement in the region had ended with the Yamasee War in 1715.[55]

Without guilds, corporations, or courts enforcing standards of quality and price, excluding strangers from the marketplace, or ruling on where trade should be conducted, these American marketplaces functioned according to a set of hierarchies exclusively rooted in property and the reputation forged through its successful accumulation. For those white men and women who were permitted to own property and recover it in court, this state of affairs was highly advantageous. Able to build powerful and profitable positions as market agents, they achieved their wealth by roving across the colonies or by rooting themselves in the towns and market hubs dotting the colonial countryside. While the lack of corporate protection proved troublesome for some white men, the disadvantages they faced were minimal compared with the barriers encountered by enslaved Africans and Native Americans, who rarely found opportunity to defend their credit. Unable to either own or recover property according to the legal regimes applied by these white male colonists, these people were themselves grist for the market's mill.

Set free from the economy of interests to roam across the vast colonial landscape, some white colonists assembled ambitious enterprises connecting multiple marketing spaces in one supply chain. Butcher John Robinson used his "five negro men butchers by trade," along with his white indentured servants, to create such a network reaching all the way from South Carolina's rural cow pens to Charleston's meat eaters. These workers purchased livestock from local plantations and drove the animals to Robinson's suburban pen, where they were slaughtered for the West Indian export market or for local consumers, who could buy the meat at his advertised "London Porter, and A La Mode Beef House," equipped to supply "families . . . with beef in small quantities every evening." Robinson was not alone in his marketing strategy. By the late 1740s butcher James Thomson owned three plantations, two of them stocked with cattle. Thomson used his enslaved herders to move cattle to his suburban pasture, where he slaughtered the beasts for the Charleston market. On the city "Neck," where Thomson's and Robinson's operations were located, some butchers even built facilities for rendering tallow and for tanning, allowing them to monopolize all aspects of the colonial cattle trade.[56]

In many ways the market networks Robinson and Thomson built were comparable to those established by Pennsylvania and Carolina merchants who specialized in the Indian trade. Baynton, Wharton, and Morgan, based in Philadelphia, relied on itinerant traders, stopping off in marketing hubs, to reach their Native customers to the west. By the 1760s the company oversaw one of the most extensive Indian trading networks in the British colonies, reaching beyond western Pennsylvania and into Illinois country. To bridge these distances, the partners employed traders to carry imported goods westward from Philadelphia and sell them in the forts and stores that supplied Indians. To further the logistics of their operation the partners bought land, and their agents established connections with farmers and traders based in Carlisle and across the countryside between. By doing so they could provision their employees with fattened cattle and feed the horses carrying packs or pulling wagons. Although operating in very different spheres of the local economy, Carolina butchers and Pennsylvania merchants both benefited from the distinctive way owning property trumped corporate controls within colonial marketing spaces. We might well label these men maestros of the market, since they almost singlehandedly orchestrated their particular branches of trade through a combination of person-to-person deals, print, and accumulation of property.[57]

By the middle of the eighteenth century, their networks were expedited by marketing hubs like those that had sprung up in almost every mainland colony. In the Chesapeake, Scottish factors opened numerous stores, rurally situated to provide plantation customers with groceries and manufactures in exchange for tobacco. John Hook's store at New London in Bedford County, Virginia, would have been a familiar sight to any Carolinian venturing northward. Occupying a lot in a village laid out as a speculative venture in 1754, Hook's store was the marketplace in a settlement that had no market incorporated into its plan. Instead, New London hosted an assemblage of retail enterprises: a tavern, other stores, and a resident midwife who was said to have delivered 1,200 children yet "never lost one woman in the operation." Passing by these other businesses to enter Hook's commodious premises, the visitor from Carolina or Pennsylvania could find a familiar array of wares on offer: a selection of essentials such as rum, nails, and salt, along with a few more refined items.[58]

Yet dealers like Hook were not quite as capable as the conductor who manages to keep his musicians in a perfect ensemble until the finale. The moments of discord occurred when the very stuff of the colonial market—the people it swept up as commodities and the regime of credit and property— rose up to challenge their power. Hook had to close his store after a few years when the revolutionary debt crisis hit his Virginia planter custom- ers. Robinson's and Thomson's enslaved workers regularly absconded from their masters, roving across the countryside and using the movable market to cut their own deals. Baynton and Wharton went bankrupt in 1769 as their entire trading network unraveled, first as unscrupulous western com- petitors undercut their prices, then as forces of war disrupted their supply chains and Indian customers faltered in their loyalty to British traders.[59]

These European colonists had created distinctive American marketing practices because it was neither advantageous nor convenient to adhere to the old rules. The new rules of property and credit allowed them to win big. But in a society that replicated neither the entrenched hierarchies of the economy of interests nor the sense of reciprocal obligation they entailed, that victory stood on uncertain ground. Whites could obtain some recom- pense if they could prove themselves men of credit in courts that functioned to uphold their power in the marketplace. Nevertheless, such avenues of legal redress were of limited utility in the vast and remote places beyond the East Coast where many Europeans traded. What is more, the narrow remit of an embryonic legal system provided few useful tools for effectively stopping Africans, Indians, and poor whites from dealing as they pleased. An American marketplace founded on property rather than place was, at least for white colonists, proving a great blessing. But such liberty to trade free from the meddling hand of government also meant that when commercial agents needed controlling, there was nowhere to turn.

CHAPTER FOUR

The Resurgence of Early Modern Market Values

By the 1760s, several of Charleston's most prominent merchants and wharf owners had served as commissioners of the city's markets. Wharfinger William Roper spent a year in the post. Created in 1737 by the Commons House of Assembly, the Market Commission was an annually elected group of four white male freeholders charged with ensuring that Charleston's meat and vegetable markets ran according to a set of regulations familiar to any English-speaking person of the time. These rules required that produce be sold only after the clerk of the market had rung the bell to signal the start of trading, that provisions on sale be fresh and of good quality, and that wares not be sold outside the spaces designated as marketplaces. Commissioners like Roper were responsible for recruiting the clerk of the market, collecting stall rents, and punishing traders who disobeyed the regulations. Punishment was usually a fine, but black traders, who constituted a large proportion of dealers, might also endure whipping or public shaming in the nearby stocks.[1]

As an enforcer of this comprehensive regulatory regime, Roper became enmeshed in a web of seemingly contradictory market cultures. His wharf and stores were the very embodiment of an individualistic, property-driven colonial market culture. Roper's waterfront lot was capacious enough for Charlestonians to store their wood supplies on it—for a fee, of course. Also for sale was "Matlock's best Philadelphia beer" and "good GUATIMALA INDICO SEED of last year's growth, small rice by the single barrel, muscovado sugar, bacon, and good butter in small casks." Like his fellow traders, Roper had used his ownership of prime waterfront property to fashion a role as a gatekeeper of the marketplace, importing, selling, and storing an array of products that he publicized colonywide using a steady stream of newspaper advertisements.[2]

While wharf owners orchestrated oceanside bazaars, however, they were becoming ever more engaged in establishing marketplaces designed for deals answering the "public good." Wharfinger Benjamin Matthews was likely involved in the 1750 establishment of the city's fruit and vegetable market, a cluster of stalls at the waterside between his wharf and Thomas Elliott's. The commissioners had purchased the land these stalls stood on from the wharfingers "for the public." As a sponsor of this market, Matthews thus happily assented to regulations calling for trade that answered the "good of the whole" while simultaneously profiting from the commerce that took place on his adjacent private property, primarily for his personal enrichment.[3]

Of course, Roper's and Matthews's British counterparts encountered similarly contrasting ways of organizing marketing as they looked inward toward the domestic market and outward over the possibilities of Atlantic commerce. John Brown, the Glasgow merchant who maintained a careful record of his commercial dealings during the 1760s, endorsed the regulation of grain prices in his home city while taking a different view on the fluctuating values of commodities he sold to America. Nevertheless, most trade physically located in the city was subject to customary forms of regulation. As a member of Glasgow's merchant guild and a freeman of the city, Brown was fully invested in an urban marketplace principally governed by corporate bodies claiming to operate for the public good through their control of wharves, shops, mills, and marketplaces. As a council member he most likely oversaw the continued development of Port Glasgow, the city's own deepwater harbor where it controlled all the wharves and collected fees from every Atlantic vessel moored there. In contemporary Charleston, however, the economic activities of its merchants were shaped by obviously clashing imperatives. While the provisions market seemed to endorse a regulated commerce for the enslaved Africans who were critical to its success, the remainder of the urban economy was structured mainly around the unvarnished pursuit of private interest on private property.[4]

Over the middle of the eighteenth century, the colonial marketplace was thus characterized by two parallel paths of development. Within cities and across rural Pennsylvania and South Carolina, privately owned commercial spaces had multiplied rapidly. Nevertheless the era also witnessed the establishment of familiar markets, fairs, and licensed peddling circuits that seemed to replicate the physical, legal, and cultural trading environments of Europe. Fully understanding the character of the early American marketplace therefore requires that we also visit the common commercial spaces springing up alongside the private wharf, the ferry inn, the country store, the newspaper's advertising columns, or the mill shop.

While documenting the creation of these spaces is important, equally critical is uncovering the dynamic that defined their relation to the "free market" places already operating in colonial landscapes. The entanglements between these two kinds of marketing structures were at the very heart of contemporary British debates about the operation of the local economy. The most explosive eighteenth-century disputes and protests were prompted by the increase in middlemen and merchants who, like their American cousins, traded away from markets and fairs. Only intellectuals like Josiah Tucker and Adam Smith were prepared to entertain an economy in which individuals trading like this for their own private interest, in privately owned spaces, could operate free from the customary marketplace. But what happened when this customary marketplace was the newcomer, as it was in Pennsylvania and South Carolina? Why did Americans seek to rebuild such markets when they had managed without them for decades?[5]

Looking closely at the interface between novel and customary marketing spaces in early America reveals a very complex, and quite particular, relationship. Here the differences between South Carolina's slave society and Pennsylvania's society with slaves—and with numerous immigrants from the German lands—become very clear. When it came to their own dealings, white Carolinians were less enthusiastic about endorsing customary markets in their colony. Instead, their efforts concentrated relentlessly on the majority of unfree, and mostly poor, Africans in their midst. As a result, customary marketing places flourished when they promised to fulfill wealthy whites' desire to control enslaved Africans. The ambition to place economic power in the hands of European colonizers also drove sustained attempts in both Carolina and Pennsylvania to introduce customary modes of commerce to the Indian trade.

Among whites themselves, regulated marketplaces acquired greater importance in Pennsylvania. There, colonists favoring the reconstruction of such marketplaces were more numerous and showed greater commitment to establishing them. While Quakers' strong communal values endeared to the brethren the idea of the economic common good, German-speakers who had experience of a domestic economy more corporate than its British counterpart also endorsed its replication in the New World. Nevertheless, customary markets in Pennsylvania still found both their practical and their ideological supremacy challenged by the interests of private property. Almost evenly matched in the Quaker colony, the two visions of the marketplace were already prone to conflict in the colonial era. Arguments over which ideal should triumph nevertheless proved inconclusive, producing a hybrid mix of marketing practices. In this respect the commercial terrain in Pennsylvania shared some characteristics with that of South Carolina, where regulated markets were undermined by colonists who would not support them ahead of their own profits.[6]

As private gain and the public good operated side by side in colonial commerce, the bitter European debate between the two modes of organizing the marketplace lost its focus in the expansive American landscape. The sheer variety of colonial marketing spaces created a spectrum of ways trade within them might be conducted. With economic growth and relative plenty characterizing the prerevolutionary era, there was often little impetus to reconcile the competing forces organizing colonial domestic marketing.

RECONSTRUCTING A REGULATED MARKETPLACE

Urban marketplaces, fairs, and a system of licensed peddling composed the bundle of customary European marketing practices. Although consumerism sponsored an increase in shops, newspaper advertising, and the secondhand trade, it also found an outlet in existing marketing spaces, which flourished as they facilitated the sale of familiar commodities alongside novelties. Given the staying power of these traditional places and practices of buying and selling, charting their reappearance within early America's eighteenth-century towns and rural areas is essential.

Without question, the establishment of urban marketplaces was the most obvious sign of the growing influence of European marketing customs in America's commercial landscape. Wherever colonists founded major towns, marketplaces were often at the center of the ground plan. By 1770, after decades of development, Philadelphia and Charleston had multiple provisions markets. Philadelphia's Market Street hosted a market stretching almost its whole length. The main market was later supplemented by the South Market, established at Lombard Street in Society Hill in 1745. Charleston's original marketplace was the beef market on one of the "four corners of the law" at the intersection of Broad and King Streets. In 1737 a fruit, vegetable, and meat market was established between wharves on the East Bay, and in 1770 a fish market was also raised at the wharfside, a few blocks northwest of the existing market building. Contemporary descriptions of these markets reveal them to be thriving spaces of trade, eventually rivaling their European counterparts in popularity. On visiting Philadelphia, Swedish traveler Pehr Kalm commented that "the town has two great fairs every year. . . . But besides these fairs there are every week two market days viz. Wednesday and Saturday. On those days the country people in Pennsylvania and New Jersey bring to town a quantity of food and other products of the country, and this is a great advantage." Philadelphia's market stood comparison with that of the metropole, reported Newcastle servant William Moraley, observing that "in the Shambles . . . are sold all kinds of Butchers Meat, as well cut and drest as at London." Another British visitor considered the place "superior to any I know in London, in point of neatness and regularity. There appeared to [be] great abundance of provisions of all sorts."[7]

Carolinians worked to establish marketplaces and fairs outside Charleston too. In February 1723 the colonial Assembly, under the influence of Governor Nicholson, passed three identical bills designed to bring these fixed spaces of government-regulated trade to three existing commercial hubs on the frontier of European society. Dorchester Town, Ashley Ferry Town, and Childsbury were targeted by rulers as suitable sites for biannual fairs and biweekly markets. As we have seen, Dorchester and Ashley Ferry would become commercial hubs, thanks to enterprising Carolinians like Mary Sureau, while Childsbury was the pet project of Joshua Child, a planter and Indian trader, who set up a ferry next to his town at the same time. The text of the three acts showed an impressive loyalty to English legislative practice. Laid out as a charter following the exact format of its metropolitan forerunners, the document provided for a master of the fair, a clerk of the market, and government officials charged with collecting tolls and policing traders. Those fairgoers who found themselves in dispute with a fellow trader could have the issue resolved before the court of pypowder, a special form of mobile commercial justice characteristic of English fairs since medieval times.[8]

Pennsylvanians also created markets and fairs outside their capital city. In contrast to Carolina, they achieved a slow but steady increase in the number of market towns until these urban spaces became regular resorts of commerce among settlers on their way to "mill and market." The growing visibility of markets and fairs as places of trade in Pennsylvania was thanks to the enthusiasm of successive post-1700 waves of European immigrants, who embraced market towns and persisted in founding them. As William Penn's early efforts to shape market practice suggested, Quakers were equally enthusiastic endorsers of incorporated towns and customary commercial instruments. While the ambitions of Penn and the Free Society of Traders went unrealized, the subsequent efforts of local communities to centralize provisioning were better rewarded.

Burlington, founded by Quakers with the support of the Pennsylvania government, was among the very earliest towns to establish a marketplace. At one of its first meetings in April 1694, following receipt of its charter, townsmen "considered and debated" the "regulation of the market," deciding that buying and selling should take place exclusively from 9:00 to 12:00 in the summer and 10:00 to 12:00 in the winter. The town's minutes suggest that the marketplace continued as a site of commerce well into the eighteenth century, and in 1730 a group of townsmen tried to improve it by replacing wooden stalls with brick ones. Other towns, mostly Quaker, embracing marketplaces included Uwchland, Newtown, Chester, and Bristol, where in 1759 the town burgesses advertised their intention to "introduce the Custom of selling and buying live Cattle at Fairs, in imitation of the Mother Country, the Advantages of which in bringing the Buyer and Seller together, promoting the Circulation of Money, and enabling People more easily and certainly to pay Debts, are so obvious and apparent." Still appreciative of the possibilities fairs offered, Bristol's town fathers sought a return to a local economy in which individuals met face-to-face to trade goods under the watchful eye of an official.[9]

In Lancaster, the establishment of a fair and marketplace at the town's incorporation in 1742 represented a happy convergence of the goals of James Hamilton, the owner of the land where the settlement was situated, local English and German colonists, and Pennsylvania's Quaker proprietors. Since 1730 the proprietors had searched for a suitable location for an inland town that might become a center of trade, justice, and government. To his great advantage, Hamilton's recently inherited tract was chosen and a town, complete with a marketplace, was duly laid out. Although English settlers like Lancaster's first chief burgess Thomas Cookson were vital to transforming the town from plan to reality, German settlers were just as critical to the project's success. German immigrants not only formed a large proportion of the corporation's officers through the 1770s, they also included almost all the butchers who populated the market house stalls, as well as the bakers who sponsored the successful establishment of a bread assize.[10]

Lancaster was not the only Pennsylvania town to implement a corporate local economy over the mid-eighteenth century. German-speaking settlers enthusiastically set up similar institutions in Schaefferstown, Germantown, and Manheim; in all three places, German populations embedded market houses and market squares within their town plans. The creation of these markets made a visible impact on townscapes and shaped the spatial and regulatory conditions under which local traders conducted exchange. Ne'er-do-well author William Moraley was suitably impressed not only by Philadelphia's market, but by those that flourished elsewhere. Noting that "the markets in all the Towns are well stor'd with all sorts of Provisions, cheaper than at Newcastle upon Tyne," Moraley went on to relate how he and an acquaintance had gone fishing and then quickly sold some of their catch in Burlington. Over time, the marketplace had become more than ideas on the statute books; it had influenced economic culture, evolving into a central space where colonists bought and sold goods according to regulations implemented to ensure orderly trade.[11]

On the ground, markets gradually developed from makeshift structures into larger and more permanent buildings in which traders were clustered according to what they sold. The improvement of Philadelphia's main market began in 1705, when the corporation improved the ground with gravel and installed stocks, whipping post, and pillory. In 1708 the burgesses ordered the construction of a new market house, in 1713 stalls between the courthouse and prison were relocated westward, and in 1720 thirty covered brick stalls were built. The corporation ordered renovations of existing stalls in 1724 and added more in 1730. In 1742 officials started to cordon off the market on market days, using chains to prevent wagons from cluttering the marketplace. In 1759 the marketplace was lit using oil lamps, with a vat for storing fuel installed under the meal market.[12]

As the existence of this meal market suggests, the Philadelphia corporation had also gradually systematized retailers. In 1710 butchers were allotted a group of stalls together, and four years later the burgesses ordered sellers of grain to stand under the courthouse and expose their meal by opening the mouths of the bags they had brought to market. In 1722 the butchers were relocated and the stalls between the prison and courthouse allotted to sellers of herbs, butter, fish, and milk. After a forty-year hiatus, organizing traders resumed when sellers from New Jersey were removed to a special "Jersey market" and wharfside stalls were demarcated as the fish market.[13]

When they diligently replaced wood with brick, paved uneven and muddy ground, managed traffic on market days, and organized traders according to what they sold, Philadelphia's burgesses shared with their American and British counterparts an endeavor of enlightened improvement and rationalization. By 1770 Charleston had three distinct beef, vegetable, and fish markets, each consisting of a covered symmetrical structure, the roof supported

by pillars. Just fifteen years after its founding, Lancaster's corporation established "a very convenient Markett house with severall convenient Stalls
therein." A 1770 list of stall rents assigned positions one through twenty
to the market's butchers, indicating that, as in Philadelphia, traders were
grouped according to what they sold. With these edicts, colonial authorities replicated the organizational strategies of their Glasgow and Newcastle
brethren, who had long sought to order trade into distinct meal, meat, and
vegetable markets, continually refining arrangements as their cities grew.
The creation of Glasgow's "merchant city" forced a succession of market
relocations as the town center shifted westward, including the founding
of a new "green" market building in 1758 after an agreement between the
Incorporation of Gardeners and the city council.[14]

Although city authorities across Britain's Atlantic world paid close attention to the infrastructure of their marketplaces, the greatest effort was
channeled into governing this commercial space. After all, brick stalls were
much easier to set in order than were the people who used them. Colonial
market regulations sought to guarantee a market that functioned for the
"public good." By enforcing rules about the price, availability, and quality of
provisions, they hoped to create a fair trade that would furnish city dwellers
with wholesome food at an affordable price. Market statutes across the colonies shared much because they diligently replicated these core methods and
values of urban commercial regulation. The clerk of the market enforced
rules dictating when and where provisions could be sold. Bells signaled the
beginning and end of market trading. Between these bells, only local householders were permitted to buy produce, but at the end of trading hucksters
could purchase provisions for resale. To ensure quality, the clerk, assisted
by other officers, inspected the wares for sale. The clerk was also the cus-
todian of an official set of weights and measures owned by the town, used
to make sure customers got what they paid for. Without exception, all of
Pennsylvania's and South Carolina's "official" marketplaces were governed
by these rules, which were also in force across Europe. In Charleston their
role in securing the economic public good was underlined by the stipulation
that goods sold in contravention of the law of the market must be seized and
donated for "the Use of the Poor of the said Parish."[15]

Equally important, however, were the regulations requiring the marketplace to be the *only* place provisions were sold. Statutes forbade those core
crimes of forestalling, engrossing, and regrating, the greatest crimes an
urban trader could commit. Eighteenth-century British pamphleteers constantly criticized these commercial offenses, arguing that the culprits were

"destructive of trade, oppressive to the poor, and a common nuisance." One writer even created a new illustrated version of the tale of Robin Hood, whom he characterized as "the terror of fore-stallers and engrossers and the protector of the poor and helpless." The continued relevance of these crimes was underlined by their inclusion in Blackstone's *Commentaries on the Laws of England* as well as in innumerable "how-to" guides for justices of the peace.[16]

Early American market regulators agreed wholeheartedly with their British brethren on forestallers, engrossers, and regrators, devoting large sections of market statutes to making their activities illegal and pursuing those who committed these offenses. By the late 1730s the practices were outlawed in Charleston; culprits faced a fine of five pounds and a 1752 newspaper notice reminded readers of the illegitimacy of hawking foods. Philadelphia's corporation introduced new legislation in 1727 after a report of "many Hucksters in this City" who "meet the people Coming to Markett at the ends of the Streets and then buy up provisions, which might be prevented by appointing an Hour, both Winter and Summer, for the Ringing the Bell." Shortly after the town's incorporation, the councilmen pronounced against peddlers, who were "not intinded to enter corporation or markett towns, not having any legal settlement there to sell their goods in prejudice of the freemen & inhabitants settled and trading in the same way." Traveling salesmen who encroached on the territory of town traders were fined five pounds. The Lancaster burgesses also heard "frequent complaint . . . of the markett being forestalled and the Privisions . . . brought to markett by the Country People being immediately bought up by some particular persons in order to retail out at an advanced price." These forestallers, lamented the town rulers, were further marked out by their "idle and disorderly" character. Over a decade later, the Lancaster authorities were still diligently pursuing their fair trade agenda, calling out butchers and other dealers for selling goods around town on nonmarket days. As the language of the Lancaster city fathers suggests, many of these efforts to regulate the urban provisions trade were rooted in the belief that the economic public good was best served when all involved respected the privileges purported to structure commerce for the benefit of lawful town residents and traders.[17]

Such values were also foundational to organizing the Indian trade. Whites were often supported in their endeavors by Indian leaders, who—in an effort to stem the tide of rum drowning their tribes—shared an ambition to regularize the commerce. At successive meetings between Native people and colonists, Indians asked European leaders to "confine your Traders"

rather than letting them wander far and wide selling rum to Native customers. When Pennsylvania's government seemed ineffective, they repeated
their wish, explaining that "they had frequently complained to the *English*
Governments, and desired that some Measures might be taken to prevent
Liquors being carried among them in such Quantities." Still insistent on
this necessity in the 1750s, they reiterated that "at the subsequent Treaties
they renewed this Request, and now fix upon three Places for the Traders
to reside, and request that none but honest and sober Men may be suffered
to deal with them."[18]

These requests aligned with the ideals of the Pennsylvania government,
which sought a trade that had all the characteristics of "fair" commerce,
conducted in fixed spaces by respectable dealers who would be closely observed by officials. Like the clerk of the market in Charleston, traders received official sets of weights and measures designed to ensure this just
price. The South Carolina government had, of course, launched successive
initiatives to regulate commerce between Indians and Europeans. In 1718,
not long after the Yamasee War, the Assembly established a public monopoly
to trade out of three fixed trading posts, at Savannah Town, Winyah Bay,
and the Congarees. The men staffing this trade were required to obtain a
license from the board of five commissioners charged with overseeing commerce from Charleston. Further acts were passed by the Assembly in 1739
and 1752, with British officials attempting to take the lead in organizational
matters at the conclusion of the Seven Years' War. All legislation called for
licensed traders to be "of honest repute and sober life and conversation."
Illegal dealing was punished by heavy fines, seizure of trade goods, and even
imprisonment.[19]

After Penn's failed efforts to regulate Pennsylvania's Indian trade, the
colony's government passed a steady stream of legislation to outlaw those
who "privately deal with the Indians, and very often back in the woods, out
of the view of any but themselves." By 1758, war brought renewed urgency
to the project of restricting commerce to spaces where European officials
could apply fair trade principles. Fort Pitt and Fort Augusta, the latter on the
former site of the Indian town of Shamokin, epitomized these efforts. By the
end of the 1750s both places housed physical stores. Fort Pitt had competing
stores as the British, Quakers, and non-Quaker Pennsylvanians all sought
to win a share of the trade. Equipped with counters, weights and measures,
and front and back rooms in which goods were carefully sorted, such retail
spaces were the physical expression of Europeans' quest to make the frontier marketplace function for the public good. The storekeepers who staffed

these enterprises were expected by their employers to act in the character of fair traders. To maintain his reputation in this respect, Dennis McCormack, clerk at the Fort Augusta store, swore that "he hath never during his having the care of the sd store given or sold ... any liquors or goods whatsoever of any kind to or with the Indians" for the money they hoped to exchange for rum.[20]

Efforts to nail down the Indian trade were thus predicated on the idea that mobile traders were suspect and needed close monitoring if there were to be any hope of their trading fairly. In the eighteenth century, colonial authorities also began applying this principle to itinerant traders who sold mainly to other colonists. Pennsylvania's act for licensing peddlers was on the books by 1730, and South Carolina's equivalent statute followed eight years later. Both pieces of legislation betrayed the lawmakers' attitudes toward the traveling salesmen in their colonies, "idle and vagrant persons" who "have greatly imposed upon many people as well in the quality as in the price of the goods" to the "great prejudice of the inhabitants of this province." Such people, explained the South Carolina legislators, paid no provincial taxes, whereas storekeepers and shopkeepers were "obliged to pay tax for their stock in trade." Peddlers thus represented unfair competition with the fixed traders of the province. In giving voice to their dislike of peddlers, early American governments were repeating ancient accusations and assumptions deeply embedded in European societies, where mobile traders were consistently vilified as the scourge of society, preying on the good intentions of the "fair trader" and taking advantage of poor consumers who could not resist wasting their money on the trinkets glittering like fool's gold in the hawker's pack.[21]

As a result of this Pennsylvania legislation, quarter sessions across the colony heard a steady stream of petitioners requesting peddling licenses. At Lancaster and Chester, courts often received multiple requests from men who insisted they were "orderly sober person[s] & fit for the imployment." In addition to bearing signatures of those who supported the petitioner's character, many of the documents took pains to explain the reasons for the application. Joseph Trout claimed that "an accident that befell your pet[itioner] severall years ago made him entirely unfit to get his necessary subsistence by his labour," while Patrick Whinnery "having broke his thigh is fallen into a consumption" and could no longer support himself in his trade as a weaver. By resorting to these strategies, Whinnery, Trout, and their fellow petitioners appealed to the notion that peddling, when licensed, could contribute to the "good of the whole" by making the poor self-sustaining and hence useful members of society.[22]

Although the early phases of colonization had produced very little in the way of regulated marketplaces that might get settlers to trade according to European values, the efflorescence of such legislation after 1720 betrayed the deep legacy of Old World models of economic organization. Now more stable and staffed by emerging elites, colonial assemblies and courts returned to the principles still underpinning much local marketing in Britain and the German lands. In doing so they ensured that colonial marketplaces would not diverge completely from their European counterparts; even if private property continued to birth new marketplaces, its influence would exist alongside spaces governed by more customary values.

TRADITIONAL MARKETPLACES IN A COLONIAL LANDSCAPE

The establishment of commercial spaces, values, and practices familiar to European colonists is important for two reasons. First, their presence reveals that the popularity of novel colonial marketing spaces did not lead to complete amnesia about the customary structures that had shaped European marketing for centuries. While the decades between 1700 and the 1760s were a time for inventing new marketplaces, they were also an era of recollecting and reviving European commercial spaces.

Second, the reappearance of these customary spaces is a clue to the emerging power structures of this growing colonial marketplace. Many historians have traced the mutually reinforcing foundations of colonial cultural and political power, built when Creole elites consolidated their influence across the middle of the eighteenth century. This power also had an economic component. Using their increased might as legislators, colonists aimed their market regulation at traders who were assumed to threaten their status in the local economy. Digging deeper into the thrust of this legislation therefore reveals much about its logic and its meaning. Traditional principles of fair trade were not applied in an obedient effort to return to the imperial vision of the Board of Trade; rather, they were the project of a Creole elite looking to secure its supremacy in the domestic marketplace.[23]

Living among an African majority, South Carolina's governing Europeans embraced the regulated marketplace most warmly when it could check the growing commercial power of the enslaved. Fixed, regulated marketplaces looked very attractive to a group of white men seeking to control black traders, both in Charleston and in the countryside. Controlling marketing involved first regulating the trade *in* enslaved people; legislators added

Africans to the customary list of livestock and provisions to be sold at fairs in the hope that the fairs would prove convenient rural slave marts while also bringing in a toll income. Since auctions had already developed as a convenient way to sell people, however, this type of regulation was not the primary concern of slaveholding legislators, who were quite happy with the way sales functioned to their financial benefit.[24]

Instead, these men devoted the best part of their efforts to creating new ways to restrict dealing *by* enslaved Africans. As we have seen, Afro-Carolinians had an important role as roving traders in the colony's rural parts. They were also highly successful market men and women in Charleston. The trade in fresh fish was conducted almost entirely by black fishermen, while enslaved and free women sold provisions and prepared food in and around the town's marketplaces. Raising, slaughtering, and butchering meat was impossible without the labor and expertise of free and enslaved African people. This trade allowed men like Leander, working in every role from herdsmen to meat marketers, to make an independent living. Leander was originally the property of Charleston clerk William Mason and his wife Susanna, but by the 1760s he had used his skill as a butcher to accumulate enough money to buy his freedom. The Masons were not willing to manumit Leander, but they did agree to sell him to successful butcher Jacob Willeman, who bought the man on the understanding that he would free him after he had earned enough to pay off his SC£900 purchase price. On October 8, 1770, Leander obtained his freedom, then continued to work as a butcher on his own account by buying stock on Charleston's wharves and butchering animals on commission from country suppliers. In reaching the pinnacle of commercial success for an African in the Carolina Lowcountry, Leander was a highly visible example of blacks' foundational role in the marketplace.[25]

In both city and countryside, market regulators responded to the success of men and women like Leander. A procession of legislation was designed to target African traders, sometimes even when it seemed to be ordering whites. While South Carolina's peddling act addressed white traders, it was written with the specific intention of making it harder for Africans to operate as market agents in the decentered rural marketplace. Titled "An Act for licencing hawkers, peddlers and petty-chapmen, and to prevent their trading with indented servants, overseers, negroes and other slaves," the 1738 law cited the number of traders going "from town to town, and from one plantation to another, both by land and water," exchanging manufactured goods for "hogs, fowls, rice, corn and other produce" with "negroes and other slaves ... to the great prejudice of the planters their masters." Peddlers were thus required to pay SC£100 for a license, which they would forfeit if found to be trading with "any slave or slaves, indented servant or servants, or overseer, without the privity or consent of his or their master or mistress." Tellingly, while Pennsylvania's law regulating peddlers accused itinerants of cheating customers as they went "from house to house," it made no mention at all of enslaved people, servants, or masters. Much more so than their northern neighbors, Carolinian rulers drafted a law that, rather than protecting the community from outsiders who imposed on the settled fair trader, shored up the authority of individual white property owners and supported their role as masters or mistresses of the market.[26]

The urge to control Africans in the marketplace also motivated the regulatory ambitions of urban Carolinians. In Charleston, marketplaces were as much containers for enslaved traders—places where Africans could be watched and punished—as spaces sponsoring fair trade for the community at large. This dual function racialized the urban marketplace in a manner particular to this slave society. Early legislation hinted at its double purpose. The 1737 market regulation act stipulated "that nothing herein contained shall extend to hinder any Planter or other Person whatsoever, from carrying any Butter, Cheese, Poultry, Milk, Fish, Fruit or Herbage to any House or Houses in *Charlestown* to sell or dispose of the same, *except,* to such Persons who buy to sell the same again undressed." Very much like the peddling act of the following year, this clause aimed at protecting planters' right to send enslaved agents into Charleston to sell produce, while at the same time keeping masterless African women from hawking produce.[27]

In the wake of 1739's Stono Rebellion, legislators began to unite urban and rural trading places in a single vision of racially inflected commercial regulation. Integral to the Slave Code that came hot on the heels of the slaves' bid for freedom were a number of clauses designed to severely limit the economic agency of blacks in Charleston's marketplace. To leave Charleston, traders of color were required to have a ticket. If they were spotted alone, without white supervision, black persons could have their goods inspected. Justices of the peace were authorized to break up "meetings" of Africans and confiscate property at will. Two sections of the code expressly forbade blacks to sell and resell goods on their own account. Clause 34 outlined the way "several owners of slaves have permitted them to keep canoes, and to breed and raise horses, neat cattle and hogs, and to traffic and barter in several parts of this Province, for the particular and peculiar benefit of such slaves, by which means they have not only an opportunity of receiving and concealing stolen goods, but to plot and confederate together, and form conspiracies dangerous to the peace and safety of the whole Province." Making traders into conspirators, the code strove to limit the economic agency of blacks all the way from Pon Pon to Port Royal.[28]

While these regulations appeared very strict, enforcing them in the watery Lowcountry landscape remained enough of a problem that whites elaborated on provisions of the 1740 code with further laws targeted at Charleston's marketplaces. In 1750 auctioneers were forbidden to sell small quantities of cloth, alcohol, and sugar, presumably in an effort to put the purchase of these resalable goods beyond the reach of enslaved traders operating in a cash economy. By the time the fish market was built in 1770, however, the racist ambitions of whites' regulatory agenda had become much clearer. The centralized fish market was obviously an effort by white authorities to increase their surveillance and control over black traders. Accompanying the new building was an act designed to remove all trade in fish from other parts of town and concentrate it under the market's eaves. This legislation stated that from November 1770 no fish was to be "offered to Sale at any Stand, Dock, Wharf, or Place, in any other Part of CHARLES-TOWN, except at the FISH-MARKET." Explaining that "the Business of fishing is principally carried on by Negroes, Mulatoes, and Mestizoes, who are apt to be riotous and disorderly," the act also legislated for stocks and a whipping post, which would be used to punish any black fishermen refusing to obey the authority of the market commissioners. Whites who did likewise could pay an SC£10 fine or endure four hours in the stocks. Black fishermen had long been subject to physical punishment and arbitrary white authority if their masters chose to enforce existing laws, but acts like these brought blatant inequalities into the realm of the community at large.[29]

As these efforts suggest, establishing customary marketplaces was a campaign by ruling whites to assert themselves over urban commerce. In a market culture grounding power in individual entrepreneurs, who might be black, whites looked for ways to prevent Africans from enjoying the same market freedoms as their owners. Race became the main grounds for discrimination in a marketplace where white traders of both genders sometimes took the initiative in using distinctions of color to assert their legitimacy. In 1752 some Charleston shopkeepers and storekeepers, men and women, came together to complain about the "several persons" who had "made a practice of sending and selling dry goods and wares about *Charles-Town*, and places adjacent, hawking and pedaling, without any license for the same, contrary to an act of the general assembly of this province." Clearly identifying the supposed transgressors as black traders, the complaint was signed by twenty-nine

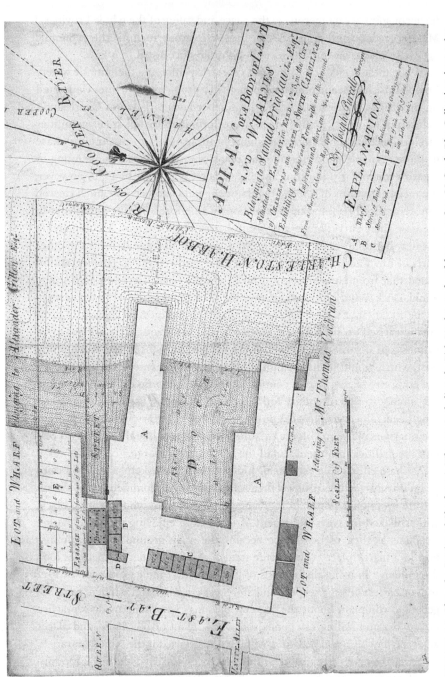

FIGURE 4.1 *Plan of a Portion of Charleston's Wharves Including the Fish Market*, undated but ca. 1780s. McCrady Plat Collection, item 0622, Charleston Register of Deeds.

tradespeople, four of them women, who promised to take the enforcement of the law into their own hands. The idea of the public good in the marketplace had become fundamentally racialized. Rather than making blacks part of a community held together by mutual obligation to the economic good, regulations sought to place them outside that community, relieving whites of any public duties toward the African traders in their midst.[30]

Black traders were targeted in early America's other cities too, but these campaigns never equaled the coherence of the sustained crusade waged by the Charleston authorities. The entangled black and white character of the poorer trading populations elsewhere made the prospect of regulation very complex. In New York City, enslaved Africans faced two waves of restriction on their trading in the wake of their 1712 and 1741 rebellions. Nevertheless an informal economy, composed of whites and blacks, women and men, evolved in and around the city's marketplaces and taverns. These networks outlasted the city authorities' efforts to regulate them. Philadelphia's corporation likewise grappled with the presence of enslaved and free black people in its marketplaces. In 1733 blacks, in concert with poor whites, were cited by the corporation for unruly behavior on Philadelphia's wharves. Throughout the colonial era, African hucksters were certainly working on the margins of the official marketplace. City authorities thus identified traders of color as a "problem" of market order, but the problem was not visible enough to attract more than sporadic attention.[31]

However, the Quaker colony, and indeed New York, shared much more with South Carolina when it came to the regulation of the Indian trade. Across all colonies, northern, Mid-Atlantic, and southern, the notion of a fair trade for the public good was an essential tool for white authorities as they sought to organize commercial space for political ends. Itinerant poor whites and those Indians willing to trade with them were universally identified as the "problem" of an Indian trade, failing because it did not answer the "good" of the British and colonial governments. Complaints about disorderly conduct were expressed in the language customarily used to condemn peddlers, middlemen, and other itinerants who encroached upon the "good of the whole" with their suspect ways.

Pennsylvania legislators claimed that Indians had been "much impoverished and abused by the forestalling traders who frequently go far up into the country . . . where they purchase their furs and skins with rum at under rates." In his 1759 analysis of the reasons behind "alienation" of Delawares and Shawnees from the British, Charles Thomson repeatedly returned to the depredations of lowlife traders who "lie, cheat, and debauch their women, even their Wives, if their husbands were not at home." Carolina agent Ludovic Grant shared Thomson's suspicions. In 1755, Grant informed Governor James Glen that, despite regulations, traders persisted "in cheating the Indians in the Prices of Goods, especially of light Goods, such as Linnings, Flannels, &c ... of false Stilliards, short yards, and little Measures." Veteran trader James May complained that Indian towns were full of "no less than 12 Traders, peddlers and idle Fellows," while one Williams raised the ire of respectable traders as he "plainly tell[s] the Indians, in Presence of the White Men that he values not the Governors either of So. Carolina and Georgia that it is what and how he pleases to trade." Complaints about trade from Indian headmen also focused on the "extravagant prices" charged by the white traders among them.[32]

In response, wealthy traders and government officials looked to reinstate obedience and hierarchy in the name of the public good. More "respectable" figures involved in the trade, such as Conrad Weiser and James Kenny in Pennsylvania or Lachlan McGillivray in South Carolina, usually attributed the disorder to poor whites. Elite imperial officials, who made pronouncements from a lofty and distant metropolitan vantage point, argued that a regulated marketplace was equally necessary to civilize Indians. In his 1755 treatise on Indian affairs, Edmond Atkin described traders as men "who have no Skill in Publick Affairs" and "are directed only by their own Interest." The only solution to the situation, argued Atkin, was for him to head up a single colonial board charged with managing the trade in the public interest. Eight years later, Carolina governor Thomas Boone sent proposals to the secretary of state for "the management of Indians in general and the conducting of the necessary commerce with them." Boone first of all explained that "repeated experience has proved beyond contradiction that neither the Indian traders nor Indians can be at all depended on, the first are the refuse of the earth, stick at nothing to obtain temporary advantage, and frequently provoke the Indians by acts of injustice . . . or if they take the other bent and endeavour to ingratiate themselves the concord that ensues tends only to engrating the arts & villanies that have expelled the traders from civilized society, upon the savage stock." The only logical course of action, Boone advised, was "that the trade should be carried on by the publick of each province," by factors, "men of character," stationed at fixed garrisons.[33]

The presence of nonwhite peoples, journeying widely and trading freely, strongly motivated elite Europeans' embrace of the regulated marketplace in the eighteenth century. Their ambition to control trade for political purposes drove ruling Europeans' negative characterization of the Indian trade, undergirding efforts to organize it for a public good. In South Carolina, the creation of regulated urban marketplaces was pushed through by whites seeking to control enslaved traders and deny them legitimate membership of the economic community. So, while a straightforward belief that markets should function for the "good of the whole" lay behind these legislative efforts, this good was in large measure interpreted through a racial lens.

DO AS I SAY, NOT AS I DO

Laws might be written and published, but getting those targeted to obey them was more difficult, as the Board of Trade knew well. That regulating trading Indians and Africans became a sustained preoccupation of whites is itself testament to the difficulties involved in translating legal ambition into reality. Historians have long recognized that slave owners and officials in the Indian trade usually relied on personal relationships, not statutes, to keep trade running for the benefit of all parties. It was only when commerce threatened to be overwhelmed by a crisis—a rebellion, a war, or something whites perceived as a major challenge to their growing supremacy—that renewed effort was channeled toward forcing obedience to existing statutes or creating new ones.

In this environment of sporadic regulation, even as lawmakers argued for the need to police the Indian trade, they admitted the difficulty of doing this over so great a territory populated by so many individuals who put their own interests first. Though the Pennsylvania government repeatedly outlawed the sale of rum to Indians, it also admitted that "the Woods have not Streets like *Philadelphia*, the Paths in them are endless that they cannot be stopt, so that it will be carried from one Country to another." In trying to impose familiar marketing regimes on the American landscape, colonists, like early imperial officials, faced challenges from those who did not wish to conform and could not be made to. Understanding the dynamic between tradition and innovation in the colonial marketplace demands discussion of these challenges. Although the apparatus of the urban marketplace was increasingly robust in these growing colonies, it continued to lack power and status compared with its European contemporaries. Charting the boundaries of the customary marketplace and exploring their origins reveals its contingent role in colonial society. Even among white colonists, the desire to trade freely challenged support for recently regulated commercial space. Whereas in Britain itinerant traders would always be interlopers to the status quo, in North America the customary marketplace was the new arrival.[34]

British corporate authorities in charge of urban markets and fairs did lose some power over trade's eighteenth-century spaces. Nevertheless, their ability to determine who could trade what, when, and where remained impressive. It might seem that Yorkshire cabbages would be an unpromising example of urban corporate power, but arguments concerning the supply and sale of that very commodity in eighteenth-century Glasgow epitomized the continued sway of institutions in the city's marketing spaces. Cabbage selling in Glasgow was regulated by the Incorporation of Gardeners, founded in 1628 and fully incorporated in 1690. The Gardeners were part of the corporate city government, meaning they had access to the Trades House court and ruled through their representative on the city council.[35]

In 1760 James Young fell afoul of the Incorporation when he offered for sale, within the city limits, "sundrey quantitys of Yorkshire Cabbage plants." The freemen gardeners claimed that Young had raised his cabbages, which were much sought-after because of a seed shortage at the time, "within the privileges of The City of Glasgow." Since Young was not a freeman, nor was he "properly a countrey gent" growing vegetables on an estate beyond the city limits, the gardeners argued that his actions were "a manifest infringement of the privileges granted to them by the honourable town councill." Young's experience reveals how seriously guilds took the city boundary as a perimeter of their jurisdiction. It also suggests an impressive surveillance network among freemen, who must surely have shared knowledge and worked together to detect the cabbages and determine their source. What is more, the gardeners had the confidence to take their case to the Trades House court, which they knew would give them a fair hearing.[36]

The provisions market and its accompanying political economy enjoyed no such supremacy in the colonial city, however. Before Philadelphia and Charleston even claimed city status, Boston's marketplace had been a disputed feature of the town for almost eighty years. By the 1660s the original site of the market house had fallen into disuse. Instead, supplying provisions was the task of an army of country traders who came into town and sold door-to-door. From the 1690s onward, as Boston endured two economic depressions caused by war and issues with the paper money supply, this system became a major source of dispute between the town's political factions. Many Bostonians advocated constructing a central marketplace for all the reasons commonly offered in early modern Europe: it held out the promise of better social, moral, and economic order and would prevent short measures, engrossing, forestalling, and regrating. Yet such reasoning was viewed with deep suspicion by many townspeople, who perceived the market's supporters as an elite hoping to use it to strengthen corporate power over the city's poorer citizens. The disagreement came to a head in 1737, when a riot in the recently reconstructed marketplace ended in a clash so fraught that it went down in Boston history. While Glaswegians were micromanaging the cabbage supply, Bostonians were fighting over the legitimacy of a central provisions market.[37]

As Philadelphia and Charleston grew to join Boston as major colonial cities, similar contests evolved over their marketplaces. Although Bostonians who supported a marketplace and incorporation had pointed to these other cities as having exemplary commercial regulation, in truth they were being highly selective with their evidence. The market's insecure status in urban trading was a feature not only of Pennsylvania's biggest city, but also of its emerging inland towns. It was a similar story in South Carolina. Philadelphia's corporation lacked clout in the marketplace because of the factious political circumstances in which it was created, while Charleston had no coherent municipal authority because local interest groups persistently thwarted efforts by governors, especially Francis Nicholson, to establish institutions that might divest them of influence. Lacking anything that resembled Glasgow's staunchly corporate economy, market spaces in all these cities and towns suffered fates similar to that of their Boston precursor.[38]

In Philadelphia the corporation had no taxing power, very little public land under its control, and no other means of raising money. Efforts to improve the marketplace relied on revenue from stall rentals. Lancaster's corporation labored under similar restrictions, since James Hamilton, who owned the land the town was built on, refused to allow it the power of taxation. The situation was no different in Charleston. When white Charlestonians decided to build their new wharfside market, the authorities were forced to buy private land from two wharfingers, the cost to be met by "the hire of the stalls to be paid in to the public treasurer till the expence of purchasing the land be reimbursed." Stallholders often fell behind on their payments, and complaints about their failure to keep up with rent were repeatedly addressed by the Philadelphia corporation. Eventually the council resorted to "all legall methods to recover all arrears of the sd Rents due." Lancaster's authorities complained of "persons [who] set up stalls and others [who] take standings to expose their goods to sale without applying to the Clerk of the Markett or entring their Names with him." In both Charleston and Philadelphia, the clerk of the market was subject to accusations of corruption either by renting out stalls twice over or by taking premiums from sellers willing to pay extra if he would reserve them a stall in advance.[39]

Quite possibly the clerk's enthusiasm for kickbacks was motivated by his low status and low pay. America's urban marketplaces had very little money to support them. Precise estimates of the poverty of urban market authorities are hard to find. However, whereas in 1755 the Glasgow Corporation received an income of £3,444 from its markets (and a total corporate income of £39,530), in 1764 Lancaster received a *total* income just short of £60. Since Glasgow had a population of 23,500 at the time and Lancaster had 2,800 inhabitants, the former had almost three shillings per head income from its markets alone, while the latter had just five pence. Lacking the financial or political influence to enforce their will, American authorities endured bold attempts to undermine their mandate over the marketplace. While contravening the "law of the market" was a persistent issue throughout the early modern Western world, directly comparing the transgressions of colonists with the dissent confronting European authorities leaves no doubt about the extraordinarily high level of disregard displayed in America.[40]

Facing persistent disobedience, struggling officials became engaged in a war of attrition with traders, who seemed incapable of remaining within the confines of the marketplace or following the basic regulations of trade. Although Charleston had two meat markets, it had no official slaughterhouse, and archaeological evidence reveals that colonists killed and sold animals in private spaces throughout the city. The July 1765 presentments of the grand jury condemned the resulting disorder, their ninth grievance deploring "the bad custom of butchers shooting cattle in or near Charles-Town, whereby many, who are near their pens, are in danger of their lives; and also, their bringing meat to market in very filthy carts, either uncovered, or so exposed to the sun and dust, or covered with very dirty blankets or cloths, to the endangering the healths of the people of this town." In Philadelphia, meanwhile, butchers "smoaked tobacco" and killed beasts within the marketplace, creating a heady and unwholesome atmosphere, while "many Hucksters in this City buy . . . Provisions in the Markett, and often meet the people Coming to Markett at the ends of the Streets and then buy up provisions." Stallholders then took it upon themselves to use their own weights and measures designed, according to the corporation, to bring about the "Impoverishment of the Poor and Needy" by selling them short.[41]

Townspeople also undermined the public marketplace when they appropriated the space for their own entrepreneurial projects. In 1736 the Philadelphia authorities found "erected in the Street, at the Front of the Court house, by Private persons, Severall Stalls, who take rent for the Same." A few years later the encroachments began again when "several persons . . . Erected Stalls in the Market Place, with Merchant Goods on market day." When the marketplace became an auction block, its customary functions were undermined again. With the marketplace taken over by a commercial mechanism that depended on a ready supply of private property to be sold according to ambiguous pricing mechanisms, the common good faded from view.[42]

While there is scant evidence that auctions were held in British marketplaces, they were common in both Pennsylvania and Carolina. As soon as Charleston's beef market opened in 1739, vendues became a regular event at which "sundry Slaves and other Goods" went under the hammer. In yet another demonstration of white economic power, enslaved market men likely worked at their butcher's blocks while watching their brethren sold on the auction block. Philadelphians also held auctions near the Meal Market, despite a ruling that only the city's official vendue master was permitted to sell goods there. Even more audacious, though it appears ultimately unsuccessful, was the effort of a group of Burlington freemen to turn their marketplace into a public-private partnership by suggesting that they might "set up Market stalls of brick after the Philadelphia manner for a Marketplace, upon condition that the inhabitants would grant to them and to their heirs the benefit that should arise from them." Lacking money, Philadelphia's corporation reacted more warmly to a similar suggestion from Joseph Wharton, who used his private funds to establish a "public" market in Society Hill. Stall rentals would, of course, go into the pockets of a select group of Society Hill gentlemen.[43]

As the Philadelphia corporation's response to Wharton's petition suggests, while colonial market authorities condemned some of these noncommunal uses of the marketplace, they ignored or actively endorsed others. Many of Pennsylvania's and South Carolina's auctions took place in the marketplace at the behest of the sheriff or government-appointed vendue master; the principles of the public marketplace were in part undermined by the authorities themselves as ideas foundational to the economic common good in the Old World became lost in the translation to a colonial setting.[44]

This failure to comprehend and fully enforce the customary political economy of the marketplace extended far beyond the city provisions market. Out west, colonial attitudes toward white peddlers were softened by the necessity for them in such an extensive landscape. As we have seen, British peddlers were subjected to endless invective as idle, cheating criminals. It is hard to overstate the ingrained nature of such characterizations, which appeared unrelentingly in both print and manuscript sources. Typical newspaper stories included a short piece in the *Manchester Mercury* in 1753 that reported how a Newcastle goldsmith had produced substandard silverware, stamped it with counterfeit assay marks, then "vended chiefly to Chapmen and Peddlers (doubtless to the Prejudice of many People)." Pamphlet writers supporting the case of resident shopkeepers spoke of peddlers in the same way, describing "thousands of Foreigners . . . *Jews, Infidels,* and *Vagabonds,* of most Countries and Nations, coming into the City in Swarms, hawking and selling . . . to the manifest Detriment of us, the *legal* and truly vested *Shop-keepers.*" Authors of advice literature warned merchants that it was their legal duty to "stop such tea, brandy, or spirits, and carry the same to the next warehouse belonging to the customs" if they were offered by a peddler.[45]

Such stereotypes were the stuff of everyday life too. Itinerant traders often found themselves in court, usually under suspicion of theft. Robert Gordon, a "tinker," was accused by Whitehaven widow Blanch Barnes of having "got into his possession divers goods" "falsely and deceitfully," while Thomas Harrison, a maltmaker turned chapman, stood accused of robbing a gentleman's house in Jesmond, a genteel suburb of Newcastle-upon-Tyne. As an itinerant trader who traveled around North East England with his common-law wife Isabelle Simpson and her six-year-old son, Harrison attracted the suspicion of James Edgar, a Newcastle cobbler with whom he had lodged at Christmastime in 1763. When a parcel of stolen goods was found in the cobbler's house, Edgar claimed Simpson had "pretended" to be Harrison's wife, while the peddler himself told him he had sold ballads at a gentleman's house that "as it stood by itself, valuable things might be got in it." Simpson, on the other hand, claimed she had found the stolen goods concealed in Edgar's house, commenting that "there's enough in there to get a man hang'd." Harrison himself tried to counter Edgar's accusation by offering a detailed itinerary of his peddling, diligently stressing the reputable nature of the people he had lodged with as well as the great distances he traveled in his efforts to make an honest living by selling books. Edgar, in the meantime, clearly believed that Harrison and Simpson's occupation made them obvious culprits.[46]

Strikingly, those white licensed peddlers who sold European manufactures to rural clientele in Pennsylvania and South Carolina did not encounter the extreme hostility meted out to their British counterparts. In a landscape so vast that mobile traders were essential and temporary rural marketing hubs were a familiar sight, attitudes toward their legitimacy had already shifted by the eighteenth century. David Jaffee has documented the surge in itinerant traders in New England bringing genteel goods and print culture to the western reaches of Massachusetts. Western Pennsylvania and Carolina were also supplied with consumables by peddlers who, as we know, were required to obtain licenses from the quarter sessions court.

Nevertheless, this legal requirement did not translate to a general environment of suspicion. Owners occasionally sought runaway servants who were said to masquerade as peddlers, but little discussion of the perils of peddling, coupled with mostly neutral references to peddlers themselves, makes it clear that these traders did not attract the ire traditionally directed at them in the Old World. This generally benign attitude is all the more conspicuous because rhetoric toward Indian traders and traders of African origin largely replicated the insults leveled against British peddlers. As in the urban marketplace, trading practices that attracted wide censure in Europe were often criticized only when done by nonpropertied whites and people of color acting independent of white elite authority.[47]

Quite possibly white peddlers met with these more benign attitudes not only because of their race, but also because they were agents of consumerism, employed by wealthy urban merchants who relied on them to reach customers far beyond the city. When applying for a license, many Pennsylvania men explained that taking portable consumer goods into rural parts was essential if they were to make a living. As frontier representatives of this world of goods, petitioners sought acceptance in the language of consumer choice developed by merchants in their numerous newspaper advertisements. Lancaster resident and prospective peddler William Baxter claimed he "[had] on hand a quantity of goods suitable for the country," while his compatriot John Hoover had "provided himself with goods very suitable for the season." Likewise, Matthias Hess described "a good assortment of goods suitable for the country people." Immersed in the language of variety characteristic of the eighteenth-century world of goods, these itinerant traders justified their license applications by stressing their ability to bring consumer opportunity to Pennsylvania's western reaches. With their legitimacy bolstered by a close connection to Philadelphia's merchants, they became creditable individuals performing a valuable service for a scattered rural clientele.[48]

The colonial condition not only had the power to repurpose European marketing practices or to change attitudes toward them, it could also erase customary spaces from the landscape altogether. The auctions, itinerant traders, newspaper advertising, and trading hubs founded by entrepreneurial individuals provided colonists with a convenient array of market opportunities tailored to their expansive settlement patterns. These places laid down a practical challenge to fixed marketplaces, which might even fail altogether if colonists preferred more recent methods of trading.

Fairs were the most visible victims of these novel commercial choices. Colonists had created fairs explicitly "in imitation of the mother country." Some fairs became long-running events, suggesting they found success. In

1753 the *Boston Evening Post* noted that the Londonderry fair date had been subject to the same confusion as its British counterparts after the change to the new calendar. In Pennsylvania the Burlington, Philadelphia, and Bristol fairs all received coverage in the *Pennsylvania Gazette,* and the Lancaster fair was a lively event attracting traders to the town in both summer and fall. By the 1760s the corporation was erecting roughly one hundred wooden stalls for its June fair, which was more popular than the fall event. These stalls were fully occupied by peddlers, hucksters, hatters, and silversmiths who are all listed as paying the five shillings rental into the town's coffers.[49]

Yet there is much to suggest that where Lancaster fair flourished others failed. Fairs in Salem, Massachusetts, in 1764 and in Philadelphia in the 1780s were ended on the grounds that they had become little more than a needless source of disorder and moral corruption. Virginia fairs were mostly an opportunity to hold horse-racing festivals. In South Carolina more flexible market networks had a particularly pernicious effect on the fairs' success. There is scant evidence that any of the fairs established with 1723's charters developed into popular resorts for traders. Occasional newspaper references to fairs at Ashley Ferry and Childsbury imply that the events did take place. Like advertisements for these events elsewhere in the colonies, however, they also describe "pretty diversions" and horse racing rather than serious dealing. Additionally, a brief run of accounts during the 1770s for the Strawberry Ferry, adjacent to the Childsbury site, show no increase in traffic around the time of the fair. Given that the colonies were agricultural economies, it is striking that fairs failed to become locations for livestock trading on the scale of their British counterparts.[50]

If we are attentive to colonists' discussion about their dealings in fairs and marketplaces, their failure to achieve the universal popularity still enjoyed in contemporary Europe becomes yet more apparent. When Lancaster apprentice William Cassel claimed in 1770 that he was incited by a unscrupulous army sergeant to steal hats from his master's shop, his case was the first to come before the county's quarter sessions naming *any* fixed retail location as the place of theft, let alone the marketplace. Courts in longer-settled urban areas all noted shops, stores, inns, and auctions as spaces where defendants accrued debts or stole goods, but markets and fairs received only infrequent references. Britons going about their commercial business, on the other hand, consistently mentioned such places. The retailing experiences of Yorkshire butcher Timothy Bawbill were typical. Defending himself against an accusation of sheep rustling, Bawbill claimed he had bought the animals at Aberford fair. After he had slaughtered them, Bawbill took the skins "on his back" to the Wakefield marketplace, where he sold them "at the end of the shambles to a stranger." These were spaces barely mentioned by colonists; when he went to the Philadelphia market, local animal trader Jacob Hiltzheimer noted that it was his first visit in two years, even though he consistently attended vendues.[51]

As infrequent visitors to customary commercial space, free white traders remained unfamiliar with markets designed to service the public good. Rather, markets were places where the rules were mostly applied to blacks and Indians, whose race allegedly made them naturally disposed to irregular commerce. Free white men and women sometimes supported marketplaces and fairs but were equally happy to undermine their political economic regimes if it suited their purposes. These purposes varied widely—from securing their living by trading in a more convenient location to checking the power of an opposing political faction. Yet however diverse their reasons for contravening the customary law of the market, the effect on these commercial spaces was the same. Fairs and provisions markets had a visible physical presence in the colonies by the mid-eighteenth century, but it was far from secure and might be challenged in any number of ways at any time.

By the 1770s, close to a century of constant growth had transformed Philadelphia from Penn's "green country town" into a major British American metropolis with some 40,000 inhabitants. That the city's success was fueled by trade is as well known as the fact of its expansion. Such a rapid increase in commerce involved growing pains, which were especially acute given the factious character of Pennsylvania politics. Philadelphia's weak corporation, its freemen, its numerous volunteer associations, and a powerful Assembly produced a "spirit of opposition" that manifested itself in myriad political disputes.[52]

Commercial spaces were not immune to this factionalism, which often flared up in discussions about who should benefit from their use and ownership. The Blue Anchor Landing, the celebrated arrival point of William Penn in 1682, was one such contested commercial space. Most prime waterfront property in Philadelphia was privately owned by merchants and wharfingers who exacted their own fees for landing or storing goods or for trading from their property. The corporation, however, could claim public ownership for a handful of landings, one of which was the Blue Anchor. As an "open and common" wharf, the Blue Anchor was supposed to be clear for the "publick service and advantage" of those people who brought "firewood, charcoal, bark, timber, boards, shingles, stones, rails, hay, and other materials, for the service of the Inhabitants of this City." In other words, it was to be preserved by the corporation as public commercial space operating for the good of city inhabitants.[53]

Yet, despite its protected status, the Blue Anchor Landing was subject to repeated attempts to make it answer to the profit of individual traders. Early efforts by Jeremiah Elfreth to "pretend" a private right to the landing were fended off by the citizens of the young town in 1692. Efforts to incorporate Philadelphia at this time were partially motivated by the quest to disallow Elfreth's claim. In 1746 the ownership of the landing was once again under dispute, this time when a question arose about the beneficiary of George Gray's will. Had Gray left his piece of the landing to the corporation or to all Philadelphians? In 1753 the status of the Blue Anchor was amended by the corporation itself, which offered it out for lease to any individuals willing to manage its use, for their own profit, on behalf of the city. The move provoked an outcry among the inhabitants, who lodged a petition claiming the right to enjoy it freely while seeing to it that a lengthy account of the previous dispute over the wharf was published in the *Pennsylvania Gazette*. The corporation was forced to back down, but there remained a seething resentment among those Philadelphians who had opposed the public-private partnership. Such was their ire that twenty years later, when the revolutionary crisis stirred up larger disputes about the ownership and order of the main marketplace, broadside author "Andrew Marvell" reminded readers of "the late Attempt of the Corporation . . . to wrest from you the Blue Anchor Landing" and the "Spirited Defence made against them by many virtuous Citizens."[54]

Spanning eighty years, the arguments over the Blue Anchor's ownership and right of use for trade revealed the precarious place, and uncertain meaning, of the public good in the city's commercial landscape. In the first instance, the Blue Anchor's status as a public wharf was so jealously guarded because it was hemmed in by individually owned landings. Already the good of the whole was at an unusually great disadvantage against individual gain compared with the panoply of corporate interests that governed English-speaking waterfronts in Europe.

It would endure further assaults. Individuals like Elfreth had no qualms about encroaching on the wharf, while even the corporation saw little harm in leasing it out to city dwellers to operate for their personal gain. In response, a noisy faction of inhabitants resorted to print in support of the common good. Unlike Durham freeman William Appleby, who was taken to court when he challenged the bishop's authority over the local marketplace in the *Newcastle Journal*, these Philadelphia protestors were permitted to voice their dissent without censure as the fluid hierarchies of white colonial society opened up fundamental economic principles to vigorous debate. Customary marketplaces could be found across Pennsylvania. Yet even in the heart of the colony's major city they did not enjoy undisputed supremacy, since their political economies were unevenly applied, broadly defined, and subjected to raucous dispute.

Retreating from the Philadelphia waterfront, we find more marketplaces designed to answer a common good redefined by its colonial American setting. Elsewhere in Pennsylvania, Lancaster's corporation was financially hamstrung at the order of the owner on whose land the town was built, while some of Burlington's city fathers proposed a marketplace operated by a public-private partnership. When they pursued a tireless campaign to shepherd poor white traders and Indians into towns and forts, Pennsylvanians and Carolinians selectively applied market regulation. Across the Carolina Lowcountry, nonwhite and unfree traders were subjected to a coordinated campaign designed to corral them in regulated space. Meanwhile white-owned commercial spaces were left to flourish even when they destroyed the viability of proposed fairs and markets or undermined the urban marketplace.

This was the state of the American marketplace by the 1760s. Shaped by the European inheritance of its traders, the landscapes confronted in their New World, and the Indian and African people alongside whom the dealers lived and traded, colonial trading spaces were a hybrid of practices structured by hierarchies that were novel but uncertain. In a trading environment driven by property ownership, white men could maneuver themselves into a powerful position. Since there were fewer corporate restrictions on their trading, women could also enjoy the fruits of this commerce. Yet the expansive landscape and the commercial power of Native Americans frequently challenged this supremacy. Europeans themselves also undermined their principles of market regulation when their individual desire to profit from their property overcame their support for a commerce that functioned for the "good of the whole." Such conflicting motivations of economic organization were bothersome, but not fatal, in a marketplace born of steady economic growth and natural abundance. The end of the Seven Years' War, however, ushered in far more uncertain times. Suddenly there was much more at stake in questioning what a marketplace should look like and for whose benefit it should operate. Unfortunately, the spaces and practices of trade that colonists had created offered few certain answers.

PART 3

Confronting the Colonial Marketplace

CHAPTER FIVE

Revolution in the Marketplace

Signing himself "John Carpenter," the author of a polemical letter to the *South Carolina Gazette* enlisted a tried and tested rhetorical strategy to anticipate the reaction of critics. His detractors, Carpenter suggested, would argue that a law of the sort he proposed "would be an infringement on the liberty of the subjects." Given that Carpenter's lengthy missive was about the government's role in regulating trade, one might think it was provoked by the Stamp Act, the Townshend Duties, or the Tea Act. But Carpenter was writing in 1763, when even the new Currency Act was only an idea. And instead of railing against British ministers, he was voicing concerns about unregulated food sales on Charleston's wharves that, he argued, had led to monopolizers' putting the price of essential provisions beyond the means of (white) working people. In the face of this "growing evil" Carpenter exhorted the provincial assembly to note that it had "ever been the policy of well-regulated governments, to keep the common necessaries of life as low as possible." Precedent demonstrated, therefore, that authorities could pass laws to govern the local marketplace, because the good of the whole was more important than individuals' right to enjoy a large profit from the traffic of their property.[1]

John Carpenter's letter raised two issues that would become critical during the imperial and revolutionary crises of the 1760s and 1770s. First he stressed the debatable role of government in organizing local trade. Colonists had come to enjoy buying and selling their property when and where they wished. Many had also come to believe that in certain instances government should regulate buying and selling in the name of the public good.

The relationship between these two parallel methods of running a market-place was not clear and was subject to public discussion. Second—and highly relevant to interactions between colonial markets and the crises afflicting the colonies after 1760—was that colonists could be very prickly about how far a government *should* dictate the terms of domestic trade. Any attempt to regulate dealing could well prompt cries that a free man's "liberty" had been infringed. White colonists of all classes were now thoroughly used to acting as individual economic agents. While they might acknowledge that they should attend to the good of the whole in the marketplace, it could be hard to persuade them to put it first. When presented with an actual situ-ation in which they had to choose between their own profit margins and buyers' right to reasonably priced, good-quality wares, colonists frequently plumped for the first option.

The freedom of white property owners to trade goods without govern-ment meddling—in the form of regulation or taxation—was now established through long experience as a central pillar of their overall liberty. Thus, when markets started to malfunction in the early 1760s, John Carpenter's letter was merely one of many opinion pieces pondering what should be done. Dis-order threatened the marketplace, and commerce was now "clogged with a disease." A postwar slump, the rapid westward movement of Europeans into territory where they were welcomed by neither Indians nor imperial offi-cials, and British rulers' determination to recover some of the debts they had run up defending the colonies all disrupted day-to-day buying and selling.[2]

Across both Pennsylvania and South Carolina, these disruptions pro-voked a strong reaction among traders dismayed by the seizing-up of their habitual channels of commerce. Their marketplaces were founded on the idea that individuals should be at liberty to trade as they pleased, but this principle no longer seemed to be enough. Finding their markets in crisis, colonists inquired into their function more closely than ever before. Mostly the chaos pushed them into heated discussion of the age-old conundrum that had preoccupied European trading people for centuries: How should private interest and the public good relate to one another in the market-place? As they pondered this question, colonists revealed the ways their dis-tinctive market culture prompted a novel approach to this long-standing puzzle. Most distinctively, while Europeans stuck with the assumption that private interest should always be a servant of the public good, many Ameri-cans were not so sure.

With the happy marriage of private interest and the public good in the marketplace now challenged to the point of chaos, some colonists began to question the legitimacy of so much free trading. Their analysis relied on a heavy investment in the belief that markets should operate for a "public good." The only questions were who was the public, and whose good should it pander to? And in what circumstances was the public good a desirable operating principle for the market? The experience of imperial crisis and the Revolutionary War raised these questions, but it could not provide definitive answers.

TRADING CALAMITIES

The imperial crisis tested the colonial marketplace well beyond its limits. It was not just the Charlestonians identified by John Carpenter who suffered. The catastrophe was keenly felt throughout South Carolina, and indeed in most of Britain's mainland American territories. To grasp just how much daily marketing experiences were disrupted, we need a proper understanding of the way events undermined the foundations on which marketing spaces were built and operated. Exactly how was domestic trade vulnerable to the events following the Seven Years' War? In what way did these crises disrupt the marketplace's smooth functioning, leaving "the Sinews of American Commerce . . . injudiciously cramp'd"?[3]

The marketplaces colonists created and frequented were a hybrid of novel and customary practices. Their smooth operation depended on the bundle of conditions and assumptions that endured until the early 1760s. Trading spaces flourished on the principle that individual property owners would enjoy the freedom to trade for their own advantage. Available credit and paper money facilitated this trade, while courts supported most free white traders when credit networks foundered. Local government intervened only to police marketing in a circumscribed group of spaces and for a distinct range of purposes, meaning that free white traders were used to a selective deployment of the regulations. In general the system worked because of the plethora of local and imported goods consistently available for sale in the marketplace. Whereas Europeans had to endure repeated food shortages in landscapes long populated, claimed, and cultivated, Americans enjoyed abundant food, land, and consumer goods that seemed to become even more accessible as Britain's colonies became better integrated into the Atlantic's trading systems.[4]

From 1763 to 1783 these systems would be severely tested by a succession of events—the protests of frontier settlers, the crisis in Indian relations, and the sequence of British legislation designed to make colonies contribute their "fair share" to the cost of their defense. The Sugar, Currency, and Stamp Acts, then the Townshend Duties and the Tea Act, followed finally by the outbreak of armed conflict in 1775, brought disarray to the domestic marketplace. Although historians have long recognized the period following the Seven Years' War as an era of economic volatility, affecting working people's wages as much as it challenged merchants' credit, the effect of these events on the actual internal mechanisms of marketing is less well understood. Thus, precisely documenting this impact is essential, because it is only by grasping the ways disorder undermined domestic trade that we can begin to comprehend how the crises challenged Americans' workaday economic practices and beliefs.[5]

This challenge was so profound because it appeared on both the western and eastern horizons of settlers' markets. Let us first look westward. In the wake of the 1763 Treaty of Paris, the frontier parts of both Pennsylvania and South Carolina became considerably more disordered as Europeans aggressively ignored the Proclamation Line. The situation was worsened by the new uncertainties about an Indian trade destabilized by political conflict. The insecurity had a major effect on the smooth operation of marketplaces hosting this trade as well as on the marketing connections between Europeans themselves.[6]

Those eastern merchants who thought they had a stable role in the Indian trade suddenly found themselves operating in a new environment where unregulated dealing promised to utterly undermine their business. At Fort Pitt, competition between colonists, the Pennsylvania authorities, and the Crown for a share of Indian custom severely affected profitability. Baynton, Wharton, and Morgan's agents at the trading post complained heartily about the situation. At the start of 1767 the Philadelphia partnership received news that "the trade of the place . . . is reduced to a most miserable state" by dealers selling goods "for less than half price, in order to take trade from this house." Bribes and "many other ways of Gaining the Indians" were in regular use. Things had not improved by 1769, when "the great number of Traders in every part of the Woods," coupled with the fact that "the Crown takes everything from you," continued to drive down profits. The situation was remarkably similar in South Carolina, where a new commissioner for southern Indian affairs, John Stuart, and veteran traders like Lachlan McGillivray complained that they were unable to prevent dealers from selling rum to Indians in complete disregard of established regulations. In 1772, Choctaws complained "of the great Quantities of Rum carried into our Towns. . . . Distraction Mischief Confusion and Disorder are the Consequences and this the Ruin of Our Nation." Meanwhile, up-and-coming backcountry farmers like Andrews Pickens set up stores on their new plantations, hoping to grab a share of the trade in this turbulent market.[7]

The breakdown of more established places and customs in the Indian trade was only partly the source of western commercial disarray. The second main cause was the intensifying pace of European settlement. As newcomers like Andrew Pickens acquired property and created communities far from the coastal centers of European power, they became dissatisfied with the weak institutional support for their efforts to establish profitable marketplaces. In both Pennsylvania and Carolina, white settlers were angry because coastal elites turned a blind eye to illegal land speculation and seemed deaf to calls from frontier people desperate to safeguard their property, order their markets, and protect themselves against Native Americans. The anger prompted the Carolina Regulators, Paxton Boys, and Black Boys to take matters into their own hands. All three touched on the problem of chaotic markets in their petitions, requesting that they be reordered for the public good of these frontier communities.[8]

Market order first became an issue among western Pennsylvania's settlers in 1764. With the Indian trade suspended by Pontiac's War, the Black Boys, led by erstwhile Paxton Boy James Smith, were outraged that Philadelphia-sponsored traders were still heading to trading posts with "warlike stores" for Indian customers. If the Indians got hold of these stores, Smith argued, it "would be a kind of murder, and would be illegally trading at the expence of the blood and treasure of the frontiers." Acting "for their King and their country's good," Smith's vigilantes, with the assistance of local justice of the peace William Smith, issued passes to traders whose goods had been inspected. Those individuals carrying only "private property" were provided with a note explaining that "none of these brave fellows will molest them upon the Road, as there is no Indian supplies amongst them." When the self-appointed clerks of the backcountry marketplace did find "warlike stores," however, they seized them and set them on fire. Although they admitted that "no law can justify, to burn our neighbors property," Smith's band nevertheless argued that "when this property is designed / To serve the enemies of mankind," such actions could be excused. Facing the reluctance of their government to regulate trade, the Black Boys took it upon themselves to make commerce conform to their own definition of the common good.[9]

Active in the later part of the 1760s, South Carolina's Regulators were less concerned with the depredations of Native Americans than with those of their fellow frontier colonists, who were a bunch of "barbarous Ruffians" executing "unheard of Cruelties" on innocent settlers. The lack of interest by Charleston elites in regulating backcountry marketing places was an important issue in their complaints. With his entrenched hostility to poor Presbyterian colonists and his close friendship with Camden storekeeper Joseph Kershaw, Anglican minister Charles Woodmason was keenly aware of the problem. In the Regulators' 1767 "Remonstrance," which he helped write, Woodmason thus noted that "Stores have been broken open and rifled . . . (wherefrom several Traders are absolutely ruin'd)."[10]

Warming to its themes, the remonstrance then explained that "No Trading Persons (or others) with Money or Goods, No Responsible Persons and Traders dare keep Cash, or any Valuable Articles by them. . . . Merchants Stores are oblig'd for to be kept constantly guarded (which enhances the Price of Goods) And thus We live not as under a British Government." Since the inhabitants of the "Metropolis" did not believe themselves "United in the same Interests" as the backcountry, settlers were doomed to live in want of trade, fair prices, and circulating cash, since no "merchant or Mecanics" would dare to live there. Instead, explained the Regulators, "when no Regular Police is establish'd, but everyone left to Do as seemeth Him Meet," "If we buy Liquor for to Retail . . . they will break into our dwellings. . . . Should we raise Fat Cattle, or Prime Horses for the Market, they are constantly carried off. . . . Or if we collect Gangs of Hogs for to kill, and to barrel up for Sale, . . . Idle, Worthless, vagrant People . . . are continually destroying them." Without "Bridewell, Whipping Post, or Pair of Stocks" (which were usually in marketplaces), the petitioners argued, their efforts to create orderly and settled commercial societies would always come to naught. Like their Pennsylvania compatriots, the South Carolina Regulators, many of whom owned mills and stores, had come to believe that in their part of the colonies commercial regulation was entirely insufficient.[11]

While the British victory over France unleashed disorder in the west's trading spaces, forces that had pushed colonists farther from the coast in the first place strained established commercial systems in the east. Prime lands close to Philadelphia and Charleston had been intensively exploited for roughly twenty years when the colonial economy started to enter a postwar trough in the early 1760s. Essential commodities, principally wood, that had always been easily available to city dwellers at a reasonable price were now becoming scarce, exactly at the moment when the colonial economy was facing a postwar depression. In Philadelphia the price of fuel became an issue deep in the winter of 1760, when a writer to the *Pennsylvania Gazette* called "Help! Help! Help!" since wood now cost "Three Pounds Ten

Shilling a Cord, a Price never before heard of!," leaving "perhaps two Hundred families" with "not a Stick to burn." A year on, in 1761, the cost once again rose precipitously, leaving "the poor . . . reduced to great Extremity and Distress."[12]

Although Charleston's winters were usually brief and mild, high prices of basic provisions nevertheless became an issue in March 1763, when a local resident complained that "the sale of Firewood has fallen into the hands of three or four persons, who command whatever price they please for it, so that a cord now costs almost, if not quite, six pounds by the time it is brought to one's door, and at exceeding bad measurement too." Although a light-touch regulatory regime had previously been tolerated in abundant urban marketplaces, by the early 1760s circumstances had combined to exacerbate the problems with a trade operating according to the maxim that "everything is worth what it will sell for."[13]

Parliament's successive attempts to levy taxes in the colonies thus merely stoked the embers of domestic discontent, smoldering even before the Currency Act. In 1764, colonists were already more aware of the conditions needed for smooth-running marketing networks—networks they had previously taken for granted. In this state of heightened alert, they quickly realized that the operation of domestic trade, so dependent on interpersonal credit networks stretched over long distances, would be severely threatened by the disappearance of paper money. The Stamp Act's threatened ability to suck up all remaining specie added insult to injury. Following news of the acts, John Dickinson painted a dire picture of what would happen to domestic marketing. Colonists, Dickinson argued, had "for a long time enjoyed peace, and were quite free from any heavy debt, either internal or external. We had a paper currency which served as a medium of domestic commerce. . . . We had a multitude of markets for our provisions, lumber, and iron. These allowed liberties . . . enabled us to collect considerable sums of money." Currency was necessary to maintain the market, noted Dickinson, because commerce was no longer confined to "a narrow strip along the shore of the ocean"; colonists had now "penetrated boundless forests, have passed over immense mountains, and are daily pushing further and further into the wilderness," so "a very extensive commerce" was needed to supply them with affordable necessities. Yet, he explained, "every restriction on our trade, seems to be a restriction on this intercourse and must gradually cut off the connection of the interior parts with the maritimes." Dickinson pleaded, "What man . . . can view without pity, without passion, her restricted and almost stagnated trade?"[14]

Other Pennsylvanians agreed with Dickinson's assessment. Philadelphia merchant Richard Waln specialized in sending provisions to the West Indies, so when the Sugar Act outlawed the lumber trade with the Caribbean, he quickly noted "an uncommon scarcity" of wood, since "the country in expectation of Little Demand have very much dropd getting it and it cannot be afforded under the present prices." With the Currency Act and Stamp Act following on the heels of the Sugar Act, Waln quickly came to believe that for Americans to refuse "a tame submission" was the only way the market might be revived. Pennsylvania's legislators were of the same opinion. In their 1766 petition to the House of Commons pleading for a repeal of the Currency Act, they painted a dismal view of the damage wrought in the marketplace over the preceding two years. "That the unhappy Effects of this Diminution of our Paper Currency are already most sensibly felt" was obvious, they claimed, since "the Price of all Kinds of Labour is lessened, the Numbers of our Poor are increased, the Value of our Estates greatly sunk, our Trade and Importations from *Britain* evidently decreased, the further Settlement of the Province obstructed, and the People reduced to greatest Distress." Like the complaints of Waln and Dickinson, this list of grievances revealed how badly British legislation in 1764 and 1765 had destabilized the domestic marketplace and how this destabilization prompted colonial outrage.[15]

By the time the Stamp Act was repealed in March 1766, the marketplace's effective function was already under pressure from a succession of events disruptive to the way it had come to operate over the past century. Western colonists and Indian traders struggled to accommodate themselves to the new order created by the departure of the French. Eastern elites seemed either unwilling or unable to return these frontier markets to a semblance of order. Farther east, the urban poor suffered winter wood shortages as prices rose beyond their reach in a marketplace that theoretically outlawed engrossing and forestalling but in reality often ignored them. Then British legislation blocked off Caribbean markets for lumber. At the same time, these new measures limited the quantity of paper currency greasing the wheels of an internal marketplace dependent on the good credit of its propertied traders.

With the repeal of the Stamp Act, small issues of nonlegal tender by colonial governments for domestic use, and legislation to satisfy western demands for law and order, colonial authorities found a salve for some of the damage inflicted on domestic marketing. But the Townshend Duties, and then the Tea Act, ensured that these wounds never healed properly. Economic instability continued to exert pressure on the smooth functioning of urban marketplaces. Ongoing imperial crisis had colluded to produce a more long-term malaise in the domestic economy, chipping away at the effectiveness of marketing mechanisms that had always seemed to function satisfactorily.[16]

These persistent problems especially plagued auctions and urban provisions markets. Although auctions had previously been widely embraced by buyers and sellers, economic dislocation rapidly transformed them into something far more troublesome. With vendues principally used to dispose of the property of the deceased and debtors, and of surplus imported goods, all sources of salable wares came under pressure. In the backcountry the vendue assumed a troubled disposition for two reasons. On South Carolina's frontier, so Charles Woodmason claimed, the haphazard rule of law made auctions a tool of swindlers. At a tavern on the Pee Dee River, the minister observed a "knott of villains" assembled in anticipation of an estate vendue, "contriving, and cooking up fictitious accounts against the estate." Since justices of the peace in the area conducted their legal work for profit rather than in service of the public good, officials overlooked the needs of the larger community.[17]

The auction's popularity was more widely tested by the increasing number of foreclosures accompanying depression and British legislation. Across Pennsylvania, auctions ceased to be an effective market as the number of sales skyrocketed while bidders' capacity to purchase evaporated. "In many instances," wrote John Dickinson, "after lands and goods have been repeatedly advertised in the public gazettes, and exposed to sale, not a buyer appears." As auctions failed in the countryside, the malaise spread to the city, where "the consumers break the shopkeepers; they break the merchants; and the shock must be felt as far as *London*."[18]

Urban marketing mechanisms came under just as much pressure as their rural counterparts. Although Philadelphia merchant Benjamin Fuller had previously seen the promise of the auction for selling British manufactures, his chosen line of business became less straightforward as repeated boycotts of imports provoked by the Townshend Duties and the Tea Act created a wildly fluctuating supply of goods. Some commentators pointed out that "the Merchants complain of vendues as destructive to their Trade": sales lowered prices and undermined their profits when shopkeepers flocked to auctions to get a cheaper deal. Others opined that since ready money was often used to pay for purchases, vendues drained precious specie from Pennsylvania as "trading adventurers and strangers" set themselves up at the auction block. Since local authorities had not managed to stop the increase in retail vendues, sales had continued to multiply and now, as tough times hit, their very nature as ad hoc markets where prices were uncertain seemed to imperil the livelihood of colonists who were already suffering.[19]

Price uncertainties increasingly plagued the city's food markets, which had already come under stress in the 1760s. The pressure built steadily through the 1770s. After the Stamp Act, and in the face of continued disruption to the provisions supply, a fragile order wholly reliant on abundance seemed to break down completely in both South Carolina and Pennsylvania. Complaints of high prices and scarcity plagued city marketplaces, often accompanied by accusations that forestallers and engrossers were behind the problem. In 1773 Carolina factor Josiah Smith remarked on "the present Extravagant Rate" charged for firewood, "which is chiefly occasioned by the scarcity of Timber Trees Convenient to the Landing places on an inland Navigation to Charlestown." "Benevolus" complained to the *South Carolina Gazette* about enslaved Africans and planters who colluded to double the price of hogs at the wharf before the beasts had even reached the marketplace. Benevolus echoed "Veridicus," who had earlier outlined the intricate strategies traders adopted as they sought maximum prices for their provisions in a tight market. "I mean those, who rent houses at the north-end of *King Street*," wrote the polemicist, "which is almost the only entrance for carts and waggons coming to *Charles-Town*, from all parts of the country . . . certain it is, that the price of butter, hams, bacon, flour, and even poultry, is exorbitantly advanced on us, by this infamous practice." Accusing the market commissioners of ignoring the extortion, Veridicus identified one of the fundamental problems of a marketplace staffed by enslaved people and policed by slave owners; the latter benefited from overlooking the law in times of scarcity, since they would profit when their enslaved agents sold plantation provisions at inflated prices.[20]

With armed conflict closing in, the situation became worse. Supply lines to urban markets grew unreliable, and observers began to assiduously record prices, horrified at how much they had risen. With the British close to Philadelphia from the start of the war, inflation quickly affected food prices. The British occupation in 1777 and 1778 brought the situation to the crisis point. Christopher Marshall, a Philadelphia apothecary and leading committeeman in the city, was already astounded to find newly imported salt selling at three dollars a bushel in October 1776. He could only conclude that the high price was a sad illustration of how "inhumane are some of our citizens to poor people." When Marshall temporarily returned before the British occupation in June 1777, the situation had worsened again, with "very ordinary meat in the markett" amid the "dirt, filth, stench & flyes." A year later, prices had still not stabilized: "butter yesterday in markett sold from 2 to 3 dollars . . . the meat of different kinds from 4/6 to 1/ lb flour little in markett £20 hund green pease from 20/ to 25/ the half peck radishes from 2/6 to 3/9 bunch, good best spirits £7.5.0 single gallon molasses sold by hogshead from £4 to £4.10 p gallon, oakwood at wharves £16 p cord hickory up to £20, house rent risen from £50 p year to £500 from £80 to £1000, 1200 etc." The intensification of conflict had a similar impact on Charleston's market prices. Although he had previously noticed little major disruption in day-to-day trade, in 1778, with the British about to launch their southern campaign, Josiah Smith noted that "the expense attending importation is very great. . . . so that for family use, we are oblig'd to pay 10/ for a Bread loaf, that is no larger than those of 1/3 formerly were, Fresh beef also sells in the market at 7/6 per lb retail, Turkey at 8£ upwards a pair."[21]

Price rises were challenging enough, but equally hard to overcome was the disruption of familiar marketing circuits. Philadelphians Christopher Marshall and his wife relied on their commercial networks to keep their house warm and their family (and its animals) fed and clothed. Marshall dealt with trusted tradesmen and frequented the city's vendue as Mrs. Marshall set off for market at 4:00 a.m. to provision the household. She also undertook the annual duty of getting in the winter's wood supply, heading down to the city's wharves toward the end of August.[22]

When the Marshalls fled to Lancaster shortly before the British arrived in Philadelphia, they both faced the problem of reestablishing these connections in a new community. Soon after they settled in their new home, Marshall noted that "we have had some Difficulties to encounter with here as the people . . . has taken offences against the Philadelphians who some off them have not behaved prudently so that at last the country folks would scarcely bring them any thing to market; but I am in hopes . . . that the Harmony yt once subsisted will return again, I've not been abell to get a load of hay or of wood as yet, nor pasture for my horse, had not my wife bought a load." The Marshalls struggled also to forge commercial connections with the farmers around Lancaster, who often sold goods promised to them before they arrived or proved reluctant to deliver them, meaning that Mrs. Marshall had to take long carriage rides to procure butter for her family. In the end, the couple had to put in months of effort rebuilding their credit with local suppliers before Mrs. Marshall could resume her patronage of the provisions market and Mr. Marshall had established a satisfactory relationship with local farmers.[23]

By the late 1770s, discussions of trade were dominated by the sentiment that a once serviceable market was now broken. Addressing his fellow Philadelphians, William Bradford detailed the situation:

> It has long been said that trade will regulate itself; yet sufficient experience has shewn that the maxim, though admittedly true in some cases, is not so in all. While monopolizers are suffered to exist, who by stepping in between the importer and the retail purchase can produce a scarcity when they chuse; or by their transporting their goods backward and forward from State to State can occasionally create a want in any or in all, or while the retailer by laying on what profits he pleases, becomes regardless of what prices he give or how much they outbid each other. In all these cases trade is deprived of its chance, and becomes clogged with a disease which, let to itself, will destroy its credit and produce its destruction.[24]

Bradford's insightful assessment of domestic trade astutely identified what had happened when the marketplace had been put under pressure from the 1760s onward. Dependent on good credit, the rule of law to support that credit, and abundance, American marketing crumbled as these foundations were gradually chipped away by crisis after crisis until they collapsed. When the foundations collapsed, so did the edifice of marketing that Americans had constructed over the previous century.

RESPONDING TO MARKETPLACE DISORDER

As Bradford recognized the disorder that crisis brought to the domestic marketplace, he documented again the two contrasting ways of organizing a market uneasily coexisting in colonial America. Operating side by side were a commerce whose success was underpinned by the creditworthiness of individual traders, dependent on the maxim that trade will regulate itself, and a marketplace governed by statutes designed to ensure that trade served the public good. The simultaneous existence of these marketing philosophies strongly shaped the way colonists responded to the crisis. Understanding their dual influence is central to appreciating how creating colonial marketplaces and trading within them would eventually produce specifically American market ideologies.

Before exploring the details of their influence, though, we must acknowledge the background to these reactions, debates, and protests. This context will once again help us comprehend what was particular to the American response. As Barbara Clark Smith has explained, these events were part of a British Atlantic tradition of popular economic protest. English-speaking people were well accustomed to reacting to an economic crisis. These reactions frequently involved crowd action, and they might be prompted by anything from new taxation promising to reduce the profits of trade, to food shortages, to inflated prices for essential provisions. As Americans faced additional taxes and high food prices, so did their British counterparts.[25]

Since many metropolitan protests shared causes with these colonial upheavals and even occurred about the same time, exploring two episodes of British market disorder yields a better understanding of the particularities of the colonial reaction. First, disputes over the Cider Tax introduced in 1763 are instructive. Contemporaries quickly recognized the parallels between the Cider Tax and the Stamp Act, which were both repealed after widespread protest. In both cases protestors argued that the duties unduly targeted a specific region, indiscriminately taxed those who could ill afford to pay, and involved too great an invasion of liberty and property. Such close parallels prompted radical Newcastle minister James Murray, who had written his *Impartial History of the War in America* after a stay in the colonies, to note that "the cyder counties tasted the same pleasure with their brethren in America, which they enjoyed at the same time, and testified their thankfulness by universall joy."[26]

Not directly united in the contemporary consciousness, but still sharing much common ground across the Atlantic, were the crowd actions elites called food riots. As the imperial crisis worsened and the cost of provisions rose, crowds in Massachusetts and New York seized goods or stopped the market until sellers consented to sell food at an agreed price. Philadelphia militiamen battled over the government's refusal to peg market prices of essential foods, the fracas eventually gaining notoriety as the Fort Wilson incident. Food riots continued to be a feature of the British marketplace in this era. In 1766 an Oxford crowd had compelled grocers to reduce the price of bacon, candles, and other provisions, observing that demand from a booming London population had caused inflated prices in the city marketplace.[27]

Critically, however, British reactions to market disorder, both when heavy taxes hampered traders and when provisions were costly or scarce, were determined by customary community hierarchies. These hierarchies structured protest as much as they structured regular exchange. The Cider Tax protests embraced all orders of society, rehearsing a familiar relationship between upper, middling, and working people as part of acknowledged patterns of popular dispute. William Dowdeswell, a West Country member of Parliament, spoke paternally for all residents of the cider counties when he condemned the tax as a burden on "the farmer, cottager, and labourer" who made cider for their own households but a fairer duty on factors, who were "as fit an object for Exise as any dealer whatsoever." The universal agreement that this tax should not target the poor–but that a tax in itself was not wrong–prompted elites staging community celebrations of the Treaty of Paris in 1763 to allow lower sorts to repurpose them as protests against the duty. The cider counties protested as a society fundamentally in agreement with central government's right to tax and regulate trade, but disagreeing with a tax targeting a single region while also contravening paternalist duties by placing an unjustly large burden on the poor.[28]

When the London market threatened to swallow up provisions destined for Oxford's consumption, protestors and authorities likewise agreed that market regulation was needed to protect the local community. Rioters were fully invested in a market that functioned for the public good, standing firm in the name of Oxford's collective good against a metropolitan public seeking to divert produce destined for Oxford's marketplace. Price regulation protecting a local public good from the encroachment of predatory "foreign" interests was a highly desirable tool of marketplace management. At no time did the Oxford protestors endorse a market that regulated itself. Indeed, their fundamental opposition to this principle was the crux of their objections.[29]

In contrast, American reactions to marketplace disorder reflected the contested status of the public good in the local economy. First of all, when leading American protestors viewed themselves as an economic "interest" distinct from the British government, their sense of difference was grounded not in their commitment to a locally regulated economy but in their long experience of a relatively *unregulated* marketplace. In this colonial space private property often ruled the day, and the right to trade it was protected only by laws allowing creditors to recover their property. The law's function as a guardian of the economic common good had fallen by the wayside in the course of the eighteenth century. Colonial protestors were defending a local interest based on individualism rather communitarianism in the marketplace. As John Carpenter had already noted in 1763, Americans feared most "an infringement on the liberty" they had enjoyed to trade in marketplaces untouched by corporate or government interests. After 1764 Americans reasoned that British legislation was illegitimate because it impeded their right to trade their property freely and to use their own courts, on their own terms, to remedy things when deals went wrong.[30]

Assuming they should be free from *any* type of government regulation, the Philadelphia Non-Importation Associators of 1769 argued that "the difficulties, under which they now labour as a trading people are owing to the Restrictions, Prohibitions & ill-advised Regulations in several late Acts of the parliament . . . injurious to property." These measures had "a tendency to prevent the payment of old Debts, or contracting new, and are of consequence ruinous to Trade." Their South Carolina brethren objected equally to "new-created commissioners of customs, placement, parasitical and novel ministerial officers" appointed to watch over "oppressive proceedings of civil law." Not only did these new officers come with burdensome quantities of regulation, they sought to come between colonists and their courts—courts that knew better than to meddle too much with a man's liberty and property. This reasoning also influenced the rhetoric of the Continental Congress, where James Duane, looking back on the late 1760s from the vantage point of 1774, recounted how the Townshend Duties were imposed when "a despotic Minister soon discovered that under the Idea of a commercial Regulation our Property might still be invaded."[31]

Americans especially felt unreasonable "commercial regulation" of their property was taking place in 1774, when the Intolerable Acts stopped Boston's trade and placed British authorities in control of its wharves. Writing in sympathy with the city's merchants, "A Carolinian" explained that the act meant "all the Wharves, Quays, Landings and Water Lots of that great Bay . . . which are the Subsistance of many Thousand People, are condemned, and little better than confiscated, as no Goods are either to be landed upon them or shipped from them by any Vessel down to the Size of a common Wherry." "Dip further into this Production of Hell," continued the Carolinian, "and you find that not so much as a Wood-Boat can enter—nor a Market Boat bring a few Cabbages or Bushels of Corn to support 60,000 People." Meanwhile, Pennsylvania lawyer Jasper Yeates decried a situation in which "the distressed People of that Town, must receive the supplies of Nature from the Points of Bayonets." By occupying the wharves the British closed down one of Boston's principal marketplaces—an action keenly felt by the individual merchants who owned them as an intrusion on property and trade, but quite possibly not even recognized as a peculiar imposition by far-away British ministers who assumed that wharves were mostly public landing places. American reactions to British government policy were fundamentally distinctive. While contemporary British protestors complained under the assumption that in any case the marketplace should be regulated, Americans worked on the principle that government had at best a questionable right to regulate their domestic trade.[32]

However, if merchants, planters, and members of the Continental Congress were pretty sure that London should not meddle in their marketplaces, how far American authorities might interfere was much more hotly contested. American reactions to the crisis were thus equally anchored in their uncertainty about the appropriate balance of individualism and communitarianism—private interest and the public good—in market transactions. The debates prompted by this uncertainty confirmed Americans' familiarity with European customary market practices but simultaneously displayed their circumscribed impact on the colonial marketplace.

Some colonists did believe that a marketplace disordered by war needed greater regulation. While backcountry people had been almost alone in their vigorous argument for more market regulation in the earliest stages of the crisis, by the late 1760s calls for adherence to the public good had rapidly spread to the centers of European power. While he called out Carolinians forestalling the marketplace on Charleston's wharves and in its suburbs, Veridicus also argued that "certain regulations are necessary for their intestine government." Such actions were justified "as particular regulations of this form take place in all the cities and towns of any consequence, both in Europe and America" and "good effect must evidently have been expected from them before they were established." "Why should *Charles-Town* be denied the privilege, of guarding its inhabitants, against the fraud of monopolizing and forestalling the necessaries of life? For surely, those who are guilty of such acts of oppression, may justly be deemed enemies to . . . society." In asking these questions Veridicus pointed out that many Charlestonians were not invested in the common economic good as he endorsed its application to the city marketplace. Because of the hybrid nature of this marketplace, Veridicus was forced to argue for the very idea of regulation, when his British counterparts needed only to be persuaded to accept a temporary strengthening of such customs universally established "since time immemorial."[33]

As the economic turmoil showed no signs of letting up, demand for market regulation intensified, eventually eliciting a response from the authorities. Veridicus's demands came four years after a 1768 Assembly statute designed to prevent the "great frauds and abuses [that] have been and still are daily committed in the sale of fire-wood in Charlestown, to the great oppression of the poor." Charleston's market commissioners were fully aware of such price hikes, initially blaming them on the free black and enslaved traders responsible for much of the town's provisioning. In May 1777 commissioners noted that citizens were being "greatly imposed on by the Free Negroes, who usually attend the Market to sell Veal, Mutton etc on Commission." Henceforth blacks were required to carry a ticket written by a free white person stipulating the highest price at which provisions could be sold, "in order that the Inhabitants may be satisfied whether the Owners or Sellers are the Extortioners." Successful free black butcher Leander was then charged with selling overpriced veal according to the new law and suffered a month in prison. By early 1780, just two months before the British laid siege to Charleston, the situation had become desperate enough for white traders to be directly targeted. The Assembly passed an ordinance "to prevent the monopolizing and for regulating the Retailers" of several imported commodities, including rum, salt, sugar, flour, butter, "negro cloth," and coarse blankets. Heavy financial penalties faced those who retailed these goods at more than a 25 percent markup on the wholesale price, either at a store or by vendue. In a further return to historic British practices, the authorities empowered the courts to prosecute monopolizers.[34]

As the clerk of the market's appeal to "owners and sellers" suggests, however, planters did not always support this drive for a regulated trade answering the public good. War and drought had disrupted the plantation economy, leaving planters without income from rice and indigo, and sometimes without enslaved laborers. Such difficulties left those who still had provisions to sell, and a way of transporting them, in an advantageous position. At Margaret Colleton's plantation a rice crop brought a good return in July 1777, but for the next two years almost all income came from renting out a schooner to sell wood, livestock, and butter on the local market. The rewards of such trade were scant compared with those from producing staples, driving planters to charge as much as they could for these increasingly valuable commodities, often by giving their enslaved proxies permission to get the highest price possible. The tough new regulations clashed with the priorities of slave owners, who were happy to put the stability of their plantations before the common good of the Lowcountry.[35]

Meanwhile, the scrap between supporters of the public good and staunch guardians of their private rights was played out more explicitly in the politically factious environment of Philadelphia. Between 1770 and 1780 town residents repeatedly locked horns in print and in the marketplace over how far the government should regulate daily economic transactions. Even in a market plagued by high prices and unreliable supply, the decision to regulate was still hotly contested.

Supporters of regulation for the public good began putting their case forward in the early 1770s after the second round of consumer boycotts. Soon after merchants once again placed their orders for British manufactures, the city became flooded with goods, and traders resorted to vendue sales to shift their surplus stock. The sudden spike in auctions drew the attention of

commentators, who insisted that now was the time to regulate sales properly. Supporters of stricter control drew on a customary interpretation of the
common good to justify their regulation, which was necessary to subjugate
private interest, protect the privileges of the resident community over outsiders, and benefit the poor. "It can seldom happen that any Regulation,"
trumpeted "Legion," "however benificial, can be devised, but what will clash
with the private Interest of Individuals, who, if they are Men of public spirit,
will acquiesce with Silent Submission; but when private Interest absorbs
public virtue, a different conduct may be expected." Thus merchants should
be prepared to sacrifice profits to a duty on auctions so that when "numerous adventurers and strangers" came from New York to auction goods, the
taxes would support the poor of Philadelphia while also discouraging the
large number of sales at which "stolen goods, and all Kind of Merchandize
procured in an unfair and underhand way" were auctioned.[36]

Now keenly alert to the issue of economic regulation, Philadelphians
again confronted the contested status of the public good just a month later
in a broadside written by the city's soap boilers, calling for government action to regulate the market for potash, an essential raw material for their
trade. The pamphlet accused John Rhea "of this City, Merchant" of going
"door-to-door" offering families and businesses a five-year fixed rate for
their ashes "under the specifious pretence of creating a new article of remit-
tance to Great Britain." Instead, the soap boilers argued, Rhea was working
as a middleman, proposing to sell the ashes back to them at an inflated
price. Labeling him a monopolizer, the broadside authors gloomily contemplated the consequences; they would suffer penury while Rhea's handsome
profits would "genteelly support his family."[37]

The soap boilers did not win government support, and existing vendue
regulations remained unchanged. But with Congress's nonimportation and
nonexportation association, and with impending war, radical revolutionary
authorities gradually warmed to the idea of regulating the marketplace for
the public good. By late 1774 Philadelphia's committees of inspection were
closely monitoring every merchant cargo arriving in the city, logging and
clearing it before owners were permitted to put it up for sale. By early 1776,
with congressionally sanctioned boycotts now firmly in place, these committees openly endorsed price setting for a range of commodities sold in the
urban marketplace. Announcing their intention to fix the price of eleven
commodities including common rum, coffee, sugar, and salt, the committee
cited "the engrossing . . . that several persons" had engaged in "at a period
of public calamity." Therefore they resolved that "bound in duty and justice

to the inhabitants of this city and province" they should "give an immediate check" to prices. Individuals who "shall be so lost to virtue, honour, and the public good, as to demand greater prices" would be rewarded with exposure "by name to public view."[38]

By September 1777 renewed calls for price controls were circulating. "A.B." chided the Continental Congress for nullifying the committee's earlier efforts to fix prices and firmly condemned the unchristian behavior of those who had made sure that "extortion, oppression, and a thirst for gain were never so extensive." Even a York Town convention at which six states met to discuss the condition of the market had settled on "a mistaken principle of leaving trade to regulate itself" and so "broke . . . up without doing any thing." The authorities' rigid adherence to this doctrine could only bring "the vengeance of heaven upon us," warned the author. The stresses of war had by then convinced many Pennsylvanians that a regulated market was the only way traders would be persuaded to conduct commerce in a manner sensitive to the common good. Whereas prewar marketing practices had involved merchants, shopkeepers, and marketing folk buying and selling wares with barely any intervention from the government, the crisis had transformed the trading environment.[39]

After the British left Philadelphia, some among Pennsylvania's government were beginning to agree with A.B. and the Committee for Inspection. The Assembly banned vendues of "goods, wares, and merchandises" across the state, citing sales "as tending to raise the price of almost every necessary article, and to depreciate the current money of the continent." In early 1778 the state government at last relented, passing "An ACT to prevent Forestalling and Regrating, and to encourage Fair Dealing." Fully buying into a customary model of market regulation that viewed "combinations of evil and designing men" as leeches on the public good, happily raising prices for their private gain, the legislation criminalized forestalling, engrossing, and regrating, and it promised that traders who committed these crimes would be "legally convicted thereof before any Court of Quarter Sessions in this State," a move restoring the common law's role as a protector of the public good in the marketplace.

Christopher Marshall, a longtime supporter of the regulated marketplace exiled in Lancaster, sought to enforce the principles of this act with the creation of a new committee of inspection in the town. The committee "Resolved, That we will . . . encourage fair and honest commerce, and suppress, to the utmost of our power, and at the hazard of our lives and fortunes, engrossing, monopolizing and forestalling, and the depreciation of our currency."

By 1780 the Lancaster, Bucks County, and Philadelphia marketplaces had all joined these efforts to fully reinstate regulated markets.[40]

As the Fort Wilson incident of 1779 suggested, however, the campaign for the economic common good remained locked in a duel with traders rather less invested in its principles. The clash, in which six men died, was partly a political standoff between Philadelphia's radical and conservative revolutionary parties but was equally prompted by militiamen who believed market regulation had come too late, and was too poorly enforced, to really benefit the public good.[41]

The militiamen's opponents were those Philadelphians who extended their dislike of government interference in commerce beyond British legislation and into the realm of local authority. They consistently spoke out against regulation from the beginning of the 1770s onward, often arguing that trade should indeed regulate itself. Regulation's advocates had to fend off critics like "A Friend to the Community," who resisted auction duties because the sales ensured "that every individual might have an opportunity of cloathing their Families upon the lowest Terms. . . . [It] is in the interest of shopkeepers to purchase their Goods on the lowest Terms, by which means they have it in their power to supply the Country much cheaper than the merchants could." The "Friend" also accused supporters of the tax of favoring "the good of the poor" over "the rest of his Fellow Citizens." In short, the "Friend" firmly believed in a trickle-down model in which competition would keep prices low for deserving working people, who would then be able to afford clothing.[42]

As the debate moved on from vendue taxes, the "Friend" and others like him turned their attention to the corporation's 1773 attempt to extend the central market. The free marketers viewed the plan as "to the Prejudice of, not only the Public Convenience but the private Property of many worthy Citizens." Two broadside authors, "A Philadelphian" and "Andrew Marvell," directly linked the imperial crisis to the actions of the city corporation, comparing the mayor's efforts to increase stall rental income to British taxation. Without doubt, factional politics that had long pitted the corporation against numerous other interest groups created an environment in which a move to expand the market could be interpreted as a power grab. Nevertheless, to an extraordinary degree both writers viewed the proposed market expansion as an encroachment on the liberty of private property on the scale of British taxation campaigns. Marvell argued that "a power so unwarrantably obtained and exercised" was undoubtedly "to the Prejudice of . . . the private Property of many worthy Citizens" and thus "ought . . . to be unanimously and vigourously opposed." The author then pondered how "citizens, who but a few Years since nobly stood forth against the whole Power of the British Parliament rather than submit to be taxed, or to have the Money taken out of their Pockets without their consent," could now permit their own corporation to check their property rights. "Can the corporation prove one Foot of Ground of any Street, to be their Property[?]" asked "A Philadelphian." Overall, the confrontation illustrated that economic crisis had made colonists keenly attuned to intrusions on their individual right to protect and increase the value of their property, even if it promised to bolster the public good.[43]

Outside of this marketplace conflict, Philadelphians questioned those who always privileged the common good over private interests. The shaky commitment of some townspeople to the good of the whole was especially clear in 1770, after the second round of nonimportation boycotts. City trader Richard Waln wrote that "it is a very general Wish amongst the Merchants" that the boycott "may continue at least one year in order that they may dispose of the great Quantity of Goods on hand . . . this is agreeable to my private Interest, but when I consider that it is inconsistent with the general good of the Brittish Empire . . . I wish the Cause of Complaint may be immediately removed." Waln was far from the only trader openly weighing the value of his own estate against the good of the whole. Benjamin Fuller pursued his private interest by establishing a trade in British goods through St. Eustatius. Fuller explained that "the channell of the Windies has been much usd . . . I am of opinion [it] will continue so, untill a general importation takes place, wch will not be till next Spring . . . , but I cannot think the Merchants in general can be so lost to themselves or the trade of the province, as to sit tamely quiet, while all the provinces round are importing in large Quantities, particularly New York, who has broke through the nonimportation agreement & will have goods out this fall." By July 1770, as Fuller had predicted, merchants in Philadelphia were beginning to break the boycott.[44]

By September of the same year, "A Freeholder" felt compelled to defend their failure to stick to the boycott on the grounds that most of their fellow traders had also resumed importation, and even smuggling. As during the Seven Years' War, the temptation to secure their estates had led many city dealers to cast aside the interests of the "public . . . [and] every person who values Liberty" to once again order the manufactures the American market craved. While commitment to the boycott of 1774 was stronger, Patriots were still alert to the idea that there could be too much economic regulation.

Indeed, it was this very sentiment that had led the Continental Congress to overrule the Philadelphia Committee of Inspection when it proposed its program of price setting in April 1776.[45]

These intense disputes formed a sustained argument over how markets should function. The conflict had its origins in colonists' long experience of trading in marketplaces that rewarded the individual credit-worthy property owner but also incorporated some sense that trade should answer the common good. When colonial society abandoned the consensus that traditional hierarchies should govern trade, the universal acceptance of market regulation had also been neglected. These debates therefore not only revealed the competing value systems and willingness to challenge received orthodoxy that developed with the hybrid marketplace, they also exposed the weak grip of elites on the instruments of economic order. Unlike their British brethren, colonial elites could not resort to the court to hang rioters, and they also found it hard to prosecute effectively for crimes against the common good. With the mechanisms for recovering debt then rendered useless by economic disorder, rulers were left with few means of ordering the marketplace and guaranteeing their authority. Elites were increasingly powerless in the urban centers and were even less able to order trade on the distant frontier. Out of crisis and disagreement in the marketplace emerged a growing consensus among white property owners that they must reformulate the idea of the public good if they were to restore their economic advantage.

TAKING BACK CONTROL?

Provoked by a prolonged crisis in their marketplaces, Americans vigorously disputed the fundamentals of the way day-to-day commerce should function. While colonial market culture was quite novel, the language of the debate was rather familiar. The idea that an economy was composed of "private interests" and a "public good" (or "common good") dated back millennia. Indeed, the emergence of a commercial society in imperial Britain had thrust discussion of these concepts into the spotlight. The publication of Smith's *Wealth of Nations* in 1776 was merely the zenith of decades of heated exchange about the place of commercial interests in an agrarian commonwealth, the good of the whole, and the regulation of trade. Since American debates were related to such quarrels, it is important to situate them within these wider deliberations. Doing so helps us locate the particularities of the American discussion, revealing its unique dimensions and highlighting the novelty of the assumptions it produced.[46]

As more and more Enlightenment thinkers weighed in on the knotty issue of political economy, debate about the role of the public good intensified. Some writers began to ponder the idea that an economy might be "self-organizing." At the same time, they examined the connection between private interests and the public good, which had previously appeared clear-cut. In a 1757 discussion of economic issues, Josiah Tucker proposed that good government should give self-interest "such a Direction, that it may promote the public Interest by pursuing its own. And then the very Spirit of Monopoly will operate for the Good of the Whole." Although Tucker did not envision an economic system in which government might step aside to make individual interests the rulers of the market, his ideas were fundamentally connected to those of his Scottish contemporaries, notably Adam Smith. Smith was willing to go much further, embracing the notion that individuals' thirst for a profit would naturally end up serving the common good. On a theoretical level, the relation between individuals and the public good, and the government's role in defining the dynamic between the two, was in flux by the 1770s.[47]

As we have seen, however, neither people on the ground nor members of the central government formulating American policy were attentive readers of Tucker and Smith. On a practical, day-to-day level, the proposition that the economy should work for the good of the whole was still strongly tied to both economic decision making and mundane market relations. It is well worth recalling here that even Bristol's and Glasgow's merchant communities continued to sponsor urban economies structured around a balance of local interests, whose duty it was to nurture the common good in times of dearth and plenty alike.[48]

Prominent authors concerned particularly with the American crisis also stuck with long-standing economic paradigms in their analysis of the imperial situation. Although they had forgotten the struggles imperial officials faced to get colonists to obey the "king's interest" some seventy years earlier, British pamphleteers remained deeply invested in the idea that Britain's economic interests constituted the "good of the whole" in the Atlantic arena. Thus, to resolve the crisis Americans needed to recognize that their economy must operate to answer Britain's common good.

With his experience as a colonial governor, Thomas Pownall was among the writers who most clearly argued that this issue was the crux of the dispute. Revised and reprinted multiple times, Pownall's *Administration of the Colonies* asserted that it was precisely "the rise and forming" of an American "commercial interest" that "constitutes the present crisis." As a result, the British government must intervene to bring the American interest into line. In particular, officials should work to revise "the general and several governments of the colonies . . . their trade, and the general British laws of trade, in their several relations in which they stand to the mother country, to the government of the mother country, to foreign countries, and the colonies of foreign countries." In sum, Pownall thought it both possible and necessary to convince Americans that their economic interest was also that of their mother country and that they should all work together to answer the common good of the realm.[49]

However, as Pownall demonstrated his continued belief that a commercial society should function for the good of the whole, he also betrayed his naïveté about the forces shaping the way colonists themselves thought about their economic interests and the public good. While Americans may have appeared to be of one voice when they objected to the Stamp Act or launched a boycott, such moments of unity papered over deep divides in popular economic thought. Never had all Americans wholeheartedly endorsed the idea that trade should answer the good of the whole. Many, as John Carpenter and William Bradford pointed out, had long believed that trade would regulate itself. Any attempt by a government to regulate trade would thus be interpreted as an invasion of individuals' liberty to deal as they pleased. Furthermore, it would be an uphill struggle to get frontier colonists and urban elites, let alone Indians or Africans, to constitute an "interest" of the sort Pownall dreamed of. Quite simply, while Britons like Adam Smith were deconstructing customary beliefs about market function from the top down, colonists had taken them apart from the bottom up. In the middle, however, were men like Pownall who were still fully invested in the old economy of interests.

As colonists debated how far the public good should be the organizing principle of trade, they revealed the way economic ideology had been reset by the colonial experience. Yet their debates simultaneously suggested that they were not fully committed to the idea that trade would regulate itself. As the crisis worsened, colonial supporters of the public good increasingly believed it might represent the solution to their economic woes. This did not mean they agreed with Thomas Pownall. Rather, propertied white men realized that redefining the public good for their own purposes might let them regain control of the American marketplace.

To take back control, these men first had to fashion themselves as the rightful governors of that American marketplace. By dismantling an economy of interests that had historically functioned to preserve the good of the

whole, white colonists had gotten wealthy and enjoyed an unparalleled freedom to trade, but they had also dispensed with the methods European elites
used to contain and manage dissenting voices in times of economic crisis.
In this respect, the nonimportation associations and eventually the committees of inspection became critical to the project of redefining the public
good; they became the means for white coastal elites to reassert their power
in the marketplace. Far from being a project that would be accomplished
before 1783's Treaty of Paris, nonimportation was the start of a much longer
process of reworking the guiding principles white freeholders used to claim
authority over their domestic marketplaces.

As the boycott's historians know, however, the participants in these actions were just as likely to be white women as to be men. Men exhorted
women to take part because they realized that, as custodians of the household economy, their enthusiasm was necessary to the boycott's success.
Given that women were foundational to the creation of colonial marketplaces in so many ways, it is unlikely that they needed much urging. At auctions and ferry landings, in taverns, at country stores, through their newspaper advertisements, and in the provisions market, women had been full
participants in creating markets. In 1765, in 1769–70, and finally from 1774
to 1776, women thus stood alongside men in the Western world's first consumer boycotts, seeking to leverage their status as buyers and sellers in a
commercial empire.[50]

While women supported the boycotts by staying away from the marketplaces they usually frequented to buy and sell imports, men focused on
the more obviously political task of refashioning the public good. The dec-
larations of association they wrote therefore expressed not only their dis-
taste for British regulations, but also their desire for greater control over
their own marketplaces. As the ongoing debates about private right and the
public good suggest, this was not a power readily accepted by all involved.
Indeed, some colonists openly sniped at the might of the committees: "NON-
IMPORTATION is the Word of the day; you must submit to it, fellow Subjects, the great Patriots tell you so; those very Patriots who tickle your Ears
with the *Words* SALVATION OF AMERICA.... Can you Doubt their absolute Right to save you in their own way?" boomed one Philadelphia dis-
senter. But as disordered marketplaces continued to worry white colonists,
and as the debates about private interest and the public good intensified, the
instruments granted to Associators for regulating trade grew more comprehensive, more geographically expansive, and more widely endorsed among
free white men.[51]

Although the boycotts were focused on stopping international trade, their success rested on the Associators' ability to regulate the domestic marketing of goods and people. Perhaps because the committees found successful regulation was not always straightforward, they developed a range of strategies to ensure compliance with the boycott, especially in 1769 and 1774. Their tactics drew on the mixed inheritance of practices and ideologies that had underpinned colonial marketing from the 1700s onward.

On the most general level, an agreement that traders needed strong government, and might even require price controls to trade fairly, tied Americans to customary European regulatory practices. Creating committees of inspection to oversee the storage and sale of imported goods bound white men together and made them into an "internal police" of importation. Committees used their announcements of support for the boycott to fashion this corporate male identity, which looked very much like its British counterpart. In 1770 the Lancaster committee members described themselves as liberty-loving "Freemen and Descendants of Britons" whose "Fellowship or Correspondence" was reserved for those who supported the boycott. When they created subcommittees to represent "six particular districts" of Philadelphia in 1774, the city Associators recruited sixty-six freeman to comprehensively regulate trade. These men were charged with "promoting the public welfare," while their Northampton County brethren noted in their correspondence that their boycott resolves had been "Enter'd into at the time of holding the Courts of Common Pleas & Quarter Sessions for the county when the most respectable of the Freeholders attended." South Carolinians constituted their committees in a similar manner. When they subsequently met in local inns to review manifests of imported goods and note down the prices fixed on them, these men came to share even more with their European brethren, who frequently did this when they sought to enforce guild regulations or transact the business of the municipal corporation.[52]

In other ways, however, the boycott's regulatory regime rested on a uniquely colonial foundation. The Associators used auctions to sell goods ordered before the boycott was enforced. They were also particularly peevish about imports' sullying their private property and went to great lengths to designate public warehouses where they kept the offending goods at a safe distance from their privately owned wharves and stores. Carolinians made resolutions acknowledging the expansive nature of their marketplace, which in its frontier parts was often populated with Loyalists. The committee specifically resolved to undertake "no Correspondence, Intercourse or Dealing" with sellers or wagoners who had no proof they had signed an association. The resolution was published in the newspaper and circulated throughout the colony.[53]

Just as print formed the kernel of a "virtual" marketplace reaching beyond colonial urban centers, it also became the foundation of a larger regulatory community united through newspapers to enforce the boycott. Since print was also crucial to white Americans' creation of a "common cause," newspapers were essential in effecting one of the centerpieces of colonial protest. As they reprinted the resolves and reports of numerous committees across their colonies and their neighboring colonies, newspaper editors brought white male readers together into a larger regulatory project, reaching many hundreds of miles. This was a project of economic management not only drawing on European practices in its quest to unite the white male body politic, but also assuming an American inflection.[54]

European inheritance and American novelty merged again when committees used print to redefine the "public good" as agreement with the Associators' regulations. In 1768 John Dickinson, in the twelfth of his "Letters from a Farmer," had asked whether "our zeal for the public good is worn out before the homespun cloaths." The subsequent rhetoric of the Associators suggested not. Through its frequent invocation, the public good became defined in numerous publications as conformity to the protocols implemented by the committees of inspection. Individuals who would not sign were named in newspapers "as inimical to the Liberties of America," while supporters declared their confidence that the committees "will act according to the best of their Judgement for the Public Good." Lancaster's committee stressed the necessity of "sacrificing our immediate gains and profits for the public good," while the proceedings of Annapolis's committee pronounced to Pennsylvania readers that they "very generously" preferred "the public good to their own private Interest." On the other hand, those who "meanly and from pecuniary motives endeavoured to subvert the grand, the glorious cause of Liberty . . . should be put on a level with, and exposed like . . . a poor wretch, of as little consequence as a *Scotch Pedler*." In other words, they could look forward to exclusion from the economic community like the itinerant trader, who was the natural enemy of the honest, resident (patriot) merchant.[55]

Although white men would be members of this community until they proved their disloyalty, women were naturally assumed to be outside it or at least on its margins. Because this was a political economic entity responsible for the public good, any sign that women thought themselves qualified for active membership met with a sharp rebuke. The ladies of Edenton, North Carolina, provoked just such a reaction when their 1774 association hinted at an active role in the body politic. By resolving "to do every thing as far as lies in our power to testify our sincere adherence" to the cause of upholding "the peace and happiness of our country" and "the public good," they crossed the line from being useful citizens to suggesting active governance. For the British and colonial men who read their statement, this sounded far too much like an attempt to muscle in on the serious business of regulating the economy. Rather, the Edenton ladies should strive to be more like their Philadelphia compatriots, whose spinning bees allowed them to "cast . . . [their] mite into the Treasury of the public good" without actually seeking to define its meaning or to wield power in its name.[56]

If white men, on the other hand, failed to throw themselves with sufficient gusto into upholding the public good, they were duly punished with vilification, and sometimes exclusion, by the community of resident traders. The belittling, humorous tone that often accompanied comment on women's political statements was quickly exchanged for more vicious action and criticism. To regain their status as members of the "public" and promoters of its good, male traders were required to apologize for their failings. Philadelphia dealer William Sitgreaves had to make profuse excuses for exceeding the prescribed limits on the price of coffee, which he claimed he would not have done had he understood it "would have been considered as injurious to the public welfare." His apology bought him readmittance to the trading community.[57]

When John Clark, a miller from Allan township in Cumberland County, refused to apologize for being "unfriendly to the Liberties of the United Colonies," the committee resolved to "have no dealings nor connections with the said John Clark." A similar fate befell Charleston dealer Benjamin Matthewes and his mother Ann: found to be selling British imports, they were duly exposed in the *South Carolina Gazette* as people "audaciously counteracting the United Sentiments of the whole Body of the People . . . and prefering their own little private Advantage to the general Good of America." Ann's actions had become serious rather than comical because she acted in consort with her son. Refusing to accept "Bills of Credit emitted by . . . Congress," Philadelphia druggist Townsend Speakman was equally dangerous and was thus held "up to the world . . . as an ENEMY in his country, and PRECLUDED from all TRADE and INTERCOURSE with the inhabitants of these colonies." In the course of the 1770s, the economic public good was remodeled as loyalty to patriot regulations governing trade, value, and legal tender. Failure to obey the rules brought exclusion from the Revolutionary—and hence the trading—community.[58]

Becoming an outsider to this trading community could come as a severe blow to those who had always enjoyed membership. Philadelphia hatter John Drinker felt his exclusion so keenly that he left off entering columns of accounts in his daybook to note in detail what had happened when the city's committee discovered in early 1776 that he had refused to take Continental currency. "This day our Store Windows were shut, and Wooden Barrs nailed across them," lamented Drinker, who went on to explain how the committee had demanded that he "should Immediately deliver our Books and Papers ... to be ... deposited in Our Stores in Trunks or Chests & then Sealed ... the Doors & Windows of our Stores & Warehouses were also to be Sealed and the Keys of them as well as of the Trunks & Chests to be delivered to them." Drinker "told them that we should not deliver," but the committeemen "persisted resolutely," eventually warning him that he could expect to "be destroyed the next day by the Mob." With this threat Drinker relented, and his stores remained locked three months later, his only income a few shillings from the sale of groceries he had kept in his house. The hatter had been reduced from legitimate trader to little more than a peddler, and an unlicensed one at that. Only when the British marched into Philadelphia later in 1777 did Drinker's trade return to its former levels.[59]

Through their committees, American patriots resurrected the public good in the marketplace and repurposed it for their cause. In doing so they returned to a familiar rhetoric in which those evil people who demonstrated "a criminal attachment to their private interest" above the "good of the whole" ("American Liberty") were viewed as illegitimate traders. Their position involved an implicit rejection of the notion that trade would regulate itself without interference from government authorities. However, this newly created public good was defined and performed in novel ways. It relied heavily on the press for its propagation and enforcement and excluded Loyalist traders. It also denied women an active role in its definition and completely ignored Africans and Indians as a legitimate constituency. In these ways the patriot public good became shorn of its historically inclusive and reciprocal qualities. Instead, it was now intimately connected to support for the American cause—the cause of propertied white men who were protesting British rule because it had threatened to divest them of their property and the absolute liberty they had hitherto enjoyed in its "truck, barter and exchange."[60]

Coherent as this public good might have been among white patriots, its ability to order the expansive American marketplace remained limited.

Newspaper pronouncements and new statutes designed to regulate the market mostly reverberated within an echo-chamber of literate East Coast residents. On Pennsylvania's western fringes, with 1768's Treaty of Fort Stanwix and the British abandonment of Fort Pitt in 1772, trade became more chaotic and riskier by the day. Alexander McCormick, a small-time merchant hoping to trade a modest herd of cattle from Shawnee Town to Detroit in late 1776, found himself swept away by the violent political disputes engulfing the region. While Pennsylvania leaders urged him to cease commerce and the British accused him of helping the king's enemies, McCormick himself pleaded that he "Could do but Little Damage" to either side's cause by selling nine cows. In the end, his dilemma was resolved when he was taken prisoner by a party of Mingo Indians before reaching his destination.[61]

Meanwhile in South Carolina, notions of regulating the Indian trade for the public good of a British imperial interest were lost as patriots and their enemies fought for the support of the Creeks and Cherokees. If Indians refused patriots' overtures, the consequences could be dire, as the Cherokees found out in 1776. Burning crops and stealing cattle as they proceeded through Cherokee towns, the Carolina militiamen sent to neutralize them soon collected enough wares to hold an auction of their booty, which lasted two days and raised "Seven Thousand Seven Hundred & 22 Pounds." This was one vendue the Charleston authorities saw little need to regulate.[62]

Indeed, white rulers' commitment to the public good remained lukewarm in a range of familiar trading spaces. Carolina planters were not the only colonists to ignore market regulation if it threatened their profits. In Pennsylvania and Carolina, wartime assemblies experimented with strict regulation of auctions. Many Pennsylvania legislators were willing to go further than their South Carolina brethren, outlawing engrossing and forestalling, banning auctions altogether, implementing quality-control laws, forbidding the export of provisions outside the state, prohibiting the use of grains to make whiskey, and fixing prices of essential provisions. Yet by the time of the Treaty of Paris in 1783 the government had repealed many of these regulations that, as one had plainly stated, "in times of peace and order . . . might be an unjustifiable limitation of private right, and productive of inconvenience." War made Americans only temporarily receptive to regulating their markets. When peace returned, traders once again became suspicious of the public good's potential to cut into their profits.[63]

Still, the experience of a disordered marketplace had forced enduring changes in Americans' beliefs about how commerce should function. The

"Declaration of Rights" opening Pennsylvania's radical 1776 constitution enumerated in its third article that "the people of this State have the sole, exclusive and inherent right of governing and regulating the internal police of the same." The doctrine of internal police "insisted that the enjoyment of personal freedom and individual rights depended on the carefully regulated society that government would construct." Under this doctrine the regulation of local trade was an essential part of a government's duties. Thus the Revolution had persuaded white male Pennsylvanians that it was they, and they alone, who had the power to order their markets. Having successfully rejected British attempts to muscle in on this role and ensured that women traders knew their subservient position in the new political economy of regulation, they then seized this right.

Equally important, however, events had persuaded Pennsylvanians that government *should* have a role in organizing the local economy. This belief evidently was shared by some Carolinians who, immediately after the peace was agreed, moved to incorporate Charleston on the grounds that "the extent, growing Trades, and opulence of this Metropolis" made it "absolutely necessary" that "its internal Police [be] regulated." Like their Pennsylvanian compatriots, white men in Carolina had simultaneously admitted the necessity of regulating the marketplace and hinted that those who could not govern (blacks and women) were the proper subjects of this ambition.[64]

Although the Revolution planted an aspiration of regulating the market in the minds of many white Americans, however, it had provided no clear answer about how to achieve it. Nor had it produced a solid definition of what the public good might actually mean in the marketplace. Indeed, it had generated multiple definitions among diverse peoples—patriots, Loyalists, frontier settlers, and city dwellers among them—who often strongly disagreed about what it was. This multiplicity of public goods would prove remarkably difficult for Americans to manage, even as they took up the reins of state government in a properly independent way in 1783.

CHAPTER SIX

Making a Republican Marketplace

Philadelphia clerk and dry goods dealer George Nelson was born in Sulgrave, Northamptonshire, in mid-December 1736. In January 1754 he struck out for America. Unlike his namesake and countryman George Washington, whose family had left the same Midlands village for Virginia one hundred years earlier, Nelson did not become a rich planter and an illustrious statesmen. Instead, the committed Baptist led a more ordinary life in the Pennsylvania metropolis, where his journal from the 1780s and 1790s provides a rare glimpse into the everyday economic life of ordinary Americans at that critical time in the nation's past. In his daily entries Nelson takes us through the commercial spaces of his hometown, buying a neck of mutton in the Philadelphia marketplace to make a medicinal broth, trudging through streets deep in wintry slush to sell salt, picking up secondhand books at an estate auction, or tucking into a plate of beef after overseeing a daylong horse auction.[1]

Through his daily recording Nelson revealed the continuities in American commerce during the closing decades of the eighteenth century. Working as a clerk to livestock dealer Jacob Hiltzheimer in the service of the Continental Army, he traversed Philadelphia's hinterland, haggling with local farmers for forage. He was also charged with selling off the Continental Army's horses at periodic vendue sales, a job that included drumming up publicity by placing advance advertisements in the newspaper. By 1790, with the war long over, Nelson had set up as a small-time salt dealer, shuttling between the wharves, wholesalers, and his store.

His business bargains punctuated a constant and familiar round of visits to the main marketplace to buy meat, vegetables, and clothing for his family. Nelson maintained relationships with city tailors and dressmakers, from whom he obtained his own shirts as well as some items for his wife. Saturdays were Nelson's day for stopping by the city's vendues, where he sometimes bought books, fabric, salt, coffee, or sugar but on other occasions "made no purchase." Friday nights and early Saturday mornings often saw him socializing with his nieces and nephews, the Tomlinsons, in town from their Bucks County farm with a wagonload of produce to sell in the market. After completing their sales, drinking tea, and sometimes accepting gifts of sugar and coffee, the Tomlinsons would set off on the journey home. Making his round of the city's wharves, inns, stores, and marketplace, dealing in both public and private spaces, Nelson perpetuated the customary modes of trade established when he was a subject and continued when he became a citizen.

But Nelson's jottings also reveal that not everything stayed the same in the Philadelphia marketplace. First, continual inflation and a scarcity of hard currency meant that poorer Americans like Nelson regularly found even essential goods beyond their means. Hoping to taste some of a prize cow Hiltzheimer had slaughtered, Nelson lamented that he "wanted to have had a piece but it was too Dear." Instead the beef was sold to the French ambassador and to George Washington, who received the best cuts. Meanwhile Nelson retreated to his cellar to smoke some of his army beef rations "to take away the ill smell of the Pickle." A few months later, however, things had gotten worse, with "very distressing times no provision to be had in this City for us that are in the Service nor any Money to purchase any Oh that God would be pleased to look down upon us and save us." Nelson could afford to buy new clothes, but each purchase was accompanied by an exclamation at the inflated price. Eventually he bought sugar, coffee, and linen simply to get rid of his Continental money before it depreciated beyond all use. Meanwhile, "many of the Country Folks [are] refusing to sell but for hard Cash and the Poor [are] unable to procure what is absolutely necessary for Family support."[2]

As runaway inflation hampered Nelson's daily marketing in the early 1780s, he kept a close eye on the debates of the State Assembly concerning the financial crisis. By the time his diary picked up again in 1790, postwar inflation had subsided and political commentary disappeared from his jottings. But Nelson's notes about his peacetime business reveal how government policy continued to shape his daily trading. Now the dealer had a bank account, a checkbook, and loan office certificates. When Congress raised the duty on salt, Nelson rushed to sell what he had in stock so as to get as much clear profit as possible. Even in the mundane daily dealings of this small-scale trader, new economic institutions and state powers had quickly intruded on both the conditions and the instruments of marketing.

Because George Nelson was a "nobody," his experiences in the marketplace would have been familiar to many Americans. The spaces and practices of marketing changed little as people continued to patronize a familiar array of vendues, newspapers, stores, mills, inns, town markets, and wharves. The beginnings of America's financial revolution, and the power of state governments over trading spaces and their institutional scaffolding, did not prompt dramatic shifts in an established marketing system.

Nevertheless, Nelson's record also reveals how the heavy burden of war debt, coupled with relentless inflation, constricted daily dealings. Most critically, these problems continued to hamper vendues, which were now more likely to be sales of debtors' property. The number of these auctions increased because state governments made it easier for sheriffs to seize that property. The expansion of sheriffs' authority was part of a larger process, both in South Carolina and in Pennsylvania, of intensive institution building at state and county levels. The core county institutions under construction—both legally and physically—were courthouses and jails, which could then be filled by the sheriffs, justices of the peace, and judges, who might help creditors bring their debtors to heel. These were not the only new institutions influencing marketing, however. A glance at the statute books reveals that in north and south alike, state governments had been busily extending their police powers, many of which involved regulating trade.

The use of police powers to regulate the market was frequently justified on the grounds that it would sustain the public good. Yet the definition of the public and its good remained as slippery as ever. Americans had turned to the idea during revolutionary disorders that had periodically disrupted the economy from the early 1760s onward. Each of these periods of crisis, as we have seen, prompted heated debate between the different factions of the community, with only some agreeing that marketing should answer a public good and many disagreeing on what constituted that good. What is more, the process of ordering the marketplace was not a postrevolutionary innovation—it was part of ongoing efforts spanning the colonial era. These efforts had frequently picked out poorer whites, blacks, and Indians as in particular need of having their commercial dealings organized for this "good of the whole." In the 1780s, governing men continued to redefine the public good. In the young nation, the ideal rapidly became embellished with a new rhetoric and ideology imagining freeholders as conscientious citizens who were organizing local trade to preserve order and a virtuous republic.

Making marketplaces was therefore swept up in the process of making the new American republic. Creating orderly local trade was considered to be both the right and the responsibility of white republican freeholders. Even more than in the colonial era, the idea that some (black, poor) people were unable to conduct themselves in the marketplace for the "good of the whole" was integral to regulation. Through both power and persuasion by government officers, such people might become orderly participants. Being orderly, however, meant obeying rules designed to protect the property and the supremacy of white men. Yet in the unstable environment of the 1780s, where the authorities themselves often lacked legitimacy and reach over a large territory, enforcing this ambition was hard. The first decade of independent peacetime government was thus a time when a new vision of domestic trade emerged as freeholders threw themselves into the creation of a republican marketplace designed to answer the "good of the whole." Drawing up a new plan of government was no less challenging in the marketplace than it was in the state Assembly, however, especially when freeholders seemed willing to break their own rules to put the preservation and increase of their own property and wealth above everything else.

CONTINUITIES

Independence did not immediately transform the American marketplace. Neither the mechanisms of trade nor the potential of inflation and war debt to destabilize them changed dramatically when the war ended. Even though state governments took steps to solve the financial crisis, it nevertheless persisted for much of the republic's first fifteen years. "Trade is in a most wretched state," complained Philadelphia merchant and vendue master Benjamin Fuller in November 1784, "and I am convinced many Bankruptcies must take place in the course of a year or two." "I have never had so much trouble in the Sale of any Goods in my Life," wrote another exasperated city trader almost a year to the day later. Fuller endured the hard times by concentrating on the West Indian trade and avoiding all European "adventures." Carolinians suffered along with their Pennsylvania countrymen and countrywomen. Inland residents complained to the state Assembly that a lack of hard currency was severely curtailing trade. The petitioners of Edgefield County identified "an almost total want of Circulating meadium," meaning "that no property amoung them will if sold for money command 1/5 or 1/6 part of its intrinsic Value." Charleston merchants suffered at the hands of British traders who had remained in the city after its occupation.

These merchants, complained the "resident" traders who had fled in 1781, used their better financial position to engage in the "practice of buying up whole stores of Goods" so as to become "general Engrocers" of city retail. What is more, this habit created "artificial scarcities of the most necessary articles," claimed the native merchants, whose patriot allegiance prompted them to lay the blame for their woes at the door of the city's Loyalist traders, even as they drew on age-old English definitions of what made a market-place fair.[3]

Inflation meant that army quartermasters found feeding and clothing soldiers as tricky during peace as in wartime. Army suppliers were still forced to accept late payment, often in a paper currency they considered worthless. The freeholders of York County, Pennsylvania, petitioned the Assembly to recover "considerable sums ... due for supplies of grain, cattle, hay, pasturage, transportation etc." Requesting that they be "put upon an equal footing with all publick Creditors as well the Army as they are Citizens in funding the Debt," the farmers pointedly remarked that they were "unacquainted with any Publick happyness unconected with property, and as the designs of Government is to make people happier, they wish to enjoy as much of their property as possible." But with the government's financial situation not improving and its money depreciating, quick payment remained elusive.[4]

A succession of Philadelphia vendues to sell off horses and wagons at first brought much-needed income to the army's coffers, but even before the peace George Nelson reported that the latest "Vendue for the sales of old Geers Waggons etc ... sold so poorly that we left of [f] at Dinner time." Aware of the army's reputation as an unreliable customer, some Pennsylvanians refused altogether to do business. David Duncan, in charge of provisioning soldiers stationed around Pittsburgh, noted that he had been unable to acquire any supplies "since the exchange came to One Hundred & Seventy five, for now the People seems not to be willing to sell their property for state money." Two months later the situation had worsened, with Duncan "very hard set to furnish the Troops with provisions" and resorting to "paying with his own notes."[5]

Persisting instability did not, however, prompt a wholesale transformation of marketing places and practices. People bought and sold goods in familiar market spaces. Market dealings between farmers, tradesmen, and the military had long been structured around ad hoc commercial relationships with individual suppliers. Duncan's arduous tours of the countryside, much like Christopher Marshall's wartime experiences in Lancaster, were common for army contractors, who relied on striking multiple bargains with farmers on their property. Whereas British military provisioning in the metropole centered on competition for long-term contracts among men whose sole business was feeding soldiers and sailors, British and American armies alike had had to be satisfied with a far more face-to-face process, characteristic of so much marketing in the expansive rural landscape.[6]

As Duncan's Pittsburgh experience also reveals, Europeans replicated familiar market spaces as they moved westward. A marketing system in which person-to-person deals, rural stores, and vendue sales combined with European-style markets became more embedded in eastern America as it also became foundational to western commerce. The hybrid marketplace had survived the conflict to continue its expansion. Its endurance meant that ordinary Americans like George Nelson maintained commercial itineraries taking them to a familiar array of fixed and transient commercial spaces.

Traders who had built up colonial trading networks revived and expanded them in the early republic. Philadelphia tanner Jonathan Meredith operated an intricate business that relied on a set of loyal suppliers and customers to keep it afloat even when he "never was in greater want of Cash." Meredith already deemed his tannery a great success before the war, since it had provided him with "every comfort that this world can produce." After sitting out the conflict on "a large farm of my own about ten Miles distant" from the city, he returned in the early 1780s to pick up where he had left off. Unencumbered by the battle for privileges waged by competing guilds in some British cities until the nineteenth century, Meredith's city tanyards were the control center of an expansive business geared toward the profitable transformation of skins into the finest leather. The tanner bought some partially tanned hides from long-standing suppliers in Montgomery County, Christiana Bridge, Carlisle, Trenton, and Lancaster County. He contracted annually with multiple city butchers to take as many hides as they could give him. Once they were cured, he shipped the skins to numerous customers, including the nationally renowned coachmaker John Bringhurst of Germantown, who used them to upholster his luxury vehicles. Meredith also sold his products to bootmakers and shoemakers in New York and Connecticut, and in the 1780s he was attempting to establish connections with Alexandria and Richmond, Virginia.[7]

Meredith's creditable status as a man of property helped him keep his marketing network running even in a troubled economy. When business associates failed to pay, he used creative and profitable methods to keep the debt out of court; Montgomery County tanner Andrew Rud supplied Meredith with free bar iron to avoid having his debts called in. For Meredith, the Revolution forced a hiatus in the expansion of his trade but had little effect on his ability to be master of an extensive and dynamic commercial network.[8]

Those marketing hubs that dotted the Pennsylvania and South Carolina countryside also came through the Revolution unscathed. Mills, ferries, and stores continued as the main means of reaching Americans scattered across the expansive (and expanding) landscape. The 1780s found Carolina storekeeper William Logan doggedly persisting in his trade, which he had pursued ever since establishing his first store at Bacon's Bridge in the early 1750s. By the time the Revolutionary War came to the Carolina backcountry, Logan was settled at Pon Pon, the "proprietor of a Lott of Land, with very large and Convenient Rice Stores & a Counting Houses thereon." But misfortune visited the dealer once again when patriot forces burned down his property in anticipation of the advancing British army. In 1785 Logan petitioned the state Assembly for compensation so he could once again re-establish his store.[9]

The need for these marketing hubs was just as strong in western Pennsylvania as it was in the south. As a merchant who made his way by supplying the inland trade, Philadelphia resident Anthony Kennedy received letters from men in want of stock to retail. David Stewart explained that he lived "in a part of the Country that would answer very well for keeping a Country Store . . . within a few perches of the Juniata River" and with "a Grist & Saw mill close by." Since "industrious" and "wealthy Germans" were in the vicinity and there was also a "mill handy to erect Boats," Stewart supposed the location "would answer you . . . to set up a Commission Store." Stewart was among many storekeepers setting up in places like Redstone, west of Pittsburgh. "There are three stores," noted Boston adventurer John May in his travel diary, "which take considerable money, but more produce, which again is sold for cash to people from Marietta, or bound to Kentucky."[10]

May had indeed been very pleased to find these stores and the small settlement of fifty houses they belonged to. In these western marchlands of European habitation, where shops or even taverns were sparse, rural people still relied mostly on itinerant traders and bargaining on the hoof for income and material necessities. Realizing this, May purchased a boat and took to peddling up and down the river goods he had hauled across country from Baltimore. Extremely satisfied with the fruits of his ingenuity, he exclaimed that he had been "busy as a bee all day. Took about $20 in cash, and this at a place where one would never think of looking for inhabitants, much less for money." May clearly thought himself a true original, but he was merely following in the footsteps of the many Europeans, Africans, and Indians who had long made their way by selling goods to anyone passing who would buy.[11]

Indeed, May was far from alone in his endeavors in these first years of independence. While they were imprisoned at Lancaster toward the end of the war, British soldiers raised the ire of American shopkeepers by sending women camp followers out across the countryside with baskets of wares "under the wholesale price at London." At Pittsburgh, meanwhile, American soldiers had "made a Common practice" of selling government grain supplies for whiskey "at every opportunity." In Upcountry South Carolina, residents noted the presence of New York peddlers importing goods from northward and siphoning off much of the region's hard currency, while a 1785 petition from the residents of St. James Santee documented the flourishing once again of "Patroons of Schooners and other small Craft" that "pass and re-pass up and own our Rivers . . . to Trade, Traffick, Barter, and Sell to and with Negroes." The westward surge of Europeans in the decade after independence merely increased the commercial possibilities for traders who were willing to roam by boat, by horse, or on foot no matter how adverse the weather or the terrain.[12]

In South Carolina such movement created more opportunities for African traders. Yet new possibilities were accompanied by the intensifying of those market mechanisms designed to make enslaved people into commodities. As one of America's most vital and singular marketing devices, auctions showed little sign of diminishing in importance in the 1780s. Certainly an increase in bankruptcy-related sales continued to undermine the auction's historical reputation as a trouble-free way of selling land, people, and goods. Nevertheless, as a method for retailing imports, livestock, and the estates of the deceased, the sales proved ever more popular. George Nelson's weekly attendance at Philadelphia's numerous auctions in search of goods both for his household and for retail sale in his grocery business reveals the vendue's enduring value in everyday commercial life.

In both Philadelphia's and Charleston's newspapers, more sales than ever were listed in each issue. Auctions dealing purely in livestock were increasingly popular. In cities, the state-appointed job of vendue master emerged as a profitable and sought-after position. Under questioning from an Assembly committee about the revenues of his office, John Bayard, Philadelphia's official auctioneer, explained that "we have frequently from 100 to 150 different persons to call out for the purchase at a Sale, this keeps two sometimes three clerks . . . employed in Collecting & I have constantly more outstanding than the whole amount of my Commissions." In rural South Carolina, the new district court system prompted more regular local sales of estates, and in Camden District alone there was roughly one sale a month. At each sale, widows and relatives purchased some of the property on offer, but with five, ten, and sometimes twenty people also buying livestock, enslaved Africans, kitchenware, tools, and clothing, the vendue was a vital opportunity for Upcountry settlers to acquire necessary items for their homes and farms. That residents could now also purchase unclaimed stray horses and cows at sales timed to coincide with court sessions made them even more useful.[13]

In the meantime, Americans placed ever more faith in traditional marketplaces designed to bring buyers and sellers together for a well-regulated commerce. Governing assemblies and townspeople collaborated to create new marketplaces and revivify existing regulatory regimes. In South Carolina citizens of Winnsborough, Belleville, Camden, and Georgetown all petitioned the Senate during the 1780s to create markets and fairs in their towns "by law." Georgetown inhabitants lodged two petitions in 1787, first requesting the power to better regulate the town and its wharves, then calling for a market square, since there was "no particular place assigned for the reception of Butchers Meat, Poultry, Butter etc that comes for sale from the Country." In Philadelphia the Assembly approved the creation of a new marketplace at Callowhill in the Northern Liberties. As Europeans swarmed into western Pennsylvania, town founders incorporated marketplaces into the new settlements designed to anchor "civilization" in the state's more sparsely occupied reaches. In their 1789 act of incorporation, the residents of Easton, Pennsylvania, provided for "two markets each week . . . and two fairs in the year."[14]

Efforts to "improve" the main provisions markets in both Philadelphia and Charleston gathered pace rapidly in the 1780s. In 1786 a new act empowered Philadelphia's wardens to extend the main market sheds from Third Street to Fourth Street. Legislation cited petitions from "the inhabitants of the city of Philadelphia and the counties bordering thereon" arguing for an extension to the marketplace, which was now too small to protect the numerous country dealers "from the inclemency of the weather." In all, the legislature had received a flood of petitions both for and against the market's extension, not only from city residents but also from inhabitants of Bucks, Chester, York, Lancaster, and Dauphin Counties. Many of the appeals reached the Assembly on printed petition templates circulated as part of one of the earliest petitioning campaigns in the state. This level of organization, coupled with the number of signatures on these appeals, suggests that the condition of Philadelphia's central market was of major concern to a large number of Pennsylvanians; levels of engagement almost matched the intensity of petitions addressing the division of counties and the relocation of county seats.[15]

The importance of Philadelphia's provisions market made it a priority for improved regulation. Previously under the control of the city's corporation, the market was left unregulated when the colonial infrastructure was abolished on the grounds that "all powers and jurisdictions ... not founded on the authority of the people became null and void." In its place, a group of elected wardens took charge, but they quickly proved ineffectual, and in 1789 a new act of incorporation once again placed the power of "the promotion of trade" and "the suppression of vice and immorality" in the hands of a mayor and aldermen. A mere three days after the city's new rulers had processed to the City Tavern and offered a solemn address to George Washington congratulating him on his "Civil Policy ... uniting civil Liberty with effective Government," they convened a committee "to prepare Rules and Regulations respecting the Markets in the City." Drawing up market ordinances and attending to the status of hawkers and hucksters then continued as the main order of business for a corporation coming to terms with its new duties.[16]

With the racial order at stake, the Charleston authorities never lost their enthusiasm for market regulation. Although the 1770s fish market was the high point of colonial market organization, its construction did not preclude ongoing improvements. Using the new police powers granted by Charleston's 1783 incorporation, commissioners set about a wholesale reorganization of provisioning. A new 1786 act for regulating the city's markets outlined an ambitious and more detailed plan for their operation. In 1788 Charles Pinckney leased a prime plot of land to the city council to construct more extensive market sheds. These sheds were completed in 1804, and the city market still stands today.[17]

Viewing the republican marketplace from the ground up therefore uncovers few drastic innovations in the spaces and mechanisms of commerce. No doubt war debt and inflation continued to jam the gears of market exchange. Nevertheless, these difficulties did not prompt a physical transformation of the market. With more stores, more mills, more expansive networks of buying and selling, a torrent of commercial print, and larger and more bustling marketplaces, the postrevolutionary commercial scene was simply a scaled-up version of its colonial predecessor. Indeed, it is very important to recognize this continuity, since it underlines that for most Europeans and African Americans the market changed only marginally in the immediate wake of independence. Although problems of money supply and inflation continued to hamper trade in the 1780s, these blockages failed to change the course of the river of commerce that had already carved its path through the American landscape over the preceding century.

FREEHOLDER CITIZENS AND INTERNAL POLICE IN THE MARKETPLACE

Surveying the spaces and mechanisms of trade after 1783 rightly conveys the structural continuities of the American marketplace. However, even as a physical status quo endured, important new processes were afoot in its regulation. Although authorities had already debated the need for a more comprehensive "internal police" of the marketplace in the 1760s and 1770s, this concept came into its own after 1783. Having seized from the British the right to act as the police of their marketplaces, ruling Pennsylvanians and South Carolinians set about fulfilling their responsibilities with gusto.

Legislative programs to order traders took shape most quickly in the urban marketplace. The concept of internal police was expansive, however, permitting regulatory activities to extend far beyond cities. Spurred on by their newly acquired power and independence, and by their dedication to creating a virtuous republic, citizens converged on the necessity of creating a marketplace that could bolster the public good. As Judge Nathaniel Pendleton explained to the Georgia grand jurors in his 1787 charge, "The close of the late war with Great Britain having established our independence" had bestowed on Americans "the exclusive power of modelling our government on principles most apparently conducive to our prosperity." Prosperity, of course, came from the orderly trade of property by its (white) owners. The quest to model effective government at state level had to encompass the regulation of commerce.[18]

The wharves of Southwark, a southerly suburb of Philadelphia, were among the earliest marketing spaces to feel the effect of such regulation. The war was not yet won, but Pennsylvania nevertheless had its own state government with, as we have seen, a constitution that prominently claimed the power of internal police over its territory. Wharves had functioned as a vital marketing space throughout Philadelphia's colonial era. Mostly privately owned and packed with various businesses designed to exploit valuable land to its full potential, these spaces embodied the free reign of private property

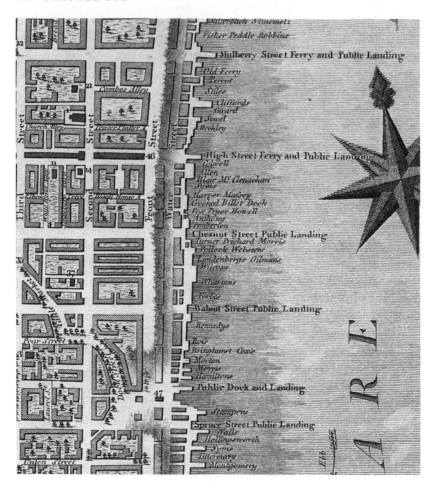

FIGURE 6.1 Public and private wharves in early national Philadelphia, extract from *This Plan of the City of Philadelphia and Its Environs (showing the Improved Parts)*, Johns Hills, Philadelphia, 1797. Library of Congress, Geography and Maps Division.

in so many corners of the American marketplace. In Southwark, with "no Public or Corporate Capacity to represent" the inhabitants, by 1769 private wharves had threatened to occupy all of the shore, since "proper care was not, nor could be taken to leave Room for public landings." With property prices spiraling higher, some men of "fortune, integrity and public spirit" stepped in to fix the bidding at the auction of a prime water lot, purchase it for a reasonable price, and manage it for the public. Such public-private partnerships could be fragile, however, and when an original purchaser's descendant claimed his share as private property in 1776, the cause of the public landing seemed lost.

Yet a renewed enthusiasm for the public good among the state's legislators saved the day. Recounting the sorry saga to the state Assembly in a 1781 "application to make sure" that the land "does not fall into private hands," the Southwark petitioners found a friendly ear in a government happy to endorse an increased role for the "public." By 1782 the Commonwealth had passed a statute mandating a trusteeship to preserve the wharf as a public landing. The trustees were permitted to levy a tax on local residents to recover the cost of buying the lot from the original owner's descendants. The act also allowed the wharf to be farmed out to a contractor who would manage it for seven years. Thus the public-private partnership was recreated, but with the force of both the law and the Commonwealth behind it to ensure that the terms of agreement would be upheld in the name of the public good.[19]

The statute securing this Southwark wharf for the commercial "good of the whole" was a mere brick in a mansion of legislation erected by state government in both Pennsylvania and South Carolina during this era. As we have seen, marketplaces, itinerant traders, and to some extent vendues and wharves had all been regulated by colonial assemblies during the 1700s. However, the last two decades of the century found local governments energetically dedicated to increasing their authority over the commercial spaces under their jurisdiction. People who frequented or owned these places thus felt the hand of government more immediately than before.

Because of their unstinting popularity as the beating heart of daily trade, marketplaces and market people were prime targets for the regulatory ambitions of an enthusiastic citizenry. In Philadelphia's growing northerly districts, new market houses at Callowhill and in the Northern Liberties were designed to foster orderly traders who abided by the clerk's commands. Callowhill's dealers were more forcefully directed beneath the eaves of the market house by a 1789 law outlawing door-to-door selling. The Charleston corporation, meanwhile, was granted ownership of the fish market, Tradd Street markets, and beef market, which were the only legitimate spaces where sellers were permitted to retail provisions. People who sold "at any other place within this city than the public markets before established" would face a fine and seizure of their property if white or a whipping and six hours in the stocks if black. With statutes rolling out identical market regulations in Belleville, Greenville, Winnsborough, Georgetown, Camden, and the new state capital at Columbia, Carolinians were much more likely than their colonial forebears to encounter the clerk of the market, hear his bell, and see his official set of weights and measures portioning out their produce.[20]

This increased oversight did not end when market people unpacked their goods in the marketplace. Sellers were used to standing with traders who sold roughly the same goods they offered or had traveled from the same region. Yet newly incorporated city authorities took a special interest in the internal order of market stalls. Charleston's commissioners reserved six places especially for planters who wished to send enslaved people to retail produce. Carlisle's corporation conducted a campaign against engrossing butter in its newly built marketplace. Philadelphia's corporation was still more exacting. As retailers of "country produce," George Nelson's Bucks County relatives were confined to "the space under the eaves of the shambles, on the south side thereof, of the breadth of five feet, beginning five feet from the west end of the court house and extending to the east line of Third-street, and from the west line of Third-street, to the east line of Fourth-street . . . leaving all the passages between the stalls open for passengers." Where they were permitted to park their wagon was also strictly regulated by this 1798 ordinance, the third concerning the main marketplace since the corporation was reestablished in 1789. Sellers of earthenware, sellers of roots and herbs, and butchers were also subject to rigorous regulation, with butchers required to ensure that any "block, benches, tubs, or other things used" extended no more than two feet six inches from the edge of the market house. The corporation minutes make it clear that the common council took its enforcement duties very seriously, spending plenty of time discussing the order of market space as well as making expeditions to Market Street.[21]

For traders in the main market shambles who were familiar with the presence of officials and rules in their commercial lives, these new regulations were often a matter of degree. In other spaces the arrival of officials with their novel decrees was more surprising. In both Philadelphia and Charleston, wharf owners had enjoyed substantial freedom to organize trade on their property. Since each wharf had its own set of scales and a variety of stores and business premises available for rent, the wharfinger largely avoided regulation of his profits. He (seldom was the owner a woman) cleared a profit every time commodities were loaded onto or unloaded from a ship, for weighing and storing goods, and for the rental of stores or warehouse space. Royal customs officers were visible on the waterfront, but their authority could easily be undermined or avoided. Perhaps the most stringent regulation was Charleston's 1768 act setting rates of wharfage and storage, a statute drawn up in response to complaints that merchants and wharfingers were often locked in dispute about the proper charges.[22]

While there was no effort to divest wharf owners of their property, with independence came a surge in waterside regulation. From the mid-1780s, Charleston's wharves were constantly surveyed by the harbor master, who was granted "full power and authority" to ascertain the tonnage of vessels, collect customs duties, and police the commercial (and other) activities of black and white seamen at the wharf. As part of the more rigorous regulation of the city's provisions markets, the wharves were recognized as an important site of retail and wharf owners were required to swear an oath that scales were accurate and would be used to "do impartial justice between buyer and seller." The city council regulated the presence of flammable naval stores at the wharves, granting the privilege of landing tar and pitch to just three of the wealthiest wharfingers. Philadelphians likewise had to accommodate themselves to a new waterfront office, occupied by seven wardens and a customs collector whose job it was to oversee trade on the bustling Delaware riverfront. Wharf owners had to adhere to regulations governing traffic at the wharves while also submitting any plans for their development to the wardens for consideration. As the city's wharves continued their expansion into Southwark and the Northern Liberties, similar regulations were rolled out in these districts.[23]

If the policing of commerce at wharves and in marketplaces, which were fixed and circumscribed in their character, was a relatively familiar and straightforward task, ordering early America's more mobile commercial spaces presented a greater challenge for its novice state governments. Rural mills and ferries, vendue sales, and itinerant traders overlaid rural Pennsylvania and South Carolina, creating a fluid network of marketplaces distributing goods among white settlers, Indians, and Africans. These were the very places where British authorities and proprietors had struggled to make traders deal according to their rules: places that colonial governments had often left to the rule of credit unless Indians and Africans were especially visible in them. Yet despite these historical challenges, some white American lawmakers were keen to apply their new policing ambitions to them as well, meaning that traders in these places confronted officials and their regulations for the first time. What is more, in South Carolina, where Africans were a majority, the policing effort was visibly more intensive.

Vendue sales had already been the subject of some colonial decrees, especially at the height of the Revolution, but in the 1780s state governments made it clear that they would now be considered proper objects not only for regulation, but also for taxation. In Philadelphia, the Northern Liberties, and Moyamensing, multiple official vendue masters were installed, giving a £2,000 bond for good behavior in exchange for the privilege of holding sales in any place that was "most convenient" to them. While such vendue masters had featured in both the Charleston and Philadelphia retail landscapes since the mid-eighteenth century, additional rules placed them in a more intricate regulatory regime. The South Carolina officeholder had to hold American citizenship, was not allowed to bid up the price at sales, and was required to keep accounts for inspection by the state government. In both states, vendue profits would now also be subject to a tax of at least 1 percent.[24]

The state's increasing interest in auctions reached further than the stoop of the city vendue master's rooms because the unstable economy caused a much larger proportion of vendue sales to be composed of debtors' confiscated property. At the height of the economic crisis in 1787, over half of all vendues advertised in the *Pennsylvania Gazette* were triggered by the seizure of property for debt. Often the property of numerous debtors was offered for sale at once. This share of sheriff-run debtor sales exceeded those advertised during the late 1760s, when the province had suffered its first credit crisis. In South Carolina, where there had been no noticeable increase in such sales before the Revolution and auctions of debtors' goods hovered at about 10 percent of total advertised sales, two-thirds of sales listed in 1787 were sheriff's auctions. In such dire economic times, the vendue had been appropriated by state-appointed officers in their quest to enforce the law and "protect" the property of creditors.[25]

The South Carolina authorities further deployed vendues to extend their influence into the rural economy, well beyond Charleston. As we have seen, the state's efforts to create a wide network of district courts brought regular sheriff-run vendues of estates to Upcountry districts such as Camden. Sheriffs and justices of the peace, selected by the General Assembly, first arrived as part of 1785's Circuit Court Act, superseded by a 1791 revision that increased the apparatus of local justice. In addition to overseeing the vendues of debtors' goods and estates of the deceased, sheriffs were also responsible for selling unclaimed stray animals, the property of tax evaders, and the labor of those prosecuted for vagrancy. Sales of people and property were held concurrently with quarterly court sessions, attracting a large crowd and occasioning no little debate about the most advantageous manner of auctioning off the horses, cows, and pigs that were in demand among Upcountry planters.[26]

The role of justices of the peace in policing the local economy was novel in rural South Carolina but not completely new elsewhere in America. By the middle of the eighteenth century, Pennsylvania's county courts were, as we have seen, already issuing licenses to peddlers and tavern keepers, while sheriffs oversaw auctions. Yet these officers did not get additional powers after the Revolution. They continued to be elected by their fellow freeholders rather than appointed by the state Assembly. When independent authorities in South Carolina finally got around to creating comprehensive institutions of local justice, they not only directly recruited officers but also gave them more power to regulate day-to-day economic transactions than other men in their position. Hence, while Carolina justices of the peace granted tavern licenses as their Pennsylvania compatriots did, they also decided which storekeepers and forge owners could sell alcohol and set the prices innkeepers charged for lodging, horse stabling, cold and hot food, hot drinks, gin, rum, punch, brandy, whiskey, madeira wine, burgundy, champagne, domestic and imported beer, and cider. In at least one county, the county clerk was given a set of weights and measures, presumably to provide an official standard in the sale of provisions, alcohol, and commodities.[27]

This new court system also gave freeholders more tools to prosecute the many mobile traders roaming around South Carolina's rural districts. White peddlers continued to seek licenses from the state government according to the 1738 peddling law, which had carefully targeted itinerant Africans and whites who were willing to trade with enslaved people. However, presumably as part of a more concerted effort to put a stop to interracial dealing, the newly appointed Upcountry justices of the peace were given additional authority over itinerant traders. They derived their powers from two statutes. A 1787 law targeted vagrancy, and the 1791 revision of the county court system created intermediate courts whose purview included the activities of free and enslaved Africans. South Carolina's new vagrancy law, designed to prosecute those people who might "become dangerous members of the community," was directed at "idle and disorderly persons" who were "a grievance to the honest and industrious" population through their "wandering from place to place without any known residence." Rather than "occupying or being in possession of some piece of land," these people made their way by "going about the country swapping and bartering horses or negroes." But court proceedings make it clear that dealing with enslaved people, rather than in them, could also result in prosecution for vagrancy. Edmond Franklin came under suspicion from his Pendleton County neighbors in 1792 when he seemed to suddenly acquire livestock. According to one witness, Franklin and his wife "had Dealings with the Negroes" belonging both to Mrs. Ropes and to "Perkins." Whereas such commercial relations might previously have been under the radar, thanks to the extended reach of the local court Franklin was now at risk of being deemed a vagrant and sold by auction into a year's servitude. The punishment meted out to the enslaved Africans involved was not recorded.[28]

By the early 1790s many fewer marketplaces operated free from the hand of government. Even South Carolina's mills were subject to a law limiting the amount of grain the miller could take in toll. Of course, for some farmers mill toll rates might have been a secondary concern, given the federal taxes on their stills and their whiskey that they had to pay in hard-to-find silver and gold. About the only marketplace left relatively untrammeled by government statute was the trade with Native Americans that, until federal intervention in the 1790s, was unencumbered by new laws. But in the brave new world of the 1780s, relations between Indians and whites were rarely friendly enough to permit the kind of commercial relationships forged in the colonial era. Indigenous people faced government-sponsored plunder and violence executed by European frontier people with the assistance of the federal government.[29]

Western markets were thus shaped not only by commercial necessity, but by Europeans' ideological ambitions of American empire building. Closer to the East Coast, market regulation was equally emerging as an ideological imperative as well as a practical one. States' attempts to order the market had two goals; to put freeholder citizens in charge of local trade and to produce rhetoric portraying the virtuous citizen as a man who took control of domestic commerce for the good of the republic. Leading officials, often judges, thus took it upon themselves not only to make new laws, but also to give officeholders practical advice concerning their enforcement duties. In his 1787 address, Judge Pendleton also reminded his audience that "it is peculiarly incumbent to interest yourselves in the conduct of all around you—you have the greatest property to loose, and your example is therefore of great weight—investigate the police of your district." Elucidating a nexus of property, power, and good order embodied in the freeholder officers of the recently established local court system, Pendleton exhorted men to work with the state and its new regulatory regime to ensure that their power was firmly rooted in the diffuse marketplaces scattered over rural South Carolina.[30]

Placing as much commerce as possible under the watchful eyes of freeholders was one option for increasing control. As we have seen, county quarter sessions had become the focus both for marketing and for its regulation.

These events thus gave white men the ideal opportunity to display their power and virtue in the local marketplace. At the sessions, freeholders held propertyless white and enslaved neighbors to account for trading with each other or tried them for swindling other citizens, selling liquor at more than the official price, or not following the correct procedures when they found stray animals. Over the same few days as the court met, the sheriff auctioned off the property of debtors and sold stray animals, which only freemen had the authority to seize, round up, advertise, or sell.[31]

Freemen's authority was then further augmented by holding court sessions on their private property. At first the Spartanburgh court met on the plantation of John Wood. It then relocated to more permanent quarters on a two-acre lot donated by local freeholder Thomas Williamson. The construction of a courthouse and jail was under way by 1787, with priority given to the erection of "jail, stocks & Pillory to be finished in the present year." The Winton county court, meanwhile, met at the "Big House" belonging to freeholder Charles Brown, where at least one convicted thief was "carried to the most Public Place in the Courtyard" so that "he should on his bare Back receive Thurty nine lashes well laid on by . . . the directions of the Sheriff." Carolina property holders used the requirements of the county court act to concentrate local commerce on their property and to ensure that it was regulated according to their application of the law. With the quarter sessions also a major opportunity to socialize and trade, income from such dealings might well end up in the pockets of the freeholder who had generously given over his property for the use of the court.[32]

In cities like Charleston and Philadelphia, opportunities for refining the role of citizen policeman also abounded. Reinvigorated corporations, charged with regulating economic life as it unfolded in a growing city's many commercial spaces, were a good prospect for men aiming to build reputations as republican citizens, on the lookout for the "good of the whole." Postrevolutionary acts of incorporation redrew these municipal bodies as expressions of republican government. As befitted a slaveholding republic, Charleston's incorporation charter entrusted the "preservation of peace and good order" to thirteen freeholder wardens, who were responsible for keeping "it in their respective wards, to issue warrants, and cause all offenders against law to be brought before them." Philadelphia's 1789 charter announced that "the intention of civil government is to provide for the order, safety and happiness of the people." By approving the document, the state Assembly ratified an incorporation devoting no fewer than eleven articles to the proper election of officers, who were subject to dismissal for misconduct so as "to avoid an entire dependence" on their positions. These upstanding freeholders were then given the authority, should they wish, of regulating brokers in the city, establishing an assize of bread, wine, beer, wood, "and other things," and, of course, regulating the markets and taking possession of the former corporation's wharves. When they welcomed George Washington to the city and took up their positions at Philadelphia's July 4 celebrations, the corporation officers cemented their role as the guardians of good order in the city. The municipal corporation's extended role in the marketplace was as much an act of republican state building by worthy freeholders as it was a project of regulation.[33]

The practice of republican citizenship in the marketplace necessitated a particular relationship between freeholders and poor whites in this space. The latter were expected to conduct commerce so as to realize the republican goal of the well-ordered marketplace. While hucksters and dealers had always been subject to surveillance and punishment, now these efforts became enmeshed in a new discourse promoting the idea of the useful and virtuous citizen. It was the duty of all citizens in the marketplace to uphold the "civil economy," explained one newspaper commentator. No doubt hoping to inculcate such values as early as possible, children's authors adapted the popular "Cries" of the marketplace series from its London original for an American audience. Philadelphia readers could enjoy picturesque portrayals of common market people such as the sellers of sweet potatoes, oysters, and milk, accompanied by a carefully composed text designed to educate the young citizen reader. "'Any matches today?'" cried the matchgirl: "They are surely cheap enough, and the poor child deserves better to be encouraged, than many other children, who hawk about the streets, apples and other fruit, which the farmers ought to sell to the people for use, and not to hucksters." However, the author did concede that a fruit seller might also be "a useful person, so long as she sells her apples, peaches . . . only when they are ripe, and to good children, for no others deserve such enjoyments." Readers were further assured that "the good woman . . . has made much money by observing the maxim 'honesty is the best policy.' She sells for small profit and never cheats." Respectful of the right of the independent yeoman to the just profits of his land, and putting aside greed in the name of a virtuous deal, the huckster would inhabit her proper place in the well-ordered market.[34]

As the *Toy Shop*'s description of the female fruit seller suggests, this market also placed its officers at the helm of a gendered order. When they rehearsed their governing duties, white male freeholders imagined a particular role for white women that recognized them as economic citizens but limited their scope for independent action. As had been the case during nonimportation, white women were permitted a measure of participation in the political economy of the marketplace, but only through the proper channels. While all-female groups of petitioners had been exceedingly rare before the Revolution, the early republic frequently saw women appealing to their government with their economic grievances. Female hucksters in Philadelphia approached the corporation "praying respectively to be permitted to sit in the market to supply the country people with breakfasts, and to sell fruit etc in the market," while Charleston's seamstresses implored the Assembly to halt the importing of the "ready made cloths & slops" that were selling more cheaply than their labor. Susanna Ford, meanwhile, was part of a group of male and female petitioners lobbying for her right to keep a ferry "for the benefit of travellers and the Publick Good." As Ford's request reveals, women often used language demonstrating their commitment to the values of the republican marketplace.[35]

Ford's petition also argued for the privilege of keeping a ferry on the grounds that she had lost both her husband and her property in the name of her "countries cause," reasoning frequently deployed by men in the same position. Yet Ford was unsuccessful, as were the other women who sought the licenses, or the legislation, that would have made them active participants in fashioning the republican marketplace. Despite multiple petitions by hucksters and proposals from both the clerk of the market and the Assembly for a licensing system, the Pennsylvania authorities were slow to authorize peddlers' presence in the marketplace. Charleston's seamstresses were similarly unsuccessful, suffering a rebuke from the South Carolina Assembly putting them firmly in their place as objects of charity as opposed to economic citizens with a right to question the wisdom of the state's tariff regime. Reporting on their situation, the house committee portrayed the women as "distressed persons" worthy of their "humane attention" but noted that "it has seldome been the policy of well-regulated states to give a monopoly of the home market to domestick industry." This may have been a veiled criticism of British mercantilism, but it was certainly not an accurate description of state policy. Perhaps the committeemen assumed that a group of women seamstresses would not know either way. Like their forebears during the nonimportation era, they could not entertain the prospect of women taking an active role in defining the economic public good but sought to keep them as subjects of an order wholly determined by men.[36]

But the Carolina committeemen also gave another reason for refusing to raise the duty on imports of ready-made clothing. "A greater duty," they argued, "would in fact amount to a heavy tax on another very numerous part of the community." Since enslaved people were in all likelihood the main market for ready-made clothing, we must assume that the slaveholding committeemen's decision was informed by the prospect of a change eating directly into their own profits. Although using language that skirted the real issue at hand, the committee's response nevertheless draws our attention to the critical way race also contributed to the construction of the South Carolina freeholders' role in ordering the market. Freeholders did not seek to eliminate enslaved people from the marketplace, a move that would damage the foundations of their wealth. Instead, good policing of blacks meant ensuring that their economic dealings would not threaten the livelihood of freeholders, nor would the enslaved conduct themselves in a manner contravening the "peace and good order" of the marketplace. In short, blacks could participate, but only within the limits dictated by whites.[37]

This vision united freeholders of different social degrees in South Carolina. Charleston's tailors embraced it with a 1794 announcement in the local newspaper on the question of slaves "renting shops, rooms or houses and carrying on trades, without being in the employment and under the directions of freemen." Inimical to those whites who are "bound to pay the state tax" and "perform all the duties of a citizen," such practices should be punished, argued the tailors, by strict application of the fines enumerated in the city council's recent ordinances. Following the example of Charleston's cordwainers, these tradesmen had recast a historic complaint concerning "unfair" competition from enslaved laborers as a source of disorder in the republican marketplace. Freeholders who encouraged the independence of black tailors were legitimate targets for punishment, though of course training and owning African tailors was permitted. Such reasoning also underpinned the city council's reserving six stalls in the provisions market for enslaved people present on behalf of their masters; this black commerce was for freeholders' gain, making it acceptable even in the heart of urban marketing.[38]

At the same time, in his 1789 charge to the city's grand jury, Justice John Faucheraud Grimké reinforced these principles by drawing freeholders' attention to "an act for the better ordering and governing of negroes and other slaves," passed May 10, 1740. "Give it an attentive perusal," said Grimké, "and if there should appear to you any defects in the policy of it; or that the law is too harsh and severe upon that unfortunate race of mankind . . . soften off its rigorous effects . . . shew to the world, that having obtained your own liberty, you well know how to prize it, and that you are truly sensible how dear it is to mankind, by extending to the coloured people in our State as much indulgence as their unhappy subordinate situation will admit of." Clothing his pronouncement in a suitable dose of sentiment and paternalism, Grimké was all the same directing freeholders to a well-known slave code decisive in its brutal determination to deprive enslaved Africans of the mobility, property, and independence integral to their successful participation in South Carolina's expansive marketing networks. Republican slaveowning freeholders, argued Grimké, would do well to follow this model, being sure to show kindness to the enslaved, but on no account to allow sentimentality to cloud their judgment so as to permit Africans to enjoy economic freedoms reserved by right for their owners.[39]

A decade after the British had given up the thirteen colonies, elected officials such as William Mifflin, first magistrate of the Pennsylvania Commonwealth, looked at what they had achieved and were pleased with the order they had brought to the local government of commerce. "The Benefits which the Citizens enjoy, under the useful regulations that have been introduced into the Police of the City since its Incorporation, are universally acknowledged," announced Mifflin in his New Year's Eve speech to the corporation's officers. Much more than in the colonial era, commercial spaces had felt the hand of institutional regulation because of the commitment by those in power to the internal police of the economy. If the desire to police the marketplace had emerged during the tumultuous decades before 1783, it took flight over the following decade, when American rulers at last had some power to realize their ambitions.

These ambitions led to the creation of what superficially, in terms of volume of regulation, might seem to mirror a British economy governed by "interests" for the common good. Yet Americans had not built an exact replica of this economy of interests. Instead, this was a freeholders' marketplace; a well-ordered commercial system that functioned according to the needs of a well-policed republic in which race, gender, and also property would determine an individual's place. This republican marketplace had a hierarchy, with freeholders at the top, the enslaved at the bottom, and white women somewhere in between. But it did not assume that those at the top had any duty to look out for those at the bottom. Rather, the "public good" was the order adopted by freeholders, and whether it was good for them or not, those at the bottom were expected to obey it.[40]

LIBERTY, PROPERTY, AND THE PUBLIC GOOD

As the continuities between early modern British market regulation and that of the early republic suggest, Americans had never completely abandoned their belief in the need for government to intervene in local trade.

Yet regarding the state of economic regulation in the early United States on a continuum from its roots in British practice and culture has also revealed that not all regulatory regimes are the same. The common good as it had operated in the European marketplace did not transfer successfully to the American setting, where for a long time the private interest of individual traders had been equally important in determining where and how commercial exchange took place. Inventing a republican *public* good was therefore a process of reinterpreting the concept and reasserting its importance to everyday trading spaces. This was achieved by creating an internal police of republican citizens to order the young nation. In this respect an internal police was the logical outgrowth of those committees that had redefined the public good during the nonimportation movements of the 1760s and 1770s.

In the colonial marketplace, and during those nonimportation boycotts, however, trading according to the "good of the whole" was often questionable for dealers who had not customarily been compelled to obey such an ideal. In the republic the idea of internal police became so important not only because governing men wanted to become virtuous citizens. These men needed a philosophy that would justify increased government to the many Americans who remained unwilling to subject their trade and their property to regulation. Such men repeatedly challenged the authority claimed by state and county governments. Used to a lightly policed trade and high levels of negotiated authority, many Americans recoiled at these new, more vigorous institutional regimes. Many had just participated in a Revolution whose outcome seemed to question government's right to intervene at all in such matters.

Some aspects of government's increased presence in the marketplace would go unchallenged by the vast majority of white Americans. Seldom did people defend the rights of landless, enslaved, Native American, or even female participants in the marketplace. Among propertied white men, however, clashes over state efforts to regulate the marketplace for the public good only increased in ferocity through the 1780s. Disagreements about how much government should interfere in everyday dealing were rife as numerous interests clamored for attention in the debt-ridden new nation. So vociferous were these arguments that when Henry Brackrenridge was elected to the Pennsylvania state legislature in October 1786 he was dispatched to Philadelphia with a petition warning that "no people can long continue in mutual police where their interests become separate." In the marketplace, the separation of these interests would take place in multiple settings, both urban and rural, north and south.[41]

Conflict over the policing of the domestic marketplace for the "general good" occurred in just about every commercial space, but it did not achieve the same intensity everywhere. In cities, where it was easier for freeholders to rally around the regulation of poorer, propertyless townspeople, debate was vigorous but for the most part eventually concluded in agreement that making urban markets work for the good of the whole required an effective municipal corporation. Rehearsing many of the same arguments that had unfolded in the 1760s and 1770s, city dwellers were on familiar ground regarding the public good in the urban marketplace. Nevertheless, defining and applying the public good seemed urgent in a new republic that feared above all else the corruption of its citizenry by private interest. Consequently, municipal corporations were still vigorously protested in the early republic, in good part for their potential to encroach on the liberty of freeholders in the marketplace.

Such fears meant that Philadelphia was without corporate governance for thirteen years, until 1789. This was not for want of effort by state assemblymen, who were checked at each turn by opponents certain that a municipal authority could only constitute too much government, often by men who had too much wealth. In 1781 "Agricola" claimed there was no need to "seek after any new plans of police" in the city because the justices of the peace had matters in hand. The 1786 Assembly agreed, refusing a petition for incorporation. Responding to the charge that crime and disorder were increasing and keen to keep their capital city status, in 1789 the assemblymen changed their tune. Yet even after its establishment the corporation faced criticism from those who felt it was falling short of its civic duty when, among other things, it failed to ensure that during a hot summer the market still offered fresh provisions with "ease and convenience." The pronouncements from men like Mifflin who supported the corporation were surely targeted at these naysayers, who continued to view it with suspicion.[42]

Perhaps because of its quick establishment in 1783, the actions of the Charleston corporation were subject to more sustained censure than those of its Philadelphia counterpart. Although the city's incorporation represented a victory for men like "John Carpenter," who had argued for it twenty years earlier before the Revolution turned the Lowcountry upside down, its realization did not draw a line under the debate about its necessity. With the municipal authorities in power for less than a year, merchant Benjamin Waller accused them of unfairly threatening him when they entered his premises to prevent an unlicensed auction. Waller's grievances were publicly supported by "Amicus," who claimed the council had prosecuted the

British merchants for contravening auction regulations out of "PRIVATE PIQUE" and suggested the city government was no better than British tyranny in its arbitrary application of justice. Then, in an article questioning the city council's conduct in the sale of valuable waterfront property, Amicus accused councilors of acting in a "spirit of FAVOURITISM, or the rapacious thirst of *gain*" when they decided to develop the lots privately after auction rather than allowing the public to receive the income from their improvement. In the fraught aftermath of Charleston's occupation, the corporation's commitment to a marketplace operating for the good of the whole was in constant doubt. The concept was relatively fragile, the economy in turmoil, and the profit of private property owners firmly ensconced in the urban marketplace. As a result, deciding where the public good ended and private gain began proved almost impossible.[43]

Both Philadelphia's and Charleston's corporations survived the challenge to their authority in the marketplace. In South Carolina the economic order of a slave society that depended on its black traders was at stake, and the corporation's right to regulate them was so thoroughly accepted that the issue never even figured in the argument. Since it was entangled with the increasingly troubled relationship between government and farmers, however, the fate of marketplace governance in the rural Lowcountry and Upcountry was much less certain. Across the American mainland, the ongoing financial crisis badly tested yeomen's belief in government's ability to pay due regard to their economic interest. In their petition for redress, indebted farmers in New Hampshire described a "Deplorable & Shocking Situation . . . Never Experienced by a Free People." They were among dozens of such petitioners contesting the economic policy decisions of urban coastal elites on the grounds that they failed to take equal account of everybody's interests in the marketplace.[44]

In South Carolina the conflict was somewhat muted as leading men like Nathaniel Pendleton appealed to Upcountry whites as fellow freeholders who must, at all costs, put "security" over dissent. Nevertheless, facing a more extensive county court system staffed by Charleston-selected officeholders, many South Carolina freeholders still balked at the new intrusions into their everyday economic dealings. Sheriffs attempting to execute debt suits and run auctions in Carolina's Upcountry districts encountered such violence that in 1786 a General Assembly committee was established to inquire into the problem. Proclaiming vociferously that "resistance to the Execution of the Laws . . . tends to the Subversion of all Order in the Community [and] total Annihilation of . . . Freedom and Happiness, which are the great Objects of all good Government," the committee of worthies promised financial support to sheriffs performing their duties as well as "all possible assistance to the Civil Officers whenever it shall be found necessary."[45]

Still, two years later residents of Ninety-Six District petitioned against the power sheriffs had to ruin "public and private credit." Meanwhile, inhabitants of Lincoln County, near the Georgia state line, claimed they did not want a court at all because it was "grievous and manifestly to the hurt of yr petitioners by laying on them a heavy tax that has been exacted of them payable in specie." These petitioners argued that the court had been established in the first place only because of a previous request "signed by a number of persons of no taxable property, mulattoes and other persons at that time resident in the state of Georgia." Whether this was true or not, petitioners perceived an unwelcome intrusion by a state designed to deprive them of their property. In the teeth of such resistance, some sheriffs resorted to holding vendue sales of confiscated property far away from the neighborhood where it had been seized. Petitioners duly complained about these evasive tactics to the General Assembly, which sent out stern instructions to sheriffs to sell debtors' property in the place where it had been taken.[46]

This was not the worst of it, however. Residents of Winton County resorted to more direct action in February 1790 when "a riotous mob" "tore down from the Court House all the Sheriff's Advertisements for Sales as Levied for Execution," then threw the court furniture and papers out in the rain and came back the next day to burn everything to the ground. The rioters were the men whose goods had been seized. This was direct action by freeholders who strongly disagreed with the state's recently acquired power to sell their property for what they perceived as a fraction of its value and to destroy their credit in the local marketplace. In the colonial era, men of credit had been happy to rely on the court to protect their property from debtors and dubious dealers when they chose to resort to the law. But the more extensive powers of state government in the local economy during the 1780s seemed to divest them of a choice they had previously been free to make independently. In the dire economic circumstances of the early republic this may have been only a choice of how they would go bankrupt, but at least it would have been their own decision.[47]

The action in Winton County was the most extreme expression of freeholders' opposition to South Carolina's new and intrusive state apparatus. Yet it paled to insignificance next to the discord afflicting Pennsylvania. While rural Pennsylvanians had been more accustomed to the involvement of legal authority in their daily dealings before the Revolution, they nevertheless expected courts to be staffed by justices of the peace, juries, and judges who shared the commercial interest of the community. Indeed, the

Black Boys had relied on the cooperation of such officials in their quest to order the Indian trade for their interest during the 1760s. The 1780s, however, witnessed both the establishment of state authorities determined to make sheriffs into more effective debt collectors and of groups more organized in their resistance to such moves. The result was a bitter conflict between authorities committed to court-ordered auctions as a means of collecting debt and debtors themselves, who still prized the liberty to hold and to trade their property on their own terms. Historians have described the ensuing conflict as a class war or the emergence of an east/west divide. Yet poorer, rural settlers were quite happy to welcome government intervention when it promised to protect their property and profits in the marketplace. Most consistently, this was a conflict about government meddling in trade.

Looking westward from Philadelphia, governing freeholders struggled to understand the interpretation of public good and private interest held by the state's farmers. As they wrestled with the desperate financial situation of the confederation during the early 1780s, both Robert Morris and his deputy Gouverneur Morris expressed a strong belief that the behavior of ordinary Americans in the marketplace was stymieing their own highly admirable commitment to the struggle for the nation's public good.

Gouverneur Morris compared the Revolution to a fermentation process in which the "dregs" had now risen to the top. These dregs, argued Robert Morris, were the type of men "who cannot find Money to pay Taxes" but "can find it to purchase useless Gew Gaws, and expend much more in the Gratification of Vanity, Luxury, Drunkenness, and Debauchery than is necessary to establish the Freedom of their Country." As they corrupted the internal police by exercising partiality in their offices as tax collectors, such men devalued paper money by refusing it in favor of specie and kept goods off the market unless they could obtain ridiculous prices paid in coin. Getting to the heart of the matter, Robert Morris exclaimed to Alexander Hamilton that "the Farmers will not give full Credit to Money merely because it will pay Taxes, for that is an Object they are not very violently devoted to; but that Money which goes freely at the Store and the Tavern, will be sought after as greedily as those Things which the Store and the Tavern contain." Philadelphia merchant Benjamin Fuller seemed to agree as he cursed "Our Country Wiseacres" who "have taken it into their heads that the bank" of America, set up by Morris, "was injurious to Trade & Country." Their resistance, claimed Fuller, "has thrown all kind of business into confusion."[48]

So while Philadelphia Federalists sought to restore domestic marketing to health by levying and collecting tax, rechartering the Bank of America, and recruiting county tax collectors, justices of the peace, and juries to do their bidding, rural people looked on suspiciously. From their perspective such efforts were interpreted not as measures designed to rescue the public good in a time of economic crisis, but as interventions between the freeholder and his liberty to trade his property freely and enjoy the full profit of it—surely what freeholders needed to do in tough economic times. If a man chose to spend the profit of a wheat sale in his local tavern, who was Robert Morris to say he should be paying his tax with it instead? Indeed, Pennsylvania's courts had not previously sought to intervene in local dealing in such a sustained manner, so struggling farmers were unwilling to recognize a government mandate for tax when their markets were already so threatened by inflation and the lack of hard currency. Faced by government intrusion into their daily dealings, rural people thus petitioned and complained, dodged, and when all else failed took direct action. Pennsylvanians reacted much as their South Carolina counterparts did when presented with stronger government of their daily marketplace dealings, but with far greater ferocity.

Free white Pennsylvanians often used petitions to express their disagreement with this increased government involvement. In 1784 Chester County's distillers opined that they labored "under many difficulties and disadvantages" caused by the commonwealth's March 1783 Excise Act, which levied a tax on alcohol producers to pay annual interest due on state bonds. Probably signed by wealthier distillers, the petition complained that the tax seemed designed to eat into their profits at every stage of retail. If producers took liquor "from their customers in payment for their labour," they would have to pay duty should they wish to sell it on for cash, thus paying a double tax. Yet producers were forced to do this because of the very shortage of cash. It was this same shortage that also prompted farmers to demand grain be paid for in liquor, which they then sold at cheaper prices than the distiller could afford by avoiding duty. The distillers thus noted that "it is extremely hard that they should be abridged in their priviledges of Disposing of their own Manufactures without being Exposed to the insults of some of the meaner Class that has no higher motives in view than to gratify a lust or fulfill their avaritious desire." From the Chester County distillers' point of view, state involvement in their trade in the form of a duty could not be tolerated because it had impinged on their liberty to profit from local commerce, which as hardworking freeholders they deserved to do.[49]

However, this principle could equally lead freeholders to demand more state action, not less. Thus, at the same time as distillers were petitioning for the freedom to profit from their "own manufactures," their neighbors were demanding an extension of Philadelphia's main marketplace—a marketplace that, as we have seen, was more intensively regulated than ever before. Many petitions from the city, Chester County, Northampton County, and Lancaster supported the marketplace's enlargement precisely because, they argued, a well-regulated central space meant better prices for produce. "The disadvantages of detached Markets must be obvious to every Man," explained a 1784 petition, "Where they happen, the Seller and Buyer are equally at a loss which to attend, and the Whole in a little Time will become useless. But where the Market is compact, it suits the Conveniency of both; the Seller knowing where to get the current Price and a ready sale for his Produce; and the Purchaser to procure what he has Occasion for, without losing their Time in running from one to another." These men were against the proposition of a rival petitioning campaign that still fully supported regulated marketplaces but preferred enlarging the South Market. The universal support for a regulated marketplace by Pennsylvanians, who were quite possibly protesting an excise tax at the same time, was no contradiction; behind both actions was a belief that government intervention in the economy was desirable only to protect the property and profits of freeholders.[50]

Such sentiments also lay behind the sustained efforts of rural people to elude both the collection of taxes and the auction of their property for unpaid duties. Like the Black Boys before them, freeholders relied on county officials sympathetic to their protecting their property from a government wanting to take a cut of their profits or to seize it altogether. Already in 1779, Northumberland County justices of the peace labeled the state legislature "a pack of damned Rascals." Men like Bedford County justice James Martin not only agreed that a meddling state was rascally but actively worked to help freeholders evade its authority. Martin played the fool to state officials, claiming he had lost his tax ledgers and "forgetting" to attend court sessions while encouraging people to sell their property and flee when he could prevaricate with revenue collection no longer.[51]

As Martin's strategy suggests, farmers were still willing to enter the marketplace if they believed the profits of a sale would go to a deserving individual (the property's owner) and not to any state agent. Pennsylvanians therefore developed numerous maneuvers to prevent the state from getting a cut of the proceeds of an auction, which had long been a regular market instrument. By the latter 1780s, freeholders across the state were veterans of the auction boycott in which "no one would bid" on "goods taken by the collectors for the taxes." In Westmoreland County alone, bidderless auctions increased from 72 to 300 between 1783 and 1786. Such action was made possible by agreements among freeholders to "bind and engage themselves together as one man" in a manner that looked very similar to the committees formed to protect the "public good" during earlier boycotting campaigns of the Revolution. If a community could not organize effectively, however, individual debtors might still be saved by friends and neighbors' helping to protect their property from the sheriff's auction. Writing in 1784, Bucks County farmer Isaac Hicks sought to keep "poor Newman" from destitution by asking a relative to "give me leave to interceed on his behalf and beg you'll still wait with him a few months longer and consider the great Scarcerty of money and that should you push the Sale . . . you will ruin a very honest Man." If creditors could be persuaded to have mercy, a freeholder's honor might be preserved.[52]

However, it was much easier to remain at liberty, free from the demands of the sheriff or tax collector, for a wealthy man with abundant credit in the community. Elites quickly realized they could mobilize valuable personal connections to protect themselves against the vicissitudes of the early republic marketplace. Philadelphia merchant Benjamin Fuller was involved with a very intricate plan to save his friends, the Mitchell family, from losing their property. Although it would place him "under more difficulty than I have experienced for a long time," in 1785 Fuller agreed to rescue them from the embarrassing and reputation-damaging prospect of a sheriff's sale. Bedridden by old age, Fuller nevertheless orchestrated a scheme whereby he would take out a loan, then put it in the hands of Randall Mitchell with instructions to buy as much of the estate at auction as possible. Then, wrote Fuller, "when there was sufficient sold, the sheriff to make me a regular sale and conveyance of the Property . . . and send it to a friend of his here who may deliver it to me . . . I woud then take the Negros & hire them out to the best advantage towards the support of Mrs Mitchell." Meanwhile, Fuller reassured the widow Mitchell that he would "prevent effectually, your Negroes, Goods & necessaries from ever being, hereafter taken by a Miserly, Griping Creditor." The plan worked; the widow remained at the farm after the sale, letting out portions to tenant farmers.[53]

Philadelphia druggist Townsend Speakman's ploy to save another man of property was less contrived. Speakman stepped in to rescue Lancaster tradesman Dr. Henry Stuben, who was under threat of being "irretrievably ruined" by an impending court action. Speakman proposed that if Stuben "would make over to me his Shop Furniture and what other Property he is possessd of as Security for so much of the Debt as it may be worth by fair appraisment," he would supply him with medicines "to enable him to go on Again." While the economic crisis saw innumerable farmers fall to the demands of their eastern creditors, those creditors saved their friends and relatives by drawing on well-established interpersonal commercial networks to keep the sheriff at bay.[54]

But eastern elites held a further trump card in the quest to regulate the marketplace without divesting themselves of their own liberty to trade and enlarge their property. These elites were not struggling to keep the state at bay, they were the state. Historians have traced the way public corporations supporting many of the early republic's infrastructure projects rarely required stockholders to give up private property that would increase in value as a result of the plans. As Andrew Schocket has argued, in the early republic "elites used the state ... to enforce their interests." More often than not, these interests centered on ensuring the security, enlargement, and free trade of their property in the marketplace.[55]

For less wealthy western freeholders, the most visible strategy elites used to protect property from state regulation was their refusal to put a stop to land speculation. Thanks to the vastness of the American continent and to British colonial legislation permitting real estate to be seized for debt from the early eighteenth century onward, land sales had long been a central pillar of marketing. As we have seen, the freedom to own land outright and to trade it at will was foundational to European Americans' market culture. When limits on westward movement fell away after 1783, neither the Pennsylvania government nor its South Carolina counterpart stepped forward to regulate the newly expanded land market with anywhere near the enthusiasm they had applied to other forms of domestic trade. The South Carolina Assembly passed two laws to halt speculation a decade apart, in 1784 and 1794, but neither was as carefully implemented as the new county court system. Pennsylvania made no effort to legislate against speculation; rather, it favored speculators when it suspended the sale of unoccupied land for unpaid taxes, also outlawing the backdating of those taxes. While officials applied themselves diligently to removing hucksters selling hot dinners from the marketplace for the "good of the whole," speculators bought up thousands of acres of western land for their private enrichment, unregulated by a state they controlled.[56]

Western freeholders were quick to note that while the tax officers and justices of the peace had been mandated to take their property and stop trade, the government did nothing to regulate land speculation among men with much more wealth than they might ever enjoy. A 1788 petition from the inhabitants of South Carolina's Chesterfield and Lancaster Counties, one of a succession on the issue, complained about the "large Quantities of Lands that are Surveyd amongst us ... which Oppress us greatly ... and dose Distress many poor Honest Families not able as yet to secure there lands, but intending to do it when able." With regulation of the land market poorly applied, such families had been gazumped by cartels of wealthy Philadelphians, including Robert Morris, who by the 1790s had bought huge tracts of Upcountry territory.[57]

The dismay of westerners only increased with the government's puny attempts to stop speculation. While the whiskey rebels were stirred up by the assault of the federal excise on their marketing freedoms, they were equally frustrated by the same government's inaction in keeping speculators' hands off "their" land. Petitioners from Westpensbro and Newton complained of the "mode of selling Back Lands in Great Quantity to Companys," arguing that "it tends to seeing themselves Deprived of Becoming Purchasers upon the same terms with the Favourites of Government." Many turned to the customary language of the common good, arguing that "the officers of government and the land jobbers were engrossing all the property of the country." "Tom the Tinker" also warned that "to prevent a great deal of trouble, it will be necessary to repeal the excise law and lay a direct tax on all located and patented land in the United States." From Pittsburgh to the Carolina pine barrens, Americans witnessed authorities happy to interfere in their daily dealings, to their financial detriment, but unwilling to legislate against speculators who seemed free to buy and sell as they pleased.[58]

America's new state governments had done a very good job of folding into their vision of a well-ordered republic the idea of a well-regulated marketplace, well-policed, operating for the good of the whole. Yet the cultures of commerce that had evolved over the colonial era meant there was little chance that this new regulatory edifice would be comprehensive and widely respected. Instead, legislation provoked another round of protests, debates, and intransigence, all too similar to revolutionary disorder. These early republican conflicts were motivated by the clashing interests of free American society: east versus west, rural versus urban, and rich freeholders versus poorer ones. Nevertheless, such divisions remained frustratingly ephemeral. More tangible was the realization that it was much easier to agree that the public good belonged in the republican marketplace than it was to get traders to obey it in their daily dealing. If state regulation of domestic commerce promised to divest men of their long-treasured liberty to trade their property at will and enjoy *all* of its profits, most freeholders, rich or poor, eastern or western, farmer or merchant, would find a way to contest it, resist it, or at the very least evade it.

In the years after 1783, Americans continued to wrestle with the question of where in the marketplace to draw the line between the "good of the whole," or "public good," and the private interest. The dire economic circumstances of the early republic made finding an answer to this perennial question into an urgent quest but also seemed to place a satisfactory solution even further out of reach. Efforts to create a virtuous economy often united European market institutions with new rhetoric, producing creative definitions and novel ideas about how public and private should relate to one another. In New York, private banks acquired legitimacy by making themselves indispensable to the state government as it sought to build the infrastructure necessary for inland commerce.[59]

Such creative elisions of public and private in the marketplace sprang up equally in South Carolina and Pennsylvania. In Upcountry Carolina, the new town of Belleville was formed with a very traditional fair charter allowing for "a court of pipowders . . . with all liberties and free customs to such fairs appertaining . . . according to the usage and custom of fairs." Yet Belleville had been created by freeholder William Thompson, who in laying out the town on his property, effortlessly combined this older interpretation of markets for the "common good" with his own entrepreneurial dealings as a property-owning American citizen.

In Pennsylvania the dissonance between ideology and profit prompted vigorous debate. Carlisle was the site of successive disputes over economic regulation, with quarrels centering on where the interest of private property owners ended and that of the public began. Inhabitants who had petitioned to prevent the fisheries from being blocked by mill dams on the Conodoguinet Creek were lambasted in the newspaper by a "farmer" who believed such a petition was antithetical to "the Democratical form of government we live under," which required that "every citizen should be strictly attentive not to his own rights and privileges only, but likewise to those of his community at large." But who was to say that the men who wanted to protect the fishery were not the ones looking to the common good? Was it those who wanted to catch fish and sell them in the local marketplace who were pursuing their private interest, or was it the mill owners who were seeking to build dams so they could enjoy the profits of Pennsylvania's lucrative wheat economy? In an American marketplace where both the fishery and the mill had long been run by individuals for their own enrichment, there was simply no right answer.[60]

Philadelphians engaged in similar debates, albeit about more commercial marketplaces. How, asked a correspondent with the printer Mr. Dunlap, should the buying and selling of "public stocks, bank and canal scrips and all other certificates" be accomplished? The author did not recommend outlawing such deals, since that would place the state at a disadvantage against neighboring New York, which had gained "immense capital" by the "avidity in dealing therein." Perhaps auctions were the answer but, as the writer pointed out, the 1 percent duty on this mode of exchange was enough "to effect a total prohibition of all sales." Indeed, if the state Assembly agreed that duty should be levied on "the dealer in paper," then it amounted to discrimination by gentlemen who had shown such "indifference . . . towards the conduct of those who, on the arrival of the melancholy news of the insurrection of the blacks in the West-Indies, engrossed and monopolized the whole of the necessary articles of rum, melasses, sugar and coffee." As the early republic's markets expanded and embraced ever more types of dealing, the task facing those who wished to distinguish between a public good and a private interest became more complex than ever.[61]

Just as Americans grappled with these contradictions in the 1780s, historians have found it fiendishly difficult to draw the battle lines of the conflict in both Pennsylvania and South Carolina. Was it rich against poor? West against east? Participants in a market economy against subsistence farmers? At least when it came to economic affairs, opposition or support for government intervention arose everywhere because all were struggling with the same question: Was regulation and taxation of everyday trade the answer? And if so, how much and by whom? The boundary between the public good and private interest was poorly defined in a country lacking long commitment to these concepts in the marketplace. At the same time, the liberty to trade property was still likely to be placed above the communitarian action demanded by "internal police" of the marketplace. State republican government could not provide a definitive solution for governing a marketplace that had for so long thrived on the free trading of private property by its owners. The job was made even harder by governing men themselves, who manipulated or ignored the regulations when they had the chance.[62]

Yet definitive answers were easier to come by in applying the "good of the whole" to traders who also happened to be propertyless, women, people of color, or a combination thereof. Especially in South Carolina, regulations dictating how such people disposed of their property, or permitting freeholders to confiscate it from them, had begun to appear on the statute books before the Revolution. The republic's creation merely hastened the process and heightened the rhetoric. Used to the same freewheeling marketplace as their free white brethren, these groups did not easily bend before such regulations; they often continued to trade in the spaces within the ever-denser tangle of European-made laws and rhetoric. At the same time, white rulers carefully constructed the idea that the marketplace was well regulated to ensure great opportunity for the virtuous. But with the marketplace in turmoil, such opportunity remained frustratingly elusive in practice.

Constitution Making and the Marketplace

Americans' colonial marketing experiences presented them with a major co-nundrum. Accustomed to trading property with minimal intervention from the many "interests" governing Europe's economies, they had created a free-trading culture Adam Smith could only dream of. What is more, they built this edifice well before the renowned political economist had formulated the ideas at the heart of his 1776 masterpiece. This decades-long experi-ence of freely exchanging goods bred a strong belief among Americans that they deserved the liberty to trade their property free of government's regula-tions, taxes, and duties—indeed, from meddling of any kind. Although the full benefits of this "free" trade could be enjoyed only by white property holders, Africans and Indians had played a major role in promoting such marketing practices, since their trading gave them an essential role in com-mercial networks.

These patterns of development *could* have created the ideal Smithian com-mercial society were it not for two important features of the colonial expe-rience. First, many people—including many American colonists—did not believe private interest was naturally capable of serving the public good in the marketplace. In Pennsylvania, the diverse and factional character of the white population created tension between those who were more and those who were less committed to the idea that some sort of public good should be visible in marketing spaces. In South Carolina, on the other hand, these early modern ideas had found their continued value and expression in regu-lating nonwhite people in the marketplace. Both colonies' governments, in agreement with the imperial authorities, strongly believed in regulating the

Indian trade to meet a public good. In a variety of marketing places, there-fore, and for a range of reasons, early modern ideas of regulated trade had met with a warm reception in their colonial setting.

Then the character of colonists' markets was challenged by the experi-ence of the Revolution. Tensions between those colonists who believed the government did have a role in regulating markets and those who felt it had no place in them at all were transformed into outright conflict by the chaos of the imperial crisis and the war. This was a revolution caused in part by the sacrosanct status of free trading among white property owners, but it could not be solved by it. Many Americans reacted so strongly to British taxa-tion policies after 1763 precisely because they intervened in trading that had been completely free from the interference of governing institutions. Yet Americans could not resolve their Revolution by a total resort to the ide-ology that, as they put it, "trade will regulate itself." As men of their time who often remained invested in the operation of the public good in the marketplace, their reaction to revolutionary market disruption necessarily involved a return to familiar tools of early modern economic management. Critically, this move required women to stop being market makers and re-cast them as subjects of a male-defined public good.

However, revolutionary goals also required patriot leaders to create an al-ternative rationale for their own dealings in the marketplace, one that added up to more than just a straightforward revival of a British-style "economy of interests." Their answer was subsumed in the Revolution's overarching republican ideology, which allowed them to redefine the public good as nec-essary to the success of their bid for independence. White American men's idea of the economic public good only partially resembled its European pre-decessor, the common good. Like its forerunner, the American public good embraced the ideal of fair trade, a determination to subjugate private inter-ests to the good of the whole, and the power of officially sanctioned market-places to give force to these ambitions. Yet it also differed in three important ways. First, this public good allowed that, if it was beneficial to white men's private interests, the latter could operate to meet the former. Second, this eli-sion allowed white property owners to preserve their wealth and apply the ideal selectively. Third, and integral to this public good in the marketplace, was its use of "internal police" by white men to ensure that others obeyed it. The turmoil of war had forced white Americans to confront the nature of their marketplace and produced a particular ideology for its government.

Nevertheless, organizing commerce to meet this ideal would prove an elusive goal in a republic so expansive and populated by so many propertied men. Many were not even sure it was necessary to regulate their dealing. For others, like James Madison, leaving trade completely alone to regulate itself posed great danger to the republic. In his notes on the "vices of the system" in April 1787, Madison began thinking through solutions to this "problem." The inability of states to effectively govern their economies and establish functioning markets meant that "paper money, instalments of debts, occlusion of Courts, making property a legal tender" became "aggressions on the rights of other states." At the same time, states' jealous protection of their own commercial interests produced "expensive & vexatious" regulations "destructive of the general harmony." Lying behind all these harmful policies, however, were state governments populated by men operating according to "ambition" and "personal interest" as opposed to "public good." "Veiling his selfish views under the professions of public good," the representative protected his private interest while enjoying the misplaced confidence of the "honest but unenlightened." Although private interest reached beyond commercial matters, Madison's own tendency to describe the factions of American society primarily as economically driven—creditors and debtors, rich or poor, husbandmen, merchants or manufacturers, or owners of different kinds of property—strongly suggests the foundational role of economic life in the debate. While some Americans accepted a rationale for government of the domestic economy, their commitment to protecting and enlarging their own property was too strong to make it stick through the economic crises and political cacophony of the 1780s. Madison had, as historians have acknowledged, put his finger on the problem.[1]

Without realizing it, as he identified the "vices" plaguing commerce and its government in 1787, Madison also revealed that Americans were confronting many of the same difficulties their former British masters had faced almost a century earlier. Madison described these difficulties in a new, republican language, yet the issues he discussed were remarkably familiar. Edward Randolph, whom we met in the late 1600s patrolling creeks and customs houses to find disobedient colonists contravening England's Navigation Acts, asked similar questions about market authority. As Madison lamented Americans' disloyalty to the republican public good, Randolph called out colonists for snubbing the king's interest and its associated common good. Madison observed how weakly enforced laws, self-interest, and the difficulty of governing such expansive and diverse polities all brought about the neglect of the public good. Randolph, meanwhile, identified crooked customs officers who neglected English law, were corrupted by the profits of smuggling, and struggled to regulate trade in such an extensive landscape. The American public good in the marketplace may not have been the king's interest ideo-logically, but practically there was not much difference: the English could not make selfish traders in a scattered marketplace pay their duties to the king; the Americans could not get them to give a cut to their own indebted government.[2]

Edward Randolph's answer to these problems was the 1696 refurbish-ment of England's Navigation Acts. The desire of Madison and his compa-triots for a solution motivated their 1787 decision to produce a federal con-stitution. Randolph was trying to work out how to govern colonies, not a sovereign nation. Madison and the other men at the Constitutional Conven-tion were working on a much grander scale. But as historian Max Edling has observed, the novelty of the American project did not necessarily mean it was trying to accomplish entirely singular goals of government.[3]

When it came to ordering domestic trade, therefore, the Founding Fathers faced an issue that had troubled their British forerunners: How do you gov-ern markets effectively in such an expansive landscape? At the convention itself, Alexander Hamilton's notes showed him fretting that "distance has a physical effect upon men's minds" while also recognizing that "execution of laws feeble at a distance from government—particularly the collection of revenue—" would be difficult for any new federal authority. To be effective on the international stage, the Constitution needed to create solid financial foundations. Doing so required constructing institutions that could success-fully harvest taxes, duties, and tolls from the daily buying and selling in a marketplace populated by a scattered people. What is more, these people were as ill disposed as ever toward government's involvement in their daily economic transactions.[4]

That the Constitution might create institutions capable of restoring order and confidence to the marketplace was a quality strenuously emphasized by its Federalist supporters. Pamphleteers in South Carolina and Pennsylvania boasted of the benefits it would confer on internal trade, hoping to win over doubters by proving the plan would protect their property *and* serve the public good. "Cato," writing in the *State Gazette of South Carolina*, was confident that ratification would create a nation able to "flourish in com-merce" rather than "sink in bankruptcy." "At this momentous crisis when so much is at stake, surely does it become every one, to act towards the general good," pleaded the author, who also exhorted freeholders to "shake off our libertinism, and wish only to be free so far, as well regulated laws will permit and defend." Americans must overcome their desire to exchange their prop-erty entirely without government intervention, argued Cato, if they were ever again to enjoy a functioning marketplace.[5]

Mired in a bitter ratification debate that had seen state representatives pursued through the streets of Philadelphia and Federalists sent scurrying by rioters in Carlisle, Pennsylvania's supporters of the Constitution were equally certain of its potential for stabilizing the marketplace. Although Revolutionary War officer George Turner did not love the Constitution, he admitted that "as a public creditor, and weighing, like many good citizens, my own private advantage against the public good, I ought to wish for the most speedy adoption of the proposed plan. . . . payment of my hopeless debt might possibly be obtained sooner under a *real government of any sort.*" "One of the People," a correspondent with the *Pennsylvania Gazette,* agreed. "Bankrupt merchants, poor mechanics, and distressed farmers are the effects of the weakness of the Confederation," he argued, claiming that "every person must long since have discovered the necessity of placing the exclusive power of regulating the commerce of America in the same body; without this it is impossible to regulate their trade." What America therefore needed, argued the author, was "a stable energetic Federal Constitution" that would "cause property again to rise to its real and true value." James Wilson, a staunchly Federalist member of the state convention and the man who had been at the center of the 1779 Fort Wilson skirmish, also saw the Constitution as a means of preventing further disorder in the domestic economy. "Suppose we reject this system of government, what will be the consequence?," asked Wilson. "Let the farmer say, he whose produce remains unasked for; nor can he find a single market for its consumption, though his fields are blessed with luxuriant abundance. . . . Go along the wharves of Philadelphia, and observe the melancholy silence that reigns." Allowing the proper regulation of trade, and bringing justice back to dealing, these men argued, were the solutions for a marketplace that had been clogged by war, and then by debt, for far too long.[6]

Once the Constitution was ratified, its supporters proceeded to promote it as the solution to the woes of an expansive, hard-to-govern marketplace. South Carolina's politicians rejoiced at its potential to restore the public good and rein in private interest, thus mending the desperate condition of Carolina trade. Renowned historian David Ramsey, in an oration planned for celebrating the ratification in Charleston, lamented how "expiring credit, languishing commerce . . . proclaimed aloud something to be fundamentally wrong" but applauded because now "America called forth her sons to meet and form a constitution for the future good government of her widely extended settlements." Ramsey predicted that "justice will again lift up her head. While legislative assemblies interfered between debtors and creditors, what security could there be for property? He that sold, did not know that he should ever get the stipulated price, he that parted with his money could not tell when it would be replaced—hence a total want of confidence and of credit . . . these evils will be done away . . . it will soon bring back the good old times under which we formerly flourished and were happy." The Constitution had saved America from the "confusion and disorder which would probably have taken place from the jarring interests of such an ungoverned multitude." Camden's Federalists certainly agreed as they toasted the ratification in June 1788. No fewer than seven of their thirteen toasts celebrated its power to restore a functioning marketplace, overseeing the growth of Columbia as "the source of good and orderly administration" and Charleston as the site of flourishing commerce.[7]

The Constitution did indeed accomplish what Federalists argued it was capable of. It was ratified in part because Anti-Federalists found it difficult to counter arguments that it might offer ordinary freeholders a way out of the desperate economic situation they found themselves in late in 1787. Restoring international confidence in the United States and allowing the federal government to assume war debt got markets moving again. While the young nation may have gained a measure of legitimacy in the eyes of the mighty European powers, however, the question of how to get ordinary property owners to lay aside their "private interest" would not go away. Many freeholders were unable to successfully oppose the Constitution's ratification, but this had not reduced their determination to prevent the federal authorities' from snatching their trading profits and impinging on the liberty they enjoyed to trade their property where, when, and how they wished. Like Edward Randolph a century earlier, the Founding Fathers still faced the problem Madison had identified in 1787 as a vice of the system and Hamilton had mused on at the convention itself: in an expansive republic with thinly policed territories, they needed to get freeholders to give up these private interests and to sponsor the public good by paying taxes and duties. Unfortunately for them, this struggle was far from over. Even though they had redefined the public good, accommodating private interest within it when necessary for the individual property owner and allowing it as a motor of trade, the struggle continued.[8]

For much of the 1790s, federal authorities thus found themselves once again fighting the battles that the British, and then the state governments, had waged against the deeply entrenched sentiment that no government had the right—or indeed the resources—to interfere with the liberty of the white American man to trade and increase his property. Two of the four chief sources of revenue for the federal government that Albert Gallatin outlined in his 1796 *Sketch of the Finances of the United States* necessitated the collection of taxes or duties: external duties on tonnage and imports and internal duties on a range of domestic goods and services. Seldom were these duties easily collected, as Americans looked for ways to hold on to the free trading spaces they were so accustomed to.[9]

As in the 1780s, the opposition was uneven but universal. Gallatin himself observed that one citizen had already brought a case to the Supreme Court against his carriage tax, looking to disallow it on the grounds it was not a direct tax. This was a minor affair, however, compared with the deals cut to make the external revenue system profitable. As historian Gautham Rao has documented, establishing and staffing the 134 customs houses charged with collecting external revenues was a herculean task. Some customs officers, and Alexander Hamilton himself, experienced acute frustration when they tried to collect the duties on time and according to the letter of the law. In the end, bringing in sufficient customs income was possible only because of the "cozy relationship between customs houses and commerce" that permitted a "manipulation of the laws." In other words, the potential opposition of merchants to the hand of government had been staved off only by another deal within the elite. Such smooth elisions of private interest and the public good not only had been the motor of British customs authority in the colonial era but were also behind merchants' ability to profit from land speculation and the republic's many improvement corporations.[10]

While persuasion could be used with merchants who were friends and business partners, Hamilton and his fellow Federalists faced much tougher resistance from those men who lived away from the urban centers of power and had not been given the opportunity to cut a deal with their friends and leaders. Responding to 1791's whiskey excise, the farmers of Edgefield County in South Carolina were certainly not in agreement with the federal government's image of an economy operating for the "good of the whole." Assembled as a grand jury in 1791, they proclaimed it to be their "Dispensable Duty" to protest a "Greivance of the most alarming nature to the Citizens of this State, we mean the late act of Congress laying an Excise on home distilled Spirits and a Tax on Stills." "All Excise Laws in the Nature of Excise Laws are repugnant to the Condition and Liberties of a free people," argued the Edgefield freeholders. Like their Revolutionary forebears, they saw a "free people" not as accepting some duties on trade in the name of the common good, but instead as viewing freedom as the right to buy and sell property with no government interference whatever.[11]

As had often been the case, Pennsylvanians, free of the "menace" of an enslaved majority, were a measure more radical in their reaction. Efforts to make western farmers pay the whiskey excise prompted a rebellion and a federal military response that together constituted a major crisis for the young nation. Especially in western Pennsylvania, opposition to the excise grew to embrace a multiplicity of protestors and causes, which historians have explored in detail. Nevertheless, as the elite Lancaster lawyer Jasper Yeates recognized, the dispute was in part about the republican state and its determination to apply its police powers to local trade. As a delegate to the meeting between the protestors and the government at Parkinson's Ferry in August 1794, Yeates explained to his wife Sally that he would do his "best to . . . contribute to the general Welfare of the great Whole," adding, "I feel that I am discharging my Duty as a good Member of society." Fully invested in the government project, Yeates believed in the Hamiltonian drive to secure the good of the whole through a well-funded central state.[12]

Yeates may have envisioned himself as a crusader for the "general welfare," persuading the assembled rebels to be good citizens and pay the duty they owed, but the rebels saw it differently. For western Pennsylvania's smallholders the tax was fundamentally another effort by the state to place itself between the freeholder and his ability to dispose of, and profit from, his property according to his own will. The long-standing, and still popular, mode of face-to-face dealing away from regulated marketplaces underpinned this belief. Electing their own court officials, Pennsylvania freeholders had effectively avoided state appointees and tax payments. The whiskey excise, however, sent in federally appointed men with a mandate to disrupt the status quo and divest farmers of their enjoyment of a duty-free trade operating according to their idea of the public good. To evade payment, the resistance revived a tactic that had served them well some thirty years earlier when the Black Boys had policed the colonial backcountry: they established their own market regulation conforming to their idea of fair trade. The regulation came in the form of "Tom the Tinker," a mysterious figure who chopped up the stills of whiskey producers who paid the excise tax. Claiming to be motivated by the "virtuous principles of republican liberty," Tinker took aim in the newspaper at one John Reed, who would suffer "the consumption of his distillery" if he did not show sufficient enthusiasm for the rebels' cause.[13]

Hamilton's definition of the public good as embodied in his whiskey tax was further undermined by growing factionalism in Congress. Jefferson and the Democratic-Republicans had become increasingly convinced that Hamilton's understanding of the economic public good was faulty. As the consensus about what federal measures would answer the economic "good of the whole" broke down, so did the fragile agreement on what that good actually might be. Hamilton proposed bounties to encourage domestic manufacturing as part of a vision boosting domestic industry and discouraging reliance on imported goods. Jefferson feared such a move would open the floodgates to luxury, undermine virtue, and set the United States on a course of corruption and failure. Once again slippery definitions of the public good, along with its uncertain status in the economy, prompted dissent and debate.[14]

Disagreements in the centers of American power were not about to be smoothed over by western expansion. If the federal government had a difficult time imposing its authority on the economic order of familiar territories, the challenge of trying to insert the state into markets stretching across the places beyond was far more difficult. As the British imperial authorities had long since realized, the farther westward one moved on the North American continent, the harder it got for a state to make its authority felt in daily trade. Even with the cooperation of colonial governments, making the Indian trade a "fair trade" was well-nigh impossible. During both the Seven Years' War and the Revolutionary War, the British had also learned that the contracting systems deployed in the metropole to provision the army were useless in their North American colonies, where they were forced to deal with individual farmers whose main goal was to drive as hard a bargain as possible. Sellers did what they wanted regardless of what custom, duty, or law might dictate. During the 1790s the federal government discovered that such dealers were not about to change their freewheeling behavior to obey its rules: What was this authority, after all, but another imperial regime?

Across these far western territories, where Indians, Americans, and Britons once again met in the marketplace, the federal government found itself ensnared in "a clash of multiple economies and the opposing values that distinguished them." On one hand, the American state was in this situation because it behaved like the British before it: certain that its interest constituted the public good, it sought to impose its framework of fair trade on the local marketplace. People in that marketplace responded as Americans used to trading freely in an expansive landscape: they evaded the authorities and refused to obey the rules that would make them "fair traders," dealing instead to achieve maximum return to the individual.[15]

This dynamic unfolded in two marketing spaces by now very familiar to Americans: the Indian trading post and the fluid networks of face-to-face dealing between merchants and farmers. Like many other trading relationships, the Indian trade had been thrown into chaos by the Revolution. Competition among state governments jealously protecting their interest had not improved the situation. By 1783 Congress had noted the chaos and resolved that "the trade with the Indians ought to be regulated & security etc given by the traders for the punctual observance of such regulations." Backed by no authority, this resolution came to nothing. And so it was that, almost two years later, the Pennsylvania government received a petition from three men laying out the woes that befell individual traders caught in the crossfire of competing regulations. James Parr and his compatriots explained that they had purchased goods to trade with Indians at Fort Detroit, having gotten New York state permits, then found they could not obtain permission to pass British ports. Caught in a bureaucratic nightmare, they were now penniless, having sold no goods yet paying duty on their stock three times over. A series of acts passed by the federal government from 1790 onward was in part designed to create a more coordinated American Indian trade that avoided such pitfalls of petty state interest.[16]

Yet, as the wording of the 1796 "Act for Establishing Trading Houses with the Indian Tribe" revealed, the federal authorities were aiming for more than the role of peacemaker to squabbling Indian traders. To stake out their authority as the American empire moved westward, they proposed to do exactly what their former British masters had done (and were still doing): establish fixed trading posts in which the dealing between Europeans and Indians could be closely observed to ensure that fairness and the public good prevailed. Just like their British predecessors, government agents in charge at each post had to take an oath to obey the regulations of trade—an oath to the president, of course, not to King George. They also had to promise to ensure that prices were regulated and that Indians were not permitted to buy or sell goods that might corrupt them. As before, "interlopers" on the trade—the private and unlicensed men—faced heavy fines should they be caught trying to make a fast buck by undercutting the official government price. Certainly this was a republican regulation of the commerce; it was a "liberal trade" in which goods should be priced so "that the capital stock furnished by the United States may not be diminished." Yet it was also hard to distinguish from a British model in which the king's interest and the wealth and power of his nation were the ultimate beneficiaries.[17]

When it came to ensuring a well-fed and well-stocked United States military force in these contested areas, the federal government's reaction was similar. It moved to make provisioning easier by recruiting contractors to guarantee the supply of an agreed quantity of food or equipment. In the Ohio Valley of the early 1790s, men like Robert Elliot and Elie Williams led networks of subcontractors and individual farmers channeling livestock, food, and alcohol to the army. The business was lucrative, with one farmer claiming he did not "care [if] the war lasts this twenty years or my lifetime," since "we have a ready sale for our beef, flour, bacon, and old horses."

Anthony Wayne's army, and the federal state he represented, was bringing westward the kind of market opportunities enjoyed earlier by those who had provisioned the British army, and the Continental Army after it.[18]

But as with with the ill-fated Braddock expedition during the Seven Years' War and Washington's hungry winter in Valley Forge, the state found itself constantly struggling against the private interest of farmers and dealers out to obtain maximum profit, as they had always done. George II had ordered "our said Deputy Quarter Master General to provide the proper Conveniences" to General Edward Braddock, who nevertheless found himself constantly short of supplies. Farmers insisted he pay over the odds for beef, then delivered it late. "This Behaviour in the People does not only produce infinite Difficulty in Carrying on His Majesty's Service," raged Braddock, "but also greatly increases the Expense of it, the Charge thereby occasion'd in the Transportation of Provision and Stores through an unsettled Country." Undersupplied, Braddock and his troops met their fate shortly thereafter.[19]

Thirty-eight years later, farther northwest in the Ohio Valley, Anthony Wayne feared his army might meet a similar end against the British because of the "logistical nightmare" he faced trying to provision his troops. Wayne's difficulties were caused by contractors' failure to deliver provisions; as soon as they saw a state customer on the horizon their subcontractors, and the farmers and merchants below them, withheld supplies to get better prices. By 1794 there were complaints of "an excessive encrease in the price of the ration." Needless to say, federal Indian factors suffered similarly as local people continued to trade with Native Americans as they had done for centuries. In this fluid marketplace, federal agents found themselves unable to compete on price, being rooted in place as roving customers completely bypassed their trading posts.[20]

Americans could create a republic and a public good. They could adapt its definition and even legitimize it with acts, trading posts, and contracts. But in this vast, still expanding empire, reining in those property owners on the ground was a different matter altogether. The Constitution did not provide the definitive solution its supporters had hoped for. Although they could point to its success in solving the nation's problems of inflation and indebtedness, the federal system ran into many of the issues that had challenged its predecessors. It could not take possession of the public good or work out just how it related to private interest. And it could not stop Americans who put their individual interest first in the marketplace from ignoring their government's efforts to prevent it.

The Colonial Marketplace's American Legacy

In the course of researching and writing this book, I spent considerable time driving through the American landscape. Having grown up in Europe, I observed this landscape as a foreigner. Time and again I was struck by the way the spatial qualities of the eighteenth-century marketplace live on in contemporary America. As I was driving down a quiet rural highway, at a crossroads a cluster of stores and gas stations would suddenly appear. Other times I would pass the classic American eatery—the solitary roadside diner or barbecue joint. With my European expectations about settlement patterns in mind, I wondered how on earth these isolated stores made a profit. There was no village or town nearby and hardly any people lived within ten miles, so they were not part of what in Europe would be recognized as a place. Yet they make perfect sense in the American context; they are the twenty-first-century incarnation of the country store or the ferry landing. Since America is now a car-owning society, they spring up where highways intersect rather than where rivers join. They are composed of Walmarts, McDonald's, CVS pharmacies, and Exxon gas stations rather than general stores and taverns. But in both their function and the logic of their location, they differ little from their eighteenth-century forerunners. The crossroads is convenient for people whose nearest real town might be very far away or those who are looking to stop and refresh themselves on long journeys through this enormous nation.

The colonial marketplace's contemporary spatial legacy is more than matched by its political and economic legacy. In Britain the mantra of laissez-faire became ever more popular after 1800, whereas in the young United

States the trend remained toward an increase in the state's involvement in trade for a "public good." For Britons the loss of America, the shift of the imperial gaze eastward, and the end of the Napoleonic Wars came hand in hand with a distinctive change in the relation between government, the marketplace, and the broader economy. Both the state and its involvement in organizing domestic trade shrank. Officials who still supported corporatism and favored prosecuting market crimes against the common good, such as engrossing, were viewed as relics of the past. Although the Corn Laws showed that political economy would never completely shed its regulatory urge, historians have charted the way successive governments looked to retrenchment and to reducing bureaucracy after the "excesses" of a century spent building a huge fiscal-military state. The arguments of prominent political economists—first Smith, then Malthus, Bentham, and Ricardo—provided vital ideological support to such ambitions. On the ground, the "rationalization" of the new Poor Law in 1834 constituted the practical impact of such ideals for laborers who had been used to having the "common good" as their safety net.[1]

While Britons were mostly devoted to dismantling state regulation of the marketplace, many nineteenth-century Americans still believed it needed elaboration. Driven by their republican agenda, legislators looked for ways they could increase their institutional commitment to the public good in the marketplace. State and city governments unleashed a torrent of statutes and ordinances, building up layers of regulation of all aspects of domestic trade. This was a comprehensive effort to make the local marketplace operate for the good of the whole. Municipal authorities—in older cities like Philadelphia and in newer ones like Chicago—would assert their right to order the market and to determine how and where marketing took place, all the while claiming the advancement of the republic as their noble goal. Public works projects such as the construction of the Erie Canal were given state support on similar grounds. Commentators like Matthew Carey argued that the federal government should also use its powers to build up a state that nurtured the public good. Carey argued that boosting manufacturing was a public good even if it involved an expansion of slavery. Meanwhile, auctioneers defended their sales against merchants' criticism on the grounds that they operated for the public good by offering choices to consuming citizens.[2]

That the public good was invoked in all these commercial contexts is testimony not only to its continued value, but also to the enduring malleability of the concept. The effort to define it in the American marketplace would remain perpetually elusive. Although minorities continued to exist firmly outside its remit and women would struggle to participate in its definition, white men engaged in a prolonged debate about its meaning and its limits in an economy where they also cherished their private interests. Yet that very elusiveness would prove advantageous in this burgeoning capitalist society where there was no ambition to pin down the concept or recreate it in its fully historical European sense. Rather, the more capacious its definition, the easier it was to co-opt the private interest and fold it into this public good. Such creative elisions were essential, moreover, when the operation of the public good in the marketplace was part of the republican project's DNA; as a guiding principle it could not be abandoned but must be constantly redefined according to the flow of factional politics and the expansion of capitalism into ever more corners of the antebellum economy. Giving up on the public good in the marketplace would require giving up on the republican project, even though hanging on to the idea meant constant buffeting by the forces of entrepreneurship and individualism, which were equally hardwired into American economic culture during the colonial era.

It is far beyond the remit of this book to continue this story into the twentieth century, and if I did so it would be a very potted history indeed, full of overgeneralizations that fail to do justice to the complexities of American capitalist culture as it developed through and beyond the Civil War. Nevertheless, patterns of discourse about the market established through the colonial and Revolutionary eras echo down the centuries in some compelling ways. Most obviously, contemporary American capitalism remains awkwardly shackled to both the common good and the private interest. Debate swings to favor one or the other, but never have Americans agreed that one should be jettisoned altogether. With Republicans in power, contemporary political debate involves much hand-wringing about the need to bring the public good back into the American economy. Abigail Disney, the grandniece of Walt Disney, who made the family fortune in the most "American" way possible—through creativity and entrepreneurialism in the entertainment industry—has committed herself to putting the public good above her private economic interest, campaigning against tax cuts for the rich and supporting charities and internet startups. Her one-woman stand is merely the most visible of many common good initiatives. As wealth inequality increases, Bernie Sanders, Elizabeth Warren, think tanks, and local community groups all plead for a return to an economy in which the common good comes first.

Yet it is apparent that they face a nation as predisposed to pursuing its private interest as it is to creating narratives justifying that interest's legitimacy, and even its potential to work for the public good. As Bethany

Moreton has shown, no one has performed this balancing act with more as-surance than Sam Walton, the founder of Walmart. An anchor of the modern roadside marketplace, the Walmart corporation found a new way to merge huge personal wealth and the public interest in one of its modern American guises—Christian values. In Walmart, the seemingly opposing forces of pri-vate enrichment and the greater good are united in a corporation that claims to do right by its employees and customers, even those female employees it failed to promote or to pay equally. And for every American who views the Waltons as the purveyors of the core values of American capitalism, there is another ready to argue that they represent everything currently corrupt about it.[3]

Critically, the story of Walmart is one of white evangelicalism and capi-talism, and therefore also of white power in the marketplace. This power constitutes the final critical legacy of the colonial marketplace; its reliance on black agents who are nevertheless divested of power within it in every way possible by white property owners. The centrality of African Americans to American capitalism remained undimmed throughout the nineteenth and twentieth centuries. Following emancipation, some black leaders viewed the marketplace as a vital source of uplift, an opinion that has endured to the present through all permutations of the freedom struggle. Yet African Amer-icans would repeatedly come up against the same problem in this quest: whites not only controlled the main sources of capital in the marketplace, they also made and enforced the regulations determining who had access to it. In the contemporary United States, these inequalities persist all too plainly.[4]

Like their colonial forebears, Americans are still wrestling with a market system that wants to allow individual economic freedom while also pro-moting a national ideal that relies on the public good for its success and its integrity. The struggle is far from unique to the American economy, but the nature of the republican project makes the stakes that much higher, while the deep colonial, racist roots of individualism make it all the more intense. This is a project that has now been under way for nearly 250 years, and it seems we have only inched closer to a satisfactory resolution of its core con-tradictions. But it is also a project that requires Americans to carry on look-ing for that elusive solution—one that will allow them to do as they please in the marketplace while also contributing to the greater good of the United States of America.

Acknowledgments

I should have started writing my acknowledgments when I started research for this book. There are so many people to thank, and I worry that I will not remember them all. If I were an eighteenth-century storekeeper, I would certainly have gone bankrupt because I hadn't organized my accounts and my inventory well enough from the beginning. So if I've left anyone out it's my fault, as are any errors in the book itself.

The book involved copious archival research, a lot of presentations of chapters or sort-of-chapters, much writing and rewriting, and unlimited support from friends and family throughout all these stages. If I organize my gratitude into these four groups, like the appraiser making an inventory of my disorganized store on bankruptcy, I have some chance of catching everyone.

The archivists should come first, because without archives we have no history. In the United Kingdom I am grateful to the staff at the National Archives, the Mitchell Library in Glasgow, the Northumberland Record Office in Woodhorn and in Berwick-upon-Tweed, the Durham Record Office, and the Tyne and Wear Archives Service in Newcastle. Dr. Tony Lewis, curator at Glasgow Museum services, deserves a special mention for his willingness to talk Glasgow history with an early Americanist and for giving me access to the museum's vast collections of maps and objects. On the other side of the Atlantic, the staffs at the Huntington Library, the Library Company of Philadelphia, the Historical Society of Pennsylvania, Lancaster History, the Chester County Archives, the Bucks County Archives, the South Carolina Historical Society, and the South Carolina State Archive all made my research trips—often brief and intense as I tried to collect as much material as I could in as little time as possible—smooth and enjoyable.

In Columbia I am eternally grateful to Connie Schultz, who provided accommodation, hospitality, friendship, and a visit to the South Carolina state fair during my time there. Her vast knowledge of South Carolina history also led to a number of valuable documentary discoveries. In Philadelphia, Sally and Dan Gordon provided a home away from home during multiple research trips. Sally's intellectual contribution to this book is also immeasurable, not least because she thought up the snappy title when I failed, once again, to think of anything the least bit exciting.

Some of the archives I worked at provided financial support too. A one-month fellowship from the Library Company of Philadelphia's Program in Early American Economy and Society (PEAES) way back in 2005 set me on the road to the marketplace. A three-month Andrew Mellon fellowship at the Huntington Library in 2011 was critical to the project's gathering momentum. The Carnegie Fund for the faculty of Scottish universities gave me two small grants that permitted one research trip to the United States and one to Northumberland. My annual research allowance from the University of St Andrews School of History also funded much work. And finally, I thank Dan Richter and the selection committee for the McNeil Center's Barra Sabbatical Fellowship. Awarding me this fellowship for 2016–17 was central to this project's completion. Indeed, it's fair to say that had I not had the opportunity to spend the year at the McNeil Center, availed of the incredible resources of the Center, its fellows, its staff, and the University of Pennsylvania, this book would have taken a lot longer to make it into print.

As I hope my readers will find out, people make institutions. This is just as true now as in the eighteenth century. The scholars at numerous universities, conferences, and workshops improved this book immeasurably by listening to talks about my research or reading draft chapters. Peter Mancall's invitation to participate in a Borchard Foundation/University of Southern California workshop gave me constructive responses to a very early version of chapter 2. Further down the road, the members of the McNeil Center seminar twice read papers on the topic, while audiences at Trinity College Dublin's Early Modern History seminar, Carnegie Mellon's Center for Africanamerican Urban Studies, the PEAES annual conference on the early American economy, the "Alternative States" workshop at the University of California, Berkeley, Yale University's Early Modern Empires workshop, The Seminar at the Johns Hopkins University, the University of Delaware's History Department seminar, and the University of Cambridge's American Seminarhad to read my work through only once.

In these audiences were many of the great scholars and colleagues who make early American history such a wonderful field to be working in. I need especially to thank some longtime supporters who have had to read far too much of my work yet somehow never flag in their ability to offer insightful questions, useful comments, and moral support. Cathy Matson, Trevor Burnard, and Mark Peterson (individually as well as in his role as American Beginnings coeditor) all deserve special mention. Plaudits equally go to the people who read the entire manuscript and gave me such great feedback on it: my St Andrews colleague Richard Whatmore and, for the University of Chicago Press, Christopher Clark and Joanna Cohen. As a reader for the book's proposal, the late, great Daniel Vickers provided some early critique that inspired me and spurred me on to see the project through. At the press, Tim Mennel has been a wonderful editor, as have the editors of the American Beginnings series, Edward Gray, Stephen Mihm, and Mark Peterson. Rachel Kelly Unger, Ruth Goring, and Alice Bennett expertly guided the manuscript (and the author) through the editing and production process.

No less important are the scholars and friends who have provided inspiration and encouragement along the way, organized geographically: in the USA, Zara Anishanslin, Nick Bonneau, Mariana Dantas, Lauren Duval, Liz Ellis, Chris Heaney, Eric Herschthal, Whitney Martinko, Melissa Morris, Alex Ponsen, Christy Potroff, Alyssa Zuercher Reichardt, Dan Richter, Jessica Roney, Carole Shammas, Andrew Shankman, Nora Slonimsky, Whitney Nell Stewart, and Yevan Terrien. In the UK, Amy Blakeway, Rachel Douglas, Max Edling, Bronwen Everill, Kate Ferris, Nicholas Guyatt, Rab Houston, Simon Newman, Katie Stevenson, and Nuala Zahedieh. And in both places, at some point or other, Jane Dinwoodie, Simon Middleton, Paul Musselwhite, and Katherine Smoak. Last, but far from least, are my family. My parents did more than their fair share of child care while I worked in the archives, even if they enjoyed trips to Los Angeles and Philadelphia in the process. My husband Daniel read the whole manuscript even though he didn't have to, since he is neither a historian nor an academic. But his insights as a working economist and an expert in the history of economic thought were invaluable, more so because they came from someone who knew little about the exact topic. His support was practical as well as intellectual: he held the fort in Edinburgh many a time when I ventured off on yet another research trip or conference. Finally he even relocated to Philadelphia for the year so I could take up my fellowship at the McNeil Center. I hope he already knows that he is an exceptional husband, father, and all-round person, but I'll say it again for the record. Aside from a recent love of Lin-Manuel Miranda's *Hamilton*, Klara and Lily have contributed less to the intellectual preoccupations of this book, but that is no matter because their very existence is enough.

Notes

ABBREVIATIONS USED IN NOTES

APS	American Philosophical Society, Philadelphia
BRO	Berwick-upon-Tweed Record Office
HL	Huntington Library, San Marino, California
HSP	Historical Society of Pennsylvania
LCHS	Lancaster County Historical Society
LCP	Library Company of Philadelphia
ML	Mitchell Library, Glasgow
NRO	Northumberland Record Office, Woodhorn
PSA	Pennsylvania State Archives
SCDAH	South Carolina Department of Archives and History
SCHGM	*South Carolina Historical Society Magazine*, manuscripts described by Helen Gardner McCormack
SHC	Southern Historical Collections, University of North Carolina
SCHS	South Carolina Historical Society
TNA	The National Archives
TWAS	Tyne and Wear Archives Service

INTRODUCTION

1. Pottinger's letter can be seen at https://stevepottinger.co.uk/coffee/.

2. Edward Luttwak, *Turbo-Capitalism: Winners and Losers in the Global Economy* (New York, 2000).

3. On Philadelphia's merchant community that directed international trade see Michelle Craig McDonald, "The Chance of a Moment: Coffee and the New West Indies Commodities Trade," *William and Mary Quarterly* 62 (July 2005): 441-72, and see other essays in this issue for further discussion of merchants and trade in the later eighteenth century; Thomas M. Doerflinger, *A Vigorous Spirit of Enterprise: Merchants and Economic Development in Revolutionary Philadelphia* (Chapel Hill, NC, 1986); Emma Hart and Cathy Matson, "Situating Merchants in Late Eighteenth-Century Port Cities," *Early American Studies* 15 (Summer 2017): 660-82; Cathy Matson, *Merchants and Empire: Trading in Colonial New York* (Baltimore, 1998); Sheryllynne Haggerty, *The British Atlantic Merchant*

Community, 1760-1810: Men, Women, and the Distribution of Goods (Leiden, 2006); Gautham Rao, *National Duties: Customs Houses and the Making of the American State* (Chicago, 2016), chap. 1. On (in)effective government and factionalism in Philadelphia see Jessica Choppin Roney, *Governed by a Spirit of Opposition: The Origins of American Political Practice in Colonial Philadelphia* (Baltimore, 2014); and Gary Nash, *Quakers and Politics: Pennsylvania, 1681-1726* (Princeton, NJ, 1968). For a more general assessment of economic life, trade, and politics in the city see Gary Nash, *The Urban Crucible: The Urban Seaports and the Origins of the American Revolution* (Cambridge, 1979).

4. Those historians who emphasized the consumption of British imports and its link to self-sufficiency include Daniel Vickers, "Competency and Competition: Economic Culture in Early America," *William and Mary Quarterly* 47 (1990): 3-29; Richard Lyman Bushman, "Markets and Composite Farms in Early America," *William and Mary Quarterly* 55 (1998): 351-74; Carole Shammas, "How Self-Sufficient Was Early America?," *Journal of Interdisciplinary History* 13 (Autumn 1982): 247-72; T. H. Breen, "An Empire of Goods: The Anglicization of Colonial America, 1690-1776," *Journal of British Studies* 25, no. 4 (1986): 467-99. Perhaps the leading proponent of the idea of self-sufficiency was James Henretta, "Families and Farms: Mentalité in Pre-industrial America, *William and Mary Quarterly* 35 (January 1978): 3-32.

5. For prime examples see David Hancock, *Citizens of the World: London Merchants and the Integration of the British Atlantic Community, 1735-1785* (Cambridge, 1995); Peter Coclanis, ed., *The Atlantic Economy during the Seventeenth and Eighteenth Centuries: Organization, Operation, Practice, and Personnel* (Columbia, SC, 2005); Jacob M. Price, *Capital and Credit in British Overseas Trade: The View from the Chesapeake, 1770-1776* (Cambridge, MA, 1980); Kenneth Morgan, *Slavery, Atlantic Trade, and the British Economy, 1660-1800* (New York, 2000); Henry A. Gemery and Jan Hogendorn, eds., *The Uncommon Market: Essays in the Economic History of the Atlantic Slave Trade* (New York, 1979). New England is the notable exception when it comes to detailed knowledge of local economies, of course, as a fascination with the cradle of American democracy focused sustained attention on its economic and political development. Margaret Newell comes closest to analyzing local market culture in a study that addresses the New England political economy at the provincial/metropolitan level. See Margaret Newell, *From Dependency to Independence: Economic Revolution in Colonial New England* (Ithaca, NY, 1998); Christopher Clark, *The Roots of Rural Capitalism: Western Massachusetts, 1780-1860* (Ithaca, NY, 1990); Stephen Innes, *Creating the Commonwealth: The Economic Culture of Puritan New England* (New York, 1995); Daniel Vickers, *Farmers and Fishermen: Two Centuries of Work in Essex County* (Chapel Hill, NC, 1994). Yet, as most historians would now agree, New England cannot stand in for the wider range of colonial American experience.

6. A major exception to the standard narrative is Ellen Hartigan-O'Connor, *The Ties That Buy: Women and Commerce in Revolutionary America* (Philadelphia, 2009). Hartigan-O'Connor has pointed out the slippages between early modern understandings of the market as a physical space and the interpretation offered by Adam Smith and has applied these insights to women's economies in Newport, Rhode Island, and Charleston, South Carolina, at the end of the eighteenth century.

7. Some works under the auspices of this field—some more explicitly than others—include Seth Rockman, *Scraping By: Wage Labor, Slavery, and Survival in Early Baltimore* (Baltimore, 2009); Seth Rockman, "What Makes the History of Capitalism Newsworthy?," *Journal of the Early Republic* 34 (Fall 2014): 439-66; Brian Phillips Murphy, *Building the Empire State: Political Economy in the Early Republic* (Philadelphia, 2015); Sharon Ann Murphy, *Investing in Life: Insurance in Antebellum America* (Baltimore, 2010); Jessica Lepler, *The Many Panics of 1837: People, Politics, and the Creation of a Transatlantic Financial Crisis* (New York, 2013); Sven Beckert, *Empire of Cotton: A Global History* (New York, 2014); Walter Johnson, *River of Dark Dreams: Slavery and Empire in the Cotton Kingdom* (Cambridge, MA, 2013); Edward Baptist, *The Half That's Never Been Told: Slavery and the Making of American Capitalism* (New York, 2014); Jonathan Levy, *Freaks of Fortune: The Emerging World of Capitalism and Risk in America* (Cambridge, MA, 2012).

8. Charles Sellers, *The Market Revolution: Jacksonian America, 1814-1846* (New York, 1991),

44; John Lauritz Larson, *The Market Revolution in America: Liberty, Ambition, and the Eclipse of the Common Good* (New York, 2009), 2–5; Daniel Walker Howe, *What God Hath Wrought: The Transformation of America, 1815-1848* (New York, 2007), 44–47.

9. In their efforts to break down the myth of self-sufficiency, historians have mostly sought to connect consumers to Atlantic markets, focusing principally on ocean-facing economic networks. For example, Hancock, *Citizens of the World*; Mark Hanna, *Pirate Nests and the Rise of the British Empire, 1570-1740* (Chapel Hill, NC, 2015). The importance of the Atlantic slave trade also has placed most attention on outward-looking trade connections on the North American continent and in the Caribbean. See Philip D. Curtin, *The Atlantic Slave Trade: A Census* (Madison, WI, 1969); Gregory O'Malley, *Final Passages: The Intercolonial Slave Trade of British America, 1619-1807* (Chapel Hill, NC, 2014). Already in 1991 John McCusker and Russell Menard noted the lack of work on internal markets and the domestic economy of colonial America. See McCusker and Menard, *The Economy of British America, 1607-1789* (Chapel Hill, NC, 1991), 277–330. David Hancock's recent call for economic histories that focus more on ordinary primary actors provides the best agenda for a new approach to colonial American economic history that moves beyond "Whiggish preoccupation with economic growth . . . and [is] not answered primarily by statistical analysis." David Hancock, "Rethinking the Economy of British America," in *The Economy of Early America: Historical Perspectives and New Directions*, ed. Cathy Matson (State College, PA, 2006), 71–106. Some historians have focused on domestic trading, but often in the context of particular groups and not under the rubric of a domestic marketplace more generally. As a result, we have targeted knowledge about economic exchange between certain groups of people at certain times and places, but no overview. See Philip D. Morgan, *Slave Counterpoint: Black Culture in the Eighteenth Century Lowcountry and Chesapeake* (Chapel Hill, NC, 1998), 318–66; Hartigan-O'Connor, *Ties That Buy*; Kathryn E. Holland Braun, *Deerskins and Duffels: The Creek Indian Trade with Anglo-America, 1685-1815*, 2nd ed. (Omaha, NE, 2008); Ann Smart Martin, *Buying into the World of Goods: Early Consumers in Backcountry Virginia* (Baltimore, 2008). A major exception here is Christopher Tomlins, *Freedom Bound: Law, Labor, and Civic Identity in Colonizing English America, 1580-1865* (New York, 2010). Tomlins traces the origins of the "free labor" myth from the earliest moments of colonization through the Civil War.

10. Ellen Hartigan-O'Connor's work on women's economies is a case in point. Women's credit networks, and their involvement in local exchange, fanned out from "housefuls" of people whose composition did not radically change with independence. Hartigan-O'Connor, *Ties That Buy*, 13–38.

11. I derive the language of "ligaments" from "Ligaments: Everyday Connections of Colonial Economies," special issue, *Early American Studies* 13 (Fall 2015). These papers constitute one of the best sources for understanding these "on the ground" economic exchanges.

12. My methodology draws on scholars who see spaces as culturally produced by the human actors who move through them, most especially Anthony Giddens. Giddens's theory of structuration proposes a "duality of structure" in which individuals and institutions are constantly in dialogue with each other, with the locations of such interactions essential as generative *"settings* of interaction." Anthony Giddens, *The Constitution of Society: Outline of the Theory of Structuration* (Cambridge, 1984), xxv. Applying Giddens's ideas to the nineteenth-century Louisiana plantation landscape, Anthony Kaye has explained how "as repetition gives a pattern to our actions' unintended consequences, rules and institutions are replicated across space and gain a place in society." Anthony Kaye, *Joining Places* (Chapel Hill, NC, 2010), 12–13. See also Andy Wood, *The Memory of the People: Custom and Popular Senses of the Past in Early Modern England* (Cambridge, 2013). Wood argues that "Landscape is, above all, a social construction, a collective way of seeing, into which are built collective ways of remembering. . . . many geographers assume that modes of production generate their own historically distinct material environments and ways of perceiving those environments" (188). Also, "landscape was not only a bearer of meaning but a site of conflict" (196).

13. On the early years of Pennsylvania and South Carolina, see Nash, *Quakers and Politics*; John Smolenski, *Friends and Strangers: The Making of a Creole Culture in Colonial Pennsylvania*

(Philadelphia, 2010); L. H. Roper, *Conceiving Carolina: Proprietors, Planters, and Plots, 1662-1729* (New York, 2004); Peter H. Wood, *Black Majority: Negroes in Colonial South Carolina from 1670 through the Stono Rebellion* (New York, 1974); Michelle LeMaster and Bradford Wood, eds., *Creating and Contesting Carolina: Proprietary Era Histories* (Columbia, SC, 2013). On Philadelphia and Charleston see Nash, *Urban Crucible*; Karin Wulf, *Not All Wives: Women of Colonial Philadelphia* (Ithaca, NY, 2000); Emma Hart, *Building Charleston: Town and Society in the Eighteenth-Century British Atlantic World* (Charlottesville, VA, 2010); Hartigan-O'Connor, *Ties That Buy*. On interactions with Native Americans see Jane Merritt, *At the Crossroads: Indians and Empire on the Mid-Atlantic Frontier, 1700-1763* (Chapel Hill, NC, 2003); James H. Merrill, *Into the American Woods: Negotiations on the Pennsylvania Frontier* (New York, 2000); Michelle LeMaster, *Brothers Born of One Mother: British-Native American Relations in the Colonial Southeast* (Charlottesville, VA, 2013); Alan Gallay, *The Indian Slave Trade* (New Haven, CT, 2002).

14. On the social similarities and differences in Britain's American colonies see Jack P. Greene, *Pursuits of Happiness: The Social Development of Early Modern British Colonies and the Formation of American Culture* (Chapel Hill, NC, 1988). On contrasting labor systems see Sharon V. Salinger, *To Serve Well and Faithfully: Labor and Indentured Servitude in Pennsylvania, 1682-1800* (Cambridge, 1987); Robert Olwell, *Masters, Slaves, and Subjects: The Culture of Power in the South Carolina Low Country, 1740-1790* (Ithaca, NY, 1998). On settlement patterns see Joseph A. Ernst and H. Roy Merrens, "Camden's Turrets Pierce the Skies! The Urban Process in the Southern Colonies during the Eighteenth Century," *William and Mary Quarterly*, 3rd ser., 30 (1973): 549-74; Kenneth E. Lewis, *The Carolina Backcountry Venture: Tradition, Capital, and Circumstance in the Development of Camden and the Wateree Valley, 1740-1810* (Columbia, SC, 2017); and Judith Ridner, *A Town in Between: Carlisle, Pennsylvania, and the Early Mid-Atlantic Interior* (Philadelphia, 2010). On varied backcountry experiences see Patrick Spero, *Frontier Country: The Politics of War in Early Pennsylvania* (Philadelphia, 2016), and Rachel N. Klein, *Unification of a Slave State: The Rise of the Planter Class in the South Carolina Backcountry, 1760-1808* (Chapel Hill, NC, 1990). On agricultural economies see James T. Lemon, *The Best Poor Man's Country: A Geographical Study of Early Southeastern Pennsylvania* (Baltimore, 1972), and S. Max Edelson, *Plantation in Colonial South Carolina* (Cambridge, 2006).

15. The English local history movement's founder was W. G. Hoskins. See Hoskins, *The Making of the English Landscape* (London, 1955), for the epitome of his approach. On the transfer of local cultures to the colonial, see David Hackett Fisher, *Albion's Seed: Four British Folkways in America* (Oxford, 1989), and Tomlins, *Freedom Bound*.

16. On the economic growth of Glasgow, Newcastle, and their environs in the eighteenth century see T. M. Devine, *The Tobacco Lords: A Study of the Tobacco Merchants of Glasgow and Their Trading Activities c. 1740-90* (Edinburgh, 1975); Catriona MacLeod, "Women, Work and Enterprise in Glasgow, c. 1740-1830" (PhD diss., University of Glasgow, 2015); David Levine and Keith Wrightson, *The Making of an Industrial Society: Whickham, 1560-1765* (Oxford, 1991).

CHAPTER ONE

1. Adam Smith, *An Inquiry into the Nature and Causes of the Wealth of Nations*, vol. 2, part 4.2.9, http://www.econlib.org/library/Smith/smWN13.html#B.IV,%20Ch.2,%20of%20Restraints%20 upon%20the%20Importation%20from%20Foreign%20Countries, accessed March 10, 2018.

2. There are numerous instances of such uses of the word. One good example is the Benjamin Fuller Letterbook AMB 3785, vol. 1, 1762-81, Historical Society of Pennsylvania (hereafter HSP). Fuller writes to correspondents that "ordinary colored linens do not answer in this market," "there is no accounting for the fluctuation of markets," and "I endeavor'd to give you a present state of our market."

3. The two vested interests Smith focused on were guilds with their apprenticeship systems and the government. Yet many more were at play in the British economy of the eighteenth century. On the political economy of interests see Perry Gauci, ed., *Regulating the British Economy, 1660–1850* (Farnham, UK, 2011). On Smith in his contemporary context see Emma Rothschild, *Economic Sentiments: Adam Smith, Condorcet, and the Enlightenment* (Cambridge, MA, 2001), 156 and 72–115.

4. Keith Wrightson, *Earthly Necessities: Economic Lives in Early Modern Britain* (New Haven, CT, 2000), 335.

5. James Davis, *Medieval Market Morality: Life, Law and Ethics in the English Marketplace, 1200–1500* (Cambridge, 2012), 410–11.

6. For a detailed survey of the agricultural marketing function of fairs and their distribution see J. A. Chartres, "Agricultural Markets and Trade, 1500–1750," in Joan Thirsk, ed., *The Agricultural History of England and Wales*, vol. 5 (Cambridge, 1990), 171–92. For the longevity of fairs through the eighteenth century see Ian Mitchell, "The Changing Role of Fairs in the Long Eighteenth Century: Evidence from the North Midlands," *Economic History Review* 60 (August 2007): 545–73; Fernand Braudel, *Civilization and Capitalism: The Wheels of Commerce* (London, 1982), 82–85 on fairs and 52–53 on hiring labor at fairs. For the Stourbridge fair quotation see Daniel Defoe, *A Tour thro' the Whole Island of Britain, Divided into Circuits or Journies* (1724), letter 1, part 3, "Norfolk and Cambridge."

7. William Owen, *An Authentic Account of All the Fairs in England and Wales, as They Have Been Settled to Be Held since the Alteration of the Stile* (London, 1756). See also *A Description of the Most Remarkable High-Ways, and Whole Known Fairs and Mercats in Scotland* (Edinburgh, 1711).

8. Manuscript timetable of local fairs, ZBU/B/5/8/22, Northumberland Record Office, Wood-horn (hereafter NRO); NRO 558/40 Notebook re fairs and population 1776; "A List of all the Fairs, fixed and moveable, in the Counties of York, Durham, Northumberland, Cumberland, Westmorland, Lancaster, and in Lincs," in *The Newcastle Memorandum Book, or Methodical Pocket Journal, for 1776*, ZS1—39, Berwick-upon-Tweed Record Office (hereafter BRO); ASSI 45 33/2/84; ASSI 45 45/28/2/54; ASSI 33/2/77-79 and 119, the National Archives (hereafter TNA).

9. For the Bute incident see *Newcastle Courant*, November 5, 1768. For another example of political culture at fairs see *Newcastle Courant*, September 9, 1758: at Weymouth "We have had an uncommon Cattle Fair, held for the first Time on Ship Board; French Cows and Horses, the Plunder of Cherburg, were sold at 10s a head, and Hogs &c in Proportion. When the Fleet sailed it was found necessary to make Neptune a Present of what was not disposed of, many of which swam ashore; and here is Plenty of French Beef, if Englishmen could eat it."

10. *Caledonian Mercury*, September 3, 1763: "That the whole principal Gentlemen, Drovers, and other Dealers in black cattle, in the West and North Highlands of Scotland, have resolved to hold TWO SEVERAL TRYSTS this season, for the sales of their cattle, both at the village of DOUN, in the county of Perth, lying five miles be west the town of Stirling, the first of these trysts October, second November.... purchasers will have it in their power, either to carry their cattle southward, by Stirling, or by the Ford of Frew, as they please."

11. *Newcastle Courant*, October 16, 1725: "We are advised from Herefordshire, That a Fair call'd, *Ring staud-Fair*, was held on Michaelmas-day last near Shepdon-Court in that County." For the Argyllshire case see *Caledonian Mercury*, May 24, 1762.

12. Haggertson MS ZHC1XIV, BRO.

13. *Owens Book of Fairs* listed all relevant acts in its opening pages. For fair regulation see also *Newcastle Courant*, May 6, 1729: "Whereas some Disputes have happen'd about the Stowers, whereof the Tents and Stalls are made, at the Fair commonly call'd Whitsunbank, this is to give Notice to all who design to set up Tents or Stalls there, that for the future, they will be allowed to cut Ground and cary off their Frames and Stowers, paying 6d yearly for each Tent or Stall, provided the Tents do not exceed four Yards in length, nor the Stalls their usual length; none will be allowed to cut Ground, without paying the said Price, and if any adventures to do it, they may expect to be prosecuted; none will be allowed to set up Tents or Stalls before the Fair Day ... unless they agree to pay the above

Price. NB Since Frames came into use, in the Place of Stowers, they have always paid 6d per Frame for them, besides Tolls, and now they are to pay but 6d Toll and all. The Stowers have always been detained since time immemorial (as an acknowledgment for cutting ground) by those who possess the Ground, as can be sufficiently proved." *Newcastle Courant,* June 16, 1753: "We hear from Barnard castle, that Wednesday last, being their new Fair, there was the greatest concourse of people ever known; Cattle of all sorts sold exceeding well, and wool much better than was expected."

14. For history of markets see Petitions to the Town Council, May 2, 1798, 163, A2/1/2/27 Mitchell Library (hereafter ML). For the fish market see May 13, 1701, in *Extracts from the Records of the Burgh of Glasgow,* vol. 4, *1691–1707,* ed. J. D. Marwick and Robert Renwick (Glasgow, 1908). On eighteenth-century improvements see "Branches of the Towns Revenue under the Management of the City Treasurer: Inventory 15th May 1755," in Treasurers and Chamberlain Accounts: Journal no. 1 of the Town of Glasgows Affairs, D-CC 1 -3-1, ML; Incorporation of Gardeners, item 4: The Green Mercat Book starting November 1758, T-TH 13, ML.

15. For examples see W. Ellis, *The Country Housewife's Family Companion, or Profitable Directions for Whateer relates to the Management and Good Oeconomy of the Domestick Concerns of a Country Life* (London, 1750); E. Smith, *The Complete Housewife, or Accomplished Gentlewoman's Companion . . . with Directions for Marketing* (London, 1766); Information of John Dale : "This informant on his oath saith that on Thursday last ye 10th Inst Decembr as he went into ye house of James Rowth of Yarme afords to put up some beef and other Marketing into his sack in order to be ready for some company that was to call upon him to goe home," December 12, 1724, ASSI 45/18/2, item 59; "Mary wife of thomas Chapman of Soth Newbald joyner says that about candlelight on Wednesday the 7th instant entring into Mrs Archers House in Wighton to deliver a message and to seek a man to carry her marketings home, she observd in the kitchin a Tankard lying upon a Coat," November 9, 1744, ASSI 45/23/1, item 14a, TNA.

16. Treasurers and Chamberlain Accounts: Journal No. 1 of the Town of Glasgows Affairs, D-CC 1 -3-1, ML.

17. On Blackett's checkered reputation and the factions of local politics see Kathleen Wilson, *The Sense of the People: Politics, Culture, and Imperialism in England, 1715–1785* (Cambridge, 2006), 315–75. For an account of the 1755 dispute see Allen Banks Hind, *History of Northumberland: Under the Direction of the Northumberland County History Committee 1896,* vol. 3, *Hexhamshire, Part 1* (London, 1896), 258–61.

18. Case papers re: payment of market tolls 1757–60 and 1763, DU 1/51/72–151, Durham County Record Office. For political dispute over marketing in an unincorporated city see the case of Manchester as discussed in Roger Scola, *Feeding the Victorian City: The Food Supply of Manchester, 1770–1870* (Manchester, 1992), chap. 7, "Market Provision."

19. Common Council Order Book, 1699–1718, tobacconists 83, enforced shop closure 89, joiners and cabinetmakers not to have shops in any public part of town p. 202, granting a shop lease p. 122, unincorporated wigmakers to stop selling wigs, p. 86, MD/NC/2/3, Tyne and Wear Archives Service (hereafter TWAS). See also Treasurers and Chamberlain Accounts: Journal No. 1 of the Town of Glasgows Affairs, D-CC 1 -3-1, ML.

20. Brodie Waddell, *God, Duty, and Community in English Economic Life* (Woodbridge, UK, 2012); quotation from chap. 2, p. 96.

21. For cases brought against itinerant traders in the Durham marketplace see DU/51/164–176, DH/T22, DU1/51/170, DU1/51/173, Durham County Record Office.

22. This act was the only way Pitt could sweeten the pill of a shop tax, which the shopkeepers accepted precisely because it promised to put peddlers out of business. See Hoh Cheung Mui and Lorna Mui, *Shops and Shopkeeping in Eighteenth Century England* (Kingston, 1989), 73–105. For derogatory comments about peddlers see *Newcastle Courant,* April 23, 1774; *Leeds Intelligencer,* July 7, 1772; *Newcastle Courant,* May 2, 1772.

23. Indeed, James Davis has suggested that the imperatives of the "moral economy" were more

prominent in the seventeenth and eighteenth centuries than in the medieval period precisely because such values were being challenged by new methods of marketing and new ideas of the market. See Davis, *Medieval Market Morality*, 136.

24. Claire Walsh, "Shops, Shopping, and the Art of Decision Making in Eighteenth-Century England," in *Gender, Taste, and Material Culture in Britain and North America, 1700-1830*, ed. Amanda Vickery and John Styles (New Haven, CT, 2007), 151-79; Jon Stobart, "Food Retailers and Rural Communities: Cheshire Butchers in the Long Eighteenth Century," *Local Population Studies* 79 (2007): 23-37; Jon Stobart and Ilje Van Damme, *Modernity and the Second Hand Trade: European Consumption Cultures and Practices, 1700-1900* (Basingstoke, UK, 2010).

25. For the ongoing importance of vested interests at national level see Julian Hoppit, *Britain's Political Economies: Parliament and Economic Life, 1660-1800* (Cambridge, 2017). For the greater influence of guilds in Scotland see Bob Harris and Charles McKean, *The Scottish Town in the Enlightenment, 1740-1820* (Edinburgh, 2014), 428-88. In Newcastle see Wilson, *Sense of the People*. For the declining influence of guilds elsewhere see Patrick Wallis, "Labor, Law and Training in Early Modern London: Apprenticeship and the City's Institutions," *Journal of British Studies* 51, no. 4 (2012): 791-819; Chris Minns and Patrick Wallis, "Rules and Reality: Quantifying the Practice of Apprenticeship in Premodern England," *Economic History Review*, 65, no. 2 (2012): 556-79.

26. For a careful examination of these supply chains in their Philadelphia and Liverpool contexts see Sheryllynne Haggerty, *The British Atlantic Trading Community, 1760-1810: Men, Women, and the Distribution of Goods* (Leiden, 2006).

27. J. A. Chartres, "Middlemen and Factors," in *Agrarian History of England and Wales, 1450-1750*, ed. Joan Thirsk (Cambridge, 1967); D. A. Baker, "The Marketing of Corn in the First Half of the Eighteenth Century: North-East Kent," *Agricultural History Review* 18, no. 2 (1970): 126-50.

28. E. P. Thompson, "The Moral Economy of the English Crowd in the Eighteenth Century," *Past and Present* 50 (February 1971): 76-136; Rothschild, *Economic Sentiments*: "Smith's opinion, as has been seen, is that laws and regulations are influenced by powerful groups; that small institutions defend insiders and exclude outsiders under the protection of these laws; and that the fluctuating jurisprudence of public laws and small institutions provides opportunity for personal vexation, against insiders as well as outsiders" (114). On Scottish courts see Bob Harris, "Scots burghs, 'privilege' and the Court of Session in the Eighteenth Century," *Urban History* 44, no. 3 (2017): 381-401.

29. Quotation from Wendy Thwaites, "Dearth and the Marketing of Agricultural Produce: Oxfordshire, c. 1750-1800," *Agricultural History Review* 33, no. 2 (1985): 131; John Bohstedt, *The Politics of Provisions: Food Riots, Moral Economy, and Market Transition in England, c. 1550-1850* (Farnham, UK, 2010); S. E. Brown, "'A Just and Profitable Commerce": Moral Economy and the Middle Classes in Eighteenth-Century London," *Journal of British Studies* 32, no. 4 (1993): 305-32.

30. "Memorial for the Magistrates and Town Council of Glasgow concerning Their Letter to Change Marketplaces in the City," in Petitions to Town Council, May 2, 1798, p. 163, A2/1/2/27, ML.

31. Jon Stobart, *Sugar and Spice: Grocers and Groceries in Provincial England, 1650-1830* (Oxford, 2012), 165-66.

32. C. Y. Ferdinand, "Selling It to the Provinces: News and Commerce round Eighteenth-Century Salisbury," in *Consumption and the World of Goods*, ed. John Brewer and Roy Porter (London, 1999), 393-411.

33. *Newcastle Courant*, October 5, 1765.

34. *Newcastle Courant*, April 6, 1776.

35. DU/51/164-176, DH/T22, DU1/51/170, DU1/51/173, Durham County Record Office.

36. Sheryllynne Haggerty, *Merely for Money? Business Culture in the British Atlantic, 1750-1815* (Liverpool, 2012); Matson, *Merchants and Empire*; Hancock, *Citizens of the World*.

37. March 24, 1651, Report of Mr Edward Man; December 18, 1651 Letter from Christopher Nicolson, both in *Extracts from the Minutes of Newcastle Merchant Adventurers* ed. F. W. Dendy (Durham, UK, 1895). Merchants of course also lobbied the national government in London. For

more on this see William Pettigrew, *Freedom's Debt* (Chapel Hill, NC, 2013); Nuala Zahedieh, *The Capital and the Colonies* (Cambridge, 2012); Steve Pincus, *1688: The First Modern Revolution* (New Haven, CT, 2009). On Glasgow's development of its corporate port facilities see James Deas, *The River Clyde: A Historical Description of the Rise and Progress of the Harbour of Glasgow and of the Improvement of the River from Glasgow to Port Glasgow* (Glasgow, 1876). For concerns about competition from Greenock see "Committee Reports of Certain Issues," p. 67, B10/15/7587-7598, ML. On the silting up of the river Avon see Kenneth Morgan, *Bristol and the Atlantic Trade in the Eighteenth Century* (Cambridge, 2004), 29-32.

38. For reports of the Bristol scheme see *Ipswich Journal*, February 13 and March 7, 1772; *Reading Mercury*, February 24, 1772; *Newcastle Journal*, December 26, 1772; "Bath Dec 14, An address, signed by 365 principal traders and shopkeepers of Bristol, relative to the many hardships they suffer from the unfair practices of hawkers and pedlars, was on Wednesday sent to their members, Lord Clare and Mr Brickdale, intreating them to endeavour to obtain an act, either totally to suppress the trade of those people, or put it under such regulations as may prevent the evils complained of." For Glasgow collection see Recollections of John Brown, Bogle MS, vol. 1 (91a), ML. On self-help clubs in tough economic times see Peter Clark, *British Clubs and Societies, 1580-1800: The Origins of an Associational World* (Oxford, 2000), 362.

39. Brown included numerous such assessments in his "Recollections." See also November 1758, "Provisions are getting cheaper thanks to a very good harvest. . . . This Bounty of Provisions has been a great relief to the Poor who was reduced to very great straits from the Long Contenuance of the dearth. . . . Trade . . . Great Britain since the Beginning of this War has flourishd. The town of Glasgow has had its Share . . . Of the American & West Indian trade"; December 1759, "Trade has been remarkably good all over Britain all this year and in all our Plantations & Colonys owing to our great success in the Warr. There has been a great sickness in Glasgow and in Severall Places . . . very frequent and Mortall, Oatmeal at 7½ per peck"; 1763, "Trade of Glasgow this year has been dull and money scarce the Low Price of Tobacco has been partly the Cause of it Tobacco selling from 1¾ to 2¼ according to the Quality." Recollections of John Brown, Bogle MS, vol. 1 (91a), ML.

40. In March 1766 he "Went to Edr and presented a petition to the Board of Trustees craving a Bounty for Introducing the Manufactory of Gunea Goods In Scotland." In September 1766, in a thoroughly disapproving tone, he reported the efforts of London's linen drapers to repeal the ban on French cambrics and lawns. Recollections of John Brown, Bogle MS, vol. 1 (91a), ML. Other traders, such as Joseph Oxley, the manager of the Seaton Delaval estate in Northumberland, also combined older and newer conceptions of the market in their trading lives. For example, "Sir I herein inclose you two bills value together £130 & on the arrival of Capt Gedling please to ship me twenty two tuns of yr best salt, with good contents. Wod you chuse to take the Dairies of old milk Cheese you had of me last year, or if a few more I can buy them. I shall be obligs to you to send me a cart load or two of Chalk & charge it to Sir, yr sevt Fowler Hickes PS Your answer by return relative to the Cheeses as Yarm Fair is on Tuesday the 20th Inst please to think of the Franks." Mr. Oxley to Mr. Dobson, Richmond, October 11, 1772, 2/DE.8, Delaval Papers, NRO.

41. Margaret Hunt, *The Middling Sort: Commerce, Gender and the Family in England, 1680-1780* (Berkeley, CA, 1996); Jane Whittle, "Enterprising Widows and Active Wives: Women's Unpaid Work in the Household Economy of Early Modern England," *History of the Family* 19, no. 3 (2014): 283-300; Amy M. Friode, *Silent Partners: Women as Public Investors during Britain's Financial Revolution, 1690-1750* (New York, 2016); Hannah Barker, *Family and Business during the Industrial Revolution* (Oxford, 2017); Jarna Heinonen and Kirsi Vainio-Korhonen, eds., *Women in Business Families: From Past to Present* (London, 2018).

42. On the problems and potential of extrapolating social and economic patterns from archaeological evidence in North America and West Africa see Joe Watkins, "Bone-Lickers, Grave Diggers, and Other Unsavory Characters: Archaeologists, Archaeological Cultures, and the Disconnect from Native Peoples," in *The Oxford Handbook of North American Archaeology*, ed. Timothy Pauketat (New

York, 2015), 28–38; Akinwumi Ogundiran, "Material Life and Domestic Economy in a Frontier of the Oyo Empire during the Mid-Atlantic Age," in "Current Trends in the Archaeology of African History," special issue, *International Journal of African Historical Studies*. 42, no. 3 (2009): 351–84.

43. On the Siin in Senegambia see Ibrahima Thiaw, "Atlantic Impacts on Inland Semegambia: French Penetration and African Initiatives in Eighteenth- and Nineteenth-Century Gajaaga and Bundu (Upper Senegal River)," in *Power and Landscape in Atlantic West Africa: Archaeological Perspectives*, ed. J. Cameron Monroe and Akinwumi Ogundiran (Cambridge, 2012), 64. On Aro markets See G. Ugo Nwokeji, *Slave Trade and Culture in the Bight of Biafra* (Cambridge, 2010), 31–79. On Segou see Kevin C. McDonald and Seydou Camara, "Segou, Slavery, and Sifinso," in Monroe and Ogundiran, *Power and Landscape*, 169–90. See also Michael Tuck, "Everyday Commodities, the Rivers of Guinea, and the Atlantic World: The Beeswax Export Trade, c. 1450–c. 1800," in *Brokers of Change: Atlantic Commerce and Cultures in Pre-Colonial Western Africa*, ed. Toby Green, Proceedings of the British Academy no. 178 (Oxford, 2012), 285–304.

44. Ogundiran, "Material Life and Domestic Economy"; Sam Spiers, "The Eguafo Polity: Between the Traders and Raiders," in Monroe and Ogundiran, *Power and Landscape*, 115–41; Robin Law, "Slave-Raiders and Middlemen, Monopolists and Free-Traders: The Supply of Slaves for the Atlantic Trade in Dahomey c. 1715–1850," *Journal of African History* 30, no. 1 (1989): 45–68.

45. Bronwen Everill, "'All the Baubles That They Needed': 'Industriousness' and Slavery in Saint-Louis and Gorée," *Early American Studies* 15 (Fall 2017): 714–39; Vanessa S. Olivera, "Gender, Foodstuff Production and Trade in Late-Eighteenth Century Luanda," *African Economic History* 43 (2015): 57–81.

46. Robin Law, "Trade and Politics behind the Slave Coast: The Lagoon Traffic and the Rise of Lagos, 1500–1800," *Journal of African History* 24 (1983): 321–48.

47. Nwokeji, *Slave Trade and Culture*, 31–59; Wood, *Black Majority*, chaps. 4 and 7.

48. Kristalyn Shefveland, *Anglo-Native Virginia: Trade, Conversion, and Indian Slavery in the Old Dominion, 1646–1722* (Athens, GA, 2016); Robbie Ethridge, "European Invasions and Early Settlement, 1500–1680," in *The Oxford Handbook of American Indian History*, ed. Frederick E. Hoxie (New York, 2016), 41–56; Ethridge, *From Chicaza to Chickasaw: The European Invasion and the Transformation of the Mississippian World, 1640–1715* (Chapel Hill, NC, 2010); Alan Gallay, *The Indian Slave Trade: The Rise of the English Empire in the American South, 1670–1717* (New Haven, CT, 2002).

49. Jean Soderlund, *Lenape Country: Delaware Valley Society before William Penn* (Philadelphia, 2014); Claibourne quotation, 63. On early relations in the region between Europeans and Native people see Mark L. Thompson, *The Contest for the Delaware Valley: Allegiance, Identity, and Empire in the Seventeenth Century* (Baton Rouge, LA, 2013).

50. Gallay, *Indian Slave Trade*; William L. Ramsey, "'Something Cloudy in Their Looks': The Origins of the Yamasee War Reconsidered," *Journal of American History* 90 (June 2003): 44–75; William L. Ramsey, *The Yamasee War: A Study of Culture, Economy, and Conflict in the Colonial South* (Lincoln, NE, 2008); David La Vere, *The Tuscarora War: Indians, Settlers, and the Fight for the Carolina Colonies* (Chapel Hill, NC, 2013). On the takeover of Ouidah and the rise of Dahomey see Robin Law, *Ouidah: The Social History of a West African Slaving "Port," 1727–1892* (Athens, OH, 2004).

51. Preceding paragraphs drawn from ASSI 45/33/1, items 4, 5, 7, October 15 and 16, 1776. TNA.

52. Samuel Fleischacker, "Adam Smith's Reception among the American Founders, 1776–1790," *William and Mary Quarterly* 59 (October 2002): 905.

CHAPTER TWO

1. Quotes from Merrell, *Into the American Woods*, 1. For differing understandings and viewpoints on the American landscape between colonists and Indians see William Cronon, *Changes in the Land: Indians, Colonists, an the Ecology of New England* (New York, 1983).

2. On the management of wood and other natural resources in the colonies see S. Max Edelson, "Clearing Swamps, Harvesting Forests: Trees and the Making of a Plantation Landscape in the Colonial South Carolina Lowcountry," *Agricultural History* 81 (Summer 2007): 381-406; Keith Pluymers, "Atlantic Iron: Wood Scarcity and the Political Ecology of Early English Expansion," *William and Mary Quarterly*, 3rd ser., 73 (July 2016): 389-426. The commitment among colonists to an "economy of interests" clearly drove the duty war that unfolded in the Lower Counties, which were a jurisdiction under dispute between the Pennsylvania and Maryland proprietors, each attempting to make trade operate for his own interest. See Gary B. Nash, "Maryland's Economic War with Pennsylvania," *Maryland Historical Magazine* 60 (September 1965): 231-44.

3. George Hammersley, "The Revival of the Forest Laws under Charles I," *History* 45, no. 154 (1960): 85-102; Paul Warde, "Fear of Wood Shortage and the Reality of the Woodland in Europe, c. 1450-1850," *History Workshop Journal* 62 (Autumn 2006): 28-57. See also petitions to the king after 1660 for restoration of woodland keepers' rights and inquiries into the use of woodland. "Order for a Commission under the ducky seal, to enquire concerning the King's rights in the woods and commons of Chaldicot and Sherenewton, co. Monmouth," November 7, 1661, SP 44/48 f. 10 TNA.

4. Quotation from John Stewart and J. G. Dunlop, "Letters from John Stewart to William Dunlop (Continued)," *South Carolina Historical and Genealogical Magazine* 32 (April 1931): 87; Letter dated 26th of 11th month 1686 at Warminghurst Place in old England in which Penn writes to William Markham, Thomas Ellis, and John Goodson, in *Pennsylvania Archives*, ser. 1, vol. 1, ed. Samuel Hazard et al. (Philadelphia, 1852), 97. See also Ben Fletcher to Wm Blathwayt, New York, November 19, 1694, Blathwayt papers, BL 191, and BL 301, Huntington Library (hereafter HL).

5. Docket of Randolph's Commission, October 1685, State Papers, Board of Trade, New England, vol. 5, 437; Randolph to Sir Robert Southwell, October 3, 1685, as cited in *Edward Randolph*, vol. 2 (Boston, 1899), 58-60. For extended discussion of Randolph's career see Hanna, *Pirate Nests and the Rise of the British Empire* (Chapel Hill, 2015), 183-250.

6. Order of King in Council, Enclosure 1: 42 i, Petition of Samuel Allen, Proprietor of New Hampshire in New England and late Governor thereof, to the King, January 18, 1700, CO 5/861, nos. 9, 9.i.CO 5/908, 422-25, TNA. For Martin Bladen's report see "Council of Trade and Plantations to the King," September 21, 1721, in *Calendar of State Papers, Colonial*, vol. 32 (1720-21), ed. W. Noel Sainsbury (London 1860-), no. 656, 408-49. For other discussions of wood supply see Thomas Bannister to the Council of Trade and Plantations: "Our woods afford all sorts of ship timber and plank, and if cut in a propper time and had a due seasoning, I believe would prove equal to that of any other countrey . . . You will judge what steps may be taken to invigorate the Parliament to promote their own and the Plantation's interest in this point also. If some method be not taken, the Crown is in danger of looseing the beneficial trade to that Plantation, and the supply of naval stores from thence," July 7, 1715, CO 5/866, no. 67, CO 5/914, 129-48, TNA.

7. Nuala Zahedieh, "Regulation, Rent-Seeking, and the Glorious Revolution in the English Atlantic Economy," *Economic History Review* 63, no. 4 (2010): 865-90; Thomas Leng, "Conflict and Cooperation in the Discourse of Trade in Seventeenth-Century England," *Historical Journal* 48 (December 2005): 933-54; Philip Stern and Carl Wennerlind, *Mercantilism Reimagined: Political Economy in Early Modern Britain and Its Empire* (Oxford, 2013); Joyce Oldham Appleby, *Economic Thought and Ideology in Seventeenth-Century England* (Princeton, NJ, 1978). The interpretation of colonial economic policy presented here rests on more recent analyses that play down earlier portrayals of it as "mercantilist" or "free trade" or that propose a fundamental incompatibility between Whiggism and imperialism.

8. Perry Gauci, "Introduction," in *Regulating the British Economy, 1660-1850*, ed. Perry Gauci (Farnham, UK, 2011), quotation on 23.

9. This newly heavy-handed approach was long ago noted by Thomas Barrow in his definitive study of the creation of the colonial customs service. See Thomas C. Barrow, *Trade and Empire: The British Customs Service in Colonial America, 1660-1775* (Cambridge, MA, 1967), 53-59.

10. Richard S. Dunn, "Penny Wise and Pound Foolish: Penn as Businessman," 37-54, and Nicholas Canny, "The Irish Background to Penn's Experiment," 139-56, both in *The World of William Penn*, ed. Richard S. Dunn and Mary Maples Dunn (Philadelphia, 1986). For a very good treatment of provincial discussions about interest see Mark Knights, "Regulation and Rival Interests in the 1690s," in Gauci, *Regulating the British Economy*, 63-82.

11. Ashley to Sayle, April 10, 1671, 311, and Ashley to Yeamans, April 10, 1671, ibid., 314; both in South Carolina Historical Society, *The Shaftesbury Papers*, with a New Preface by Robert M. Weir (Charleston, SC, 1999). Both as quoted in Thomas Leng, "Shaftesbury's Aristocratic Empire," in *Anthony Ashley Cooper, First Early of Shaftesbury 1621-1683*, ed. John Spurr (Ashgate, UK, 2011), 108-9.

12. Stephen Innes, *Creating the Commonwealth: The Economic Culture of Puritan New England* (New York, 1995), 182.

13. Frame of Government of Pennsylvania, May 5, 1682, http://avalon.law.yale.edu/17th_century/pa04.asp, accessed March 12, 2018. William Penn to Lord North, July 24, 1683, in *Papers of William Penn*, vol. 2, ed. Richard S. Dunn and Mary Maples Dunn (Philadelphia, 1982), 414-15; "Certaine Conditions or Concessions agreed upon by William Penn Proprietary & Governor of the Province of Pensilvania, & those who are the adventur[ers] and purchasers in the same Province the 11 of July 1681," ibid., 99-100; see also *The Statutes at Large of Pennsylvania*, vol. 1, *Regular Session of 1693* (Harrisburg, PA, 1896), chap. 115, 219-20, "The Law about Trading with Indians in which divers persons who are non resident & unsetled come into this province & privately & clandestinely deal & trade with the Indians who by reason of their non residence . . . are not carefull in Maintaining a fair Correspondence," http://www.palrb.us/stlarge/browse/getpage.php?volno=1&typedoc=act&sessyr=1693&ss=0. The law therefore proposed that Pennsylvania residents should face a penalty if they "presume to deal or trade with the Indians in the woods at their towns or wigwams after any private or Clandestine manner but at their respective Mansion houses which said Dwelling houses shall be adjudged so to be, by the respective Court."

14. A court of pypowder, or piepowder, was a special mobile court established at fairs since medieval times to dispense commercial justice. It is not clear whether these courts still took place in the eighteenth century, but the clause allowing them still appeared in all fair charters, new and existing. The *Fundamental Constitutions of Carolina*, March 1, 1669, http://avalon.law.yale.edu/17th_century/nc05.asp, accessed March 12, 2018: "Forty-four. The high steward's court, consisting of a proprietor and his six councillors, called comptrollers, shall have the care of . . . fairs, markets . . . and also setting out and appointing places for towns to be built on in the precincts. Ninety-two. All towns incorporate shall be governed by a mayor, twelve aldermen, and twenty-four of the common council. The said common council shall be chosen by the present householders of the said town; the aldermen shall be chosen out of the common council; and the mayor out of the aldermen, by the palatine's court. Ninety-three. It being of great consequence to the plantation that port-towns should be built and preserved; therefore, whosoever shall lade or unlade any commodity at any other place than a port-town, shall forfeit to the lords proprietors, for each ton so laden or unladen, the sum of ten pounds sterling; except only such goods as the palatine's court shall license to be laden or unladen elsewhere. Ninety-four. The first port-town upon every river shall be in a colony, and be a port-town forever." Early boosters of settlement put a similar emphasis to Penn on developing marketplaces as a manifestation of early colonial success. Thomas Ashe's *Carolina, or A Description of the Present State of That Country* of 1682, explained that Charles Towne's new location meant that "the Planters may bring their Commodities to the Town as to the Common Market and Magazine both for Trading and Shipping." Quoted in A. S. Salley, *Narratives of Early Carolina, 1650-1708* (New York, 1911), 157-58; Grant to Henry Earl of St. Albans, John Lord Berkeley, Baron of Stratton, Sir Wm. Moreton, and John Tretheway, May 8, 1669, C 66/3109, no. 6, TNA.

15. "And a great many other things which towns and markets would supply" and "The merchants live better than any others in the country, but suffer many inconveniences which might be

avoided if they had towns, markets and money." Henry Hartwell and others to William Popple, October 20, 1697, CO 5/1309, nos. 31, 31I, CO 5/1359, 129-96, TNA. This report was a response to John Locke's request for information on the state of Virginia and was part of his project to reverse slavery in the colony. For details of this project see Holly Brewer, "Slavery, Sovereignty, and 'Inheritable Blood': Reconsidering John Locke and the Origins of American Slavery," *American Historical Review* 122 (October 2017): 1038-78. It is clear that Whig Locke disagreed with Tories about the absolute power of both monarchs and slave owners and was seeking to address it with this plan. Nevertheless I would argue that, although these factions disagreed on an imperial level, when it came to local government of the marketplace there was more common ground. The construction of towns and imperial government continued to be an issue in Virginia. For discussion see Paul Musselwhite, "Annapolis Aflame: Richard Clarke's Conspiracy and the Imperial Urban Vision in Maryland, 1704-8," *William and Mary Quarterly*, 3rd ser., 71 (July 2014): 361-400; Musselwhite, *Urban Dreams, Rural Commonwealth: The Rise of Plantation Society in the Chesapeake* (Chicago, 2018), 56-85.

16. Gary Nash, "The Free Society of Traders and the Early Politics of Pennsylvania," *Pennsylvania Magazine of History and Biography* 89 (April 1965): 147-72; William Penn, "Certaine Conditions or Concessions agreed upon by William Penn Proprietary & Governor of the Province of Pensilovania, & those who are the adventur[ers] and purchasers in the same Province The 11 of July 1681," *Papers of William Penn*, 1:99-100. William Penn to the Emperor of Canada, June 21, 1682, "I have sett up a Society of Traders in my Province to traffick with thee and thy people for your Commodities that you may be furnished with that which is good at reasonable rates." Dunn and Dunn, *Papers of William Penn*, 2:261; Nicholas More and James Claypoole, "The Articles, Settlement, and Offices of the Free Society of Traders in Pennsilvania," *Pennsylvania Magazine of History and Biography* 5, no. 1 (1881): 37-50. For a contemporary endorsement of the economic order that might be created by the Free Society see Thomas Budd, *Good Order Established in Pennsylvania and New Jersey Being a true account of the Country; With its Produce and Commodities there made* (Philadelphia, 1685).

17. October 6, 1692, *Journals of the Common House of Assembly*, September to October 1692; November 20, 1695, *Journal*; September 28, 1698, and October 4, 1698, *Journal*; Stewart and Dunlop, "Letters," *South Carolina Historical Society Magazine*, manuscripts described by Helen Gardner McCormack (hereafter *SCHGM*) 32 (April 1931): 87 and 98.

18. Governor Nicholson to Lords of Trade and Plantations, March 18, 1696, CO 5/714, nos. 1, 2 to CO 5/725, 1-3, TNA; Col. Quary to the Council of Trade and Plantations, October 15, 1703, CO 323/5, nos. 19, 19.i.-iv to CO 324/8, 349-71, CO 5/970, no. 13, CO 5/1262, nos. 52.i, ii, TNA; Attorney General of New York to Governor the Earl of Bellomont, June 30, 1698, CO 5/1040, no. 77 to CO 5/1116, 97-101, TNA.

19. Innes, *Creating the Commonwealth*, 160-236.

20. Minutes of the Provincial Council of Pennsylvania, 28th of 12th month 1688-89; June 13, 1693; July 18, 1693; October 1, 1693; May 26, 1694; February 14, 1699-1700. All in *Pennsylvania Archives: Colonial Records*, vol. 1, *Minutes of the Provincial Council, 1683-1700* (Philadelphia, 1852). Colonists were also slow to establish marketplaces outside Philadelphia. For a petition for a fair at Chichester see 14th of 12th month 1700; for Germantown see 2nd of 6th month 1701.

21. March 7, 1706, Nathaniel Johnson address to the House, *Journal of the Commons House of Assembly, March 6, 1705/6-April 9, 1706*, ed. A. S. Salley (Columbia, SC, 1937), 11.

22. Complaint against Jacob Hall for selling rum to the Indians, 9th day 10th month, 1685, in *Records of the Courts of Quarter Sessions and Common Pleas of Bucks County, Pennsylvania, 1684-1700* (Philadelphia, 1943), 32; Entry for May 16, 1704, in *Pennsylvania Archives, Colonial Records*, vol. 1, *Minutes of the Provincial Council, 1683-1700*; petition from the Free Society of Traders, June 15, 1685, in Dunn and Dunn, *Papers of William Penn*, 3:58-59. For an instance of the society coming into conflict about trade with local residents of the Lower Counties (and losing) see March 11,

1684, and June 10, 1684, "A protest made by Benjamin Blagg, Mr of the Ship Society agst the detainment of A parcell of oyle & Whalebon" and The Free Socyety of Traders vs Henry Bowman, both in *Records of the Courts of Sussex County Delaware, 1677-1710*, vol. 1, *1677-89*, ed. Craig W. Horle (Philadelphia, 1991).

23. *Statutes at Large of Pennsylvania*, vol. 2, *1700-1712*, 236-37, http://www.palrb.us/stlarge /browse/getpage.php?volno=2&typedoc=act&sessyr=1705&ss=0; BPRO Colonial Entry Book, vol. 22, September 10, 1685; and BPRO Colonial Entry Book, vol. 22, Whitehall this September 30, 1683, both in A. S. Salley, *Records in the BPRO relating to South Carolina*, vol. 1 (Atlanta, 1928-29), 67 and 16; 31st of 3rd month 1701, the Proprietary and Governour, Provincial Council Minutes proposal for reforming the Indian trade, *Pennsylvania Archives*, vol. 1. On trade and the Yamasee War see Jessica Yirush Stern, *The Lives in Objects: Americans, British Colonists, and Cultures of Labor and Exchange in the Southeast* (Chapel Hill, NC, 2016), 62-80.

24. Randolph also explained that American customs officers would "suffer vessels carrying provisions in cask to load in any river, no matter how distant from the office." See "An account of several things whereby illegal trade is encouraged in Virginia, Maryland and Pennsylvania, with methods for preventing the same, submitted to the Commissioners of Customs by Edward Randolph," August 17, 1696, CO 323/2, nos. 6, 6, I-XII; Col. Quary to the Council of Trade and Plantations, October 20, 1699, CO 5/1260, nos. 1, 1-I, CO 5/1288, 176-79. In 1697 Nicholson also observed a "forestalling of the market" that was "a great prejudice to merchants and traders." Governor Nicholson to Council of Trade and Plantations, July 13, 1697, CO 5/714, nos. 25, 25 I-XIII | CO 5/725, 119-37, 113, 114, 142-43, 138-41, 144-48, 161-63, all TNA.

25. William Popple to Charlewood Lawton, April 16, 1702, CO 5/1289, 431-35, TNA; "nothing is more easie than putting in...." from "Reasons for Settling a Port and Appointing Custome house officers at Port Royall in South Carolina," anonymous and undated but estimated 1690-1710, Port Royal SC MS (T) ca. 1690-1710, South Caroliniana Library; South Carolina Judgment Rolls, July 30, 1714, Richard Wigg vs. Miles Harding, July 29, 1714, Wigg vs. Capt. Godfrey, November 25, 1714, Wigg vs. Joseph Swaddle, South Carolina Department of Archives and History, Columbia, SC (hereafter SCDAH); Bladen, "Council of Trade and Plantations to the King," September 21, 1721, Sainsbury, *Calendar*, vol. 32. See also "Thomas Mower late master of the Brigantine Mayflower loaded twenty barrells of rice onto his boat at anchor on the North Edisto river without the proper customs duties being collected," Judgment Rolls July 12, 1712, SCDAH.

26. For protectionist measures in the later seventeenth century see "An Act against importing cattle from Ireland and other parts beuond the seas, and fish taken by foreigners," January 18, 1667, SP 29/188 f. 190, TNA. For new markets see "Petition of Sir Willm. Fenwick, Bart., to the King, for change of the Hexham market to Monday instead of Tuesday, and for grant of an additional Tuesday market, once a fortnight in the summer..." May ?, 1662, SP 29/54 f. 9, TNA. On British smuggling see Paul Monod, "Dangerous Merchandise: Smuggling, Jacobitism, and Commercial Culture in Southeast England, 1690-1760," *Journal of British Studies* 30 (April 1991): 150-82; Hoh-Cheung Mui and Lorna H. Mui, "Smuggling and the British Tea Trade before 1784," *American Historical Review* 74 (October 1968): 44-73; R. C. Nash, "The English and Scottish Tobacco Trades in the Seventeenth and Eighteenth Centuries: Legal and Illegal Trade," *Economic History Review* 35 (August 1982): 354-72.

27. Col. Quary to the Council of Trade and Plantations, March 26, 1702, CO323/3, no. 20 CO324/8, 86-106, TNA.

28. Up to 1710, Pennsylvania put thirty laws on the books concerning economic regulation while Carolina managed just sixteen. See *Statutes at Large of Pennsylvania* and *Statutes at Large of South Carolina*, 10 vols., ed. Thomas Cooper and David J. McCord (Columbia, SC, 1836-41). This was far fewer laws related to the regulation of the domestic economy than those passed by the English Parliament in just three years of William III's reign. See *Statutes Passed into Law under William III, Including the Civil List Act of 1697 and the Act of Settlement of 1701*, ed. John Raithby (London,

1820), http://www.british-history.ac.uk/source.aspx?pubid=353. On factionalism in early colonial government see Nash, *Quakers and Politics*; Roper, *Conceiving Carolina*.

29. Entries for April 27, 1691, and September 30, 1693, in *Extracts from the Records of the Burgh of Glasgow*, vol. 4, *1691-1717*, ed. J. D. Marwick (Glasgow, 1908); Entry for May 25, 1688, Berwick guild minute books, B1/13, Berwick-upon-Tweed Archives; Entry for January 17, 1703, concerning tobacconists, Long Order or ByLaw as to their not Setting up Stalls &c, MD/NC/2/3, Common Council Order Book, 84, TWAS.

30. Midsummer Hexham 1680—unsatisfactory innkeeper Rothley; Christmas at Morpeth 1681—unlawful tailoring; Christmas at Morpeth 1685—threats to the exciseman at Buteland, smuggled goods Hexham, smuggled goods and plight of a carrier, Hexham, theft of a cow hide in Alnwick market, unlicensed badgers, butchers and drover etc.; Michaelmas Alnwick 1687—petition of three poor people against indictment of trading not having been apprenticed; Christmas at Morpeth 1688—forestalling in Westgate; Michaelmas Alnwick 1693—order to pay excise duty Alnwick; Christmas at Morpeth 1695—driving and stealing cattle on common land at Bickerton, taking sheep to market and bribery by Country Keeper; Midsummer at Hexham 1696—seizure of Jersey cloth from James Watson, dyer, on pretext it was Scots, whereas it was Northumberland at Hexham; assault by Barbary Best accusing of selling undrinkable ale at North Shields; Michaelmas at Alnwick 1696—grain prices; Christmas at Morpeth Jan 1697—salt officer assaulted and abused while delivering salt North Shields; Midsummer Hexham 1697—failure to register price of three buckskins Hexham. Christmas at Morpeth 1698—Disposal of underweight butter in Monkseaton and North Shields; Easter Morpeth 1698 grain prices and ditto 1699; Michaelmas Alnwick 1699—confusion over ale house license at Lucker, grain prices, offenses by tanners Hexham and Allendale; Michaelmas at Alnwick 1700—trouble in Wooler marketplace, grain prices, petition that inclosure of Sandoe be allowed to stand because the fair held there should be held on Stagshaw Bank as formerly, though this is now overgrown, cost of inclosure £400; unlawful seizures for sale Hartside and Greenside Hill; Wrongful seizure of wool near Morpeth. Selected from Handlist of Northumberland Quarter Sessions Papers 1663-1834, NRO. On Hexham manor market regulation see Allendale MSS, part 3, M11: 1729-40, NRO. On the continued importance of manor authority in this period see Brodie Waddell, "Governing England through the Manor Courts, 1550-1850," *Historical Journal* 55, no. 2 (2012): 279-315; R. A. Houston, *Peasant Petitions: Social Relations and Economic Life on Landed Estates, 1600-1850* (Basingstoke, UK, 2014).

31. For the general increase in credit litigation in this era see Craig Muldrew, *The Economy of Obligation: The Culture of Credit and Social Relations in Early Modern England* (London, 1998); Alexandra Shepherd, *Accounting for Oneself: Worth, Status, and the Social Order in Early Modern England* (Oxford, 2015).

32. Twelfth day of 1st month 1689, Bucks County Court of Common Pleas, pp. 113-14, *Records of the Courts of Quarter Sessions and Common Pleas of Bucks County, Pennsylvania, 1684-1700* (Bucks County, PA, 1943); Entry for 3rd day of 1st week of 7th month 1687, Chester County Court Records; * September 1685 at Dover, Sussex County records; Francis Le Jau to ?John Chamberlain, April 20, 1714, in Frank J. Klingberg, ed., *The Carolina Chronicle of Dr. Francis Le Jau, 1706-1717* (Berkeley, CA, 1956) 54; John Brown v. Eleana Wright, February 16, 1717, in *Records of the Court of Chancery of South Carolina, 1671-1779*, ed. Anne King Gregorie, American Historical Association, American Legal Records, vol. 6 (Washington, DC, 1950), 179.

33. Lois Green Carr and Lorena S. Walsh, "The Planter's Wife: The Experience of White Women in Seventeenth-Century Maryland," *William and Mary Quarterly* 34 (October 1977): 542-71; James E. McWilliams, "Butter, Milk, and a 'Spare Rib': Women's Work and the Transatlantic Economic Transition in Seventeenth-Century Massachusetts," *New England Quarterly* 82 (March 2009): 5-24; Denise Bossy, "Godin & Co.: Charleston Merchants and the Indian Trade, 1674-1715," *South Carolina Historical Magazine* 114 (April 2013): 96-131.

34. October 4, 1698, resolution that "every body may buy Skinns at their owne plantations for their owne use from their neighbour Indjans" was repeated on February 20, 1701 (*Journal of the Commons House of Assembly*), but after the Yamasee War Virginian interlopers and unlicensed traders still ignored efforts to confine trade. See *Journal of the Commissioners of the Indian Trade, 1710-18* (Columbia, SC, 1955), vol. 1; 2nd of 6th month 1686, Case of Nicholas Skull Lower Counties resident whose house was been broken into by Indians and speculation is because he was trading with them, including rum, and they were taking goods they presumed owed to them, *Pennsylvania Archives: Provincial Council Minutes*, vol. 1; "The Govr and Councill unanimously insist upon the first bill about persons Trading with the Indians for Rum, &c., apprehending that the latter Renders the End proposed ineffectual & have appointed two of the Council to go to the assembly or meet any Committee, by them to be appointed to Confer further about the same. Silvester Garland of New Castle acknowledges, &c., in £100. Upon Condition that he the said Silvester will not at any time hereafter Sell, Barter or Exchange Rum or any other Strong Liquor with any Indian or Indians, at any Indian Town or other place in ye woods, within this Govmt, for Skins or Peltry, &c., that then &c. Otherwise, &c.,—Acknowledged ye 13 of October, 1701, Before Justice Shippen," *Pennsylvania Archives: Minutes of the Provincial Council*, vol. 1; entries for July 28, 1707, and July 31, 1711, *Journals of the Commissioners of the Indian Trade of South Carolina, Sept. 20, 1710—April 29, 1718*, ed. W. L. McDowell (Columbia, SC, 1955); John Seabrook v. Jane Bray September 8, 1702, in Gregorie, *Records of the Court of Chancery*; Soderlund, *Lenape Country*; John Lawson, *A New Voyage to Carolina* (London, 1709), 16.

35. June 6, 1706, *Pennsylvania Archives: Minutes of the Provincial Council*, vol. 2 (Philadelphia, 1852).

36. As discussed in Martha Zierden, Suzanne Linder, and Ronald Anthony, *Willtown: An Archaeological and Historical Perspective*, Charleston Museum Archaeological Contributions 27 (Charleston, SC, 1999), 34.

37. William Hatton, "Some Short Remarkes on the Indian Trade in the Charikees and in Management Thereof since the Year 1717," ed. Rena Vassar, *Ethnohistory* 8 (Autumn 1961): 401-23.

38. April Hatfield, *Atlantic Virginia: Intercolonial Relations in the Seventeenth Century* (Philadelphia, 2004), 8-38; Susan Sleeper-Smith, *Indigenous Prosperity and American Conquest: Indian Women of the Ohio River Valley, 1690-1792* (Chapel Hill, NC, 2018), chap. 3, quotation on 128.

39. As cited in Morgan, *Slave Counterpoint*, 367.

40. On African cattle herders see Wood, *Black Majority*. On West African canoemen see Jeffrey Bolster, *Black Jacks: African American Seamen in the Age of Sail* (Cambridge, MA, 1998), chap. 1; advertisements of Sarah Sommerville and Elizabeth Miles, June 28, 1735, and June 22, 1734, *South Carolina Gazette*. See also *South Carolina Gazette* September 24, 1737, May 11, 1735, and November 5, 1737, for further activities of African boatmen.

41. Lawson, *New Voyage*, 9.

42. Trial of Joseph Trivithan 28th of 6th month 1690, *Records of the Courts of Quarter Sessions and Common Pleas of Bucks County, Pennsylvania, 1684-1700* (Bucks County, PA, 1943), 146.

43. Hatton, "Short Remarks," 14.

44. Winthrop as quoted in Innes, *Creating the Commonwealth*, 128; Le Jau to Philip Stubs July 3, 1707, in Klingberg, *Carolina Chronicle of Dr. Francis Le Jau*, 29; John Stewart likewise accused Carolinians of putting private interest before the public good, including in a discussion of Skirving and Smith; the former he described as "not so fire to owne in publick yea scarce in privat the Stress and interests of what he owns as to Government; not forward to show himself to the world a zealot in a publick concerne." Letters of John Stewart, SCHGM, 96.

45. William Penn to Robert Harley, ca. April 1701, *Papers of William Penn* 4:42-44. William Penn to Matthew Birch, Philadelphia, June 2, 1700, ibid., 3:602-3; Governor the Earl of Bellomont to Council of Trade and Plantations, New York, May 18, 1698, NA CO 5/1040, nos. 64, 64 I.-VI| CO 5/1115, 312-20; Bladen, "Council of Trade and Plantations to the King," *Calendar of State Papers, Colonial, America, and West Indies*, vol. 32 (London, 1933).

46. Governor Nicholson to Council of Trade and Plantations, March 27, 1697, CO 5/714, no. 16 |CO 5/725, 51-68; Copy of Col. Quary's Answer to Mr. Penn's complaints against him (June 18), June 23, 1702, CO 5/1261, no. 118|CO 5/1233, no. 38|CO 5/1290, 71-87, TNA. Quotation from Jonathan M. Beagle, "Remembering Peter Faneuil: Yankees, Huguenots and Ethnicity in Boston, 1745-1900," *New England Quarterly* 75 (September 2002): 394.

47. Charles Gookin to Opessah, June 15, 1715, *Pennsylvania Archives: Minutes of the Provincial Council*, vol. 2 (Pennsylvania, 1852).

48. For discussion of these shifts in economic thought at the end of the seventeenth century see Joyce Appleby, *Economic Thought and Ideology in Seventeenth Century England* (Princeton, NJ, 1978); On Mandeville see John Sekora, *Luxury: The Concept in Western Thought from Eden to Smollett* (Baltimore, 1977).

CHAPTER THREE

1. Steven Laurence Kaplan, *Provisioning Paris: Merchants and Millers in the Grain and Flour Trade during the Eighteenth Century* (Ithaca, NY, 1984); Bohstedt, *Politics of Provisions*, 103-64; "To the Printer &c.," January 3, 1758, *Manchester Mercury and Harrop's General Advertiser*.

2. This figure for the number of mills is the estimation of Michael V. Kennedy, "'Cash for His Turnups': Agricultural Production for Local Markets in Colonial Pennsylvania, 1725-1783," *Agricultural History* 74 (2000): 587-608. On Pennsylvania mill development see Brooke Hunter, "Rage for Grain: Flour Milling in the Mid-Atlantic, 1750-1815" (PhD diss., University of Delaware, 2001); Potts Family Furnaces Collection, 212 Forges and Furnaces Collection, HSP, John Potts Ledgers items 693, 694, 695, and item 691 Pottstown mill wastebook 1772-73; "Whereas it has been found . . . ," December 17, 1761, *Pennsylvania Gazette*.

3. Examples are too numerous to list, but see Philadelphia County Quarter Sessions, Petition of the Inhabitants, March 3, 1755; Petition of John Sellers who has "near finished a mill," December 5, 1757; Petition of the Inhabitants of Abington, December 10, 1761, City Archives, Philadelphia; *Pennsylvania Gazette*, October 6, 1763, and April 13, 1774. On the establishing of mills in the South Carolina backcountry see Lewis, *Carolina Backcountry Venture*, chap. 6.

4. Dennis Baker, "The Marketing of Corn in the First Half of the Eighteenth Century: North-East Kent," *Agricultural History Review* 18, no. 2 (1970): 126-50; Ilje van Damme and Jon Stobart, eds., *Modernity and the Second-Hand Trade: European Consumption Cultures and Practices, 1700-1800* (London, 2010). Careful examination of eighteenth-century British newspaper advertisements in the British Newspaper Archive (https://www.britishnewspaperarchive.co.uk/) reveals that auctions were held almost exclusively at inns or dedicated auction rooms in towns. On the continued importance of urban corporations see Wilson, *Sense of the People*, 287-302; Rosemary Sweet, "Freemen and Independence in English Borough Politics, c. 1770-1830," *Past and Present* 161 (November 1998): 84-115; J. David Clemis, "Government in an English Provincial Town: The Corporation of Ipswich, 1720-1795" (PhD diss., University of Leicester, 1999). See Stobart, *Sugar and Spice*, 165, for the Postlethwayt quotation. Stobart also notes that English grocers often favored trade cards over newspaper copy because they cost less and could be distributed in person to those potential customers considered desirable; Troy Bickham, "Eating the Empire: Intersections of Food, Cookery and Imperialism in Eighteenth-Century Britain," *Past and Present* 198 (2008): 71-110; C. Y. Ferdinand, *Benjamin Collins and the Provincial Newspaper Trade in the Eighteenth Century* (Oxford, 1997).

5. ASSI 45/18/1, August 20, 1719, Mathre Hebron's testimony; 45/18/4—33, information of Josias Lancashire of Midleton in the County of Lancaster, butcher, September 6, 1726, and (48) Thomas Tate of Clifford in West Riding, husbandman, September 8, 1726; 45/18/6 (16), Information of Hannah Batley of Leeds, April 23, 1729; 45/18/4 (12), Examination of Thomas Coopland of Harwood November 15, 1726; 27/1/52 Deposition of Eli Longbothom September 4, 1762, TNA.

6. Transactions between free white men and their families are indeed the best documented by early American historians, who spent many decades forensically dissecting local economic interactions in search of the transition to capitalism. Nevertheless, the qualitative aspects of these interactions were sparsely documented because the main purpose was establishing the fact of trade as opposed to the qualitative features of bargaining. Historians asked *when* farms became tied into a market, not *if* the farm itself constituted a marketplace and, if it did, the significance of this double role. For an excellent summary of the issues see Richard Bushman, "Markets and Composite Farms in Early America," *William and Mary Quarterly* 55 (July 1998): 351-74. Bushman recognizes that farms produced for sale and for family consumption simultaneously, but he does not explore the possibility that the way these farms functioned was unusual within the broader early modern context; Vickers, *Farmers and Fisherman.* See also Thomas Rutherford to James Burd, October 21, 1751, for an explanation of how person-to-person deals between white farmers operated. "I recd ye kind letter wherein you desire a day appointed for ye comeing for the cattle and mare you are to have of me on account of Mr Shippen I am Loath to disapoint you and therefore pitch on the 30th of the instant where I shall be at home and ready to doe all in my power to doe Mr Shippen suffice and recommend my self to his and yr better opinion." Burd-Shippen Papers, box 1, series 1, Correspondence, B B892, American Philosophical Society (hereafter APS).

7. Lancaster County Quarter Sessions, September 1772, F010, November 1772, F009, Lancaster History.org; Lancaster County Historical Society; hereafter LCHS); Jacob Hiltzheimer diaries, 28 vols., MSS B.H56d, APS, and Am.0804, HSP; "Journal of James Kenny, 1761-1763," *Pennsylvania Magazine of History and Biography* 37, no. 1 (1913): 1-17.

8. As cited in Morgan, *Slave Counterpoint,* 340; Lynne B. Harris, *Patroons and Periaguas: Enslaved Watermen and Watercraft of the Lowcountry* (Columbia, SC, 2014), chap. 5, "The Plantation Patroon."

9. Account of Charles Cattell with Mary Sureau, South Carolina Court of Common Pleas, Judgment Rolls S136002, 1757, no. 13A, box 432, SCDAH; Advertisement of Richard Park Stobo, *South Carolina Gazette,* October 4, 1760; Strawberry Ferry Account Book, SCDAH. I have assumed that "boy" meant a young person of African origin, since there are instances in which "white boy" or "white groom" is designated. Likewise, most accounts specify when the (free white) account holder was traveling by listing "self" along with other people and animals in the account entry. I have thus counted all entries where "white" and "self," or the name of a relative, white employee, or "overseer" does not appear on potential journeys. Typically, there are also many entries in which carriages and animals seem to cross the ferry autonomously but were undoubtedly driven by unnamed enslaved Africans.

10. Merrell, *Into the American Woods;* Robert Paulett, *An Empire of Small Places: Mapping the Southeastern Anglo-Indian Trade, 1732-1795* (Athens, GA, 2012).

11. John W. Jordan, ed., "Bishop J. C. F. Cammerhoff's Narrative of a Journey to Shamokin, Penna., in the Winter of 1748," *Pennsylvania Magazine of History and Biography* 29, no. 2 (1905): 169; Charles Thomson, *Causes of the Alienation of the Delaware and Shawanese Indians from the British Interest* (London, 1759; repr. 1876): 31, 74, 75.

12. William McDowell, ed., *Documents relating to Indian Affairs,* vol. 2 (Columbia, SC, 1970): 650, 42, 105; Peter Mancall, *Deadly Medicine: Indians and Alcohol in Early America* (Ithaca, NY, 1997); Bossy, "Godin & Co.," 96-131.

13. On Indians in European towns see Joshua Piker, *The Four Deaths of Acorn Whistler: Telling Stories in Colonial America* (Cambridge, MA, 2013); author's database of advertisements for auctions in the *Pennsylvania Gazette.* As table 3.1 demonstrates, auctions were more widely advertised in America than in Britain, although in Scotland auctions were also popular. This was because the "roup" was a Scottish legal instrument used to dispose of estates of the deceased and leases on corporate property. Many of the sales listed in the *Aberdeen Press and Journal,* for example, were

for salmon fishing rights along the river Dee; https://www.britishnewspaperarchive.co.uk/. In the eighteenth century, commercialization meant that roups proliferated and also became used for selling other types of leases and property. On the popularity of auctions see Ellen Hartigan-O'Connor, "Public Sales and Public Values in Eighteenth-Century North America," *Early American Studies: An Interdisciplinary Journal* 13 (Fall 2015): 749-73. On the mechanisms of property law that allowed frequent land sales see Claire Priest, "Creating an American Property Law: Alienability and Its Limits in American History," *Harvard Law Review* 120 (December 2006): 385.

14. Hartigan-O'Connor, "Public Sales and Public Values," 749-73; Sheryllynne Haggerty, "The Structure of the Philadelphia Trading Community on the Transition from Colony to State," *Business History* 48 (April 2006): 171-92; Hartigan-O'Connor, *Ties That Buy*; Hart, *Building Charleston*.

15. The phrase "stuck on hand" was frequently used by merchants to discuss goods they could not shift. See Robert Pringle to James Maintru & Co., London, Charleston, June 12, 1740, "The gold lac'd hatts per Ayers stick likewise on hand. They are sold much cheaper in town than your's can be afforded with any advance on the cost, & I think much better likewise than yours in quality," in Walter B. Edgar, ed., *The Letterbook of Robert Pringle*, vol. 1, April 2, 1742 (Columbia, SC, 1972); Benjamin Fuller to Mr. John Scott at Mr. James Hendersons Merct in Belfast, Philadelphia, August 26, 1768, Benjamin Fuller Letterbook AMB 3785, vol. 1, 1762-81, HSP; Peter N. Moore, ed., *The South Carolina Diary of the Reverend Archibald Simpson, Part 1* (Columbia, SC, 2012), entry for December 31, 1760, 160.

16. Statistics from auction databases. I have compiled two databases of auction advertisements in the *Pennsylvania Gazette* and the *South Carolina Gazette* from 1732 to 1765. Repeat notices are not counted. Each database has more than two thousand entries. *Pennsylvania Gazette*, March 27, 1753, "To be sold, at publick vendue."

17. This figure does not include *all* Africans sold at auction. Many advertisements failed to specify the exact number of people offered for sale. A quarter of all South Carolina advertisements merely described them as "a parcel," and others were similarly vague. This number is therefore much lower than the total number of Africans who were sold at domestic auctions. Overall, 55 percent of Carolina auctions included Africans in the property listed for sale.

18. "Monday 23rd Sept 1765—Clear and warm went a board of a Dutch ship and bought a man named John Lambe; December 28th 1767—Monday rain sent all the snow off again Bought of Saml Shoemaker a little Dutch Girl 8½ years old, Name Cathran Dieterichin for £9 for Which Sum she is to Serve 9 years and a half; Nov 1 1771 went aboard of a Dutch ship belonging to Willing and Morris with Danl Clymen and he bought a boy for £25 for which said boy Peter Oden Kirchen is to serve six years ten months and seven days he was bound before John Gobson." Diary of Jacob Hiltzheimer, APS and HSP. See also Billy G. Smith and Susan Klepp, eds., *The Infortunate: The Voyage and Adventures of William Moraley, an Indentured Servant* (University Park, PA, 1992), for the experiences of William Moraley, an indented servant; Aaron Leaming Diary, AM 0923, vol. 2, beginning 1761, HSP.

19. *Pennsylvania Gazette*, May 7, 1761. The notice mentioned that the people were "lodged at Mr. Daniel Cooper's ferry on the Jersey shore."

20. Emma Hart, "A British Atlantic World of Advertising? Colonial American For Sale Notices in Comparative Context," in "Before Madison Avenue: Newspaper Advertising in Early America," special issue, *American Periodicals* 24 (Fall 2014): 110-27.

21. Max Edelson has discussed the *South Carolina Gazette* as a mechanism for land sales. For a full analysis of these sales see Edelson, "Statistical Tables," in *Planting Enterprise in Colonial South Carolina* (Cambridge, MA, 2006), 371-86.

22. *Pennsylvania Gazette*, February 28, 1760.

23. T. H. Breen has labeled them thus. See Breen, *The Marketplace of Revolution: How Consumer Politics Shaped American Independence* (New York, 2005). Other work on colonial newspaper advertisements has noted their role in the consumer economy but has not considered them in a gen-

uinely transatlantic framework. See Carl Robert Keyes, "Early American Advertising: Marketing and Consumer Culture in Eighteenth-Century Philadelphia" (PhD diss., Johns Hopkins University, 2007); Richard Bushman, "Shopping and Advertising in Colonial America," in *Of Consuming Interests: The Style of Life in the Eighteenth Century*, ed. Cary Carson, Ronald Hoffman, and Peter J. Albert (Charlottesville, VA, 1994), 233-51. Ellen Hartigan-O'Connor, "Collaborative Consumption," in Vickery and Styles, *Gender, Taste, and Material Culture*, 125-50.

24. Max Edelson, *The New Map of Empire: How Britain Imagined America before Independence* (Cambridge, MA, 2017); Martin Brueckner, *The Geographic Revolution in Early America: Maps, Literacy, and National Identity* (Chapel Hill, NC, 2006); Paul Mapp, *The Elusive West and the Contest for Empire, 1713-1763* (Chapel Hill, NC, 2011).

25. On the Enlightenment mapping project in the British provinces see J. B. Harley, "The Remapping of England, 1750-1800," *Imago Mundi* 19 (1965): 56-67.

26. A2 Papers relating to the town of Glasgow, 22-29: dated March 1, 1779, ML. A dispute over the construction of a sawmill on the Molindenar burn by James Hamilton in 1764 is also instructive. The corporation permitted Hamilton to build the mill, then knocked it down because they claimed he had constructed it in such a way as to pollute the burn, had encroached too far on a common green, and had also built his own private wharf to land materials for the mill's construction. See George MacGregor, *The History of Glasgow from the Earliest Period to the Present Time* (Glasgow, 1881), 333-34.

27. Houston, *Peasant Petitions*, 110. For a complete history of truck legislation see George W. Hilton, *The Truck System, Including a History of the British Truck Acts, 1465-1960* (Cambridge, 1960). Pennsylvania legislation did outlaw the sale of alcohol at ironworks stores, but it did not make the stores themselves illegal; in 1726 "Better Regulating the Retailers of Liquors Near the Iron Works and Elsewhere," *Statutes at Large of Pennsylvania*, 4:65-67, and in 1736 "Regulating Retailers of Liquors Near the Irone Works," ibid., 4:301-3. Customary rights, privileges, and institutions were entwined with the running of English landed estates in so many ways that it is not possible to rehearse them all here. For discussions of these issues see Wood, *Memory of the People*.

28. Kenneth Morgan and William Ashworth, who discuss the wharves of Bristol and London in their work on trade and customs in the eighteenth century, both describe wharves as spaces that were controlled by a number of urban authorities who ensured that informal dealing in provisions would not take place there. See Morgan, *Bristol and the Atlantic Trade*, and William J. Ashworth, *Customs and Excise: Trade, Production, and Consumption in England, 1640-1845* (Cambridge, 2003); Morgan, in Daniel Maudlin and Bernard Herman, eds., *Building the British Atlantic World* (Chapel Hill, NC, 2016). For Glasgow regulation see "Regulations for the Shoremaster, 29th December 1788," C2/1/1, p. 150, ML; "Regulations for the Broomielaw," Glasgow, ML. Also Newcastle City Council minutes, p. 137, December 16, 1771, p. 304, December 16, 1778, MD/NC/2/6: October 1766 to September 1785, TWAS. See also entries in the Berwick-upon-Tweed guild book February 13, 1740, "Mr Mayor acquainted the guild that he and some gentlemen of the council had one day this week gone down to the pier of our harbour and found that some people have taken upon them to win and load every limestones from off the pier which is a great prejudice to the same and in time must be very injurious to the harbour," and March 13, 1740, "Mayor produced to guild a plan of old and new keys dividing the same into eight shares for laying timber tar and other merchantizes on which the guild approve off and do hereby desire mr mayor and justices to meet some time before the head guild in order to give the merchants an offer of the said keys and that they make their report to that guild." Berwick Guild Minute Book, B1/16A, BRO. Also see the diaries of Newcastle apprentice Ralph Jackson, in which he meticulously records his movement through the city and on the "key"—where he buys oysters on only two occasions in a period of years. Ralph Jackson wrote nineteen volumes of diaries. He started to write in 1749, and although there is a hiatus between 1753 and 1756, he resumed his habit toward the end of his apprenticeship and continued to write for the rest of his life. His diaries are at the Teesside Archives

in Middlesborough and are available online from the Great Ayton Historical Society at http:// greatayton.wikidot.com/ralph-jackson-diaries. They are labeled alphabetically from A (1749-50) through U (1787-90).

29. The debate about the size and capitalist character of English farms in the eighteenth century is long-running and severely hampered by real regional differences in farm size. For a good overview, see Leigh Shaw-Taylor, "The Rise of Agrarian Capitalism and the Decline of Family Farming in England," *Economic History Review* 65 (February 2012): 26-60. As Shaw-Taylor shows, tenancy rates reached 80 percent in many areas of England by the end of the eighteenth century. Lucy Simler demonstrates that while tenancy did exist in colonial Pennsylvania, rates stood at 20-25 percent by the Revolution. Simler, "Tenancy in Colonial Pennsylvania: The Case of Chester County," *William and Mary Quarterly* 43 (October 1986): 542-69. The work of Sung Bok Kim on New York's manors is also relevant here. As Kim demonstrates, the commercial nature of colonial society, coupled with labor shortages, resulted in a landlord-tenant relationship that was much different from its British contemporary. See Sung Bok Kim, *Landlord and Tenant in Colonial New York: Manorial Society, 1664-1775* (Chapel Hill, NC, 1978). For road construction linked to mill development see, for example, PI.2 17, undated petition, "that some years ago a road was laid out by consent of the neighbours for the use of the Cattles going out and in: and since the Petitioners have build three mills; found the said road not passable for waggons and carts; it was necessary to make one other road through one of the peittioners Land. . . . Mathis Adams, Niclaus Rittinghouse, John Vanderen, Herry Rittenhouse," A-304: Quarter Sessions Court Road Petitions fols. 1-9, Philadelphia City Archive.

30. Wragg Plantation Journal, Middle Plantation, River Side, and Wampee, MS 11/466/15, South Carolina Historical Society (hereafter SCHS). Morgan's research on such local trade and the involvement of Africans in it is exhaustive and provides a detailed account of how plantations functioned as marketing spaces. See Morgan, *Slave Counterpoint*, 358-76; Edelson, *Plantation Enterprise*, 230-31; Ellen Hartigan-O'Connor, "Collaborative Consumption," in Vickery and Styles, *Gender, Taste, and Material Culture*, 125-50.

31. Part of the 1750 "Act for Keeping the Streets Clean" did touch on wharf regulation, but it did not encroach on the privileges that were accorded to private owners. See "Act for Keeping the Streets Clean," July 9, 1750, *South Carolina Gazette*. See also Henry to James Laurens, Westminster, November 27, 1773, exhorting James to hire "a careful young man" who would "keep the purchasers from improperly intermedling in the Weights" at the plantation wharf where rice was to be sold; David R. Chesnutt, ed., *The Papers of Henry Laurens*, vol. 9, *April 19, 1773—Dec. 12, 1774* (Columbia, SC, 1981).

32. *South Carolina Gazette*, June 29, 1765. The Court of Common Pleas records contain a number of unpaid accounts for wharf charges that reveal how wharfingers profited from the use of their facility. For example, Judgment Rolls 162A February 13, 1765, John Neufville, merchant, vs. Nelson and Wilson, wharfingers, for an unpaid account from December 1763 to October 1764 totaling £302.2.11 for landing and weighing rice, storage, barrels, landing coal, putting the coal in cases, landing wine and three bales of goods, and 7½ months rent for a store, vessel wharfage, and storage of coals "lying on the wharf." For examples of advertisements for wharf services see *South Carolina Gazette*, November 12, 1772, and November 26, 1772.

33. Aaron Leaming diary, AM 0923, and Records of the Callowhill markets, both HSP. See also the diary of Christopher Marshall: entries in September 1775 when he records going down to the wharves to buy in wood for the winter, making it clear that it was a customary annual task. Marshall Remembrancer, HSP. Auctions advertised in the *Pennsylvania Gazette* from 1730 to 1765 noted sales taking place on the following wharves: Mr. Turner's, Bourn's wharf in Capt Stevenson's store, Mr. Hamilton's (multiple), Thomas Griffiths, Oswald Peel's, Andrew Hamilton's, Par's, Fishbourne's, John Parrock's, John Stamper's, Mr. Inglis's, Mr. Plumsted's, Rees Meredith's, Market Street, Thomas Gordon's house on Peel's wharf, public wharf on Drawbridge, Arch Street,

Carpenter's, John Pole's, Hasell's, Pemberton's, Lloyd's, Thomas Clifford's, Charles Edgar's, William Allen's, Walter Goodman's, Okill's, store of Robinson on Powell's wharf, William Williams's.

34. Paul R. Huey, "Old Slip and Cruger's Wharf at New York: An Archaeological Perspective of the Colonial American Waterfront," *Historical Archaeology* 18, no. 1 (1984): 15-37; Hendrik Hartog, *Public Property and Private Power: The Corporation of the City of New York in American Law, 1730-1870* (Chapel Hill, NC, 1983). To view the Ratzer map see https://digitalcollections.nypl.org /items/510d47d9-7ad5-a3d9-e040-e00a18064a99, accessed September 5, 2018.

35. On this type of settlement in a southern context see Joseph Ernst and H. Roy Merrens, "Camden's Turrets Pierce the Skies! The Urban Process in the Southern Colonies during the Eighteenth Century," *William and Mary Quarterly* 30 (October 1973): 549-74; Kennedy, "Cash for His Turnups." Ernst, Merrens, and Kennedy document the creation of these hubs but, as with plantations and farms, have not regarded them in the larger context of early American marketing and its relation to European marketing practices. Hence they have overlooked the distinctiveness of their property and legal regimes and have not taken them into account when assessing their significance in the larger history of American market culture.

36. For mention of mills and businesses at Pennypack see *Pennsylvania Gazette*, April 5, 1750; *Pennsylvania Gazette*, October 11, 1759; *Pennsylvania Gazette*, April 1, 1762; Elizabeth Thomas selling cloth: *Pennsylvania Gazette*, June 25, 1767; "in a good neighborhood . . . ," *Pennsylvania Gazette*, March 9, 1769; Road Petition from Pennypack December 1761, and Petition for road from Thomas Livezey's mill at Roxbury, June 6, 1763, both Philadelphia County Quarter Sessions Docket, 21.2, City Archive, Philadelphia.

37. Steven C. Hahn, "'The Indians That Live about Pon Pon': John and Mary Musgrove and the Making of a Creek Indian Community in South Carolina, 1717-1732," in *Creating and Contesting Carolina: Proprietary Era Histories*, ed. Michelle LeMaster and Bradford Wood (Columbia, SC, 2013), 343-66; Henry A. M. Smith, "Edmundsbury and Jackson Borough," *South Carolina Historical and Genealogical Magazine* 11 (January 1910): 39-49. In 1741 Alexander Moon and John MacKenzie are running a store there: *South Carolina Gazette*, January 29, 1741; "TO BE SOLD for Cash, or 6 Months credit, by *George Livingston* at *Ponpon* bridge, an extraordinary good billiard-table, formerly mr. *Samuel Davison's*, once reckoned the best in the province, and is so still had it a new cloth, which is all it wants," *South Carolina Gazette*, April 17, 1749; "THE Subscriber having taken Parker's-Ferry at Ponpon . . . ROBERT MCMUR," *South Carolina Gazette*, April 6 1747.

38. Judgment Rolls 206A, January 7, 1755; 152A February 12, 1765; Will of Leah Pimento, South Carolina Wills and Probate, WPA transcript, Wills, vols. 11-13, 1767-71, 301-2, March 11, 1768, SCDAH.

39. Lewis, *Carolina Backcountry Venture*; James H. Merrell, "'Shamokin, the Very Seat of the Prince of Darkness': Unsettling the Early American Frontier," in *Contact Points: American Frontiers from the Mohawk Valley to the Mississippi, 1750-1830*, ed. Andrew Cayton and Fredrika Teute (Chapel Hill, NC, 1998), 16-59.

40. Forges and Furnaces Collection, HSP, includes numerous ledgers documenting the trade and industry under way at these Pennsylvania places. On the development of the Carolina equivalent see Zierden, Lindner, and Anthony, *Willtown*; William B. Barr, "Strawberry Ferry (38K1723) and Childsbury Towne (38K1750): A Socio-economic Enterprise on the Western Branch of the Cooper River, St. John's Parish, Berkeley Country, South Carolina," Research Manuscript Series, South Carolina Institute of Archaeology and Anthropology (1996).

41. *Pennsylvania Gazette*, July 23, 1767, and July 30, 1767; Judgment Rolls, 206A, January 7, 1755, SCDAH.

42. Le Jau to John Chamberlain, April 20, 1714, "Things are not in this province as when I came near 8 yeares ago but our Shopkeepers having contrived to make certain Tickets pass for current Coyn we are come by degrees to See nothing else current which considering how they sell all things reduce our Sallaries to be very inconsiderable so that 100£ of those tickets is hardly equal

to 20£ Sterling," and then Le Jau to secretary April 20, 1714, "we suffer from both planters and shopkeepers," in Klingberg, *Carolina Chronicle of Dr. Francis Le Jau.*

43. Hartigan-O'Connor, *Ties That Buy*; Toby L. Ditz, "Shipwrecked, or Masculinity Imperiled: Mercantile Representations of Failure and the Gendered Self in Eighteenth-Century Philadelphia," *Journal of American History* 81 (June 1994): 51–80; Muldrew, *Economy of Obligation*; Alexandra Shepherd, *Accounting for Oneself* (Oxford, 2015); Hunt, *Middling Sort.*

44. On women and credit in Britain see Amy Froide, *Silent Partners: Women as Public Investors during Britain's Financial Revolution, 1690-1750* (Oxford, 2016); Cornelia Hughes Dayton, *Women before the Bar: Gender, Law, and Society in Connecticut, 1639-1789* (Chapel Hill, NC, 1995), 69–104; Hartigan-O'Connor, *Ties That Buy.*

45. Thomas Pownall, *The Administration of the Colonies, 1765*, 2nd ed., AM 1765 1494.0, Library Company of Philadelphia (hereafter LCP), 72. As Laura Edwards has observed, "localized law grew out of the patterns of everyday life" in the early modern English common law tradition that governed both Britain's provinces and its colonial possessions. Edwards, *People and Their Peace*, 63. The major exception here is efforts by Pennsylvania quarter sessions to restrict the sale of alcohol. Courts were rigorous in issuing tavern licenses and were willing to prosecute those who attempted to sell alcohol to their neighbors without them.

46. Northumberland Quarter Sessions, handlist of cases, NRO; Newcastle Quarter Sessions, QS/NC/1/7—MF2043/2044, TWAS. A variety of Scottish courts heard similar cases. The city's burgh court and the high court in Edinburgh both received a succession of cases concerning corporate economic rights and privileges through to the end of the eighteenth century. See A2 Legal papers defining powers and involving city interests: 1. Reports memorials and opinions of counsel, 1726-1851, 5 vols. (Inv 1913 XIII 5), ML; Peter Rushton and Gwenda Morgan, eds., *The Justicing Notebook of Edmund Tew, Rector of Boldon*, Surtees Society, vol. 205 (Durham, UK, 2000).

47. There are no South Carolina quarter sessions records surviving, which means my analysis here has to be confined to Pennsylvania. Lancaster, RG 02-00 0908 1745-57, RG 02-00 0908 Quarter Session 1758-69; Chester County Quarter Sessions, Chester County Archives; Philadelphia County Quarter Sessions dockets and papers and 130.1 Philadelphia Mayors Court Dockets, 1759-64 and 1774-80, City Archive, Philadelphia.

48. William Stone vs. William Logan, 1761-62, no. 4, July 19, 1762, Chancery Court Bills, SCDAH. See also Judgment Rolls 64A, box 33, April 7, 1752, where Alexander Cramahe and Co. bring Logan to court for unpaid debts for merchandise purchased to supply his Bacon's Bridge store; George William Logan, *A Record of the Logan Family of Charleston, South Carolina* (Sacramento, CA, 1874).

49. The store may have been previously occupied by Smith and Scott, who traded in enslaved people and offered a "parcel" for sale in the *South Carolina Gazette* on December 11, 1755. Smith and Scott were still there in 1760, after Logan's store had been offered to let. *South Carolina Gazette*, January 5, 1760.

50. Stone vs. Logan, Chancery Court Bills, SCDAH.

51. Estate of Mary Sureau vs. Charles Cattell, 1757 no. 13A S136002, box 432; Thomas Linthwaite is also indebted to the estate of Mary Sureau for a note for £23.12.8 and for an account February to October, 1755, for 17.5.0 for calf skins, butter, candles, leg of veal, legs of beef, harslet, veal, more beef, butter tongue, shoulder of veal, beef, a shank and more beef, 158A, May 11, 1756, Judgement Rolls, SCDAH. Inventory of Mary Sureau, January 16, 1756, WPA transcript, p. 751, SCDAH; Inventory and estate sale of Mrs. Mary Seabrook, February 3, 1753, WPA transcripts, pp. 97-98, SCDAH.

52. Twenty-nine bakers are listed in Glasgow's directory for 1787; only one was a woman, and there were no female fleshers (butchers) listed. See *John Tait's Directory for the City of Glasgow*, https://digital.nls.uk/directories/browse/archive/85274816, accessed September 15, 2018. There were women butchers at work in Glasgow at one point in the eighteenth century. For the dealings

of Elizabeth Glen, identified as a butcher, see Letters, June 15, 1734, from James Findlay; note of June 24, 1734; Letter from Glasgow October 1742 of John Reid, October 18, 1742; receipt from Elizabeth Glen, flesher in Glasgow. Hamilton of Barns Papers, ML. Interestingly, Reid's letter seemed to be an effort to cast doubt on Glen's creditability, though this did not prevent Hamilton from dealing with her subsequently. In Newcastle Order of May 5, 1709, that apprentices *can* go down to Shields and sell as much meat as they like "notwithstanding but that no brother shall send down any Woman servant to sell such meat on pain of ten shillings for each offence . . . order of 12th Sept 1706, which restrains Women Servants from Selling rutting or Breaking Meat in the shops by the foresaid." MF2069: Order Book/Gu/Bu/4, TWAS.

53. Houston, *Peasant Petitions*; Bohstedt, *Politics of Provisions*. See also petitions by the poor for assistance to the Northumberland quarter sessions, NRO. Benjamin Franklin, *Father Abraham's Speech to a Great Number of People, at a Vendue of Merchant-Goods* (Philadelphia, 1758), 14.

54. Inventory and vendue of William Perriman, second vendue held August 2, 1746, 1-3; inventory and vendue of Jeremiah Knott, February 1, 1757, vendue held March 22, 1757, 109-19, both in WPA transcripts of Inventories, SCDAH; William Stone vs. William Logan, 1761-62, no. 4, July 19, 1762, Chancery Court Records, SCDAH; advertisement of Thomas Stone, *South Carolina Gazette*, September 13, 1760.

55. "Journey of an Indian Trader," in *Documents relating to Indian Affairs*, vol. 2, *1754-57*, ed. William L. McDowell Jr. (Columbia, SC, 1958), 66.

56. *South Carolina Gazette*, October 24, 1768, and July 5, 1740. A succession of advertisements in the *South Carolina Gazette* describe Thomson's properties and his workforce. Material in the Court of Common Pleas Records also reveals accounts with Charleston customers for the supply of meat. See *South Carolina Gazette*, March 4, 1745, January 19, 1747, July 13, 1747, and December 10, 1750. South Carolina Judgment Rolls, box 24, 18A, April 3, 1744. An advertisement placed by butcher James MacKelvey also hints at a complex supply network based around the expertise of enslaved workers and a plantation-city nexus owned by one individual. See *South Carolina Gazette*, June 1, 1745: "Run away, about the 6th of *April* last, from *James MacKelvey* of *St. John's* Parish, Planter, a Negro Man, middle siz'd, about 25 Years of Age, this Country born, known by the Name of *Little Toney*, formerly belonging to the Estate of *James Goodby* deceas'd, and used to be employ'd for a Hunter at *Peedee Cowpen* Also a young Negro Fellow, named *Scipio* bought of the Executors of the same Estate. Whoever takes up the said Negroes and brings them to their Master at *Santee*, or the Gaol, Work house, or *James MacKelvey* Butcher in *Charlestown*, shall have *Twenty Pounds* Reward for *Toney*, and *Five Pounds* for *Scipio*, besides all reasonable Charges." For examples of butchers engaging in multiple branches of the trade see accounts between Thomas Fullalove, butcher, and Thomas Nightingale, Judgment Rolls, box 11A, November 17, 1764, and 16A, November 17, 1764, for "carting your barrelled beef to town," "7 beer barrels, 2 hogsheads to salt your beef £3, storage for salting and storing your beef 18 months £30," and pasturage charges in a suburban plot; SCDAH.

57. For examples of correspondence that includes detailed discussion of trade networks and logistics, see John Irwin, July 26, 1766; "Instructions to Mr John Irwin, Carlisle, June 27, 1766"; Joseph Rigby writing from Carlisle May 28, 1768; Joseph Rigby, June 11, 1768, at Carlisle; From Mr. Trent at Carlisle June, 1764. Baynton, Wharton and Morgan MS, mfm, reel 4, Pennsylvania State Archives (hereafter PSA), Harrisburg. For discussion of the company's networks see also Judith Ridner, "Relying on the 'Saucy' Men of the Backcountry: Middlemen and the Fur Trade in Pennsylvania," *Pennsylvania Magazine of History and Biography* 129 (April 2005): 133-62.

58. Ann Smart Martin, *Buying into the World of Goods: Early Consumers in Backcountry Virginia* (Baltimore, 2008), 28-33; *Virginia Gazette*, November 2, 1769, and July 18, 1766.

59. Morris K. Turner, "The Baynton, Wharton, and Morgan Manuscripts," *Mississippi Valley Historical Review* 9 (December 1922): 236-41; Ridner, "Relying on the 'Saucy Men.'"

CHAPTER FOUR

1. *South Carolina Gazette*, April 30, 1737. See also *South Carolina Gazette*, May 1, 1755, for a notice enumerating the considerable duties involved in being a commissioner.

2. *South Carolina Gazette*, October 31, 1765, for wood storage; April 13, 1747, for beer; March 25, 1753, for groceries; January 2, 1742, for "good Flour, white and brown Bread, Butter, Onions, Soap and Barrel Beer."

3. Elliott's wharf accommodated many stores from which shopkeepers sold "just imported" goods; see advertisement of Jacob Whitewood, *South Carolina Gazette*, March 27, 1749. For a detailed archaeology and history of this market wharf site see Nicholas Butler, Eric Poplin, Katherine Pemberton, and Martha Zierden (the Walled City Task Force), "Archaeology at South Adger's Wharf: A Study of the Redan at Tradd Street," *Archaeological Contributions* (Charleston Museum), no. 45, (2012): 137-55.

4. See chapter 1 for a discussion of Brown's trading habits and economic opinions. For the city council's endeavors in creating and managing wharves see James Deas, *The River Clyde: A Historical Description of the Rise and Progress of the Harbour of Glasgow and of the Improvement of the River from Glasgow to Port Glasgow* (Glasgow, 1876); Materials relating to Port Glasgow, B10/15/7587-98, ML; Committee reports of certain issues, C2/1/1, 67, ML.

5. Peter N. Miller, *Defining the Common Good* (Cambridge, 1994), 404-12.

6. Geoffrey Plank, *John Woolman's Path to a Peaceable Kingdom: A Quaker in the British Empire* (Philadelphia, 2012), 73-96; "Forum: Quakers as Political Players in Early America," *William and Mary Quarterly* 74 (January 2017): 35-144; Sheilagh Ogilvie, *Institutions and European Trade: Merchant Guilds, 1000-1800* (Cambridge, 2011); Ogilvie, *State Corporatism and Proto-industry: The Württemberg Black Forest, 1590-1797* (Cambridge, 1997).

7. Adolph B. Benson, ed., *Peter Kalm's Travels in North America* (New York, 1937), 1:30; Smith and Klepp, *Infortunate*, 68, 105; Butler et al., "South Adger's Wharf"; on the Lombard Street market see Wharton Family Papers, Ledger Book B, where Joseph Wharton discusses his financial support of and involvement in the construction of the market from 1745 to 1770, HSP. Johann David Schoepff, a postoccupation visitor to Charleston, found the city's markets worth comment but claimed that "the Charleston market can by no means be called equal to that of Philadelphia, either as regards the plenty or the quality of provisions," in *The Travelers' Charleston: Accounts of Charleston and Lowcountry, South Carolina, 1666-1861*, ed. Jennie Holton Fant (Columbia, SC, 2016).

8. "An Act for Settling a Fair and Markets in Childsberry Town in St John's Parish in Berkley County," in Cooper and McCord, *Statutes at Large of South Carolina*, 3:204-5; "An Act for Settling a Fair and Markets in the Town of Dorchester, in Berkley County, Being a Frontier in That Part of the Country," ibid., 214-17; "An Act for Settling a Fair and Markets in Ashley River Ferry Town, in Berkley County, for the Better Improvement of the Said Ferry, It Being a Principal Ferry Leading to Charlestown," ibid., 217-19. This initiative was part of Governor Nicholson's ongoing effort to improve colonial institutions to bring the territories under more effective British control. For more on Nicholson and his goals see Paul Musselwhite, "Annapolis Aflame: Richard Clarke's Conspiracy and the Imperial Urban Vision in Maryland, 1704-8," *William and Mary Quarterly* 71 (July 2014): 361-400. On March 23, 1738, the *South Carolina Gazette* noted that the General Assembly had passed "an Act for settling a Fair and Markets in Radnor in the Parish of St Helena in Granville County," but no evidence of this act exists anywhere else. These charters remained the only effort to promote the market and fair outside Charleston until the 1780s.

9. Burlington Town Book, HSP. David Pinkerton, "By Order of the Burgesses and Common-Council of the Borough of Bristol, May 5, 1759," *Pennsylvania Gazette*, May 10, 1759.

10. Minutes of the Borough and City of Lancaster, LancasterHistory.org, and Jerome H. Wood Jr., *Conestoga Crossroads: Lancaster, Pennsylvania, 1730-1790* (Harrisburg, PA, 1979), 23-71.

11. For more on the physical and institutional expressions of German influence see Diane Wenger, *A Country Storekeeper in Pennsylvania: Creating Economic Networks in Early America, 1790-1807* (College Station, PA, 2008); Stephanie Grauman Wolf, *The Urban Village: Population, Community, and Family Structure in Germantown, Pennsylvania, 1683-1800* (Princeton, NJ, 1980); Diane Wenger and J. Ritchie Garrison, "Commerce and Culture: Pennsylvania German Commercial Architecture," in *Architecture and Landscape of the Pennsylvania Germans, 1720-1920*, ed. Sally McMurry and Nancy Van Dolsen (Philadelphia, 2011). "Fish is so plentiful, that large Perch and Roach are sold for three-pence a Dozen, and trouts at the same price. . . . One day one John Houghton of Burlington and myself, being distress'd for a Sunday's Dinner, went a fishing and in twenty Minutes caught between us 140 perch and Roach; and in returning home to his Father's to get 'em dress'd, we sold five dozen of them for Fifteen pence, and the Remainder serv'd six people for Dinner." Smith and Klepp, *Infortunate*, 105.

12. Crissy and Markley, *Minutes of the Common Council of the City of Philadelphia, 1704-1776* (Philadelphia, 1847).

13. Ibid.

14. T-TH 13, Incorporation of Gardeners, item 4, The Green Mercat Book, starting November 1758, ML.

15. Order of Thomas Willing, mayor, *Pennsylvania Gazette*, February 2, 1764; Crissy and Markley, *Minutes of the Common Council*, Philadelphia; Act for Regulating Markets, *South Carolina Gazette*, April 30, 1737.

16. *The Exploits of the Renowned Robin Hood, the Terror of Fore-stallers and Engrossers and the Protector of the Poor* (London, 1760); *A Letter to a Member of Parliament Proposing Amendments to the Laws against Forestallers, Ingrossers, and Regraters and Recommending* MEANS *to Prevent for the Future Extravagant High Prices of Corn* (London, 1757). The statute law against forestalling, etc., was annulled in 1772, but this caused national outrage and failed to end traders' being tried for the crime, since it remained prosecutable under common law and there were many who supported the principle. William Blackstone, *Commentaries on the Laws of England: A Facsimile of the First Edition of 1765-1769* (Chicago, 1979), 4:158; Douglas Hay, "The State and the Market in 1800: Lord Kenyon and Mr Waddington," *Past and Present* 162 (February 1999): 101-62.

17. Crissy and Markley, *Minutes of the Common Council*, Philadelphia, March 22, 1727. Lancaster corporation minutes meeting of January 25, 1746, and March 5, 1761, LCHS.

18. Both Jessica Stern and Jane Merritt have emphasized the enthusiasm of Indian leaders, in Carolina and in Pennsylvania, respectively, for greater government control of the trade. See Jessica Yirush Stern, *The Lives in Objects: Native Americans, British Colonists, and Cultures of Labor and Exchange in the Southeast* (Chapel Hill, NC, 2017), and Jane Merritt, *At the Crossroads: Indians and Empires on a Mid-Atlantic Frontier, 1700-1763* (Chapel Hill, NC, 2003); Thomson, *Causes of the Alienation of the Delaware and Shawanese Indians*, 32, 75.

19. The comment is attributed to the 1736 "Act to Settle and Regulate the Indian Trade," 1718; "Act to Better Regulate the Indian Trade by Appointing a Commissioner," 1720; "An Act for Preserving Peace and Continuing a Good Correspondence . . . ," 1739; "An Act for Preserving Peace and for Continuing a Good Correspondence with the Indians Who Are in Friendship with Government of South Carolina, and for Regulating the Trade with the said Indians," 1752. All in Cooper and McCord, *Statutes at Large of South Carolina*, vol. 3.

20. 1701 act against selling rum and other strong liquors to Indians, *Statutes at Large of Pennsylvania*, 2:168-70; Journal of James Kenny, HSP; "Instructions to Mr John Irwin, Carlisle, June 27, 1766," Baynton and Wharton MSS, PSA; July 17, 1762; Affidavit of Dennis McCormack the clerk to Col James Burd, B B892 Burd-Shippen Series 1, Correspondence, box 3, APS.

21. "An Act for Regulating Peddlers, Vendues &c.," 1730, *Statutes at Large of Pennsylvania*, 4:141-45; "An Act for Licencing Hawkers, Pedlars and Petty-Chapmen, and to Prevent Their Trading with Indented Servants, Overseers, Negroes and Other Slaves," March 11, 1738, in Cooper and

McCord, *Statutes at Large of South Carolina*, 3:487-90; Laurence Fontaine, *History of Pedlars of Europe* (Durham, UK, 1996).

22. Unfortunately, quarter sessions records for colonial South Carolina no longer survive, and I have been unable to find any clues to whether the system of licensing peddlers in the colony was successfully implemented. Petition of Casper Lay, Lancaster Quarter Sessions, May 1760, F001, LCHS; Petition of Joseph Trout, August 1758, RG 02-00 0908 Quarter Session, 1758-69, LCHS; Petition of Patrick Whinnery of Kennett, Chester County Peddler's Petitions, 1750, Chester County Historical Society. For a defense of peddling that deployed such ideas see James C___l, *A Second Letter from a Hawker and Pedlar in the Country, to a Member of Parliament at London* (London, 1731).

23. On the idea of a Creole elite sustained through political and cultural power, see Trevor Burnard, *Creole Gentlemen* (New York, 2005); Phyllis Whitman Hunter, *Purchasing Identity in the Atlantic World: Massachusetts Merchants, 1670-1780* (Ithaca, NY, 2001); Rhys Isaac, *The Transformation of Virginia, 1740-1790* (Chapel Hill, NC, 1982); John C. Coombs, "The Phases of Conversion: A New Chronology for the Rise of Slavery in Early Virginia," *William and Mary Quarterly* 68 (July 2011): 332-61.

24. For fair charter see Child Family Muniments, 1704-1801, 502/14, 502.00, SCHS.

25. Misc. records OO:385, 387, SCDAH, as cited in Emily Blanck, *Tyrannicide: Forging an American Law of Slavery in Revolutionary South Carolina and Massachusetts* (Athens, GA, 2014), 62-63; "Benevolus," *South Carolina Gazette*, November 26, 1772; *Gazette of the State of South Carolina*, May 12, 1777; Olwell, *Masters, Slaves, and Subjects*, 141-80; Morgan, *Slave Counterpoint*; Harris, *Patroons and Periaguas*.

26. "An Act for Regulating Peddlers, Vendues &c.," 1730, *Statutes at Large of Pennsylvania*, 4:141-45; "An Act for Licencing Hawkers, Pedlars and Petty-Chapmen, and to Prevent Their Trading with Indented Servants, Overseers, Negroes and other Slaves," March 11, 1738, in Cooper and McCord, *Statutes at Large of South Carolina*, 3:487-90. There is, of course, a rich literature on the activities of Africans in the colonial marketplace, especially in South Carolina and the Caribbean. This paragraph relies on the conclusions of these historians: Morgan, *Slave Counterpoint*; Philip D. Morgan, "Black Life in Eighteenth-Century Charleston," *Perspectives in American History*, n.s., 1 (1984): 187-232; S. Max Edelson, *Plantation Enterprise in the Colonial South Carolina Lowcountry* (Cambridge, MA, 2005); Olwell, *Masters, Slaves, and Subjects*; Emma Hart and Trevor Burnard, "Charleston, South Carolina and Kingston, Jamaica: A New Look at Urbanization in the American Plantation South," *Journal of Urban History* 39 (March 2013): 214-34.

27. "CHARLESTOWN, WHEREAS the several Commissioners for putting in Execution an Act . . ." *South Carolina Gazette*, April 30, 1737. See also "Whereas several Offences have been committed against the Law for regulating the Market of Charlestown . . . ," *South Carolina Gazette*, December 22, 1739. Unfortunately, the full text of the law this article refers to does not survive and does not appear to have been reproduced in the newspaper.

28. South Carolina Slave Code of 1740, in Cooper and McCord, *Statutes at Large of South Carolina*, 7:397-417.

29. The "Act for Keeping the Streets" specified that neither "cloth, woollen or linnen" "nor wines or rum in less quantity than a pipe, hogshead or tierce; nor beer or other liquors, in less quantities than a barrel; or bottled liquor, than by the hamper or cask; nor loaf sugars, than one hundred weight; nor other sugar, than by the barrel." The same act also moved to improve the infrastructure of Charleston's wharfside provisions market. *South Carolina Gazette*, July 9, 1750. For details of the fish market legislation see *South Carolina Gazette*, November 1, 1770.

30. "Whereas several persons . . . ," *South Carolina Gazette*, March 30, 1752.

31. Serena Zabin, *Dangerous Economies: Status and Commerce in Imperial New York* (Philadelphia, 2009), 57-80; Leslie M. Harris, *In the Shadow of Slavery: African Americans in New York City, 1626-1863* (Chicago, 2003), 11-47; Candice Harrison, "The Contest of Exchange: Space, Power, and Politics in Philadelphia's Public Markets, 1770-1859" (PhD diss., Emory University, 2008), 11-60;

Minutes of the Common Council, August 17, 1741: "Frequent Complaints having been made to this Board that many Disorderly persons meet every Evening about the Court House this City, and great numbers of Negroes and other Set there with Milk pails and other things late at Night, and many Disorders are there Committed against the peace and Good Government of this City."

32. Act of February 28, 1710/11. Thomson, *Causes of the Alienation of the Delaware and Shawanese Indians*, 56. Thomson also reported that Indians said, "When these Whisky-Traders come, they bring thirty or forty Cags, and put them down before us, and make us drink, and get all the Skins that should go to pay the Debts we have contracted for Goods bought of the Fair Traders, and by this Means we not only ruin ourselves, but them too" (76). Ludovic Grant to Governor Glen, Cherokees at Tomatly Town, March 27, 1755; James May to Governor Glen, Cowee, September 27, 1755; James Beamer to Governor Glen, Estertoe by Kewohee February 21, 1756. The Little Carpenter's Speech to Capt. Raymond Demere, delivered at Fort Prince George Keowee, July 13, 1756, all in William McDowell, *Documents relating to Indian Affairs*, vol. 2.

33. "To the Lords Commissioners from Edmond Atkin," May 30, 1755, LO578, box 13, Loudon Papers m LO-1-6999, HL; C05/375 item 390, Boone to Secretary of State, November 23, 1763, TNA.

34. Thomson, *Causes of the Alienation of the Delaware and Shawnese Indians*, 31.

35. Nonincorporated industrial cities and the rising consumer economy represent the best example of these processes of corporate decline. See Maxine Berg, "Small Producer Capitalism in Eighteenth Century Britain," *Business History* 35, no. 1 (1993): 17–39, for a description of an urban economy operating with few corporate restrictions in Birmingham; Patrick Wallis, "Labour, Law and Training in Early Modern London: Apprenticeship and the City's Institutions," *Journal of British Studies* 51, no. 4 (2012): 781–819.

36. "Complaint of the Gardeners vs James Young," 1760, T-TH 13 Incorporation of Gardeners, ML. Note that this was just one of many Glasgow and Newcastle episodes of this nature that could be recounted. For example, the struggle between butchers and tallow chandlers over collection of offal from slaughtered animals in the Glasgow market rumbled on for over a century; see T TH 11/1/1: Minutes of the Incorporation of Fleshers and TTH 11 Fleshers—Legal Papers: 36 legal and other papers on dispute between fleshers and candlemakers 1779-1844, ML.

37. This paragraph relies on the discussion of the political economic dimensions of Boston's market dispute in Jonathan M. Beagle, "'The Cradle of Liberty': Faneuil Hall and the Political Culture of Eighteenth-Century Boston" (PhD diss., University of New Hampshire, 2003), 56–115. See also Barbara Clark Smith, "Markets, Streets, and Stores: Contested Terrain in Pre-industrial Boston," in *Autre Temps, Autre Espace/An Other Time, An Other Space*, ed. Elise Marienstras and Barbara Karsky (Nancy, France, 1986), 172–97.

38. Beagle, "'Cradle of Liberty,'" 86; Roney, *Governed by a Spirit of Opposition*, chap. 2; Nash, *Quakers and Politics*; Hart, *Building Charleston*, chap. 1.

39. For problems with market order in Philadelphia see November 24, 1718, April 16, 1722, October 29, 1722; *Minutes of the Common Council* (Philadelphia, 1847). On March 1, 1755, Philadelphia's clerk of the market was accused of renting out a stall twice over and pocketing the extra proceeds and was thus "guilty of some unwarrantable exactions"; ibid., 584. "Persons [who] set up stalls . . . ," May 30, 1743, at meeting of the Lancaster burgesses and also see September 13, 1779 complaint of butchers' not paying stall rents both in Borough and City Council Minutes, LCHS; *South Carolina Gazette*, May 1, 1755.

40. Treasurers and Chamberlain Accounts: Journal No. 1 of the Town of Glasgows Affairs, "Branches of the Towns Revenue under the Management of the City Treasurer: Inventory May 15, 1755," ML; Statistics derived from annual accounts in Minutes of the City and Borough of Lancaster, LCHS. This calculation does not take into account that Lancaster's accounts may have been stated in Pennsylvania currency, not sterling. It is not clear in the town book which currency is being used. A Pennsylvania pound in the 1760s was worth roughly 1.62 times the British pound,

meaning that the difference in expenditure per head would only be greater. Valuation from John McCusker, *How Much Is That in Real Money?* (Worcester, MA, 2001).

41. *South Carolina* Gazette, October 24, 1768, advertising a butcher's pen for rent; Martha A. Zierden and Elizabeth J. Reitz, "Animal Use and the Urban Landscape in Colonial Charleston, South Carolina, USA," *International Journal of Historical Archaeology* 13 (September 2009): 327–65; Presentments of the Grand Jury, published in *South Carolina Gazette*, June 8, 1765; October 29, 1772, for "smoak tobacco," *Minutes*, 222; March 22, 1727, for "many hucksters," *Minutes*, 279; for inaccurate weights and measures in the Philadelphia market see *Pennsylvania Gazette*, February 2, 1764.

42. Ibid., September 20, 1736; May 4, 1743.

43. For a discussion of auctions and value in colonial America see Hartigan-O'Connor, "Public Sales," *Early American Studies*, Fall 2015, 749–73. There are examples of auctions in Charleston's marketplace; goods for sale in a 1764 advertisement for a stock of shop goods included 1764 silverware ladle, 1764 lot of Carolina sole leather, 1744 likely young negro boy (examples extracted from author's auction database); "To be Sold to the best Bidder, on Wednesday the 11th of October next, at the Market house on Dorchester Green, a choice Parcel of Plantation Slaves (about 40 in Number) the Purchaser to have 12 Months Credit, giving good Security, and paying Interest from the Day of Sale"; *South Carolina Gazette*, September 28, 1738; Burlington Town Book September 30, 1730, HSP. Wharton Papers, HSP; and "20th May 1745—Petition from people in the South Part of the city," in *Minutes of the Common Council* (Philadelphia).

44. Generalizations derived from author's databases of South Carolina and Pennsylvania auctions.

45. *Manchester Mercury*, April 17, 1753; *Ipswich Journal*, January 24, 1746; "A Liveryman," *An Ax Laid to the Root of the Corrupt Tree, or An Essay on the Hard Case of the Retale-Traders, Citizens, Shopkeepers &c. of the City of London in regard to Their TRADE, as at present invaded by HAWKERS and PEDLARS* (London, 1740), 6. Timothy Cunningham, *The Merchant's Lawyer, or The Law of Trade in General . . . To Which Is added, a Complete Book of Rates*, 2nd ed. (London, 1762),2:456.

46. ASSI 45/28/2 61, April 7, 1766, and ASSI 27/2/46–48, August 18, 1764, and January 11, 1764, TNA.

47. Extensive searching of both Pennsylvania and South Carolina newspaper databases, as well as searches of *Early American Imprints*, failed to yield solid evidence of negative stereotypes of peddlers in both colonies. Finding negative depictions of peddlers in Britain, on the other hand, is very easy indeed. For discussion of Massachusetts peddling see David Jaffee, "Peddlers of Progress and the Transformation of the Rural North, 1760-1860," *Journal of American History* 78, no. 2 (1991): 511-35, although Jaffee does not elaborate on the novelty of this in the context of early modern peddling more broadly. Also see Laurence Fontaine, *History of Pedlars of Europe* (Durham, UK, 1996). Fontaine argues that itinerant traders in Europe also sold consumer goods but still remained pariahs in settled society. See Danielle van den Heuvel, "Policing Peddlers: The Prosecution of Illegal Street Trade in Eighteenth-Century Dutch Towns," *Historical Journal* 58, no. 2 (2015): 367–92, on tensions between peddlers and settled traders in the Netherlands.

48. William Baxter Petition, August 1757, RG 02-00 0908 1745-57; John Hoover, Petition, November 1758; Matthias Hess Petition May 1762, folder 1, RG 02-00 0908, 1758-69, all Lancaster Quarter Sessions records, LCHS.

49. For a collection of fair advertisements see Mary R. M. Goodwin, *Eighteenth Century Fairs*, Colonial Williamsburg Foundation Library Research Report Series—RR0069; *Boston Evening Post*, October 8, 1753, 81, http://research.history.org/DigitalLibrary/View/index.cfm?doc=ResearchRe ports%5CRR0069.xml#p70, accessed August 15, 2018. For accounts of Lancaster's fair see Borough and City Council Minutes, LCHS.org.

50. Goodwin, *Eighteenth Century Fairs*; *Pennsylvania Gazette*, March 6, 1764. See also Silas Deane to Elizabeth Deane, July 15, 1775, while at the Continental Congress. Deane discusses his reluctance to talk "in a Mixed Company," but he follows "a brother Delegate" to "a late Fair" where

there was "a vast crowd of girls." The delegate tells him he will give a guinea to the first girl that Deane says "has a pretty face." But despite strolling "thro the whole Fair," he cannot find one. The whole episode suggests a fair that wholly consists of leisure elements rather than real commercial functions. Paul H. Smith, ed., *Letters of Delegates to Congress*, vol. 1 (Washington, DC, 1976), 626.

51. William Cassel, December 1770, folder 8, RG 02-00 0908, 1758-69, Lancaster Quarter Sessions papers, LCHS; ASSI 45/26/3 35, Examination of Timothy Bawbill, butcher of Himsworth, March 14, 1759, TNA; Jacob Hiltzheimer diary, APS and HSP.

52. Roney, *Governed by a Spirit of Opposition*.

53. *Pennsylvania Gazette*, February 20, 1753.

54. Roney, *Governed by a Spirit of Opposition*, chap. 1; *Pennsylvania Gazette*, February 20, 1753; *Minutes of the Common Council*, 1746, 1753; "Andrew Marvell," Philadelphia, June 10, 1773, "To my Fellow Citizens, Friends to Liberty and Enemies to Despotism." The pseudonym Andrew Marvell was likely used to conjure up parallels with the poet and politician's 1667 piece "Last Instructions to a Painter," in which he attacked the corruption he saw as having taken over the Restoration government during the second Anglo-Dutch war. Marvell was a pseudonym for William Goddard. See Harrison, "Contest of Exchange," 44-45.

CHAPTER FIVE

1. John Carpenter to Mr. Timothy, *South Carolina Gazette*, March 5, 1763.

2. Quotation from "The Address of the Committee of the CITY and Liberties of Philadelphia, to their Fellow-Citizens throughout the United States," William Bradford, chairman, Committee Room, June 26, 1779, Du Simitiere, LCP. On the general malaise that affected the colonial economy after 1763 see Marc Egnal, *New World Economies: The Growth of the Thirteen Colonies and Early Canada* (Oxford, 1998); John McCusker and Russell Menard, *The Economy of British America, 1607-1789* (Chapel Hill, NC, 1980); Marc Egnal and Joseph A. Ernst, "An Economic Interpretation of the American Revolution," *William and Mary Quarterly*, 3rd ser., 29 (1972): 3-32; Nash, *Urban Crucible*; T. H. Breen, *Tobacco Culture: The Mentality of the Great Tidewater Planters on the Eve of Revolution* (Princeton, NJ, 1985).

3. Philadelphia Association of 1769 draft preamble, Pennsylvania Stamp Act and Non-Importation Resolutions Collection, MSS 973.2.M31, APS.

4. For a detailed list of food shortages and riots in Britain and France see Bohstedt, *Politics of Provisions*; Cynthia Bouton, *The Flour War: Gender, Class, and Community in Late Ancien Régime French Society* (University Park, PA, 1994).

5. On economic depression and reactions to it see Nash, *Urban Crucible*; Woody Holton, *Forced Founders: Indians, Debtors, Slaves, and the Making of the American Revolution in Virginia* (Chapel Hill, NC, 1999); Breen, *Tobacco Culture*; Billy G. Smith, *The Lower Sort: Philadelphia's Laboring People, 1750-1800* (Ithaca, NY, 1990), 126-75; Terry Bouton, *Taming Democracy: "The People," the Founders, and the Troubled Ending of the American Revolution* (New York, 2007), chap. 1.

6. Edelson, *New Map of Empire*; Patrick Spero, *Frontier Country: The Politics of War in Early Pennsylvania* (Philadelphia, 2016); Klein, *Unification of a Slave State*.

7. John Irwin to BWM, January 5, 1767, and John Campbell, March 20, 1767, Baynton, Wharton and Morgan, PSA; Jeff W. Dennis, *Patriots and Indians: Shaping Identity in Eighteenth-Century South Carolina* (Columbia, SC, 2017); quotation at chap. 3, p. 9.

8. The political protests these groups mounted are tales well told. Taking a dim view of the unwillingness of Philadelphia and Charleston elites to enforce the rule of law and protect them from Indians and thieving mobs, white men took the law into their own hands to demand proper protection for their families and their property. See Spero, *Frontier Country*, 175-87; Kevin Kenny, *Peaceable Kingdom Lost: The Paxton Boys and the Destruction of William Penn's Holy Experiment* (Oxford,

2009); Matthew Ward, *Breaking the Backcountry: The Seven Years' War in Virginia and Pennsylvania, 1754-65* (Pittsburgh, 2003); Klein, *Unification of a Slave State*; Peter Silver, *Our Savage Neighbors: How Indian War Transformed Early America* (New York, 2008), 191-260.

9. James Smith, *An Account of the Remarkable Occurrences in the Life and Travels of Colonel James Smith* (Philadelphia, 1834), 109. See also Spero's discussion of Smith in Patrick Spero, "Recreating James Smith at the Pennsylvania State Archives," *Pennsylvania History* 76 (October 2009): 171-83. Song composed by Mr. George Campbell, as printed in Smith, *Remarkable Occurrences*, 110-11; *Pennsylvania Archives*, ser. 1, 4:222-30.

10. Richard J. Hooker and Charles Woodmason, eds., *The Carolina Backcountry on the Eve of the Revolution* (Chapel Hill, NC, 1953), 214.

11. Ibid., 214-27. On the development of mills and stores at Camden, the home of Joseph Kershaw, a leading Regulator and close friend of Woodmason, see Lewis, *Carolina Backcountry Venture*.

12. Nash, *Urban Crucible*, 246-48. *Pennsylvania Gazette*, January 10, 1760, and January 7, 1761. See also advertisement of Peacock Biggar for sale of his estate at Charles Town, Maryland, highlighting the cheapness of wood at three or four shillings a cord compared with higher Philadelphia prices. *Pennsylvania Gazette*, September 6, 1759.

13. John Carpenter to Peter Timothy, *South Carolina Gazette*, March 5, 1763. In 1761 the grand jury in Charleston had also cited "the want of a proper officer whose sole duty shall be to see that the fire wood sold in Charles-Town be duly measured, and to prevent forestalling the same, to the extreme detriment of the poor." "Presentments of the Grand Jurors," *South Carolina Gazette*, November 14, 1761. About this time, complaints from the grand jury also started to focus on how much authority wharfingers had over the marketplace. See, for example, "9th, We present as a grievance, that proper care taken to regulate the public scales and weights on the wharves of Charles-Town; for want of there had been frequently found a very considerable difference in weight," and similar 11th grievance, *South Carolina Gazette*, November 9, 1767.

14. For discussion of silver and the Stamp Act see Staughton Lynd and David Waldstreicher, "Free Trade, Sovereignty, and Slavery: Toward an Economic Interpretation of American Independence," *William and Mary Quarterly* 68 (October 2011): 597-630; John Dickinson, "The Late Regulations respecting the British colonies on the continent of America considered, in a letter from a gentleman in Philadelphia to his friend in London," 1765, 58, https://archive.org/details/cihm_20384/page/n5.

15. Richard Waln to his brother, November 5, 1764, and also see Waln to David Barclay and Sons, May 18, 1764; Waln to Edmund Skinner, October 31, 1765, Waln Letterbook, Richard Waln Papers, HSP. Petition of the Pennsylvania House to the House of Commons, *Pennsylvania Archives*, ser. 8, 7 (January 14, 1766): 5825-87. This petition echoed Franklin's view, detailed in chapter 3, that in the American marketplace individuals were in extreme peril if their credit should fail, because of the absolute dependence of trade on it. "That by the Policy of the English Laws, the Person of every Debtor remains as a Security to his Creditor for the Performance of the Contract, and Discharge of the Debt: And should the Legislature of this Province be restrained from making Paper Money a lawful Tender to the Creditor; in Discharges of the Body of the Debtor, the Person of every *American* is liable to Duress and Imprisonment, at the Will and Pleasure of his Creditor." For a broader discussion of the Currency Act's effect on the colonies see Jack P. Greene and Richard M. Jellison, "The Currency Act of 1764 in Imperial-Colonial Relations, 1764-1776," *William and Mary Quarterly* 18 (October 1961): 485-518. See also Justin DuRivage and Claire Priest, "The Stamp Act and the Political Origins of American Legal and Economic Institutions," *Southern California Law Review* 88 (2015): 875-912. DuRivage and Priest highlight the way the act undermined colonial regimes of property and law that were at the heart of the marketplace.

16. On the economic depression of the Revolutionary era see Allan Kulikoff, "Such Things Ought Not to Be," in *The World of the Revolutionary American Republic: Land, Labor and the Conflict for a Continent*, ed. Andrew Shankman, Routledge Worlds (New York, 2014), 134-64.

17. Charles Woodmason, "The Justices of the Peace," sermon, 1771, Hooker and Woodmason, *Carolina Backcountry*, 124.

18. Dickinson, "Late Regulations," 30–32. I rely here on Terry Bouton's account of Pennsylvania's first auction crisis. Bouton also quotes Dickinson. Bouton, *Taming Democracy*, 23–25.

19. "Legion," *Pennsylvania Gazette*, January 23, 1772; "Philadelphus," *Pennsylvania Gazette*, January 23, 1772; "A Friend to the Community," *Pennsylvania Gazette*, January 16, 1772. There was no similar complaint about auctions in South Carolina, and sales of debtors' goods did not dramatically increase. It appears that the nonimportation action of 1769–70 may have reduced the number of Africans brought into the colony, since they were included by the 1769 association, and this meant auctions for enslaved people were still buoyant owing to owners' selling their enslaved people on the domestic market. The currency crisis was not as acute. There was still a lot of demand for land, too. Josiah Smith certainly seems to have had no problem with selling by auction in 1771–74, when his letterbook records numerous vendue sales in his capacity as a factor for a wide range of businesses (Smith Letterbook, SHC). It is also possible that Carolinians bought more Africans from the Caribbean because of the transatlantic boycott—they bought many more from this source in 1771–74. See Gregory E. O'Malley, "Beyond the Middle Passage: Slave Migration from the Caribbean to North America, 1619–1807," *William and Mary Quarterly*, 3rd ser., 66 (January 2009): 125–72.

20. To Mr John Smith Jr., Antigua, January 12, 1773, Josiah Smith Letterbook, SHC. "Benevolus," *South Carolina Gazette*, November 26, 1772; "Veridicus," *South Carolina Gazette*, November 12, 1772. These articles were preceded by a succession of grievances from the grand jury concerning the state of the marketplaces. See especially *South Carolina Gazette*, November 12, 1764, third grievance, and November 9, 1767, sixth grievance.

21. Entries for October 12, 1776, June 24, 1777, and May 30, 1778, Christopher Marshall Sr. Diary, HSP. Josiah Smith to Mr. John Ray, New Jersey, March 7, 1778, Smith letterbook, SHC; As Allan Kulikoff has commented, "The military market was neither reliable nor lucrative" and so was hardly a substitute for a peacetime market. See Kulikoff, "Such Things Ought Not to Be," 138.

22. Christopher Marshall Sr. Diary, HSP, August 29, 1776: "Fine sunshine my wife rose early to visit the wharfs for wood, all heard 1 vessell with 23 cord of hickiry & oak just sold before she (got there—illegible insert) for 29/ hickory 2 of for oak"; 30th my wife rose early to visit wharfs on accot of winters wood"; August 3, 1776: "Wife rose early to goe to market I rose past 6 as our folks begun to get their winters fire wood & were piling in ye years . . . paid £10 for 11 cord & ½ of oak fire wood hauling company and piling 42/10½."

23. Ibid., July 1, 1777: "a bushel of bran or shorts cant be procurd but am in hopes after Harvest we shall get supplyd as I intend to visit some of the Farmers. I just give this note by way of moments to remember some of our Difficulties etc."; August 14, 1777: I went by my self out of Town to John Moyers about a cow fire wood & hay, the two first these was a prospect of getting the later had none to spare from there near 8 calld at his fathers who were mowing but I could not persuade him to promise me any hay but he would some time hence send me two cord of fire wood."

24. "The Address of the Committee of the CITY and Liberties of Philadelphia, to their Fellow-Citizens throughout the United States," William Bradford, chairman, Committee Room, June 26, 1779, Du Simitiere, LCP.

25. Barbara Clark Smith, "Food Rioters and the American Revolution," *William and Mary Quarterly* 51 (January 1994): 3–38.

26. James Murray, *An Impartial History of the War in America: From Its First Commencement, to the Present Time* (Newcastle, 1782), 77.

27. Clark Smith, "Food Rioters," 7; Wendy Thwaites, "Oxford Food Riots: A Community and Its Markets," in *Markets, Market Culture and Popular Protest in Eighteenth-Century Britain and Ireland*, ed. Adrian Randall and Andrew Charlesworth (Liverpool, 1996), 147.

28. David Walsh, Adrian Randall, Richard Sheldon, and Andrew Charlesworth, "The Cider Tax, Popular Symbolism and Opposition in Mid-Hanoverian England," in Randall and Charlesworth, *Markets, Market Culture and Popular Protest*, 74-75.

29. Thwaites, "Oxford Food Riots." I am not arguing here that Britain was permeated by cosy paternalism in which the rich looked out for the poor and the poor were suitably grateful for their protection. Rather, I agree with English historians who argue that wealthy local elites were canny enough to manage protest in this way because they felt a duty to do so but also realized it was the best route to maintaining their power. The poor saw such protests as the best means of achieving a result but also recognized that if they acted outside customary norms magistrates might marshal the courts to prosecute rioters and send them to the gallows or a transport ship. For discussion of this "give and take" see Wood, *Memory of the People*, 120-87.

30. This argument is of course connected to (and inspired by) Lynd and Waldstreicher's assertion that the Revolution was "basically a colonial independence movement and the reasons for it were fundamentally economic." Lynd and Waldstreicher, "Free Trade, Sovereignty, and Slavery," quotation on 599. See also Timothy Pitkin, "The late John Adams, in his history of the disputes of the parent country with America, from the year 1754 ... from that time to this, the general sense of the colonies has been that the authority of parliament was confined to the regulation of trade and did not extend to *taxation*, or *internal legislation*."Timothy Pitkin, *A Political and Civil History of the United States* (New Haven, CT, 1828), 92.

31. Non-importation Agreement March 10, 1769, no. 89, Scraps, Du Simitiere, LCP. Another draft of this agreement in the American Philosophical Society explained that "we still hope, the Parliament may by Proper Information be convinced, that the True Interest of the Mother Country, will hereafter in a great Degree depend, on their relieving us from these unnatural and useless Fetters, with which the Sinews of American Commerce have been so injudiciously cramp'd." Pennsylvania Stamp Act and Non-importation Papers, APS; Charleston Non-importation Agreement, *South Carolina Gazette*, July 22, 1769, and James Duane's speech to Committee on Rights, Set 8, 1774, *Letters of the Delegates to the Continental Congress*, 1:51. When it came to executing nonimportation agreements, merchants' strong belief that the British must not be allowed to control their private property was also apparent. Writing in 1773, "Regulus" argued that "every American [is] indispensably obliged to oppose, by all prudent means, the Landing of it. No Man, therefore, who has any Pretension to Freedom, can, consistent with such Pretension allow his Wharf, stores, or Dwelling to be made Use of, in the landing or securing the ministerial Adventure—If it is deprived of a Footing here, which must be the case, if we determine to preserve our Wharves and Stores inviolate, Administration will be puzzled how to levy their Tribute; and, in all probability, will be reduced to the Necessity of treating the Americans in future, as Men who are worthy of Liberty; as Men, who, at all Events, are determined to enjoy it." "To the Freemen of Pennsylvania," LCP. See also Lynd and Waldstreicher, "Free Trade, Sovereignty, and Slavery," 608.

32. "A Carolinian," "To the Inhabitants of the Province of South-Carolina, "*South Carolina Gazette*, June 20, 1774. The writer also explained, "For it must be wholly at the King's Pleasure, whether I shall make a Wharf or Landing on my Land or not, or, if I do, whether I shall make my Use of it, the Nature of the Property is wholly altered. Is that my Land which I cannot improve as I please, or on which I am not allowed to land Goods even that have paid the Duty"; Yeates Papers, HSP, folder 8, draft of an intended address to the people at the meeting at Lancaster, July 9, 1774, in order to send a committee to Philadelphia. A Petition signed by Henry Laurens and a number of Americans resident in London at the time made a similar point, arguing that "the Bill takes away, immediately, from the Inhabitants of the Town, the use of Property to the amount of several Hundred Thousand Pounds, vested in Quays, Wharfs, Stores, etc., etc. That it will restrain many thousands of his Majesty's Subjects, from subsisting themselves & their Families, by their usual Employments." March 28, 1774, in David R. Chesnutt, ed., *The Papers of Henry Laurens*, vol. 9 (Columbia, SC, 1981), 370-72.

33. "Veridicus," *South Carolina Gazette,* November 12, 1772.

34. "An Act for Regulating and Ascertaining the Rates of Wharfage of Ships and Merchandise and Also for Ascertaining the Rates of Storage, in Charlestown," April 12, 1768; *Gazette of the State of South Carolina,* May 5, 1777, and May 12, 1777; ibid., February 9, 1780, "An Ordinance" and also "An Act to empower the holding of Special Courts," *Gazette of the State of South Carolina,* September 15, 1777.

35. Margaret Colleton papers, South Caroliniana Library. See letter of estate manager to Mr. Allen Swainston, Charlestown, February 17, 1781: "It was however impossible to employ the Negroes to advantage without a Boat the Estate depending upon the Freight to Watboo and Wood sent to Market, having lost the crop of Rice, and did not make sufficient Privisions for the use of ye Plantation owing to the dryness of the season . . . w the consent of Mr Kinloch I purchased another Schooner for £22,000 which has been employed ever since, except when the Town was besieged and a short time after." In her letters Eliza Wilkinson describes people fleeing trading centers such as Jacksonboro–PonPon and Willtown, as well as discussing the plundering expeditions of the British and American forces that deprived plantations of provisions. Carolina Gilman, ed., *Letters of Eliza Wilkinson during the Invasion and Possession of Charlestown, S.C., by the British in the Revolutionary War* (New York, 1839), 24–25. The nature of the war in South Carolina caused much greater disruption to food supplies and local trade than did the war in Pennsylvania. As Sylvia Frey has argued, Carolina endured a "triagonal war." Frey, *Water from the Rock* (Princeton, NJ, 1991), 108–42.

36. "Legion" and "Philadelphus," both in *Pennsylvania Gazette,* January 23, 1772.

37. To The Inhabitants of the City PHILADELPHIA, and Parts Adjacent," broadside, Philadelphia, February 15, 1772. Also "Navis" in *Pennsylvania Gazette,* February 16, 1774, arguing against the monopoly the king granted on building "raft ships, saying it was unfair because it was "an exclusive privilege, granted by the king to particular persons. . . . a designing Ministry to subjugate the Liberties of America."

38. Subcommittee Log Book 3, December 5, 1774, APS; Committee Chamber, March 6, *Pennsylvania Gazette,* March 13, 1776. "To the Printers of the Pennsylvania Gazette" from "A.B." *Pennsylvania Gazette,* September 3, 1777. This article is notable for its religious allusions—they make it extraordinary, since few others sought to place Christian duty so centrally in their calls for greater regulation.

39. "An Act to Prevent Forestalling and Regrating and to Encourage Fair Dealing," January 2, 1778, *Pennsylvania Statutes at Large,* 9:177–80.

40. An Act to Prevent Forestalling . . . Enacted into a Law at Lancaster, January 2, 1778; "At Town Meeting . . . ," *Pennsylvania Gazette,* July 7, 1779. The minutes of the Bucks County Committee of Observation noted: "The Committee being apprehensive that certain shopkeepers within this County have not been sufficiently attentive to the Continental Association respecting the price of Goods, the Clerk is directed to publish the ninth Article of sd association with the following preamble annexed viz This Committee desirous as much as possible to prevent evry species of Imposition and extortion which designing persons prompted by a sordid attachment to private Interest and the present scarcity of sundry Articles of Merchandize may be tempted to commit have directed the republication of the ninth Article of the Continental Association: And all shopkeepers and other retailers of Goods, are requested to be particularly attentive thereto, as a wilful violation thereof will necessarily incur the penalties recommended in this and the eleventh Article of said Association." Minutes of the Bucks County Committee of Observation, December 26, 1775, Bucks County Historical Society.

41. John K. Alexander, "The Fort Wilson Incident of 1779: A Case Study of the Revolutionary Crowd," *William and Mary Quarterly,* 3rd ser., 31 (October 1974): 589–612.

42. "A Friend to the Community," *Pennsylvania Gazette,* January 16, 1772. See also "Civis," *Pennsylvania Gazette,* January 30, 1772. Civis claimed he had heard complaints about the vendues not from consumers "but from those that have been long accustomed to large Profits on their

Importations, and who seem to take it hard, that there is a Sett of Men lately sprung up, who have introduced Innovations, both in the Profits on Business, and Mode of Selling, when, I suppose, they expected both the one, and the other, were to be as unalterable as the Laws of Medes and Persians." He also denied that vendue masters encouraged thievery.

43. "A Philadelphian," "To the FREEMEN, CITIZENS of *Philadelphia*," May 29, 1773, "To my fellow citizens friends to liberty and enemies to despotism"; "Andrew Marvell," June 10, 1773; Roney, *Governed by a Spirit of Opposition*. There was a similar tussle between city dwellers in October 1772 over the Leather Act, which sought to regulate the quality of leather by appointing an inspector who would stamp good leather. "A Country Shoewearer," who opposed it, agreed with the principle of some regulation but argued that shoes should be inspected, not leather.

44. Richard Waln to Harford and Powell, Philadelphia, April 18, 1769, Waln Letterbook, HSP; Benjamin Fuller to Mr. John Scott Jr., Philadelphia, September 5, 1770, Fuller Letterbook AMB 3785, vol. 1, 1762–81, HSP. In this letter Fuller was also pondering "a Swedish scheme" that may well have been a plan to import tea regularly sold at auction by the Swedish East India Company. These auctions were one of the biggest sources of smuggled tea in Britain until Pitt abolished duties. On this trade see Hanna Hodacs, *Silk and Tea in the North: Scandinavian Trade and the Market for Asian Goods in the Eighteenth Century* (London, 2016).

45. "To the Freeholders, Merchants, Tradesmen and Farmers, of the City and County of Philad.," *Pennsylvania Gazette*, September 26, 1770; "In Congress, April 30, 1776," *Pennsylvania Gazette*, May 8, 1776.

46. S. J. Thompson, for example, has explored debates about enclosure from 1730 to 1780 in which "a primarily *political* model of a commonwealth of yeoman farmers" was replaced "by a more overtly *economic* model of a society in which the progress of commerce was privileged above all other consideration." Thompson, "Parliamentary Enclosure, Property, Population, and the Decline of Classical Republicanism in Eighteenth-Century Britain," *Historical Journal* 51 (September 2008): 621–42, quotation on 626.

47. As quoted in Jonathan Sheehan and Dror Wahrman, *Invisible Hands: Self-Organization and the Eighteenth Century* (Chicago, 2015), 245. Indeed, Peter Miller has suggested that the concept of a single common good had been placed under severe pressure by the American Revolution and the spread of religious toleration in British society itself. See Miller, *Defining the Common Good*.

48. Thompson, "Parliamentary Enclosure."

49. Pownall, *Administration of the Colonies*, 38–39; Miller, *Defining the Common Good*, 211–13.

50. Linda Kerber, *Women of the Republic: Intellect and Ideology in Revolutionary America* (Chapel Hill, NC, 1980); Mary Beth Norton, *Liberty's Daughters: The Revolutionary Experience of American Women, 1750–1800* (Ithaca, NY, 1980), 155–96; Breen, *Marketplace of Revolution*.

51. The notable exceptions here include Gautham Rao, who has observed that merchants were using commercial regulation to object to commercial regulation (Rao, *National Duties*, 45–46), and Richard Buel Jr., "The Committee Movement of 1779 and the Formation of Public Authority in Revolutionary America," in *The Transformation of Early American History: Society, Authority, and Ideology*, ed. James A. Henretta, Michael Kammen, and Stanley N. Katz (New York, 1991), 151–69. See also Lynd and Waldstreicher, "Free Trade, Sovereignty, and Slavery," 608, though they skip over nonimportation and move straight to the Continental Congress. It is also pertinent to contemplate why Americans launched a boycott when Europeans did not. Irish patriot leaders initiated a boycott in 1779, after the American actions, but Americans were the first to engage in such behavior in the Atlantic world. See Padhraig Higgins, "Consumption, Gender, and the Politics of 'Free Trade' in Eighteenth-Century Ireland," *Eighteenth-Century Studies* 41 (Fall 2007): 87–105; J. H. Elliott, *Empires of the Atlantic World: Britain and Spain* (Cambridge, 2007), 316–17. I would argue that it was the strong individualist strand in colonial economic culture that allowed Americans to view themselves as independent consumers, apart from any corporate interests, who could then organize themselves into an entirely new constituency. "This is true *Liberty*. . . ." Philadelphia,

September 18, 1774. This broadside was undoubtedly part of the extreme factionalism of Pennsylvania politics—but it nevertheless appeared at a time when the patriots were more united in their committees of inspection than they had ever been previously. See Richard Alan Ryerson, *The Revolution Is Now Begun: The Radical Committees of Philadelphia, 1765–1776* (Philadelphia, 1978), 89–116. In South Carolina dissent came in the form of Drayton's *Letters from an American Freeman*, which described the associations' actions as "arbitrary and unjust." See letters and response to them, "Out of Thy Own Mouth Will I Condemn Thee," *South Carolina Gazette*, September 28, 1769.

52. *Pennsylvania Gazette*, December 7, 1774; "Resolutions of a Mass Meeting of Freeholders and Freemen of Philadelphia, June 18 to July 11, 1774, box 2, Du Simitiere, LCP. *South Carolina Gazette*, November 21, 1774. Frequent references to "strangers"—in the Philadelphia agreement of March 10, 1769 (Du Simitiere, LCP), and by the Charleston committee ("Charles-Town, December 8," *South Carolina Gazette*, December 7, 1769)—only increased the sense that the committees functioned much like urban corporations or guilds enforcing regulations over a resident community. Sometimes the potential scale of the state apparatus needed to regulate trade overwhelmed colonists little used to enforcement. In "Considerations on the Impropriety of Exporting Rice to Great-Britain," Charleston, January 11, 1775, (Charles-Town, 1775) the author pondered the issues that might stop the implementation of a plan to help disadvantaged indigo planters by exchanging indigo for rice. "Perhaps the difficulty will be at least as great, to gain the consent of individuals to this, as to a qualified non-exportation. But how is it to be executed? Where are the numerous committees to be found, who unpaid, shall take the endless task of inspecting every barrel of rice, and every pound of indico, that comes down to market, and to ascertain its specific value? Where is the court, daily to preside over the constant Barter, and to decide the numerous disputes which must arise between man and man? Where are the open offices in which all this vast business is to be transacted? Where are the free stores, in which the produce must lay after the decision?"

53. *South Carolina and American General Gazette*, December 30, 1774: "Cargoes of two vessels arrived at New York . . . have been sold by Auctions agreeably to the Association"; *South Carolina Gazette*, December 26, 1774: "Committee . . . continue selling such Goods at public vendue"; *South Carolina Gazette*, September 7, 1775; Resolution 7, "Resolutions of a mass meeting of Freeholders and Freemen of Phila." June 18 to July 11, 1774, 965.F.9, LCP.

54. Rob Parkinson, *The Common Cause: Creating Race and Nation in the American Revolution* (Chapel Hill, NC, 2016).

55. "Letters from a Farmer in Pennsylvania to the Inhabitants of the British Colonies. Letter XII," *Pennsylvania Gazette*, February 18, 1768; *South Carolina Gazette*, March 27, 1775; "To the PUBLIC . . . ," Broadside, Philadelphia, July 4, 1770.

56. Petition quoted at length in Kerber, *Women of the Republic*, 41; *Pennsylvania Gazette*, July 26, 1770.

57. Item 107, Sitgreaves to Committee of Inspection and Observation, April 2, 1776, Du Simitiere, LCP.

58. *Pennsylvania Gazette*, July 24, 1776; *South Carolina Gazette*, June 7, 1770. See also notes of Christopher Marshall, April 9, 1776, for "meeting at which Townsend Spikeman attending ownd he refust & could not take the continental money. He refusd to appear." Marshall also included two incidents in 1775 when a similar punishment was exacted on traders for the same crime. One was paraded through the streets in a cart—the Associators at least protected him from tarring and feathering by the mob. Christopher Marshall Sr. Diary, HSP.

59. Entries for Philadelphia February 15-19, 1776, and subsequent entries for 1776 and 1777 in John Drinker Account book Amb 2945, HSP; Christopher Marshall noted the treatment of Drinker in his diary, "30th Jan 1776 after 5 went to committee room philosophical hall came away past 9 raining and freezing so as their was great difficulty to walk the street at this meeting complaint was made against john Drinker hatter for refusing taking continental money who being [sorry? Soo?] for acknowledg he did & yt in point of conscience he refust it upon which he as to be

censured agreeable to the resolve of congress published but to be referd for one week in order for him to consider well off &c." Christopher Marshall Sr. Diary, HSP.

60. *South Carolina Gazette and Country Journal*, July 3, 1770. Quotation from Adam Smith, *The Wealth of Nations* (1776) book 1, chap. 2, "Of the principle which gives occasion to the division of labour," https://oll.libertyfund.org/titles/237#Smith_0206-01_246, accessed January 7, 2019.

61. Yeates Papers, HSP.

62. George Galphin to Henry Laurens, Silver Bluff, February 7, 1776, in Chesnutt, *Papers of Henry Laurens*, vol. 11 (Columbia, SC, 1988), 93-95; Council of Safety to Georgia Council of Safety, Charles Town, July 24, 1775, *Papers of Henry Laurens* (Columbia, 1985), 10:243-45; Christina Snyder, "Conquered Enemies, Adopted Kin, and Owned People: The Creek Indians and Their Captives," *Journal of Southern History* 73 (May 2007): 255-88; Colin G. Calloway, *Revolution in Indian Country: Crisis and Diversity in Native American Communities* (Cambridge, 1995), 182-212; Spero, *Frontier Country*, 206; Yeates Papers, folders 13, 14, 15, HSP; Account from Diary of Arthur Fairies of an expedition to the Cherokees, mfm, SCDAH.

63. "An Act to Repeal Divers Acts of Assembly of this Commonwealth herein after mentioned, for preventing forestalling and regrating . . . making of Whiskey," chap. 904, *Statutes at Large of Pennsylvania*, passed March 22, 1780. For a reprinting of "The Bill intituled 'An Act for the effectual suppression of Public Auctions and Vendues, and to prohibit white male persons, capable of bearing arms, from being pedlars or hawkers," see "Philadelphia. In General Assembly, Nov. 16, 1779," *Pennsylvania Gazette*, December 1, 1779.

64. This is Gerstle's definition. See Gary Gerstle, *Liberty and Coercion: The Paradox of American Government from the Founding to the Present* (Princeton, NJ, 2015), 57. See also William J. Novak, *The People's Welfare: Law and Regulation in Nineteenth-Century America* (Chapel Hill, NC, 1996). Most political scientists trace the term "police" and the idea of police power to William Blackstone's 1769 volume of *Commentaries*, in which he explained, "By the public police and economy I mean the due regulation and domestic order of the kingdom: whereby the individuals of the state, like members of a well-governed family, are bound to conform their general behaviour to the rules of propriety, good neighbourhood, and good manners; and to be decent, industrious, and inoffensive in their respective stations." Blackstone, *Commentaries on the Laws of England* (Oxford, 1769), book 4, chap. 13, "Of Offenses against the Public Health, and the Public Police or Economy," item 5, 162. See also Santiago Legarre, "The Historical Background of the Police Power," *University of Pennsylvania Journal of Constitutional Law* 9 (2007): 745; March 16, 1783, Report of the Committee appointed to consider expediency of incorporating Charles Town, SCDAH; *Ordinances of the City Council of Charleston* (Charleston, SC, 1789).

CHAPTER SIX

1. Diary of George Nelson, Am. 107, HSP.

2. Ibid.

3. Benjamin Fuller to Francis West, in London, Philadelphia, November 17, 1784; Fuller to James Doyle, October [no day] 1784, explained that he had avoided "any Adventure from Europe save a triffling one . . . most of my views have been to the West Indies & I have in some measure succeeded." Benjamin Fuller Letterbook, Amb.3485, HSP. For the troubling circumstances Philadelphia merchants faced in the 1780s see Thomas M. Doerflinger, "Capital Generation in the New Nation: How Stephen Girard Made His First $735,872," *William and Mary Quarterly* 72 (October 2015): 628; Bouton, *Taming Democracy*; Petitions of the Inhabitants of Edgefield County, Ninety-Six District, undated but labeled 1789, SCDAH; Charleston merchant petition, January 27, 1783, SCDAH. On the merchant conflicts that arose in occupied and postoccupation Charleston see Jennifer Goloboy, *Charleston and the Emergence of Middle Class Culture in the Revolutionary Era* (Athens, GA, 2016).

4. Petition March 2, 1784, Petitions to the Pennsylvania Assembly, PSA. In his role as chief financier Robert Morris faced constant requests for money to pay army suppliers and spent much time putting them off. See, for example, letter to Morris from Quartermaster General Timothy Pickering at Camp Verplanks Point, New York, September 19, 1782, 404-5; Morris to George Washington, Office of Finance, September 25, 1782, 435-36, both in *The Papers of Robert Morris*, vol. 6, *July 22 to Oct 31, 1782*, ed. James E. Ferguson and John Catanzariti (Pittsburgh, 1984).

5. Diary of George Nelson, Wednesday, June 20, 1781, HSP; For Duncan's complaints see Duncan to Mr. Reed, Pittsburgh, June 9, 1781, 200-201; Duncan to Reed, Pittsburgh, August 30, 1781, 380-81, both in *Pennsylvania Archives*, vol. 13, *Minutes of the Supreme Executive Council, 1781-83* (Harrisburg, PA, 1853). It appears that things in western Pennsylvania were still bad in 1789; on Tuesday, April 26, 1789, John May commented: "Spent the day at Pittsburg, found money affairs here at a low ebb. Everybody unwilling to part with money but very anxious to get it. You cannot buy anything without putting money in hand, nor sell it & receive your pay back." In "Journal of Col. John May, of Boston, relative to a Journey to the Ohio Country, 1789," *Pennsylvania Magazine of History and Biography* 45, no. 2 (1921): 116.

6. For a discussion of the logistics of feeding military forces and issues specific to America see Kulikoff, "Such Things" 134-64; Ward, *Breaking the Backcountry*, chap. 6; Wayne Bodle, *The Valley Forge Winter: Civilians and Soldiers in War* (State College, PA, 2002). The Loudon Papers in the Huntington Library also contain numerous items detailing the difficulties the British army encountered in provisioning its forces during the Seven Years' War. See, for example, Council of War Minutes at Oswego, September 18, 1755, on the constant shortage of provisions and the difficulty of transporting them, and "Remarks on Affairs in North America," George Montagu to Second Earl of Halifax concerning "the manner of producing a necessary Supply of Provisions, and Stores and battoes and carriages for transporting them. In all former expeditions undertaken in America, wherein the Crown has born a share, this part of the expence has been required of the Colonies. But the manner in which the supply has been and always will be given, has proved and ever will prove an insurmountable Obstacle to the execution of the Service"; box 14, L0649 and L0722, Loudon Papers, HL.

7. For the intensity of corporate conflict in the British animal trades see Emma Hart, "From Field to Plate: The Colonial Livestock Trade and Development of an American Economic Culture," *William and Mary Quarterly* 73 (January 2016): 107-40.

8. Meredith noted that it was harder to get workers in the 1780s than it had been earlier on. It is not clear whether this was because slavery had come to an end in Pennsylvania. Quotations from Meredith to Andrew Rud, Marlborough Township, Montgomery County, September 29, 1786, Jonathan Meredith Papers, HSP.

9. Petition of William Logan of Charleston, March 1, 1785, Senate Petitions, SCDAH.

10. David Stewart to Anthony Kennedy, Huntington County, December 16, 1794, Anthony Kennedy Papers, HSP. "Journal of Col. John May," *Pennsylvania Magazine of History and Biography: PMHB* 45 (April 1921): 114-15; On the increase of stores in western Pennsylvania after the Revolution see Wenger, *Country Storekeeper in Pennsylvania*; Wenger and Garrison, "Commerce and Culture"; John Bezis-Selfa, *Forging America: Ironworkers, Adventurers, and the Industrious Revolution* (Ithaca, NY, 2004).

11. "Journal of Col. John May," 122.

12. June 12, 1782, *Freeman's Journal*; A McFarlane to John Perry at the New Store, April 3, 1781, *Pennsylvania Archives*, 13:5-6; Complaints by the grand jury of Ninety-Six District, November 1794, folder 2, Grand Jury Presentments, SCDAH; Petition of Sundry Inhabitants of St James Santee to the South Carolina General Assembly, dated 1785 by the archive, SCDAH.

13. "An Act to Authorize the Governor to Appoint and Commission an Auctioneer, for the Express and Sole Purpose of Selling Horses, Cattle and Carriages, within the City of Philadelphia," April 10, 1799, *Statutes at Large of Pennsylvania*, 16:313-14; broadside, "Public Auction on

Thursday the 23d of November next, . . . 43 valuable high blooded colts, mares, and Phillies . . . "
(hand-dated 1787), SCDAH; petition of John Bayard to the Pennsylvania Assembly, Philadelphia,
September 20, 1781, PSA; South Carolina Court of Ordinary, Camden District Inventories, ap-
praisements and sale books 1782-87 (Kershaw County), SCDAH.

14. Reference to March 1787 Act for Creating Market at Winnsborough can be found in the
December 17, 1803, "Act Improving the Government of the Market at Winnsborough," in Cooper
and McCord, *Statutes at Large of South Carolina*, 5:468; Act for Creating a Market at Georgetown,
ibid., 5:22. This act also created a market at Camden: Act for Improving Government of Columbia,
December 21, 1798, ibid., 5:333. See also "An Act for Establishing Fairs and Markets in the Town
of Winnsborough," March 7, 1786, ibid., 4:652-54; petition of John Winn, Richard Winn, and John
Vanderhorst to the Senate of the State of South Carolina requesting that "a market may be by law
established" in Winnsborough, February 19, 1784, SCDAH; "An Act for Establishing a Fair and
Markets in the Town of Belleville, on the Congaree River, in This State," March 16, 1783, in *Statutes
at Large of South Carolina*, 4:557-59; "An Act for erecting the town of Easton, in the country of
Northampton, into a borough . . . " as reproduced in *Pennsylvania Gazette*, July 8, 1789. On town
founding in this region see Diane Wenger and Jan Taylor, *Schaefferstown and Heidelberg Township,
Lebanon County [PA]* (Mount Pleasant, SC, 2014).

15. Petition from Northampton County, February 10, 1784; undated petition against erecting a shambles in Dock Street, ca. 1783/84; petition against extending the market from Third to
Fourth Street, Philadelphia, February 15, 1784; then numerous petitions through the 1784 and
1785 sessions from York, Dauphin, Lancaster, and other counties both for and against the market
extension; Chester County Petition "That from the vast increase of the city of Philadelphia, and
the number of strangers coming among us for the purpose of sharing the blessings of Freedom,
Liberty and Independence, we conceive that the present Market Place is but far too small for the
accommodation of the people from different parts of the country resorting," November 4, 1785; all
RG7 0257 Petitions, reel 1, PSA.

16. "An Act to Incorporate the City of Philadelphia," passed April 8, 1785, *Statutes at Large
of Pennsylvania*, 13:193-214; Minutes of the Philadelphia City Council, 1789-94, AM3570, HSP.

17. Ordinance 38, October 11, 1786, in *Ordinances of the City Council of Charleston*; Report of
the City Council and agreement relative to the cession of Markett Street and Indenture, March 28,
1788, between Charles Cotesworth Pinckney, John Deas, Thomas Jones, Sims White, John Wyatt
and Mary Lingard . . . and the City Council," both Pinckney Family Papers, 1765–1915, (495.00),
SCHS.

18. The Honorable Judge Pendleton's Charge to the Grand Juries of Georgetown, Cheraws, and
Camden Districts. This was widely reproduced in Charleston's *City Gazette*, 1788, but appeared
earlier in *American Museum* 1 (June 1787): 423-26.

19. Petition from Southwark residences March 23, 1781, Petitions, reel 1, PSA; STATE OF
PENNSYLVANIA. IN GENERAL ASSEMBLY, SATURDAY, AUGUST 17, 1782, The bill, titled
"An Act to enable the Commissioners therein named to purchase public Landings in the District
of Southwark, in the County of Philadelphia, and for raising a Fund to pay the purchase Monies
thereof," stated that "the rapid improvement of the water lots in the district of Southwark, of the
late years, hath rendered them of great value, and unless timely care is taken to procure convenient
places for public landings for the unlading of wood, hay, boards, timber, sand and stone, and other
bulky and heavy articles, brought into the same by water for the use of the inhabitants, the public
may in time be deprived of the benefit of access to the water for such purposes, to their injury, by
increasing their land carriage." *Pennsylvania Gazette*, August 28, 1782.

20. "Act in aid of the Callowhill market in the township of the Northern Liberties," by outlawing hucksters and people going door-to-door to sell goods, March 18, 1789, *Statutes at Large of
Pennsylvania* 13:225-26; "Act for building a town house and market place between Coates Street
and Poplar Lane, . . ." March 27, 1795, ibid., 15:252-56. In Philadelphia—clerk of the market must

enter in £200 bond, regulating brokers as well as hucksters and position of stall holders, 1790 ordinance—no selling goods on brick pavements, no piling goods in he streets and placing them there; 1790—"no oysters in their shells shall be sold in the city, or at the wharves thereof, in any other manner, than by count, or tale"—1798 sees the the third market ordinance in nine years. All in City Council Minutes 1789-94: AM3570, HSP; Charleston market ordinance 38, no. 71, better ordering negroes, in *Ordinances of the City Council*; "Act for fair establishing a fair and markets in the town of Greenville, at the Long Bluff, Peedee River," no. 1253, 1785, 649-52, and "An Act for establishing fairs and markets in the town of Winnsborough," no. 1255, 1785, 652-54, both in Cooper and McCord, *Statutes at Large of South Carolina*, vol. 4; "An Act for the better regulating the streets and markets in the town of Winnsborough . . . ," no. 1819, 1803, 468-69; "An Act for establishing a Market in the town at Georgetown; and for empowering the Commissioners therein named to sell and dispose of a lot of Land in the said town; and for appointing and authorizing Commissioners for the Town and Markets of Camden . . . ," no. 1369, 1787, 21-24, both in Cooper and McCord, *Statutes at Large of South Carolina*, vol. 5.

21. "An Ordinance for the Regulation of the Market Held in the High-Street, Chapter XXXI," March 29, 1798, as reprinted in *Ordinances of the Corporation of the City of Philadelphia; to Which Are Prefixed, the Original Charter, the Act of Incorporation, and Other Acts of Assembly relating to the City* (Philadelphia, 1812), 149-60. See City Corporation Minutes, HSP, June 5, 1789, in which cedar coopers and earthenware sellers petition the council not to be removed from their current selling positions; June 23, 1789, where councilmen visit the market at 8:00 a.m. to inspect selling places of stallholders from Passyunk and Moyamensing.

22. An Act for Regulating and Ascertaining the Rates of Wharfage of Ships and Merchandise . . . in Charlestown," April 12, 1768, in Cooper and McCord, *Statutes at Large of South Carolina*, 4:286-93. On the contested authority of customs men in an early American context see Thomas M. Truxes, *Defying Empire: Trading with the Enemy in Colonial New York* (New Haven, CT, 2008). Pennsylvania's 1773 act also recruited wardens, yet their duty mostly related to the "security of the . . . navigation and commerce" and as such was concerned with harbor pilots, with issuing bills of credit to extend piers into the Delaware to secure vessels during the winter freeze, and with collecting provincial duties. The actual wharf and its owner were not dealt with in this act. See "An Act Appointing Wardens for the Port of Philadelphia, and for Other Purposes Therein Mentioned," February 26, 1773, *Statutes at Large of Pennsylvania*, 8:264-83.

23. Ordinances 38, Market, 60, Ascertain Duties of Harbourmaster, and 35, Naval Stores, in *Ordinances of the City Council of Charleston*; "An Act for the further regulation of the Port of Philadelphia, and enlarging the power of the wardens thereof," April 1, 1784, 320-30, and "Supplement," September 23, 1784, 384-85, both in Cooper and McCord, *Statutes at Large of South Carolina*, vol. 11; "An act to establish a board of warden for the port of Philadelphia and for other purposes therein mentioned," October 4, 1788, *Statutes at Large of Pennsylvania*, 13:97-126; "A Supplement to an act entitled "An act to establish a Board of Warden for the Port of Philadelphia and for other purposes therein mentioned," March 27, 1789, ibid., 13:269-74; "An Act respecting the public landings and wharves in the township of the Northern Liberties, in the County of Philadelphia," April 4, 1796, ibid., 15:468-69.

24. For Pennsylvania auction regulations see "An Act to Revive and Continue in Force the Acts of Assembly Regulating Sales by Public Auction, and for Other Purposes Therein Mentioned," December 9, 1783, in *Statutes at Large of Pennsylvania*, 11:225-27; "A Supplement of the Several Acts of General Assembly respecting Public Auctions and Auctioneers," March 19, 1789, ibid., 13:228-30; "Additional Supplement to Several Acts. . . . ," March 27, 1790, ibid., 13:467-68; "Further Supplement . . . ," February 26, 1791, ibid., 13:14-15; For South Carolina auction regulation see "An Ordinance for imposing a tax of two and a half per centum on Goods, Wares, and Merchandizes, exposed to public sale; and for regulating public auctions" (2.5 percent tax does not apply to sale by sheriff, deceased's estates or prize goods, vendue masters and owners forbidden to bid at

auction), ordinance 1134, 1779, Cooper and McCord, *Statutes at Large of South Carolina*, 4:497-99; "Ordinance for regulating public vendues in this state, and for repealing part of an ordinance ..." (requires that auctioneers must be citizens—sale of ships, lands, slaves, houses 1 percent, and horses, cattle goods, wares, merchandise 2.5 percent—1783 was 2.5 percent on all—except on sales that are property of insolvent debtors or deceased, or decree of court of chancery—vendue masters must keep a book and must remit tax every three months), ordinance 1270, 1785, ibid., 670-73; "An Act for Regulating Sales under Execution," no. 1293, 1785, ibid., 4:710-12; "An Act to alter and amend an Act for the more effectual relief of Insolvent Debtors" (land and slaves can be seized for unpaid taxes after two years and sold at vendue), 1311, 1786, ibid., 4:727-28; "An Act for Levying and Collecting Certain Duties and Imposts Therein Mentioned" (auction duty goes to 1 percent and 3 percent), no. 1350, 1787, ibid., 5:8-11.

25. I arrived at these estimates by searching online databases of the *Pennsylvania Gazette* and South Carolina newspapers for 1787, then comparing proportions with the statistics produced by my colonial-era auction advertisement databases.

26. "An Act concerning Estrays," no. 1473, 1789, in Cooper and McCord, *Statutes at Large of South Carolina*, 5:137-39; "An Act for the Promotion of Industry, and for the Suppression of Vagrants and Other Idle and Disorderly Persons," which states that "Offender to be sold at auction!" ("Before the last day of court, make known to the inhabitants by an advertisement stuck up at the door of the court-house or gaol of the district or county where he or she was apprehended, that the services of the offender will be sold at public sale on the last day of the court, for a space of time not exceeding one year; and the person so purchasing the services ... shall receive a certificate"), no. 1376, 1787, ibid., 5:41-44.

27. For Pennsylvania regulation of itinerant traders see "Regulating Peddlers, Vendues etc.," 1730, *Pennsylvania Statutes at Large*, vol. 4; "Repealing a Part of an Act Entitled An Act for Regulating Peddlers ...," 1774, ibid., vol. 8; "Prohibit the sale of goods, wares and merchandises ...," 1777, ibid., vol. 9, which prevents men who can bear arms from being peddlers; "Regulating of Hawkers and peddlers," 1784, ibid., vol. 11, in which peddlers must be recommended for a license by local justices to central government as in 1730; "Supplement to an Act Entitled An Act to Regulate Hawkers and Peddlers ...," 1799, ibid., vol. 16 (here only citizens of the United States who are disabled can become peddlers; that is, it becomes a form of charity to poor white people). On the central recruitment of justices in South Carolina see General Assembly Committee Reports, in which the house committees are in charge of coming up with a statewide list of candidates for justice of the peace who will be exempt from militia and patrol duty, 1783, no. 20. Suitable men are listed in the document, as well as the 1785 list of justices selected by Assembly for new county court, both box 1, House Committee Reports, SCDAH. The Assembly also viewed disobedience to officers they had appointed as subversion of government. A house committee thus stated that resistance to the sheriff in his duty to execute the law "tends to the Subversion of all Order in the Community to the total Annihilation of that mutual Support, Freedom & Happiness, which are the great Objects of all good Government: That it is therefore a Crime against the State of a most atrocious alarming Nature to the Suppression of which it becomes this House, in duty to its Constituents, to use every Exertion of legal Authority. Your Committee therefore recommend that his Excellency the Governor be desired to give every necessary Support to the Sheriff in his Discharge of his Duty, use all lawful means of bring to Punishment every Person Guilty of Opposition to him in the Execution thereof and that his Exc be authorized to draw from the Treasury such Sums of Money as may be requisite to defray the expence of enabling the Sheriff to overcome all unlawful Opposition and that this House recommends the good Citizens of this State to perform their Obligations to the Community by lending all possible Assistance to the Civil Officers whenever it shall be found necessary to call upon them for it," 1786, nos. 69-77, Committee Reports, SCDAH. William Poole iron master license to sell alcohol, June 20, 1786, in Brett Holcomb, ed., *Spartanburgh County Minutes of the County Court, 1785-99* (Easley, SC, 1980), 19; Grievances of the Fairfield

County Grand Jury, January 1786, "that a Hundred of Weights and measures are not provided and put into the hands of the Clerk of the County," ibid., 14–15; For licenses for storekeepers to sell alcohol see January 14, 1792, ibid., 49. I acknowledge that Laura Edwards has presented local justice in early republic South Carolina as being a flexible affair based on shared community values. It may appear this way if one looks back from the nineteenth century, but placing the new court system of the 1780s in the context of what had come before in the colonial era, it instead appears to be more a reflection of a new centralized and hierarchical power; Edwards, *People and Their Peace*.

28. Charge of Judge Champion to the Lancaster County Grand Jury, *State Gazette*, February 1788; Trial of Edmond Franklin, charged with being idle disorderly and vagrant, June 8, 1792, Pendleton County County and Intermediate Court Misc Papers from 1790–98, SCDAH; 1787—Act to promote industry and for the suppression of Vagrants and other Idle and Disorderly Persons. See also Presentment of the Edgefield Grand Jury, October 12, 1786, "Number of white men strolling and we not being sensible how they get their living." Also 1794 Ninety-Six District November complaint about hawkers and peddlers "who bring their goods by land from New York, or some of the Northern States, without paying any Taxes or duty for the same in this State, they trade for None of our produce they depreciate all proper Circulation, as they deal for nothing but Gold and Silver."

29. On the violence of this era in the Ohio River Valley see Sleeper-Smith, *Indigenous Prosperity and American Conquest*. See the epilogue of this book for further details of Indian trade regulation.

30. Charge of Judge Pendleton to the Grand Jury of South Carolina, as reproduced in *American Museum*, 1 (1787): 483–87.

31. See Brett Holcomb, ed., *Winton (Barnwell) County, SC, Minutes of County Court and Will Book 1, 1785–91* (Easley, SC, 1978).

32. Holcomb, *Spartanburgh County Minutes for the County Court 1785–99* (Easley, SC, 1980), 7, 34; Holcomb, *Winton (Barnwell) County Minutes*, 2, 18.

33. "Act to Incorporate the City of Philadelphia," 1789, *Pennsylvania Statutes at Large*, 13:193–214; Minutes of the City Council of Philadelphia, HSP. Compare with the 1701 incorporation document, in which there were no provisions on the conduct of elections at all, a vagueness that of course produced a corporation that was viewed by many as governed by an oligarchy.

34. "Civil economy," in Ironicus to Mr. Fenno, *Gazette of the United States*, September 15, 1795; Jacob Johnson, *A Toy Shop for Children* (Philadelphia, 1804), American Antiquarian Society. Marcellus Laroom's 1687 *Cryes of the Citie of London* is the beginning of the genre, which then evolved and which eventually London artist Paul Sandby depicted in his 1760 series of watercolor sketches. Sean Shesgreen, *Images of the Outcast: The Urban Poor in the "Cries of London"* (Oxford, 2002).

35. July 2, 1790, minutes of the Philadelphia Corporation, HSP; Committee Reports of the South Carolina Assembly, 1789, box 3, folders 81–90, SCDAH; Petition of sundry freeholders and other inhabitants of St Paul's and St Bartholomew's Parrishes, 1786, Petitions to the Senate, SCDAH. Ferry licenses were also granted in colonial South Carolina, but it appears that the policy was not as vigorously pursued, meaning that women like Mary Sureau could openly keep unlicensed ferries.

36. For a Pennsylvania example of petitioners for public office who used patriotism and service to justify their preferment see petition of James Rowan "that your Petitioner has been a Zealous friend to the Cause of American Freedom since the Commencement of the Hostilityes between Great Britain and America in which contest he has not only taken his Tour of duty . . . but has offerd his Services Voluntarily," November 20, 1778, Petitions, reel 1, PSA. House Committee Report, 1789, nos. 81–90, SCDAH. Judge Pendleton considered "keepers of ferries" to be among those officers "bound in duty to your country." Presumably this made the job unsuitable for a woman. Charge of Judge Pendleton to the Grand Jury, *American Museum*, 1787.

37. For use of this common phrase, see "Publicus," "I should have thought, had you been acquainted with the Duties of a good Citizen, or preferred the Peace and good Order of the Province to Tumult and Sedition . . . ," in "To the Bird of Passage," *Pennsylvania Gazette*, January 20, 1773.

38. Meeting of the Master Taylors, *South Carolina State Gazette*, January 1, 1794; Ordinances of the Charleston City Council (Charleston, 1789), Library of Congress.

39. Judge Grimké's Charge to the Grand Jury of Charleston, October Sessions, 1789, as reprinted in the *Pennsylvania Gazette*, December 16, 1789; South Carolina Slave Code of 1740, in Cooper and McCord, *Statutes at Large of South Carolina*, 7:397–417.

40. Minutes of the Philadelphia Corporation, HSP.

41. As quoted in Owen S. Ireland, *Religion, Ethnicity, and Politics: Ratifying the Constitution in Pennsylvania* (University Park, PA, 1995), 188.

42. "Agricola," *Pennsylvania Gazette*, June 13, 1781; *Pennsylvania Gazette*, October 25, 1786, for failure of petition and bill to incorporate; *Pennsylvania Gazette*, November 5, 1788, for fears that Congress would leave a disordered city; *Pennsylvania Gazette*, February 24, 1790, for complaints about the new corporation not fulfilling its duties; *Pennsylvania Gazette*, June 18, 1794, for inaction on provisions markets.

43. Benjamin Waller, notice, *City Gazette and Daily Advertiser*, July 10, 1784. "Amicus," *State Gazette*, August 16, 1785. "Amicus," *State Gazette*, July 12, 1785. In a previous article in the *State Gazette* on July 9, 1785, Amicus had also insinuated that the city council members were not managing the public funds derived from taxes and lotteries satisfactorily and were keeping the money for themselves. He suggested that the solution was to force the council to publish its accounts for public scrutiny.

44. Ruth Bogin, "Petitioning and the New Moral Economy of Post-Revolutionary America," *William and Mary Quarterly*, 3rd ser., 45 (July 1988): 391–425, quotation on 408; Klein, *Unification of a Slave State*; Bouton, *Taming Democracy*.

45. Petitions to the General Assembly, 1786, folders 69–77, SCDAH; Petitions, "Your Memorialists therefore pray that the Sheriff Sale Act may Be Removed; That Revival of the Act Respecting the Recovery of Old Debts may Take Place; That your Honourable House will use such ?[blot] as will place the Creditor & debtor on a more Equal Footing; and that proper Measures may be pursued for Restoring and preserving public and private Credit." The creditor has been placed at the mercy of the debtor, which has "greatly injured both public and private Credit"; 1787 Petition, Ninety-Six District; Petition from the Inhabitants of Edgefield County, 1789, noting the "good intention of the late legislature" in their "truly imbarassed situation" with the recent law giving debtors a grace period to pay debts before execution, that it was nevertheless ineffective, since "it is a fact Notorious to every Canded and impartial mind that the principal cause of the distress of your peers and generality of the good Citizens of this State is an almost total want of Circulating medium . . . so severely felt . . . that no property amoung them will if sold for money command 1/5 or 1/6 part of its intrinsic Value."

46. Petition from inhabitants of Ninety-Six District, undated but noted 1788; petition from inhabitants of Lincoln County, undated but marked 1788, both SCDAH. See also petition from the inhabitants of the village of Pendleton, who had never experienced "any inconvenience from not having the village aforesaid incorporated—on the contrary, that your petitioners, have, in more instances than one, observed the injurious effect which have arisen from the incorporation of small towns, in creating discord & dissention among the citizens, & thereby exciting an unnecessary exercise of power in those who may be entrusted therewith." Petition 1787, SCDAH. Note that Klein argues for the complexity of protest against courts, and the related petitions to the General Assembly. The South Carolina Assembly did take more measures for debtor relief than its Pennsylvania counterpart, and this undoubtedly kept the situation under control to some degree—though some measures such as the Pine Barren Act that favored rich planters did much to annoy poorer ones—the Assembly had great difficulty in pleasing all of the people all of the time. Here

I am not trying to demonstrate the existence of constituencies of protestors—Lowcountry vs. Upcountry, rich vs. poor. Instead, I want to illustrate the resentments that all sorts of white Carolinians felt about the newly powerful presence of state authorities in their commercial lives. Klein, *Unification of a Slave State*, 109–48.

47. Holcomb, *Winton (Barnwell) County Minutes*, 102.

48. Gouverneur Morris to Matthew Ridley, Philadelphia, August 6, 1782, 147–48; Robert Morris to Jonathan Trumbull, governor of Connecticut, Philadelphia, July 31, 1782, 111–12; Robert Morris to Alexander Hamilton, Office of Finance, August 28, 1782, 271–72; Robert Morris to Alexander Hamilton, October 5, 1782, 499–500. All in *Papers of Robert Morris*, vol. 62; Benjamin Fuller to Robert Totten, Philadelphia, April 21, 1785, Fuller Letterbook, HSP. Meanwhile, Lancaster lawyer Jasper Yeates characterized the Whiskey Rebellion protests as "wild Projects of a few intemperate Minds." Yeates to Sally Yeates, August 22, 1794, Pittsburgh, Yeates Papers, HSP. The question of monetary policy and financing the public debt also became caught up in these same arguments about where the public good ended and private interest began. These debates have been discussed in detail by historians including Woody Holton, "Did Democracy Cause the Recession That Led to the Constitution?" *Journal of American History* 92 (2005–6): 442–69. Bouton, *Taming Democracy*; Max Edling, "So Immense a Power in the Affairs of War": Alexander Hamilton and the Restoration of Public Credit," *William and Mary Quarterly*, 3rd ser., 64 (April 2007): 287–326; George William Van Cleve, "The Anti-Federalists' Toughest Challenge: Paper Money, Debt Relief, and the Ratification of the Constitution," *Journal of the Early Republic* 34 (Winter 2014): 529–60. The debates were connected to domestic marketing because they were about government policy toward an issue that affected Americans' ability to effectively enter the marketplace. However, they did not fundamentally affect the marketplace itself—as long as the money supply problem and indebtedness remained nothing changed—and are thus tangential to the issues under consideration here.

49. Petition from Chester County distillers, January 21, 1784, Petitions, reel 1, PSA.

50. Ibid., petition for the extension of the main market, undated but probably late 1784.

51. Articles of impeachment against Wilton Atkinson and Benjamin Wiser, November 25, 1779, petitions, reel 1, PSA; Bouton, *Taming Democracy*, 152–53.

52. Bouton, *Taming Democracy*, 157–59; Letter from Isaac Hicks to unknown relative, June 10, 1784, Hicks Papers, folder 37, Bucks County Archives.

53. To Mr. Randle Mitchell Bow Hill, Philadelphia, January 29, 1785; To Randall Mitchell, February 7, 1785; to Mrs. Mitchell at Spring Brook, February 12, 1785, and February 22, 1785; to Capt. John Mitchell at Charleston, Philadelphia, April 9, 1785; all Benjamin Fuller Letterbook, HSP. Fuller is inconsistent in his spelling of Randall/Randle.

54. Townsend Speakman, Philadelphia, October 24, 1783, to Yeates; Yeates Papers, folder 23, HSP.

55. Andrew M. Schocket, "Thinking about Elites in the Early Republic," *Journal of the Early Republic* 25 (Winter 2005): 547–55, quotation on 552.

56. "An Act for establishing the mode and conditions of surveying and granting the vacant lands within this State," in Cooper and McCord, *Statutes at Large of South Carolina*, 4:590–94; "An Act to Close the Land Office for and during the term of four years, under certain limitations; and for other purposes therein mentioned," ibid., 5:233–35; "An Act to suspend for six months the powers of the commissers of the several counties of this state to make sale of unseated lands for nonpayment of taxes," September 22, 1788, SCDAH. See also Bouton, *Taming Democracy*, 197–215.

57. Petition to the Senate, December 22, 1788, SCDAH; Klein, *Unification of a Slave State*, 178–202.

58. Westpensbro and Newton Resolves, as quoted in Cornell, *Other Founders*, 211; Bouton, *Taming Democracy*, 237; *Pennsylvania Gazette*, August 6, 1794.

59. Murphy, *Building the Empire State*.

60. "An Act for establishing a fair and markets in the town of Belleville, on the Congareer river, in this State," no. 1178, 1783, in Cooper and McCord, *Statutes at Large of South Carolina*,

4:557–60; "A Conodoguinet Farmer" to the *Carlisle Gazette*, February 18, 1794; the town was of course a hotspot of the whiskey rebellion and also the location of a riot over the ratification of the Constitution.

61. *Dunlap's Gazette*, January 11, 1792.

62. Klein, *Unification of a Slave State*; Ireland, *Religion, Ethnicity, and Politics*; and Cornell, *Other Founders,* have all commented on the difficulty of clearly laying down these divisions of class or geographical conflict during the 1780s. The obvious answer to their difficulties is that the fault line among freeholders lay elsewhere, that is, the line between a "public good" and the increase of their own property.

CONCLUSION

1. James Madison, "Vices of the System," April 1787, https://founders.archives.gov/documents /Madison/01-09-02-0187, accessed March 16, 2018.

2. Madison, "Vices of the System"; "An Account of several things whereby illegal trade is encouraged in Virginia, Maryland and Pennsylvania, with methods for preventing the same, submitted to the Commissioners of Customs by Edward Randolph," August 17, 1696, C0323/2, nos. 6, 6 I-XII, TNA.

3. Max Edling, *A Revolution in Favor of Government: Origins of the U.S. Constitution and the Making of the American State* (New York, 2003).

4. For Hamilton material see Rao, *National Duties*, 59–60.

5. "Cato," *State Gazette of South Carolina*, November 26, 1787.

6. George Turner to Winthrop Sargent, November 6, 1787, 209; James Wilson speech, 580, both in Merrill Jensen, John P. Kaminski, and Gaspare J. Saladino, eds., *Ratification of the Constitution by the States*, vol. 2, *Pennsylvania* (Madison, WI, 1976), http://digital.library.wisc.edu/1711.dl /History.DHRCv2, accessed March 16, 2018; *Pennsylvania Gazette*, October 17, 1787;

7. David Ramsey Oration, June 5, 1788, and Camden Federalists Toast, both in John P. Kaminski et al., eds., *Documentary History of the Ratification of the Constitution: Ratification of the Constitution by the States*, vol. 27, *South Carolina* (Madison, WI, 2016), http://digital.library.wisc.edu/1711.dl /History.DHRCv27, accessed March 16, 2018.

8. Ireland, *Religion, Ethnicity, and Politics*; Cornell, *Other Founders*.

9. Albert Gallatin, *Sketch of the Finances of the United States*, 11, https://babel.hathitrust.org/cgi /pt?id=pst.000055528382;view=1up;seq=9.

10. Rao, *National Duties*, 69 for customs officer numbers, 88 for quotation.

11. Grand Jury Presentments, 1791, nos. 1–3, Edgefield County, April 1791, SCDAH.

12. Jasper Yeates to Sally Yeates, Pittsburgh, August 17, 1794, Yeates Papers, HSP. For full treatments of the Whiskey Rebellion and the larger context of Hamilton's fiscal policy see Thomas P. Slaughter, *The Whiskey Rebellion: Frontier Epilogue to the American Revolution* (New York, 1988); Bouton, *Taming Democracy*, 216–43; Edling, "So Immense a Power in the Affairs of War."

13. *Pennsylvania Gazette*, August 6, 1794, and October 8, 1794; Patrick Griffin, *American Leviathan: Empire, Nation, and the Revolutionary Frontier* (New York, 2007), 221–26.

14. Andrew Shankman, *Original Intents: Jefferson, Madison, Hamilton and the American Founding* (New York, 2018); Drew McCoy, *The Elusive Republic: Political Economy in Jeffersonian America* (Chapel Hill, NC, 1980); Joanna Cohen, *Luxurious Citizens: Consumption and Civic Belonging in Nineteenth-Century America* (Philadelphia, 2017).

15. Bethel Saler, *The Settlers' Empire: Colonialism and State Formation in America's Old Northwest* (Philadelphia, 2014), 122.

16. US assembled in Congress, Wednesday October 15, 1783—Report of the Committee of Congress digested into a resolution etc transmitted to the General Assembly January 29, 1784, in

Petitions to the Pennsylvania Assembly; Memorial of James Parr, Michael Kimmell, and John Lauman, September 10, 1785, both Petitions, reel 1, PSA.

17. "Act for Establishing Trading Houses within the Indian Tribes" and "An Act to Regulate Trade and Intercourse with the Indian Tribes, and to Preserve Peace on the Frontiers," both in *Acts of the Fourth Congress of the United States*, April 18, 1796, 452-53, and May 19, 1796, 469-74. PDF downloaded from https://www.loc.gov/law/help/statutes-at-large/4th-congress.php.

18. This section is based on William Bergmann, *The American National State and the Early West* (New York, 2011), quotation on 66.

19. November 25, 1754, Secret Instructions for Edward Braddock from George II, contemporary copy, Loudon papers, box 11, LO—1-6999, HL; LO581 Braddock to Sir Thomas Robinson, June 5, 1755, Fort Cumberland at Will's Creek, HL.

20. Bergmann, *American National State*, quotations on 62 and 72.

EPILOGUE

1. Hay, "State and the Market in 1800," 101-62; Philip Harling and Peter Mandler, "From 'Fiscal-Military' State to Laissez-Faire State, 1760-1850," *Journal of British Studies* 32 (January 1993): 44-70; Philip Harling, *The Waning of "Old Corruption": The Politics of Economical Reform in Britain, 1779-1846* (Oxford, 1996); Ellen Frankel Paul, "Laissez Faire in Nineteenth-Century Britain: Fact or Myth?," *Literature of Liberty: A Review of Contemporary Liberal Thought* 3 (Winter 1980): 7-38; E. P. Thompson, *The Making of the English Working Class* (London, 1963).

2. Novak, *People's Welfare*; Harrison, *Contest of Exchange*; Helen Tangires, *Public Markets and Civic Culture in Nineteenth-Century America* (Baltimore, 2003); Robert Gamble, "Civic Economies: Commerce, Regulation, and Public Space in the Antebellum City" (PhD diss., Johns Hopkins University, 2014); Cohen, *Luxurious Citizens*; Robin L. Einhorn, *Property Rules: Political Economy in Chicago, 1833-1872* (Chicago, 1991); Murphy, *Building the Empire State*; Andrew Shankman, "Capitalism, Slavery, and the New Epoch: Matthew Carey's 1819," in *Slavery's Capitalism: A New History of American Economic Development*, ed. Sven Beckert and Seth Rockman (Philadelphia, 2014), 43-261.

3. Bethany Moreton, *To Serve God and Wal-Mart: The Making of Christian Free Enterprise* (Cambridge, MA, 2009).

4. N. B. D. Connolly, "Black and Woke in Capitalist America," https://items.ssrc.org/black-and-woke-in-capitalist-america-revisiting-robert-allens-black-awakening-for-new-times-sake/, accessed September 10, 2018.

Index

Act of Frauds, 45
Act of Union, 56
advertisements. *See* newspapers: advertising in
African peoples, 34–36; Aro, 34; Dahomey, 34; Oyo, 35; Segou, 35; Siin, 34
Africans and trade: colonial, 6, 60–62, 73, 86–87, 114–19, 150–51, 181, 188–89; enslaved, 77–78, 225n9, 240n17
Annapolis, MD, 63, 161
Anne (queen), 56
Anti-Federalists, 210–11
assizes. *See* courts
Atkin, Edmond, 120
auctioneers. *See* vendue masters
auctions, 26, 174–75; advertisements of, 239n13; boycotts, 151–53, 160, 196–97; British, 71; creating mobile marketplaces, 75; debtors' property, 143, 169, 193–94; Pennsylvanian, 75, 153, 171, 194, 196, 255n42; regulation of, 181–82, 192–94; slave and servant, 77, 125, 240n17; South Carolinian, 90, 164, 192–93

Bacon's Rebellion, 60
Bank of America, 194
Baynton, Wharton & Morgan, 100–1, 138
Belleville, SC, 175, 179, 200
Bellomont, Earl of (Richard Coote), 49, 63
Berwick-upon-Tweed, 52, 55, 241n28
Birmingham, England, 26, 38
Black Boys, 139, 194, 196, 210

Blackett, Walter, 23
Blackstone, William, 111, 258n64
Bladen, Martin, 43, 46, 53, 63
Blue Anchor Landing, 129–30
Board of Trade, 43, 47, 49, 53, 63, 114, 121
Boston, MA, 63, 89, 122–23, 149, 249n37
boycotts. *See* protests
bread: bread assize, 50, 54, 108, 186; high price of, 31, 69, 145
Bristol, England, 3, 157; markets in, 31; Society of Merchant Venturers, 31
Bristol, PA, 108, 128
broadsides, 20–21, 90, 130, 152, 154
Bucks County, PA: bankruptcy in, 197; court in, 51, 61; farming in, 168, 180; marketplaces in, 154; non-importation in, 255n40; petitions from, 175
burghs (Scottish towns), 26, 27, 31, 55

cabbages, regulation of trade in, 122–23, 149
Callowhill, PA, 89, 175, 179
Camden, SC, 6, 36, 91, 140, 175, 179, 182, 208
Carlisle, in Westmoreland, 37–38; in PA, 100, 172, 180, 200, 207
Carolina. *See* South Carolina
cattle. *See* cows
Charles I (king), 21–22
Charles II (king), 44
Charleston: African trade in, 115–17; auctions, 77, 164; committees, 162; corporations, 191–92; enslaved people in, 188;